A Professional Approa

Outlook Core

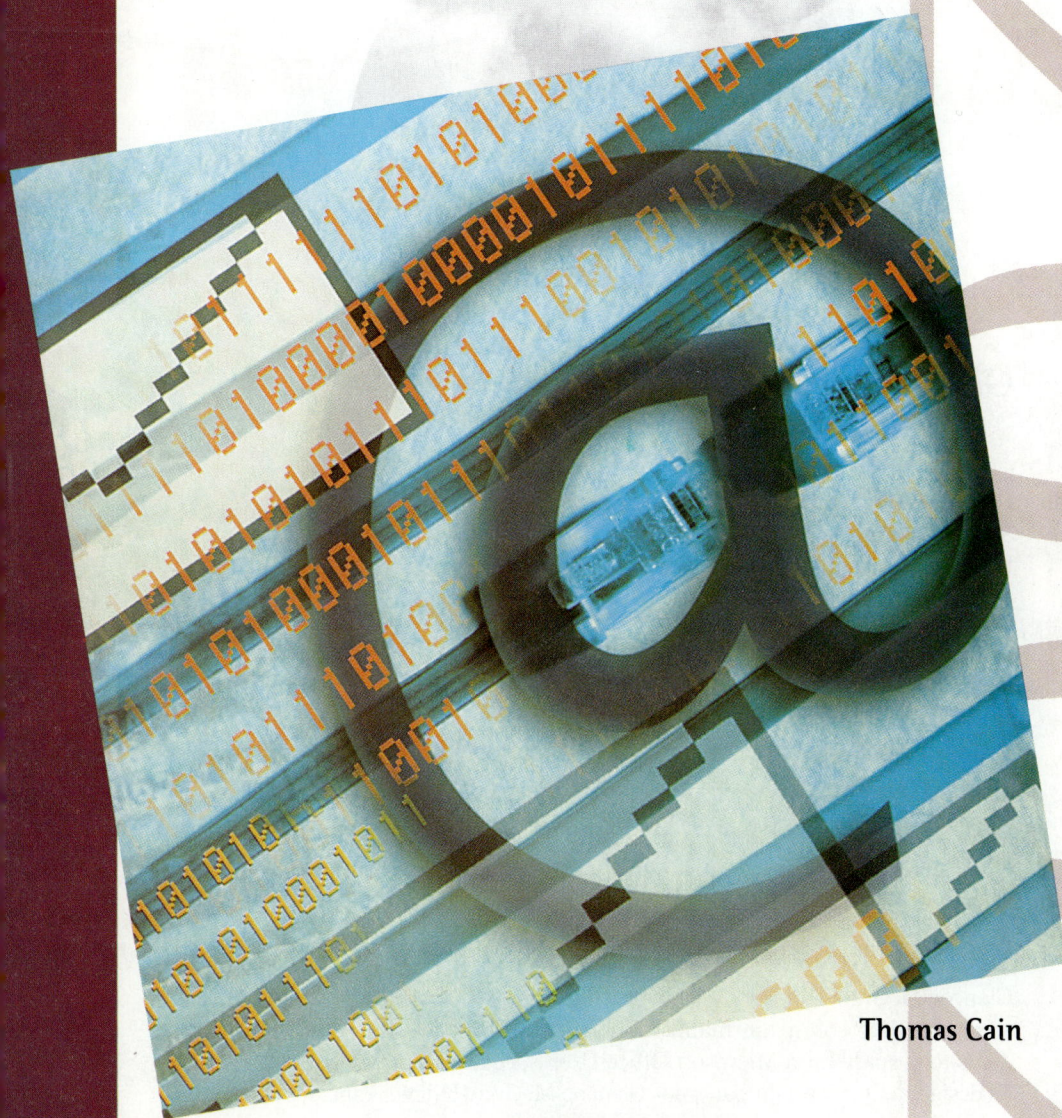

Thomas Cain

Mc Graw Hill **Glencoe McGraw-Hill**

New York, New York   Columbus, Ohio   Chicago, Illinois   Peoria, Illinois   Woodland Hills, California

This program has been prepared with the assistance of Gleason Group, Inc., Norwalk, CT.

Editorial Director: Pamela Ross

Copy Editor: Malinda McCain

Composition: The Format Group LLC; Creative Ink, Inc.

Design: Leggitt Associates; Creative Ink, Inc.

Screens were captured using FullShot V6 For Windows from Inbit Incorporated, Mountain View, CA.

Glencoe/McGraw-Hill

A Division of The **McGraw·Hill** Companies

Outlook 2002: A Professional Approach, Core
Student Edition
ISBN 0-07-827391-9

2   3   4   5   6   7   8   9   10   079/079   06   05   04   03   02

Microsoft, Microsoft Outlook, Microsoft Word, Windows, and the Microsoft Office User Specialist logo are either registered trademarks or trademarks of Microsoft Corporation in the United States and/or other countries.

PostScript is a registered trademark of Adobe Systems, Inc.

Glencoe/McGraw-Hill is independent from Microsoft Corporation, and not affiliated with Microsoft in any manner. This publication may be used in assisting students to prepare for a Microsoft Office User Specialist Exam. Neither Microsoft, its designated review company, nor Glencoe/McGraw-Hill warrants that use of this publication will ensure passing the relevant exam.

Between the time that Web site information is gathered and published, it is not unusual for some sites to have closed. URLs will be updated in reprints when possible.

Visit the Professional Approach Series Web site at www.pas.glencoe.com

Contents

Unit 1

OUTLOOK BASICS — 5

Unit 2

MANAGING E-MAIL EFFICIENTLY   89

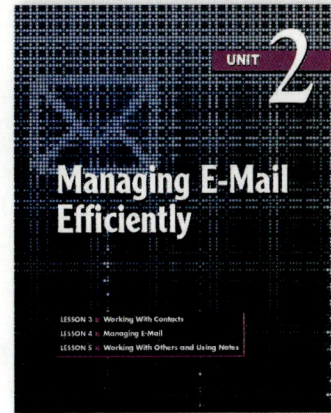

UNIT **2**

Managing E-Mail Efficiently

LESSON 3 :: Working With Contacts
LESSON 4 :: Managing E-Mail
LESSON 5 :: Working With Others and Using Notes

Unit 3

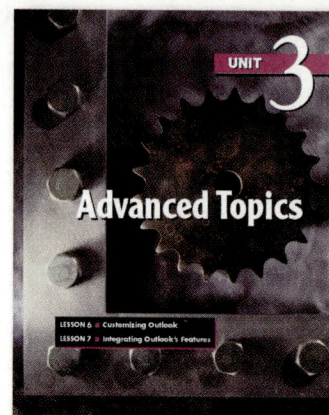

Appendices   A-1

Glossary   G-1

Index   I-1

Preface

Outlook 2002 is written to help you master Microsoft Outlook for Windows. The text takes you step-by-step through the Outlook features that you're likely to use in both your personal and business life.

Case Study

Learning about the features of Outlook is one thing, but applying what you learn is another. That's why a *Case Study* runs through the text. The Case Study offers the opportunity to learn Outlook in a realistic business context. Take the time to read the Case Study about AllWood Mills, Inc., a fictional business located in Dubuque, Iowa. All the documents for this course involve AllWood Mills.

Organization of the Text

The text includes three *units*. Each unit is divided into smaller *lessons*. There are seven lessons, each building on previously learned procedures. This building block approach, together with the Case Study and the features listed below, enable you to maximize the learning process.

Features of the Text

- ☑ *Objectives* are listed for each lesson
- ☑ Required skills for the *Microsoft Office User Specialist (MOUS) Certification Program* are listed for each lesson
- ☑ The *estimated time* required to complete each lesson (up to the "Using Help") is stated
- ☑ Within a lesson, each *heading* corresponds to an objective
- ☑ Easy-to-follow *exercises* emphasize "learning by doing"
- ☑ *Key terms* are italicized and defined as they are encountered
- ☑ Extensive *graphics* display screen contents
- ☑ *Toolbar buttons* and *keyboard keys* are shown in the text when used
- ☑ *Large toolbar buttons in the margins* provide easy-to-see references
- ☑ Lessons contain important *Notes*, useful *Tips*, and helpful *Reviews*
- ☑ *Using Help* introduces you to a Help topic related to lesson content
- ☑ A *Lesson Summary* reviews the important concepts taught in the lesson
- ☑ A *Command Summary* lists the commands taught in the lesson
- ☑ *Concepts Review* includes true/false, short answer, and critical thinking questions that focus on lesson content
- ☑ *Skills Review* provides skill reinforcement for each lesson

☑ *Lesson Applications* ask you to apply your skills in a more challenging way

☑ *On Your Own* exercises lets you apply your skills creatively

☑ *Unit Applications* give you the opportunity to use the skills you learn in a unit

☑ *Appendices*

☑ *Glossary*

☑ *Index*

MOUS Certification Program

The Microsoft Office User Specialist (MOUS) certification program offers certification at two skill levels—"Core" and "Expert." This certification can be a valuable asset in any job search. For more information about this Microsoft program, go to www.mous.net. For a complete listing of the MOUS skills for the Outlook 2002 "Core" certification exam (and a correlation to the lessons in the text), see Appendix E: "MOUS Certification."

Professional Approach Web Site

Check out the Professional Approach Web site at www.pas.glencoe.com. A helpful *Task Reference List*—handy for remembering how to perform many Outlook tasks—is available for downloading.

Conventions Used in the Text

This text uses a number of conventions to help you learn the program and save your work.

- Text to key appears either in **boldface** or as a separate figure.

- Filenames appear in **boldface**.

- Options that you choose from menus and dialog boxes appear in a font that is similar to the on-screen font; for example, "Choose P̲rint from the F̲ile menu." (The underline means you can press Alt and key the letter to choose the option.) Hyperlinks also appear in blue text, as they appear on-screen.

- You're asked to save files with your initials, followed by the exercise name. For example, an exercise might end with this instruction: "Save the file as *[your initials]*5-12."

If You Are Unfamiliar with Windows

If you're unfamiliar with Windows, review *Appendix A: "Windows Tutorial"* before beginning Lesson 1. This tutorial provides a basic overview of the program and shows you how to use the mouse. You might also want to review *Appendix B: "File Management"* to get more comfortable with files and folders.

Screen Differences

As you practice each concept, illustrations of the screens help you follow the instructions. Don't worry if your screen is different from the illustration. These differences are due to variations in system and computer configurations.

Acknowledgments

We thank the reviewers of this text for their valuable assistance: Susan Olson, Northwest Technical College, East Grand Forks, MN; Eric Ecklund, Cambria Rowe Business College, Johnstown, PA; Debi Griggs, Bellevue Community College, Bellevue, WA; Mary Davey, Computer Learning Network, Camp Hill, PA.

Installation Requirements

You'll need Microsoft Outlook 2002 to work through this textbook. Outlook needs to be installed on the computer's hard drive (or on a network). Use the following checklist to evaluate installation requirements.

Hardware

☑ Pentium computer with between 32 MB and 72 MB of RAM depending on the version of Windows installed

☑ 3.5-inch high-density disk drive and CD-ROM drive

☑ 245 MB or more of hard disk space for a "Typical" Office installation

☑ Super VGA or higher-resolution video monitor

☑ Printer (laser or ink-jet recommended)

☑ Mouse

☑ Modem (if needed for Internet access)

Software

☑ Outlook 2002 (from Microsoft Office XP)

☑ Windows 98 (or later) or Microsoft Windows NT 4.0 with Service Pack 6 installed

☑ Browser

☑ Internet Service Provider

Prerequisites

The following assumptions have been made for all the exercises in this text. In order to use this text, it is necessary to configure your computer and your class, as specified below as well as to

- This text assumes that Word (WordMail) is the default e-mail editor. This is the Outlook system default. This means that the default message format for new messages is HTML. You will be directed to change the format to Plain Text in most exercises when you create e-mail messages. If Word is not the e-mail editor, you won't need to change the default message format.

- To send and receive e-mail, you must have a valid e-mail address. You will also need a list of valid e-mail addresses for other students in the class.

- In Lesson 6 you are required to change Outlook's defaults. You will also be required to change *back* to the system defaults at the end of the lesson. Make sure you do this. Otherwise, other students using your computer will have problems.

Installing New Features

Some lessons take advantage of Outlook or Office features that may require installation on your computer. For example, using Speech Recognition Technology as described in Appendix C, requires installing features that are not part of the typical installation. (These features can be found in **Office Shared Features/Alternative User Input**.)

To install a feature that is not part of the typical installation:

1. Close all programs.
2. Click the Windows **Start** button, point to **Settings**, and click **Control Panel**.
3. Double-click the **Add/Remove Programs** icon.
4. Do one of the following:
   - For Windows 98 and Windows NT:
     If you installed Microsoft Office, click **Microsoft Office** on the **Install/Uninstall** tab and then click the **Add/Remove** button. If you installed Word individually, click the program name on the **Install/Uninstall** tab and then click **Add/Remove**.
   - For Windows 2000 and Windows Millennium Edition:
     If you installed Microsoft Office, click **Microsoft Office** in the **Currently installed programs** box and then click the **Change** button. If you installed Word individually, click the program name in the **Currently installed programs** box and then click **Change**.
5. With **Add or Remove Features** selected, click **Next**.
6. Click the plus sign to the left of an Office feature to expand the options. Click the down arrow to the right of a feature you want to add and choose **Run all from My Computer**. When you have finished choosing features, click **Update**. Follow the on-screen instructions (which include loading the Office CD-ROM).

APPROVED COURSEWARE

What does this logo mean?

It means this courseware has been approved by the Microsoft® Office User Specialist Program to be among the finest available for learning Outlook 2002. It also means that upon completion of this courseware, you may be prepared to become a Microsoft Office User Specialist.

What is a Microsoft Office User Specialist?

A Microsoft Office User Specialist is an individual who has certified his or her skills in one or more of the Microsoft Office desktop applications of Microsoft Word, Microsoft Excel, Microsoft PowerPoint®, Microsoft Outlook® or Microsoft Access, or in Microsoft Project. The Microsoft Office User Specialist Program typically offers certification exams at the "Core" and "Expert" skill levels.* The Microsoft Office User Specialist Program is the only Microsoft approved program in the world for certifying proficiency in Microsoft Office desktop applications and Microsoft Project. This certification can be a valuable asset in any job search or career advancement.

More Information:

To learn more about becoming a Microsoft Office User Specialist, visit www.mous.net

To purchase a Microsoft Office User Specialist certification exam, visit www.DesktopIQ.com

To learn about other Microsoft Office User Specialist approved courseware from Glencoe/McGraw-Hill, visit www.pas.glencoe.com

---

* The availability of Microsoft Office User Specialist certification exams varies by application, application version and language. Visit www.mous.net for exam availability.

Microsoft, the Microsoft Office User Specialist Logo, PowerPoint and Outlook are either registered trademarks or trademarks of Microsoft Corporation in the United States and/or other countries.

CASE STUDY

AllWood Mills, Inc.

There's more to learning a program like Microsoft Outlook than simply writing and replying to e-mail messages. Not only do you need to understand how to use Outlook's e-mail feature, but you need to know how to use all the integrated features of Outlook in a real-world situation. That's why all these lessons relate to everyday business situations.

As you work through lessons, imagine yourself working as an intern for AllWood Mills, Inc., a furniture manufacturer based in Dubuque, Iowa.

AllWood Mills, Inc.

Starting with a table saw in his garage, Rob Connelly has grown his furniture-making hobby into a chain of six retail furniture stores in five Midwestern states. Even as a teenager, Rob spent much of his free time building tables, desks, and bookcases. He continued his hobby through his college years, and he eventually left medical school to pursue his passion for making furniture. His period designs and attention to fine detail created a demand for his furniture that stretched far beyond his first modest storefront in Dubuque, Iowa.

AllWood Mills designs, manufactures, and sells custom-made furniture. As reflected in their name, AllWood makes only wood furniture.

AllWood sells furniture for the bedroom, living room, and dining room. They also sell products for computer and media storage. Their furniture is available in four different styles: Mission, Shaker, Colonial, and Contemporary. In keeping with Rob's earliest pieces, each AllWood product is individually crafted in the style of a fine antique. Over the years, AllWood has found great favor with customers who want hand-crafted furniture at affordable prices.

In addition to their Dubuque store, AllWood also has retail outlets in Chicago, Minneapolis, Milwaukee, St. Louis, and Kansas City. (See Figure CS-1 for the location of AllWood's retail outlets.) AllWood's strategy is to locate

FIGURE CS-1
AllWood Mills Retail Outlets

a retail outlet in a major metropolitan center because the company expects to draw most of its customers from an area within 150 miles of its retail outlet. AllWood's headquarters and manufacturing facility is located in Dubuque, a central location for the other retail outlets.

AllWood MILLS, INC.

In your work as an intern at AllWood, Inc., you will have a chance to meet many of the people who work at AllWood. You will certainly interact with the key employees shown in Figure CS-2.

All of the work you do with Microsoft Outlook in this course will relate to AllWood, Inc. You will also discover that your work in this course will involve e-mails sent to, and received from, your fellow classmates. For the purpose of this class, treat your classmates as interns at AllWood. As you work through the course, take the time to notice the following things:

- The types of e-mail and Outlook tasks required in a small business to carry on a day-to-day business.

- The format and tone used for e-mail (see the "Guidelines for Using E-mail" on the next page).

- The types of business that are appropriately conducted using e-mail.

- The way that a business can increase efficiency by using the integration available between the various Outlook components.

As you use this text and become more experienced with Microsoft Outlook, you will also gain an understanding of how small businesses actually use the integrated components of Microsoft Outlook.

FIGURE CS-2
Key Employees

WILL MCCARTHY
Head of Design Dept.

ROB CONNELLEY
President

JASMINE JONES
Head of Sales Dept.

PAUL EPSTEIN
Head of Manufacturing Dept.

MARIA LOPEZ
Head of Administration Dept.

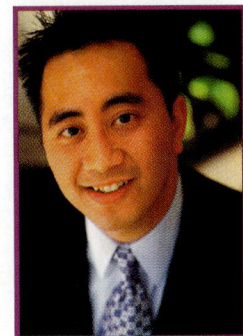

JOHN YU
Head of Marketing Dept.

AllWood Mills, Inc.

Memo

Guidelines for Using E-Mail

■ Send your messages only to people who need to see it. Some people receive a large volume of e-mail, and unnecessary e-mail is annoying.

■ Never send unsolicited ads or other material that the recipient is likely to regard as junk mail.

■ Try to give your messages a meaningful subject heading. This helps the recipient quickly determine if an immediate response is required.

■ Keep your messages short and to the point. Try to avoid composing messages that exceed the length of one screen.

■ Restrict your message to one subject. Send two separate messages instead of covering two topics in a single message.

■ Use short, single-spaced paragraphs. Do not indent the opening line of paragraphs. Leave one blank line between paragraphs.

■ Avoid the use all-capital letters in your messages, which is considered the equivalent of shouting. Follow the standard rules of capitalization.

■ As in any business communication, keep the tone of your message professional and courteous.

■ Edit and proofread your messages carefully. Messages containing errors in style, punctuation, grammar, and spelling reflect poorly on the sender.

■ Never send a message composed in anger. If you receive such a message, ignore it rather than respond in kind.

■ Do not pass messages on to others unless you are sure the sender will not object.

■ Exercise discretion in discussing confidential topics in your messages. The privacy of e-mail messages you send cannot be guaranteed.

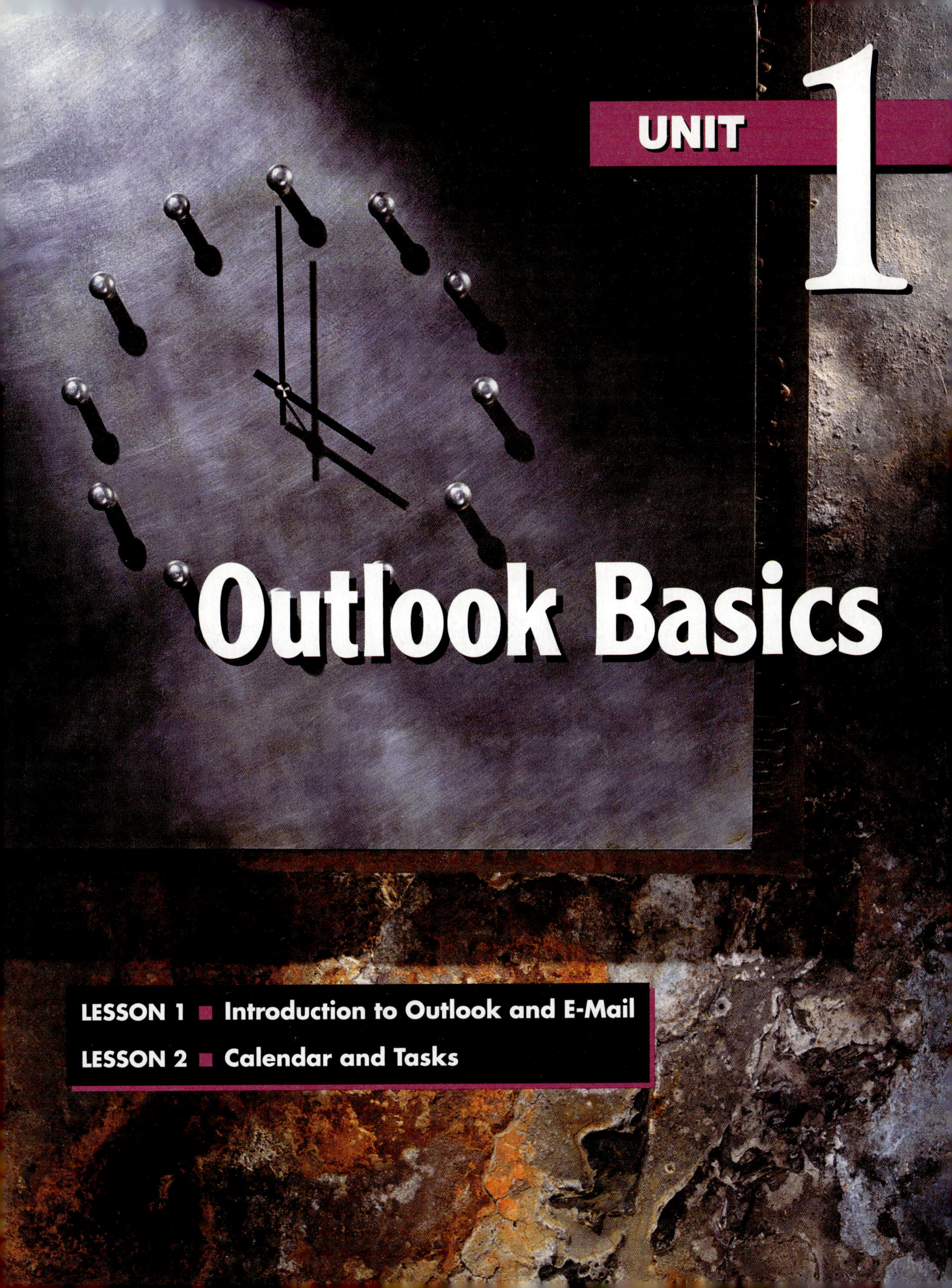

UNIT 1

Outlook Basics

Introduction to Outlook and E-Mail

After completing this lesson, you will be able to:

1. Start Outlook and identify parts of the Outlook window.
2. Address, compose, send, and receive e-mail.
3. Use contacts to address e-mail.
4. Read e-mail.
5. Send attachments to e-mail.
6. Use e-mail features.
7. Print e-mail and contacts and close Outlook.

Estimated Time: 1¾ hours

Microsoft Outlook is used to send and receive e-mail, as well as to manage messages, appointments, contacts, and tasks. This lesson begins with an overview of the Outlook screen. Then you learn how to compose, send, receive, and read e-mail, how to create contacts, and how to print contacts and e-mail messages.

NOTE: The e-mail messages, contacts, appointments, and tasks you create in this course relate to the Case Study (pages 1–4) about AllWood Mills, Inc. a fictional furniture manufacturing company.

Starting Outlook and Identifying Parts of the Outlook Window

FIGURE 1-1
Shortcut icon
to start Outlook

There are several ways to start Outlook, depending on your system setup and personal preferences. For example, you can use the Start button on the Windows taskbar or double-click an Outlook shortcut icon if one is on your desktop.

After you've started Outlook, you can become familiar with it by navigating through the program and identifying its components. Then you can learn to use the various menus, commands, and toolbars.

Outlook's major components include the Inbox, Calendar, Contacts, Tasks, Journal, and Notes. Information in Outlook is stored in folders. There is a folder for each of Outlook's major components.

EXERCISE   1-1   Start Outlook

You can start Outlook by using the Start menu or by clicking an icon on the Windows desktop.

1. Turn on your computer. Windows loads.

2. Click the Start button **Start** on the taskbar and point to Programs.

FIGURE 1-2
Starting Outlook
from the
Windows taskbar

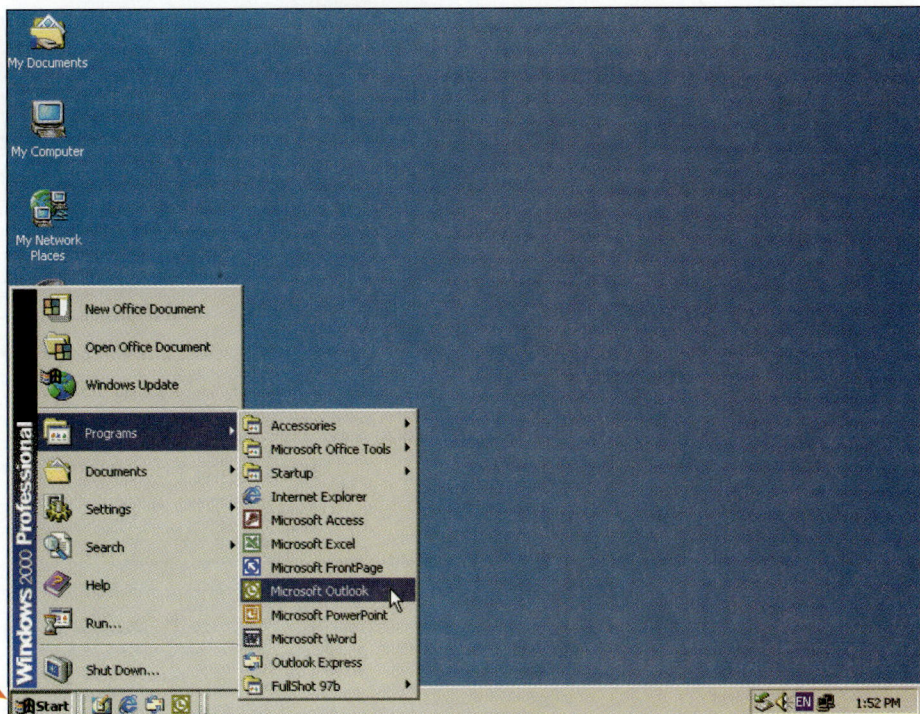

Start button

NOTE: Windows provides many ways to start applications. If you have problems, ask your instructor for help. Your screen might differ from Figure 1-2, depending on the programs installed on your computer.

3. On the <u>P</u>rograms menu, click **Microsoft Outlook.** In a few seconds, the program is loaded and the Outlook window appears. The Inbox is the default window when Outlook first appears.

TABLE 1-1   **Parts of the Outlook Window**

PART OF SCREEN	PURPOSE
Title bar	Displays the name of the current Outlook folder. The opening folder is always the Inbox.
Menu bar	Contains the menus you use to perform various tasks. You can open menus by using the mouse or the keyboard.
Toolbar	Contains buttons you click to initiate a wide range of commands. Each button is represented by an icon.
Outlook Bar	Displays shortcuts to frequently used folders. The Outlook Bar is located as a column on the left side of the program window.
Inbox	Displays received e-mail messages.
Shortcut group	Shows groups of related shortcuts on the Outlook Bar.
Shortcut	Allows quick access to a folder or feature. Shortcuts are found in the Outlook Bar.
Table view	Displays a list of Outlook items in rows and columns. The attributes for each item are arranged in the columns.
Item	Describes the basic element of Outlook information. An item can be an e-mail message, a task, an appointment, a contact, or a note.
Status bar	Displays information about the current folder. The status bar is located at the bottom of the Outlook program window.

FIGURE 1-3
The Inbox in the
Outlook program
window

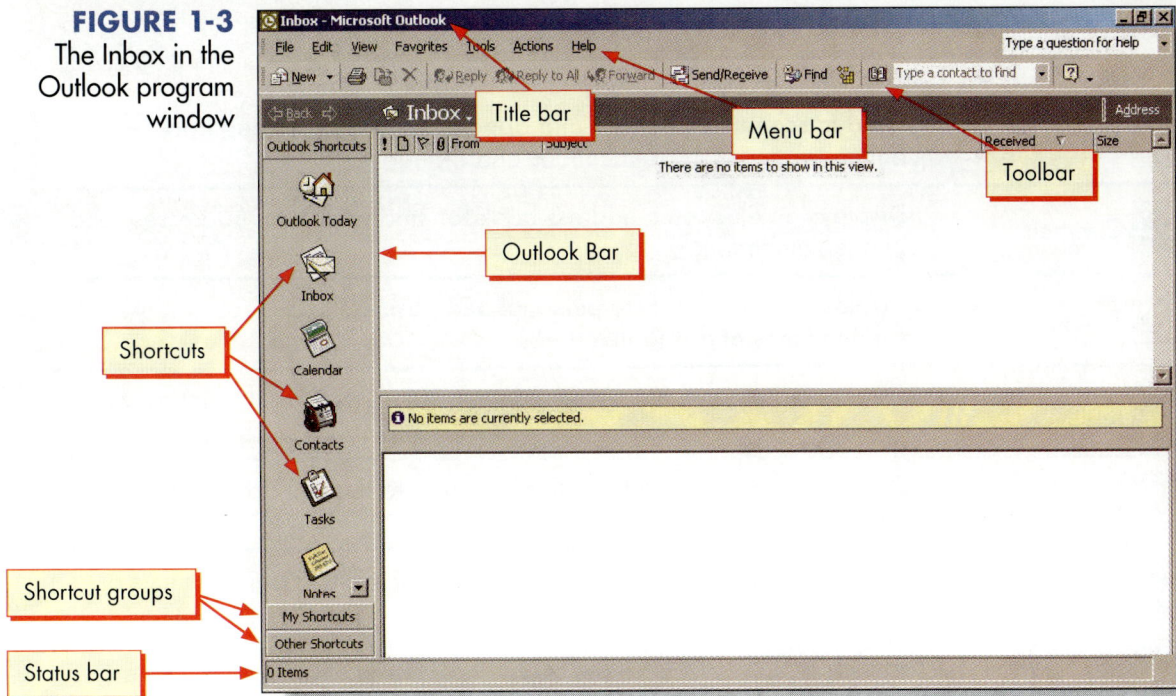

FIGURE 1-3
The Inbox in the
Outlook program
window

NOTE: Your program window might differ from the one shown in Figure 1-3, which shows the Inbox with no messages. Your program window might show a different part of Outlook, or your Inbox might already contain messages.

EXERCISE **1-2** **Navigate in Outlook by Using the Outlook Bar**

A convenient way to navigate among Outlook's components is by using the *Outlook Bar*. This is the column on the left side of the Outlook window and shows groups of shortcuts, including Outlook shortcuts.

1. If the Outlook bar is not displayed, you can display it by choosing <u>V</u>iew from the menu, and then choosing <u>O</u>utlook Bar. The Outlook Bar appears as a column on the left side of the Outlook window.

TABLE 1-2   **Outlook Shortcuts in the Outlook Bar**

ICON/NAME	PURPOSE
Outlook Today	Provides a quick overview of your day, showing how many new e-mail messages you have, your appointments, and any pending tasks.
Inbox	Shows received e-mail messages, with a preview of the currently highlighted message.

continues

TABLE 1-2   **Outlook Shortcuts in the Outlook Bar**   *continued*

ICON/NAME	PURPOSE
Calendar	Used to schedule meetings and appointments and to keep track of annual events such as vacations and birthdays.
Contacts	Displays an electronic address book for storing names, addresses, and phone numbers.
Tasks	Displays a "to-do" list for personal and business tasks. You can use it to set deadlines and prioritize tasks.
Notes	Used to write quick notes, reminders, or ideas you want to jot down quickly.
Deleted Items	Displays all deleted Outlook items, similar to the Windows Recycling bin.
Journal	Records actions related to specific contacts, such as appointments or e-mail messages.

2. If the Outlook shortcuts are not displayed, click **Outlook Shortcuts** in the Outlook Bar. The Outlook shortcuts provide quick access to all the major components of Outlook: Outlook Today, Inbox, Calendar, Contacts, Tasks, and Notes.

FIGURE 1-4
Outlook Bar

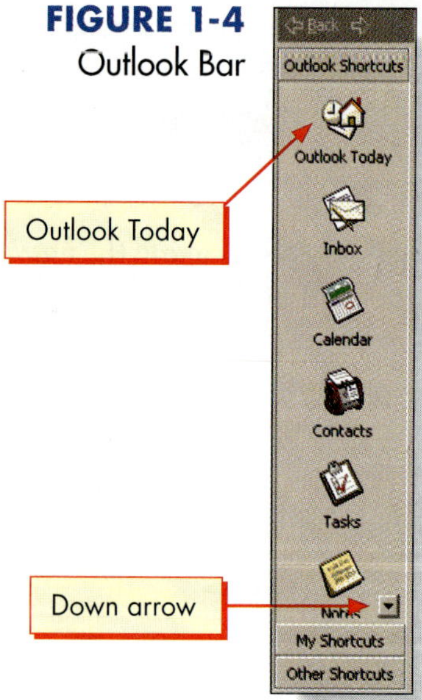

Outlook Today

Down arrow

3. Click the Outlook Today shortcut, which is the first icon in the Outlook Bar. Outlook Today provides a summary of information you've entered in Outlook that is relevant for today and the next few days. It shows a count of new e-mail messages, your appointments, and pending tasks. It is empty because you've not yet entered any information or received any e-mail messages.

4. Click the Inbox shortcut in the Outlook Bar to redisplay the Inbox.

5. Click the Back button above the Outlook Bar. This displays the previous Outlook folder.

6. Click the Forward button. The Inbox reappears. Two additional shortcut groups are listed at the bottom of the Outlook Bar: My Shortcuts and Other Shortcuts.

7. Click **My Shortcuts** to display the My Shortcuts group. See if anyone has added any shortcuts to this computer.

8. Click **Other Shortcuts** to display the Other Shortcuts group, which contains shortcuts for folders and utilities on the Windows desktop.

9. Click **Outlook Shortcuts** to redisplay the Outlook shortcuts. Depending on the size of your computer monitor, you might see a down arrow near the

bottom of the Outlook Bar (see Figure 1-4). The arrow indicates there are more shortcuts in this shortcut group.

10. If it's visible, click the down arrow ▼ to see the remaining Outlook short-cuts. Notice the Deleted Items shortcut, which contains items you delete in Outlook. An up arrow ▲ might appear near the top of the Outlook Bar.

11. If it's visible, click the up arrow ▲ to redisplay the Outlook Today shortcut.

EXERCISE   1-3   Navigate in Outlook by Using the Folder List

Outlook saves all information you create in a data file known as the *Personal Folders* file. The Personal Folders file contains folders for all of Outlook's components. Your messages, tasks, and appointments are stored in these folders. You can use the <u>V</u>iew command to view these folders and to navigate in Outlook.

The basic element for storing information in Outlook is referred to as an *item*. Every appointment, meeting, contact, message received, sent message, and so on, is an Outlook item. And within each item are various units of information, which are known as *fields*. For example, the fields for a received message include the message subject, the sender, and the date sent.

1. From the <u>V</u>iew menu, choose **Fol<u>d</u>er List** if the folder is not already displayed. Outlook displays all the file folders associated with the program. Notice under Outlook Today - Personal Folders that Outlook lists the folders for the My Shortcuts group along with all the folders on the Outlook Bar. (See Figure 1-5 on the next page.)

NOTE: Depending on your screen resolution, some of the labels in the folder list might be truncated. Use the scroll bar at the bottom of the folder list to see all the labels.

2. Click the folder for **Sent Items** to display the contents of the Sent Items folder. The folder is empty because you haven't sent anything yet. The name in the folder banner identifies it as Sent Items.

3. Click the **Inbox** folder to display the contents of the Inbox folder.

4. From the <u>V</u>iew menu, choose **Fol<u>d</u>er List** once again to turn off the display of the folder list, or click the folder list's Close button ✕.

5. Click **Inbox** in the folder banner. Outlook displays the folder list. This is an alternative to using the <u>V</u>iew, **Fol<u>d</u>er List** command to temporarily open the folder list.

6. Click anywhere outside the folder list to close it.

EXERCISE **1-4** **Identify Menus, Commands, and Buttons**

Each component of Outlook has a menu bar near the top of the window, and a toolbar underneath. The commands and buttons on the menu bar and toolbar might be different, depending on the part of Outlook. To identify a toolbar button by name, point to it with the mouse and Outlook will display a *ScreenTip*—a box with the button name.

You can move around Outlook by using the mouse or keyboard shortcuts. Some components of Outlook have mouse functions or keyboard shortcuts that are applicable only to that area of Outlook. Other mouse functions and keyboard combinations work in all areas of Outlook.

1. Click the Inbox shortcut 🔲 on the Outlook Bar to display the Inbox, if the Inbox is not already displayed.

2. Move the mouse pointer to **Edit** on the menu bar. Click the left mouse button to open the menu. Outlook displays a short version of the menu, showing only the most commonly used commands. If you take no action for a few seconds, the short version of the menu expands to the full version.

3. If the short version of the menu is still displayed, click the down arrows at the bottom of the menu to expand the **Edit** menu. Notice the additional commands in the expanded menu.

NOTE: Outlook's short menus are adaptive--they change as you work, listing the commands you use most frequently.

4. Without clicking the mouse button, move the pointer to <u>V</u>iew on the menu bar. Point to <u>T</u>oolbars, and notice the list of additional toolbars.

FIGURE 1-6
Displaying Toolbar menu options

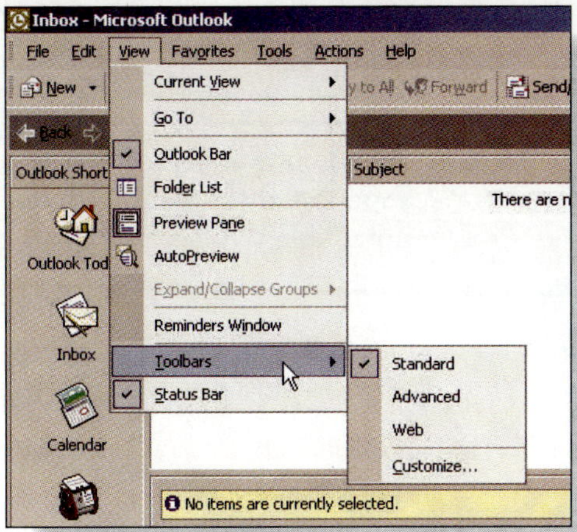

5. Without clicking, move the pointer slowly across the menu bar to display the <u>H</u>elp menu.

6. Click <u>H</u>elp on the menu bar to close the menu. You can also close a menu by clicking within the text area of the screen or by pressing [Esc].

7. Click <u>V</u>iew to open the <u>V</u>iew menu and choose <u>T</u>oolbars. The submenu shows the Standard toolbar is the only currently selected toolbar.

8. Click a blank text area of the screen to close the menu.

9. Position the pointer over the <u>N</u>ew button [icon] on the Standard toolbar. A ScreenTip appears, describing the button as New Mail Message. The text of the ScreenTip varies based on the folder currently displayed.

FIGURE 1-7
Identifying a toolbar button with a ScreenTip

10. Move the pointer over each of the remaining toolbar buttons, observing the ScreenTip for each.

Addressing, Composing, Sending, and Receiving E-Mail

To send a new e-mail message to someone, you must know the recipient's *Internet e-mail address*. This consists of a user name and a domain name, with the two separated by the "at" sign (@). The *domain name* is the mail system of the recipient and consists of two or more elements separated by periods or dots. For example, if your Internet Service Provider (ISP) is America Online, their domain name is aol.com. To receive e-mail, the recipient must have an e-mail address. You can send an e-mail message to one or more recipients at a time.

When you create information to store in Outlook, you use a *form*, which is a window to display and collect information. There are forms for each type of Outlook item. For example, when you create a message, you use a Message form. When you create a new contact, you use a Contact form.

TABLE 1-3 **Recipient Boxes**

BOX	PURPOSE
To	Sends a message directly to the recipient.
Cc	"Carbon copy." Sends a copy of the message to the recipient, with the recipient's name visible to other recipients of the message.
Bcc	"Blind carbon copy." Sends a copy of the message to the recipient, with the recipient's name not visible to other recipients of the message.

EXERCISE 1-5 Send and Receive E-Mail

Outlook lets you create and send new e-mail messages in several different ways. You can use:

- Menu commands
- Toolbar buttons
- Keyboard shortcuts

1. Click the **New** button on the toolbar. The Message form appears. (See Figure 1-8 on the next page.)

2. On the Formatting toolbar, click the down arrow next to the **Message format (HTML)** box, and choose **Plain Text**. This option controls the format of the text you type in the Message form. The Plain Text format is a Courier font.

NOTE: It is good practice to always use Plain Text as the message format for messages you compose. The recipients of your e-mail messages might have e-mail programs that only read messages written in Plain Text. Other message formats such as HTML might be unreadable or produce unpredictable errors. Message formatting is described in more detail later in this book.

3. In the To text box, key *[recipient's name]@[ISP]*

NOTE: Your instructor will provide you with a list of e-mail addresses to use for the To and Cc text boxes.

4. Press Tab to move the insertion point to the Cc text box.

5. Enter a second e-mail address by keying *[recipient name]@[ISP]*. This will send a copy of the message to the recipient in the Cc text box. In both the To and Cc textboxes, you can enter multiple e-mail addresses, following each address with a semicolon to separate it from the next one.

FIGURE 1-8
Message form for a
new message

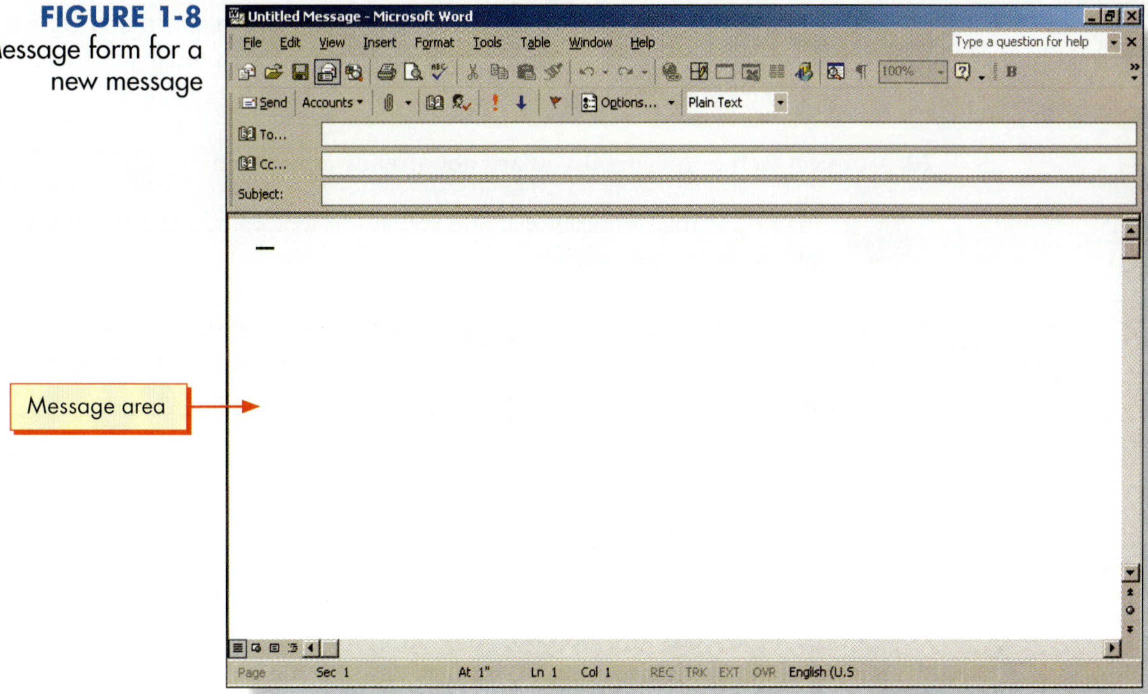

Message area

6. Press Tab to move the insertion point to the **Subject** text box.

7. Key **Traditional Homes Ad Campaign** and press Tab.

8. Begin your message with a salutation that addresses the recipient(s) by name, such as "Hi, Bill," or "Bill:" or some other appropriate greeting. For the body of the message, key the text shown in Figure 1-9, starting on the line below the salutation.

NOTE: You can use all basic word-processing editing features in the Message area of the Message form.

FIGURE 1-9

John was contacted by Traditional Homes magazine this past week about an article they are preparing on historic homes. The profiled homeowners have made significant use of AllWood furniture. John has asked that we prepare some advertising campaigns based on this article. Let's get together for a brainstorming session.

9. Read through your message to check for errors after you finish keying the body of the message. Check that you have the correct e-mail address in the To and Cc text boxes.

TIP: It's a good idea to double-check the addresses in the To and Cc text boxes before you send your e-mail. Errors in the address result in the return of e-mail or in delivery to the wrong person.

10. Connect to the Internet if you are not already connected.

NOTE: Your instructor will give you instructions on how to connect to the Internet from your computer.

11. Click the <u>S</u>end button on the Message form toolbar. Outlook sends the message to the specified recipients. The Message form closes and the Inbox appears.

12. Click Inbox in the folder banner. Outlook displays the folder list.

13. Click Sent Items in the folder list. The Sent Items folder appears, showing a listing for the message you just sent.

14. Click the Inbox shortcut 📧 in the Outlook Bar to display the Inbox.

15. Click the Send/Re<u>c</u>eive button on the Standard toolbar. The Outlook Send/ Receive Progress box briefly appears while the operations are in progress. Outlook first sends any messages in your Outbox and then checks your mail server for any messages that might have arrived for you. A tone sounds when new messages arrive, and they automatically appear in your Inbox. The Inbox shortcut shows a number in parentheses indicating the number of unread messages in your Inbox.

FIGURE 1-10
Inbox with a
received message

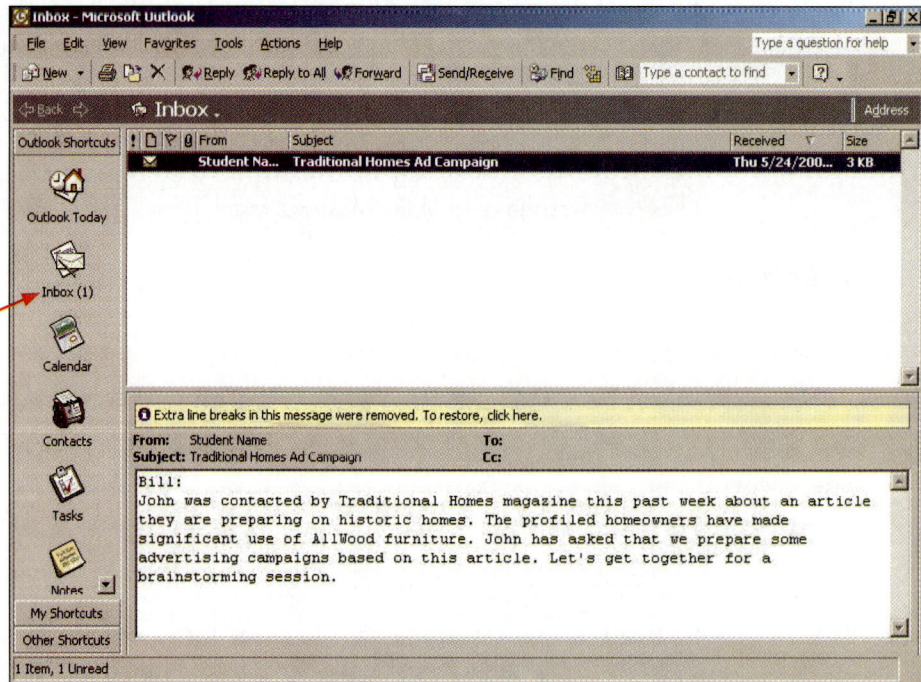

Number of unread messages in Inbox

Using Contacts to Address E-Mail

The Contacts component of Outlook is an electronic address book. You can use it to store information about *contacts*—individuals and businesses with whom you communicate. You access Contacts by clicking the Contacts shortcut 📇 in the Outlook Bar or by opening the Contacts folder in the file list. The Contacts folder displays the *contact list*, which is the list of people and organizations with whom you communicate.

EXERCISE   **1-6**   **Create Contacts**

In addition to contact names, you can also store job titles, phone numbers, e-mail and postal mail addresses, and notes. Contact information is stored in the contact list in the Contacts folder. When you create a new contact, you add it to your contact list.

1. Click the Contacts shortcut 📇 in the Outlook Bar. The Contacts folder is displayed, but the contact list is empty.

2. Click the **New** button 🔲 on the Standard toolbar. The Contact form appears.

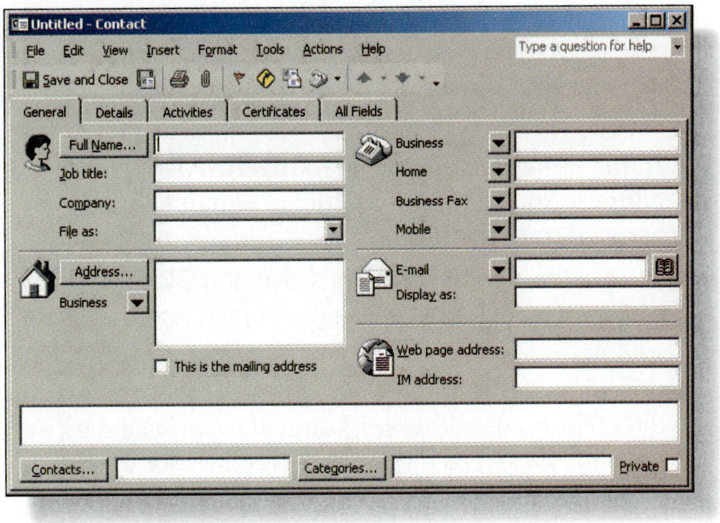

FIGURE 1-11
Contact form

3. Click the **General** tab, if it is not already displayed, and then click **Full Name**. The Check Full Name dialog box appears.

> ⭐ **TIP:** When creating new contacts, use the Check Full Name dialog box to ensure a name is identified correctly for sorting, filtering, or mail merge.

4. Click the down arrow next to the <u>T</u>itle text box and choose **Mr.**

5. In the <u>F</u>irst text box, key **Frank**. You can enter two names in the <u>F</u>irst text box by including the word "and" or the ampersand (&) between the names, as in "Frank and Susan."

6. In the <u>L</u>ast text box, key **Young** and click **OK**. The Contact form reappears.

7. Click **A<u>d</u>dress**. The Check Address dialog box appears.

8. For <u>S</u>treet, <u>C</u>ity, S<u>t</u>ate/Province, and <u>Z</u>ip/Postal code, key:

240 Montgomery Street

Dubuque

IA

52003

9. Click **OK**. The Contact form reappears. Under **A<u>d</u>dress**, Outlook shows this as a Business address.

10. Click the down arrow under **A<u>d</u>dress** and note that the other choices include **Home** and **Other**. If there are multiple addresses, you can specify the one to use as the mailing address by selecting **This is the mailing add<u>r</u>ess**.

11. In the phone area of the dialog box, click the down arrow in the topmost text box. Select **Assistant** and key **(319) 555-1234**. Specify the second phone text box as **Business** and key **(319) 555-1235**.

> **NOTE:** As you key a phone number in the phone text boxes, Outlook underlines the number. Outlook also formats the number properly even if you type the digits without spaces, parentheses, or a hyphen. You can see details of the number and enter a country code by double-clicking the underlined phone number.

12. In the E-mail text box, key **fyoung@ISP.isp**. This is the contact's e-mail address. You can enter additional e-mail addresses by clicking the down arrow next to the text box.

13. To save the contact, click the **<u>S</u>ave and Close** button on the Contact form toolbar. Outlook saves the new contact, and the Contacts folder appears.

14. Add the contacts shown in Figure 1-12 on the next page, but do not key the comments in red, which indicate if the information is home or business data. For home addresses, you will need to change the text box from Business to Home. For home addresses, be sure to select the **This is the mailing add<u>r</u>ess** option.

> **TIP:** When entering multiple contacts, use the Save and New button on the Contact form toolbar when you've finished with one contact and are ready to begin another. This button saves the current Contact form and displays a new one.

FIGURE 1-12

Mr. Tom Campbell   ABC Graphics *(Enter as company)*

123 Pleasant Street *(Home)*   1600 Main Street *(Business)*

Dubuque, IA 52002   Dubuque, IA 52001

(319) 555-1111 *(Home)*   (319) 555-1199

E-mail: tcamp@ISP.isp   E-mail: abcgraph@ISP.isp

Ms. Doris Jones   Dr. Henry Williams

240 Cedar Avenue *(Business)*   1200 Sunset Road *(Home)*

Dubuque, IA 52002   Dubuque, IA 52003

(319) 555-1231 *(Business)*   (319) 555-1119 *(Home)*

15. Add another student in your class as a contact. Your instructor will supply you with a list of e-mail addresses to use in the E-mail field of the Contact form.

FIGURE 1-13
Contacts folder
with new contacts

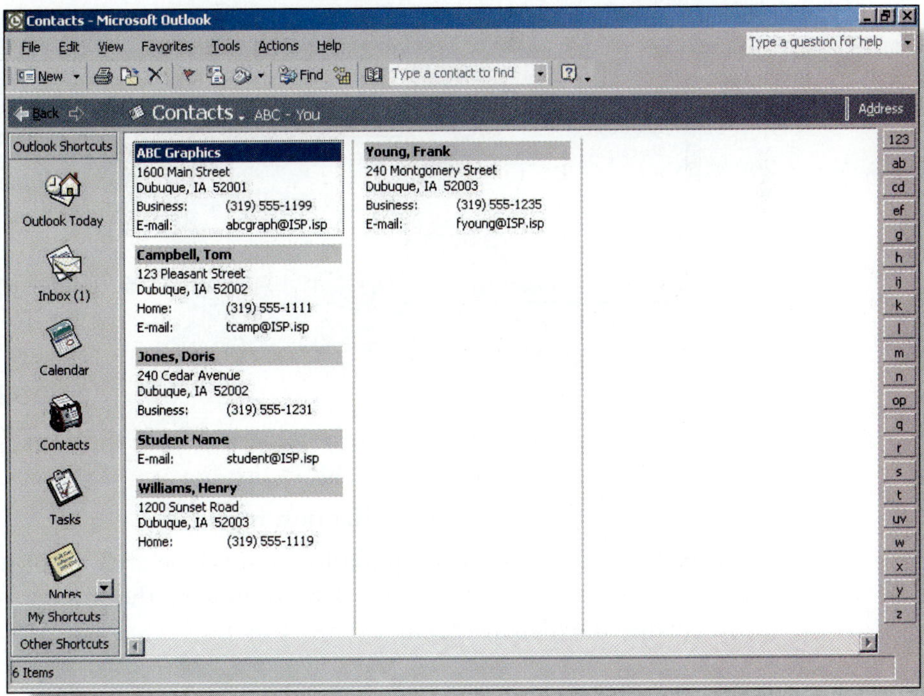

NOTE: Your Contacts folder might not look the same as the one shown in Figure 1-13, depending on the name you use as your student contact. Outlook alphabetizes the contact list, based on last names.

EXERCISE **1-7** **Send an E-Mail to a Contact**

If you want to send an e-mail message to a contact, you can enter the contact's address in the Message form by selecting it from the contact list instead of keying it.

1. Click the Inbox shortcut 🖼 in the Outlook Bar. The Inbox folder appears.

2. Click the **New** button 🖼 on the Standard toolbar. The Message form appears.

3. Click the **To** button, which is just to the left of the **To** text box. The Select Names dialog box appears. The dialog box shows the entries in your contact list that contain e-mail addresses. (Some of the contacts you entered did not have e-mail addresses.)

4. At the top of the dialog box, click the down arrow next to the **Show Names from the** text box and select **Contacts**, if it is not already displayed.

FIGURE 1-14
Select Names
dialog box

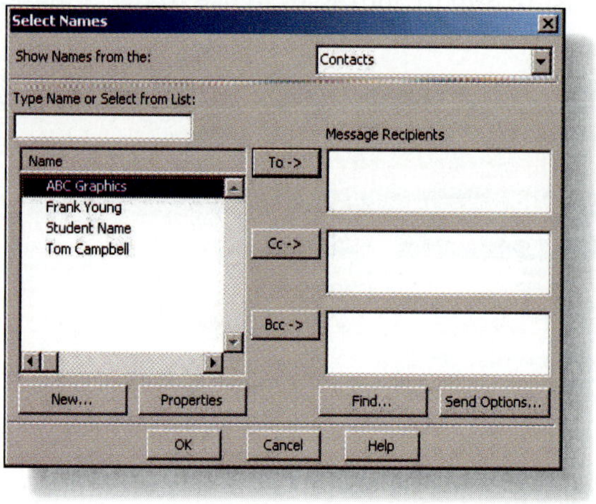

5. Under **Name**, select the name of the student in your class whose name you entered in the previous exercise.

TIP: You can select multiple names by holding Ctrl and then clicking the names.

6. Under **Message Recipients**, click **To**. The selected name appears as a message recipient.

7. Click OK. The Message form reappears, with the e-mail address of the student's name entered in the **To** text box.

8. For Subject, key **New collection input**

9. Position the insertion point in the message area of the Message form. You'll create the body of the message by copying the contents of a Word document into the message area.

NOTE: You can copy text for e-mail messages from any existing Word document by using the *Office Clipboard,* which is a feature that lets you collect text from one document or program and paste it into another.

10. From the File menu, choose Open. The Open dialog box appears.

11. Click the Word file **Email1** once to select it, and then click Open. The Word file Email1.doc opens.

12. From the Edit menu, choose Select All. The entire document is selected.

13. From the Edit menu, choose Copy. The selected text is copied to the Office Clipboard.

14. Close the Email1 document by clicking the Close button ☒ on the Word title bar. The Message form reappears.

15. Position the insertion point in the message area of the Message form if it is not already located there.

16. On the Formatting toolbar, click the down arrow next to the **Message format** box and change the message format to **Plain Text**.

17. From the Edit menu, choose Paste. The contents of the Clipboard are pasted into the message area of the Message window.

18. Move the insertion point to the end of the pasted text and replace "Student Name" with your name.

19. If you are not already connected to the Internet, make the connection now.

20. Click the Send button on the Message form toolbar. Outlook sends the message to the specified recipient. The Message form closes and the Inbox appears.

21. Click the Send/Receive button on the Standard toolbar. New messages automatically appear in your Inbox.

Reading E-Mail

The items in Outlook's Inbox are the e-mail messages you've received. The fields for messages include the message subject, the sender, and the date received, as well as other items of information.

Each component of Outlook has a set of standard *views,* which are ways of presenting the same information in different arrangements and formats. For example, items might be presented in a table, in a timeline, or as icons, depending on the Outlook folder. Inbox information appears in the Table view. Each item (message) is a row of the table, and details about the messages are in columns. Some of the columns use symbols as their headings. Figure 1-15 on the next page shows the Inbox column headings.

FIGURE 1-15
Parts of the Inbox

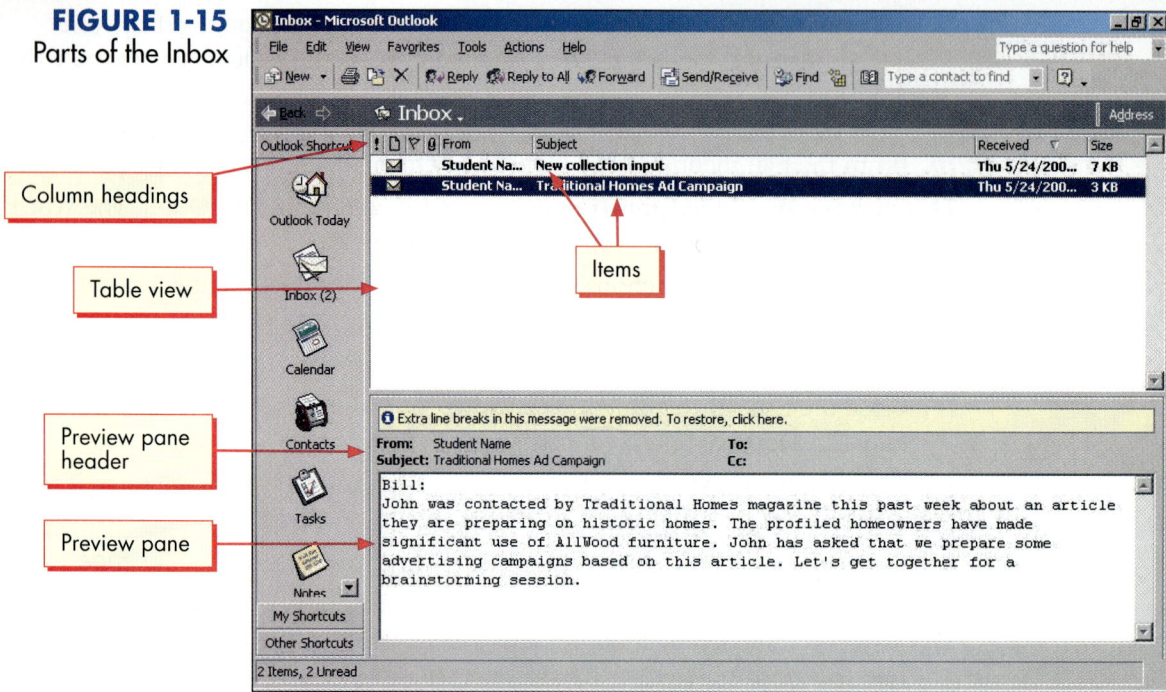

Column headings

Table view

Preview pane header

Preview pane

Items

TABLE 1-4   Inbox Column Headings Symbols

SYMBOL		PURPOSE
❗	Importance	Shows the importance of a message.
🗋	Icon	Indicates status of item (unopened or opened mail messages, for example).
▽	Flag Status	Shows messages that are flagged.
📎	Attachment	Indicates if a message has an attachment.

EXERCISE   1-8   Read E-Mail and Navigate in Messages

You can read shorter messages by just selecting them in the Inbox and viewing them in the preview pane. Opening the message enables you to read longer messages and use various viewing options.

1. If the Inbox is not already displayed, click the Inbox shortcut 📧 in the Outlook Bar. Inbox messages are arranged in the order in which they were received.

2. If it is not already selected, select the first message you received, which is the "Traditional Homes Ad Campaign" message. Notice that you can read the contents of the message in the preview pane without actually opening the message. Use the scroll bar in the preview pane to read any portion of the message not visible in the preview pane.

3. Double-click the "New collection input" message to open it. The Message form appears. Although you can read a message in the preview pane, the Message form gives you more options for responding to a received message, and you can enlarge the viewing area of the screen.

FIGURE 1-16
Message form for a received e-mail

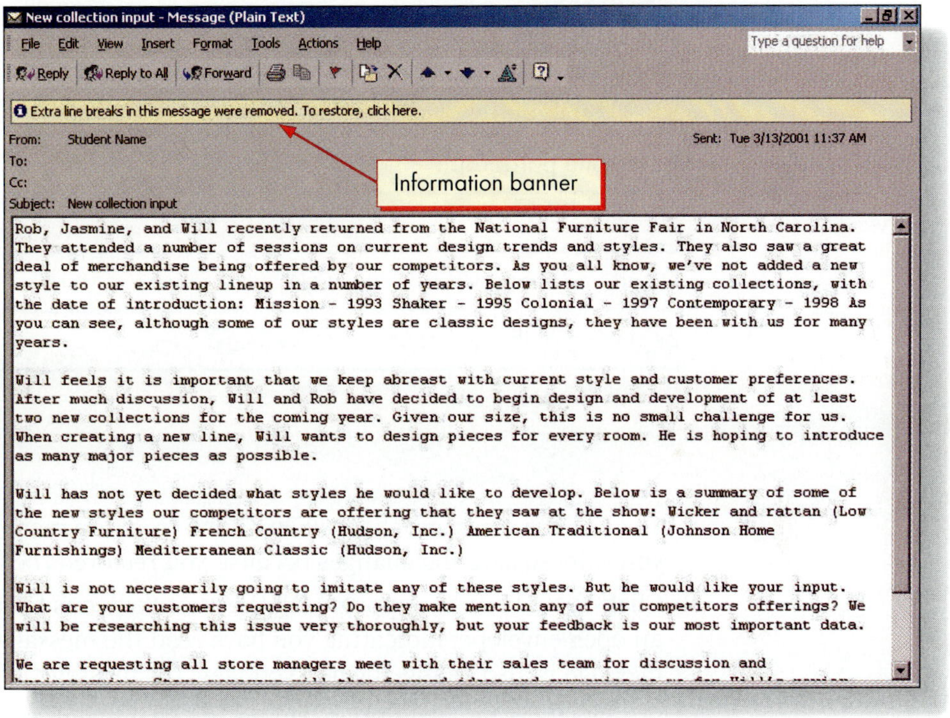

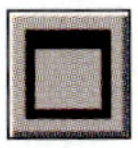

4. Click the Maximize button ▢ in the Message form title bar to enlarge the viewing area if the window is not already maximized. The Message form will remain maximized for all subsequent messages that you view.

5. Use the scroll bar to read the message. (Depending on the size of your screen and its resolution, the entire message might display without scrolling.) Notice that the information banner under the toolbar indicates that line breaks were removed in the message.

6. Click the banner to restore the line breaks. The message now has more blank space, and the line breaks are restored in the collection list in the first paragraph.

7. Press [Ctrl]+[End] to move the insertion point to the end of the message. Table 1-5 lists other keystrokes you can use to move the insertion point.

TABLE 1-5   **Keys to Move the Insertion Point**

TO MOVE	PRESS
One word to the left	[Ctrl] + [←]
One word to the right	[Ctrl] + [→]
Beginning of the line	[Home]
End of the line	[End]
Up one paragraph	[Ctrl] + [↑]
Down one paragraph	[Ctrl] + [↓]
Up one window	[PgUp]
Down one window	[PgDn]
Beginning of the document	[Ctrl] + [Home]
End of the document	[Ctrl] + [End]

8. To close the message, choose <u>F</u>ile, <u>C</u>lose from the menu. Outlook asks you if you want to save the changes because you restored the line breaks.

9. Click **Yes**. The Inbox appears. Notice that the icons for both messages show an open envelope, indicating you have read the message. The status of the message is also changed when you view the message in the preview pane.

10. Double-click the "Traditional Homes Ad Campaign" message to open it. The message appears in the Message form.

11. Click the Previous Item button [▲] on the Message form toolbar to display the "New collection input" message. This message appears just before the "Traditional Homes Ad Campaign" message.

12. Click the Next Item button [▼] on the toolbar. The "Traditional Homes Ad Campaign" message appears again.

13. Click the Close button [X] on the Message form title bar. The Inbox appears.

Sending Attachments to E-Mail

You can send an e-mail message with one or more files attached to the message. Recipients can then read the e-mail and store the file separately on their computers. In essence, the attached file is copied from your computer to the recipient's computer.

Outlook blocks certain types of attachment files that might contain viruses, such as files with the .bat, .exe, and .vbs extensions. Another issue in message attachments is file size. Depending on your Internet connection and the recipient's Internet connection, it might not be practical (or even possible) to send or receive very large files that tie up the lines for a long time. Some Internet Service Providers also limit the number of attachments that can be sent or received with a single e-mail message.

EXERCISE | **1-9** | **Send an Attachment with an E-Mail**

When you attach a file to an e-mail message, you see only the filename, not the file's contents. It's a good idea to take a look at the file before you send it. In this exercise, you attach a Word document to an e-mail, so your first step is to look at the Word document you intend to attach to your e-mail.

1. Click the Start button [Start] on the taskbar and point to <u>P</u>rograms.

2. On the <u>P</u>rograms menu, click Microsoft Word. The Word window appears.

3. Choose <u>F</u>ile, <u>O</u>pen from the Word menu. The Open dialog box appears.

4. Select the Word file **Renovate** and click <u>O</u>pen. The Word file Renovate.doc appears.

5. Key your name following "From." To save the file, choose <u>F</u>ile, Save <u>A</u>s from the menu, key *[your initials]*1-9 in the File <u>n</u>ame text box, and then click <u>S</u>ave.

6. Click the Print button [printer icon] on the Word toolbar to print the document.

7. Close Word. (Click No if you are asked to save the changes in the file.)

8. In Outlook, click the <u>N</u>ew button [New]. The Message form appears.

9. In the To text box, key *[recipient's name]@[ISP]*

   NOTE: Your instructor will provide you with a list of e-mail addresses to use for the To text box.

10. In the Subject text box, key **Power shutdown** and press [Tab].

11. On the Formatting toolbar, click the down arrow next to the Message format box and change the message format to Plain Text.

12. For the body of the message, key the text shown in Figure 1-17 on the next page.

FIGURE 1-17

Valerie has asked me to notify all office staff that the power will be off between 8 and 9 p.m. Sunday evening for the re-wiring of the conference room audio-visual equipment. Attached is a renovation schedule for next month.

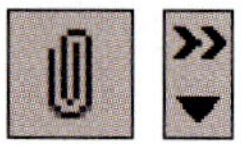

13. Click the Insert File button ⌾ on the toolbar (use the Toolbar Options button ❯ if the Insert File button does not appear on your toolbar). The Insert File dialog box appears.

14. Select the Word file *[your initials]***1-9**, and click **In**s**ert**. Outlook attaches the document to the message. The Word icon and the name of the attached file appear in the **Attach** text box.

FIGURE 1-18
Message form with attachment icon and filename

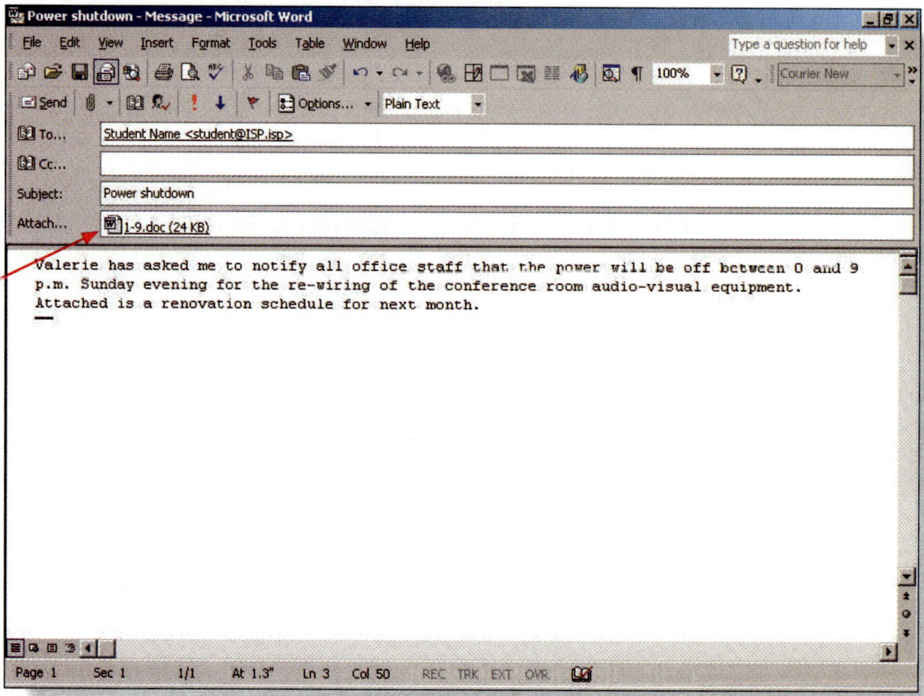

Attachment icon

> **TIP:** If you attach a file to a message and decide before you send it that you don't want to attach the file, you can click the attachment icon and press Delete to remove the attachment.

15. Click the **S**end button to send the message to the specified recipient. The Inbox reappears.

16. Click the Send/Re**c**eive button [Send/Receive]. New messages automatically appear in your Inbox. Messages with attachments show an attachment icon next to the sender's name.

17. Log off the Internet if your instructor tells you to do so.

EXERCISE **1-10** **Open a Message with an Attachment**

You can open the attachment by clicking the attachment icon in the message header of the preview pane or by opening the attachment from within the message itself.

1. Double-click the "Power shutdown" message. The Message form appears. The message header shows that the message includes a Word file attachment.

2. Double-click the Word icon in the Attachments field. The Opening Mail Attachment dialog box appears. Outlook displays this dialog box as a precaution to remind you that attachments might contain viruses. You have a choice of opening the attachment or saving it. Unless an attachment is from a known source, it is considered safer to save an attachment to your hard drive and scan it by using an anti-virus program before opening it.

FIGURE 1-19
Opening Mail
Attachment
dialog box

3. Select **Open** it. Because you know this file is from a safe source, it is safe to open it.

4. Click **OK**. The Word file opens.

5. Close the Word file and Word, and then close the "Power shutdown" message.

Using E-Mail Features

Outlook includes features that help you manage e-mail efficiently. For example, when you receive an e-mail message and reply to the sender, Outlook includes a copy of the sender's message in your response. You can also forward a received e-mail message to a third party.

EXERCISE 1-11 Forward an E-Mail Message

You may forward a message from the Inbox or while viewing it in the Message form. A toolbar button for forwarding a message is available in both locations.

1. Display the Inbox, if it is not already displayed.

2. Open the "Traditional Homes" message. The message appears in the Message form.

3. Click the Forward button on the Message form toolbar. The Message form toolbar changes and Outlook prefaces the title with "FW," indicating that this is a forwarded message. The "FW" prefix precedes the Subject text as well. The original message has been reformatted, clearly delineating the original text from text you might add to the body of the message.

FIGURE 1-20
Message form for a message that will be forwarded

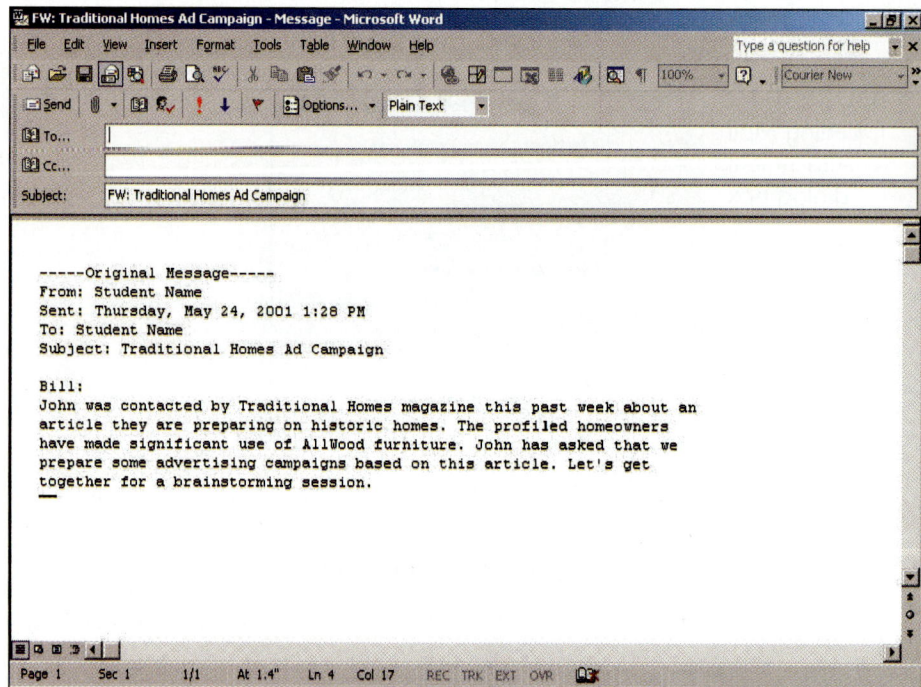

```
-----Original Message-----
From: Student Name
Sent: Thursday, May 24, 2001 1:28 PM
To: Student Name
Subject: Traditional Homes Ad Campaign

Bill:
John was contacted by Traditional Homes magazine this past week about an
article they are preparing on historic homes. The profiled homeowners
have made significant use of AllWood furniture. John has asked that we
prepare some advertising campaigns based on this article. Let's get
together for a brainstorming session.
```

4. In the To text box, key *[recipient's name]@ISP* or click the To button and use the student name in your contact list.

NOTE: Your instructor will provide you with a list of e-mail addresses to use for the To text box.

5. Press Tab until the insertion point is in the Message area, above the original message. Begin the message with a salutation addressing the recipient by name. Then key the text shown in Figure 1-21.

FIGURE 1-21

John wants us to develop some ideas for an ad campaign based on the
Traditional Homes article. Could you supply us with the ad copy of any ads
we've run in different publications in the last few years? Thanks!

6. Click the Send button. Outlook sends the message to the specified recipient, and the Message form redisplays the original message as it was before you forwarded it. Outlook adds a comment at the top of the message indicating you forwarded it.

7. Close the Message form. The status icon has changed to indicate that you've forwarded this message. Note that you can forward a message without opening it by using the Forward button on the Standard toolbar.

TIP: It is good e-mail etiquette to delete unneeded portions of a forwarded message to make your e-mail smaller and thus faster to download.

EXERCISE 1-12 Reply to an E-Mail Message

You can reply to an e-mail message from the Inbox or while viewing it in the Message form. A toolbar button is available in both locations for replying to a message.

1. Display the Inbox, if it is not already displayed.

2. Select the "Power shutdown" message without opening it. You do not have to open a message to forward or reply to it.

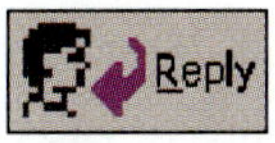

3. Click the Reply button on the Standard toolbar. Outlook reformats the original message, similar to the way it reformats a forwarded message. Both the subject and the message title are prefixed with "RE" to indicate that this is a reply message. Outlook automatically places the sender's e-mail address in the To text box, so you don't need to re-key it.

> Reply to All

> ⭐ **TIP:** If you receive a message that was sent to other individuals besides yourself, you can use the Reply to All button to send your reply to everyone who received the original message.

4. Place the insertion point in the Message area if it is not already positioned there. Key a salutation addressing the message recipient by name, and then key the text shown in Figure 1-22.

FIGURE 1-22

```
You might want to tell everyone to power down their computers before they
leave on Friday. The workers might be repeatedly turning the power on and
off, and this is not good for computer equipment.
```

5. Connect to the Internet if you are not already connected.

6. Click the **Send** button. Outlook sends the message to the specified recipient and the Inbox reappears. Like a forwarded message, the original message now contains a comment indicating that you replied. The status icon shows that you've replied to this message.

7. Click the **Send/Receive** button. New messages automatically appear in your Inbox.

8. Log off the Internet if your instructor tells you to do so.

Printing E-Mail and Contacts and Closing Outlook

Printing an e-mail message or a contact is easy. You can use any of the following methods:

- Click the Print button 🖨 on the Standard toolbar.
- Choose **File**, **Print** from the menu.
- Press Ctrl + P.

The menu and keyboard methods open the Print dialog box, where you can select printing options. Clicking the Print button 🖨 sends the message or contact directly to the printer.

There are several ways to close Outlook:

- Click the Close button ✕ button in the upper right corner of the Outlook title bar.
- Choose **File**, **Exit** from the menu.
- Press Alt + F4.

EXERCISE **1-13** **Configure Basic Print Options**

Outlook lets you print individual messages and contacts or the entire Inbox or contact list. Depending on what you are printing, you use a combination of paper and page settings to determine the look of the printed material. These settings are called a *print style*. Outlook has two built-in print styles: the Memo style and the Table style.

1. Display the Inbox, if it is not already displayed.

2. From the File menu, choose Page Setup. The submenu shows choices for two built-in print styles. Use Table Style to print the Inbox, which is in Table view. Use Memo Style for an individual item, such as an e-mail message.

3. Choose Table Style. The Page Setup: Table Style dialog box appears.

FIGURE 1-23
Page Setup: Table
Style dialog box

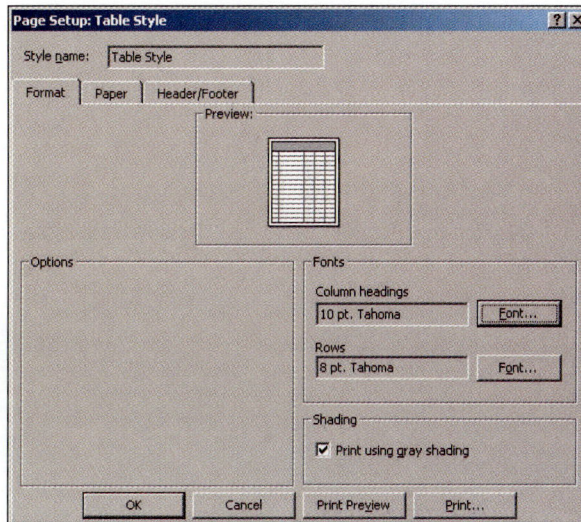

4. Click the Format tab, if it is not already displayed. You can set the fonts of the rows and columns in this tab.

5. Click the Paper tab. You can set page orientation in this tab.

6. Click the Header/Footer tab. The default is for a footer that includes the User Name, the page number, and the date.

7. Replace the User Name in the footer with your name, and key your name in the center section of the header.

TIP: Buttons under the Footer section on the Header/Footer tab can be used to automatically insert a page number, the total number of pages, or the date, time, or user's name in a header or footer.

8. Click Print Preview to display the Inbox as it appears when it is printed.

9. To zoom in (magnify) the preview so you can see the details, position the pointer over the section of the document you want enlarged and click. The preview enlarges. Click again to reduce the size.

10. Click Close on the Print Preview toolbar to close the preview. The Inbox reappears.

11. From the File menu, choose Page Setup once again, and then select Memo Style. The Page Setup: Memo Style dialog box appears. Outlook uses Memo style for printing individual messages. The options in this dialog box resemble the Table Style dialog box.

12. Click the Header/Footer tab and key your name in the center section of the header.

13. Click Print Preview. Outlook shows a preview of the selected message. Zoom in to view the details of the preview. Then click Close.

EXERCISE 1-14 **Print E-Mail and Contacts, Delete a Contact, and Close Outlook**

1. Display the Inbox if it is not already displayed.

2. From the File menu, choose Print. The Print dialog box appears.

FIGURE 1-24
Print dialog box

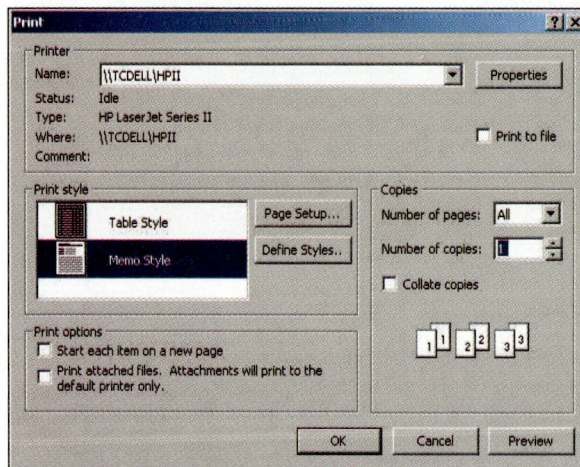

3. Choose Table Style as the print style.

4. Click OK. Outlook prints the Inbox.

5. Select the Inbox "Power shutdown" message without opening it.

6. Click the Print button on the Standard toolbar. Outlook prints the "Power shutdown" message. The printout includes the Word icon and attach-

ment filename. You can print e-mail items from the Sent Items folder as well as from the Inbox.

7. Click the Contacts shortcut 📇 on the Outlook Bar to display the contact list.

8. Select the listing for Tom Campbell without opening it.

9. From the File menu, choose Print. The Print dialog box appears. Notice that there are various print styles available for printing contacts.

10. Select Memo Style.

11. Click Preview. The Print Preview appears. In addition to clicking in the document, you can also use Print Preview toolbar buttons to zoom in and out.

12. If the preview appears as one page, click the Actual Size button 🔍 on the Print Preview toolbar to zoom in. If the preview appears as actual size, click the One Page button 🗒 to zoom out.

13. Click the Print 🖨 button on the Print Preview toolbar to return to the Print dialog box.

14. Click OK. The selected contact prints in Memo Style.

15. If it is not already selected, select the Tom Campbell contact and click the Delete button ✖ on the Standard toolbar. The contact is deleted. You can use this button to delete any item in Outlook.

16. Close Outlook by clicking the Close button ✖ in the Outlook title bar.

USING HELP ❓

Online Help is available to you as you work in Outlook.

Get acquainted with Microsoft Outlook Help:

1. Start Outlook.

2. Locate the Ask a Question box in the upper right corner of the screen. (See Figure 1-25 on the next page.) Click the box to activate it, and then key **get Help**

3. Press Enter. A list of Help topics appears. Click See more at the bottom of the list to see additional topics. Notice that the mouse pointer is shaped like a hand.

4. Click See previous to return to the first group of topics.

5. Click the topic Guidelines for searching Help. The Help dialog box opens.

6. Click each of the topics listed in blue text.

7. Close Help by clicking the Help window Close button ✖.

FIGURE 1-25
Using the Ask a
Question box

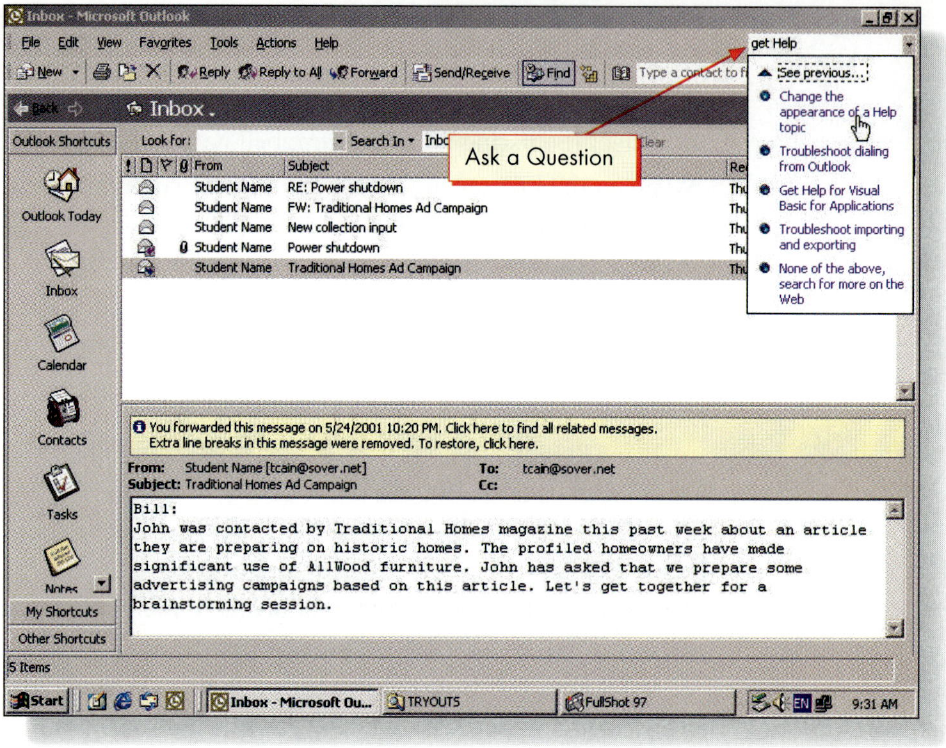

LESSON 1 Summary

> Start Outlook by clicking the Start button [Start] on the Windows taskbar, pointing to **P**rograms, and clicking **Outlook**.

> Use the Outlook Bar to navigate among Outlook's components.

> To navigate among the Personal Folders files, use the menu command **V**iew, **Folder List** to view Outlook folders. You can also click the folder name in the folder banner to display the folder list.

> Click the commands on the menu bar to open a menu. Click the down arrows at the bottom of the menu to display all the options. Press Esc or click a blank area of the screen to close a menu.

> Move the pointer over a toolbar button to display a ScreenTip that describes the button.

> Use the Message form to address and compose new e-mail messages. Enter the recipient's Internet e-mail address in the **To** field. The Sent Items folder contains a list of sent messages.

➤ The Contacts folder is an electronic address book that stores information about individuals and businesses in a list called a contact list.

➤ Enter new contacts in the Contact form. Information in a contact includes the name, title, phone number, e-mail address, and postal address, among other information.

➤ You can use an entry in the contact list to address an e-mail message. You can use the Office Clipboard to copy text for an e-mail message from another program.

➤ The Inbox contains received e-mail messages, displayed in a Table view, showing fields for message subject, sender, date received, and other information.

➤ You can read Inbox items in the preview pane or open them by double-clicking the message. Use the scroll bar to read longer messages, and click the information banner to restore line breaks.

➤ You can send e-mail messages with one or more files attached. Recipients can open the message and store the attachment on their computers.

➤ When a file is attached to a message, the filename of the attachment is displayed, not the contents of the file.

➤ Double-click the attachment icon displayed in the message header to open an attachment to a file. Outlook displays a precautionary message warning of potential viruses in file attachments.

➤ The subject of a forwarded message is given the prefix "FW."

➤ The subject of a reply is given the prefix "RE."

➤ Print styles define page and paper settings for printed material. Outlook has print styles that vary depending on the Outlook folder.

➤ Click Preview in the Print dialog box to display a preview of the printed item, and click toolbar buttons to enlarge or reduce the image. Delete items by using the Delete button ☒.

LESSON 1 Command Summary

FEATURE	BUTTON	MENU	KEYBOARD	SPEECH
Print	🖨	File, Print	Ctrl + P	✓
Send/ Receive All	Send/Receive	Tools, Send/Receive Send and Receive All	F9	✓

continues

LESSON 1　Command Summary　*continued*

FEATURE	BUTTON	MENU	KEYBOARD	SPEECH
New Message/ Contact		File, New	Ctrl + N	✓
Close Message	X	File, Close	Alt + F4	✓
Exit Outlook	X	File, Exit	Alt + F4	✓
Reply	Reply	Actions, Reply	Ctrl + R	✓
Forward	Forward	Actions, Forward	Ctrl + F	✓
Reply to All	Reply to All	Actions, Reply to All	Ctrl + Shift + R	✓
Insert File		Insert, File		✓

Concepts Review

TRUE/FALSE QUESTIONS

Each of the following statements is either true or false. Indicate your choice by circling T or F.

T F   *1.* You can use the Standard toolbar to start or exit Outlook.

T F   *2.* The Outlook Bar is a column on the right side of the Outlook window.

T F   *3.* You can click Other Shortcuts in the Outlook Bar to see shortcuts for Windows desktop items such as My Computer.

T F   *4.* You can send a message to more than one person at a time.

T F   *5.* When you create a contact, you can use only one first name.

T F   *6.* The icons in the Inbox for a message change when you reply to or forward a message.

T F   *7.* You must open a message to reply to it.

T F   *8.* Outlook has only one default print style, the Table Style.

SHORT ANSWER QUESTIONS

Write the correct answer in the space provided.

1. Which Outlook Bar shortcut presents you with a quick overview of your day, showing you new Inbox messages, tasks, and appointments?

_____

2. Which character is used to separate multiple e-mail addresses in the To and Cc fields?

_____

3. What feature enables you to send a file with an e-mail message?

_____

4. What button on the toolbar do you click when you're reading a message in the Message form and want to go to the next message in your Inbox?

_____

5. What button on the Message form toolbar would you use to reply to everyone whose names appeared as a recipient of an e-mail message?

_____

6. A forwarded message includes a comment that indicates the message was forwarded. Where does this comment appear?

_____

7. What prefix appears in front of the subject text for a message to which a reply has been sent?

_____

8. What prefix appears in front of the subject text for a forwarded message?

_____

CRITICAL THINKING

Answer these questions on a separate page. There are no right or wrong answers. Support your answers with examples from your own experience, if possible.

1. It is considered good e-mail etiquette to delete unnecessary portions of a forwarded e-mail message. Can you think of other good practices in using e-mail? Do you think appearance and content are important in e-mail messages? Why or why not?

2. You can send e-mail messages to multiple individuals. How do you decide if someone should be included as a recipient of the message? Is it desirable to limit the number of people you include as recipients? Why?

Skills Review

EXERCISE 1-15

Navigate in Outlook; address, compose, and send an e-mail message.

1. Start Outlook by following these steps:
   a. Click the Start button on the Windows taskbar.
   b. Point to Programs. Point to Microsoft Outlook and click it.
2. Click the Outlook Today shortcut on the Outlook Bar. Observe the number of new messages listed in your Inbox, if any.
3. Click the Inbox shortcut in the Outlook Bar to redisplay the Inbox.
4. Address and compose a new e-mail message by following these steps:
   a. Click the New button on the Standard toolbar.
   b. On the Formatting toolbar, click the down arrow next to the Message format box and choose Plain Text.
   c. In the To text box, key *[recipient's name]@[ISP]*

NOTE: You will send your message to your instructor. Your instructor will supply you with the appropriate e-mail address.

    d. Press Tab twice to move the insertion point to the **Subject** text box.

    e. Key **Conference room arrangements** and press Tab.

    f. Begin the message with a salutation, addressing your instructor by name. For the body of the message, key the text shown in Figure 1-26:

FIGURE 1-26

Per your request, I have made arrangements for the monthly store managers'
meeting to take place off site this month. I have reserved a conference
room at the Lodging International Hotel on Grant Road in Dubuque from 9
a.m. until 5 p.m. next Monday.

nd the message by following these steps:

    Connect to the Internet.

    b. Click the **Send** button on the Message form toolbar to send the message to the recipient.

    c. Log off the Internet if your instructor tells you to do so.

EXERCISE 1-16

Read an e-mail message, create a contact, use a contact in addressing an e-mail message, and send an e-mail message with an attachment.

NOTE: This exercise uses the e-mail message you received in Exercise 1-5. If you do not have this message in your Inbox, complete Exercise 1-5, addressing the message to yourself.

1. Read an e-mail message by following these steps:

    a. Click the Inbox shortcut on the Outlook Bar if the Inbox is not already displayed.

    b. Double-click the message whose subject is "Traditional Homes Ad Campaign."

    c. Click the Close button in the Message form title bar to close the message.

2. Create a contact by following these steps:

    a. Click the Contacts shortcut on the Outlook Bar.

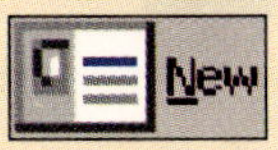

    b. Click the **New** button on the Standard toolbar.

3. From the <u>F</u>ile menu, choose <u>P</u>rint.

4. Under Print st<u>y</u>le, select **Memo Style**.

5. Click **Page Set<u>u</u>p**, and click the **Header/Footer** tab if it is not already displayed.

6. If it is not already present, key your name in the center section of the header, and then click **OK**.

7. Click **OK** again.

Lesson Applications

EXERCISE 1-19

Navigate between Outlook components, create a contact, read an e-mail message, and send a new e-mail message to the contact.

NOTE: This exercise uses the e-mail message you received in Exercise 1-7. If you do not have this message in your Inbox, complete Exercise 1-7, addressing the message to yourself.

Will McCarthy, AllWood's VP of Design, has asked you to help him develop a new line of furniture. You need to get some information from your colleagues.

1. Open Outlook and display the Outlook Bar, if it is not already displayed.
2. Display the Contacts folder.
3. Create a new contact.

NOTE: You will enter your instructor's name and address as your new contact. Your instructor will provide you an appropriate address. If you have already entered your instructor's address in a previous exercise, your instructor will give you a different address to use.

4. Display the Inbox and open the "New collection input" message. Locate the portion of the message with the text "Mediterranean Classic," and make note of the company that manufactures furniture in this style. Close the message.
5. Create a new e-mail message, addressing the message from the contact list. Use the contact name you created in step 3. Key the subject of the message as **Information request**
6. For the text of the message, key the text shown in Figure 1-28, substituting the company name you noted in step 4 in the blank:

FIGURE 1-28

```
I would like to compare our current lines to the Mediterranean style
manufactured by _____. Could you send me their current catalog?
Thanks!
```

7. Connect to the Internet and send the message.
8. Log off the Internet if your instructor tells you to do so.

EXERCISE 1-20

Navigate between Outlook components, create and print a new contact, and use the contact to address, send, and print a new e-mail message.

A new AllWood employee has just started working with you on a project for the Marketing Department. You'll need to enter your coworker's name in your contact list and send him a message.

1. Display the Contacts folder and create a new contact with the following information, specifying the address and phone number as Home and the address as the mailing address:

   John Smith

   555 Third Street

   Dubuque, IA 52001

   (319) 555-9999

2. Enter your instructor's e-mail address for the new contact.

   NOTE: Your instructor will supply you with an appropriate e-mail address.

3. Print the contact, using a Memo Style print style and using your name as a centered header.

4. Compose a new e-mail message, addressing the message from the contact list (use the contact you created in step 1). Key the subject of the message as **Discuss sales input**

5. Set the message format as Plain Text. For the text of the message, key the information in Figure 1-29:

FIGURE 1-29

```
John:

Rob has given me the feedback he received from the store managers. He has
asked that we organize the material and prepare a presentation for the
senior managers. Let's meet to discuss this.
```

6. Connect to the Internet and send the message.

7. Display the Sent Items folder and select the message you just sent. Print out the message, using a Memo Style print style with your name as a centered header.

8. Log off the Internet if your instructor tells you to do so.

EXERCISE 1-21

Open an e-mail message, forward it with an attachment, and print the sent message.

> **NOTE:** This exercise uses the e-mail message you received in Exercise 1-7. If you do not have this message in your Inbox, complete Exercise 1-7, addressing the message to yourself.

John Yu, AllWood's VP of Marketing, has asked you to work with him in developing some print advertising. You need to send some information to a colleague who is also working on the project.

1. Display the Inbox and select the message with the subject "New collection input."

2. Click the For**w**ard button. In the **To** text box, key your instructor's e-mail address.

> **NOTE:** Your instructor will provide you with an appropriate e-mail address.

3. In the message area, delete everything after the first paragraph in the original reformatted message. Position the insertion point above the remaining text, and key a salutation that addresses your instructor by name. Then key the message in Figure 1-30:

FIGURE 1-30

```
John gave me a list of what we're offering in the Shaker line. I've
attached the file. Could you add our other three collections to this
document?
```

4. Attach the Word file **Shaker1** to the message, connect to the Internet, and send the message.

5. Display the Sent Items folder and select the message you just sent. Print the message, using a Memo Style as the print style and using your name as a centered header. Close the message after printing it.

6. Log off the Internet if your instructor tells you to do so.

EXERCISE 1-22 ✚ *Challenge Yourself*

Open a received e-mail, forward it to another recipient, create a simple Word document as an attachment, and print the sent message.

> **NOTE:** This exercise uses the e-mail message you received in Exercise 1-9. If you do not have this message in your Inbox, complete Exercise 1-9, addressing the message to yourself.

You've been assigned to work with Maria Lopez, AllWood's VP of Administration. She wants you to manage the computer equipment affected by a pending power shutdown.

1. Display the Inbox and select the "Power shutdown" message.

2. Forward the message to your instructor. Your instructor will provide you with an appropriate e-mail address. Key a salutation addressing your instructor by name, and then key the message shown in Figure 1-31 above the reformatted text.

FIGURE 1-31

Valerie will need some help Monday morning bringing all the office equipment back on line again. Attached is a list of equipment that will need to be turned on and tested. You might want to assign different people to help out.

3. Open Word and create a simple file to use as an attachment to this message. Key the text shown in Figure 1-32.

FIGURE 1-32

Equipment Affected by Power Shutdown

Reception area - 1 computer and printer
Administrative area - Copy machine, 3 computers, 2 networked printers
First floor offices - 4 computers, 4 printers, 2 scanners, 1 fax machine
Second floor offices - 3 computers, 2 networked printers, copy machine
Conference room - 1 computer and printer

4. Save the Word file as *[your initials]*1-22, print the document, and close Word. (Click No if you are asked to save the changes in the file before you exit Word.)

5. Delete the attachment that was part of the original message and attach the Word file you created in step 3.

6. Connect to the Internet and send the message.

7. If the message is still open, close the message and display the Sent Items folder. Select the message you just sent. Print the message, using a Memo Style print style and using your name as a centered header.

8. Log off the Internet if your instructor tells you to do so.

On Your Own

In these exercises you work on your own, as you would in a real-life work environment. Use the skills you've learned to accomplish the task—and be creative.

EXERCISE 1-23

Have a friend with Internet access and an e-mail account send you a short e-mail message. Forward the message to your instructor. Locate the forwarded message in your Sent Items folder and print it.

EXERCISE 1-24

Enter the name of a friend or family member into your contact list, and then send an e-mail message to the contact. Locate the message in your Sent Items folder and forward it to your instructor. Locate the forwarded message in your Sent Items folder and print it. Print the contact.

EXERCISE 1-25

Have a friend with Internet access and an e-mail account send you a short e-mail message. Reply to the message. Locate your reply in your Sent Items folder and forward it to your instructor. Locate the forwarded message in your Sent Items folder and print it.

Calendar and Tasks

After completing this lesson, you will be able to:

1. **Navigate within the Calendar.**
2. **Schedule appointments.**
3. **Use reminders.**
4. **Schedule events.**
5. **Print the Calendar.**
6. **Create and update tasks.**

Estimated Time: 1½ hours

When your workday is filled with appointments and tasks, you can use Outlook's Calendar and Tasks to help you keep track of everything you have to do. You can use the Calendar to schedule appointments and events. You can set reminders for yourself and print your Calendar. With Outlook's Tasks, you can also create a task and follow it until it's completed.

Navigating Within the Calendar

Outlook's Calendar is accessed from the Outlook Bar as well as from the folder list. As with other Outlook components, the Calendar has its own file folder, and all items associated with the Calendar are stored there.

Navigating within the Calendar is similar to navigating within other components of Outlook. You can use the mouse, keyboard shortcuts, or menus to access Calendar functions. You can display the Calendar in a variety of time frames, ranging from a single day to an entire month.

EXERCISE   2-1   Navigate Within the Calendar

The Calendar is divided into several different areas. The *Appointments Calendar* occupies most of the left half of the screen. It divides the day into half-hour segments and shows any scheduled appointments, meetings, and events. The upper right portion of the Calendar is the *Date Navigator,* which shows two complete months of the year. The lower right portion of the Calendar contains the *TaskPad,* which is an abbreviated list of current tasks.

1. Click the Calendar shortcut in the Outlook Bar. The Calendar folder appears.

FIGURE 2-1
Calendar folder

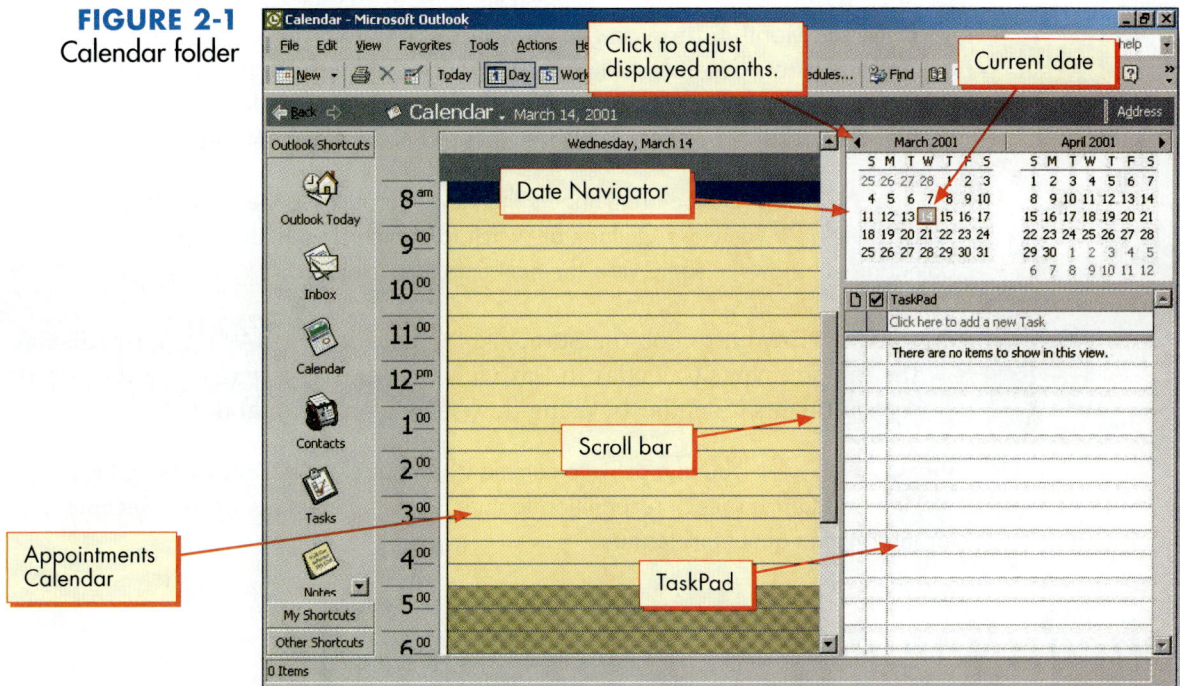

2. Drag the scroll bar on the right side of the Appointments Calendar to display the hours at the beginning and the end of the day. The normal work hours are shown in bright yellow and are displayed by default.

3. In the Date Navigator, click the date of the next business day. Notice that the Appointments Calendar changes to that date. The current date is shown in a red box. Click the T<u>o</u>day button on the Standard toolbar to return the Appointments Calendar to the present day.

4. Position the pointer over the current month title at the top of the Date Navigator. Click and hold briefly. Notice that you can adjust the month by using the displayed menu. You can also click the arrow keys next to the month titles to adjust the months sequentially.

5. Click the Wo<u>r</u>k Week button on the Standard toolbar (or press [Alt]+[R]). The Appointments Calendar displays an appointment schedule in Work Week view for the current week, without the weekends.

REVIEW: If some buttons do not appear on your toolbar, click the Toolbar Options button to see additional buttons.

6. Click the <u>W</u>eek button on the Standard toolbar (or press [Alt]+[W]). The Appointments Calendar displays in Week view, which includes weekends. If the Appointments Calendar is displayed in Week view, it automatically changes to Day view when you click a date in the Date Navigator.

7. Click the <u>M</u>onth button on the Standard toolbar (or press [Alt]+[M]). The Appointments Calendar displays in Month view. Notice that the space available for the display of appointments is necessarily smaller than in previous views, and the TaskPad and Date Navigator are not displayed.

NOTE: Outlook remembers the view you apply to the Appointments Calendar. If you close Outlook or switch to another folder, the Appointments Calendar will show the same view the next time it is displayed.

8. Click the Da<u>y</u> button on the Standard toolbar (or press [Alt]+[Y]) to redisplay the Appointments Calendar in Day view. You can also change the view of the Appointments Calendar by using the <u>V</u>iew menu command.

NOTE: You can activate commands and toolbar buttons by using the Microsoft Office speech recognition feature. See Appendix C, "Speech Recognition," for information about this feature.

Scheduling Appointments

An *appointment* is an activity occurring at a specific day and time that does not require inviting people to attend or reserving a room (or other resources). For example, a meeting with your supervisor could be considered an appointment. You can specify that an appointment should appear automatically in your Calendar at specified intervals. You can also have Outlook remind you of appointments.

Outlook gives you the option of letting others look at your Calendar, which is useful when other people are trying to schedule meetings with you. For this reason, you can control how others see your Calendar. For example, the time when an appointment takes place can be shown as "busy" or "out of the office."

EXERCISE   **2-2**   **Schedule an Appointment**

You can add a new appointment by using the Appointment form or by entering the appointment directly in the Appointments Calendar.

1. Click the date on the Date Navigator one week from the current date. Notice that the Appointments Calendar automatically displays this date.

2. Choose File, New and then choose Appointment (or click the New button [icon] on the Standard toolbar). The Appointment form appears, using the date displayed in the Appointments Calendar as the default date for the appointment.

FIGURE 2-2
Appointment form

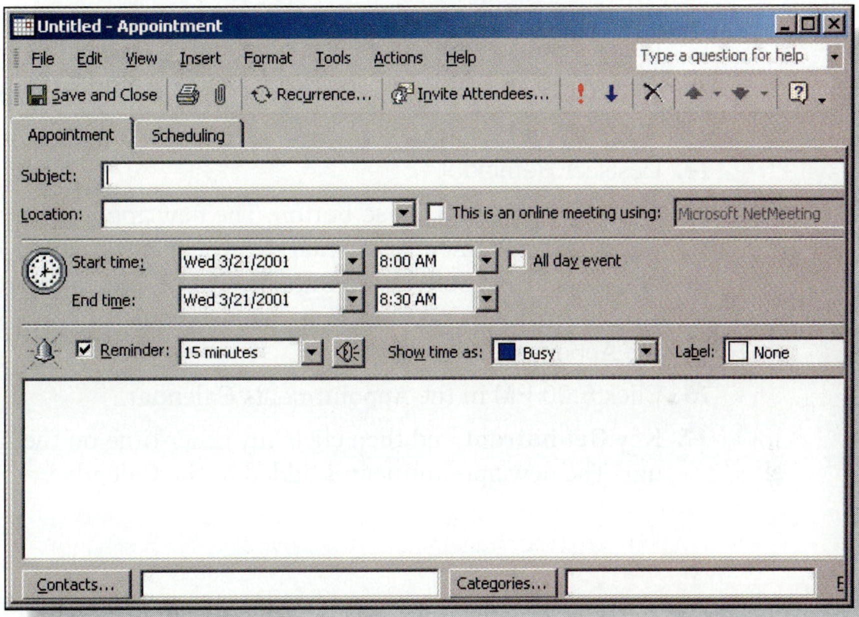

3. In the Subject text box, key **Weekly meeting with Will**

4. Press [Tab], and in the Location text box, key **Will's office**

5. Click the down arrow next to the Start time: text box for the time of the appointment, and set the starting time at 10:00 AM. Notice that the End time is automatically set at 10:30 AM. Leave this time for now.

6. Deselect Reminder.

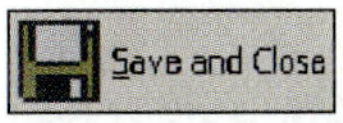

7. Click the Save and Close button on the Appointment form toolbar. The Appointment form closes. Notice that the new appointment now appears in the Appointments Calendar for that date.

8. Click the <u>N</u>ew button ⊞▾ (or press [Ctrl]+[N]). The Appointment form appears.

9. In the Subject text box, key **Meet with Valerie**, and in the <u>L</u>ocation text box, key **My office**

> **TIP:** Outlook saves locations that you key in the <u>L</u>ocation text box. Clicking the down arrow next to the text box displays a drop-down list of previously keyed locations. You can use this feature for frequently used locations, such as "My office."

10. In the Start time: text box for the date of the appointment, click the down arrow to the right of the date box. A drop-down calendar appears.

11. Select a date roughly three weeks from the current week. The selected date appears in the date portion of the Start time: text box.

12. For the starting time of the appointment, click the down arrow next to the time box and select 1:00 PM. The appointment is one-half hour in length, so there is no need to set the End time.

13. In the text area of the Appointment form, key **Show her how to access my calendar.**

14. Deselect <u>R</u>eminder.

15. Click the <u>S</u>ave and Close button. The new appointment has been added to your Appointments Calendar. Notice that the date for this appointment now appears in bold in the Date Navigator, indicating that you have an appointment on that date. You can also enter an appointment directly into the Appointments Calendar.

16. Click 5:00 PM in the Appointments Calendar.

17. Key **Get haircut** and then click any other time on the Appointments Calendar. The new appointment is added to the Calendar.

EXERCISE   **2-3**   **Edit an Appointment**

You can make changes to existing appointments. You can open an appointment to change its time or location. You can also change the time of an appointment in the Appointments Calendar by simply dragging its *move handle*, which is the left border of an appointment in the Appointments Calendar.

An existing appointment can be opened in one of several different ways. You can open it by:

- Double-clicking the appointment.
- Selecting the appointment and then choosing <u>F</u>ile, <u>O</u>pen, <u>S</u>elect Items from the menu.

- Selecting the appointment and pressing Ctrl + O.
- Right-clicking the appointment and choosing <u>O</u>pen from the shortcut menu.

1. Display the day in the Appointments Calendar for the first appointment you entered in Exercise 2-2, the "Weekly meeting with Will" appointment.

2. Position the pointer over the appointment's move handle (the left blue border). The pointer changes to a four-pointed arrow ✛. You can move an appointment to another time by dragging the move handle.

3. Drag the move handle, moving the appointment to 11:00 AM.

4. Double-click the appointment to open the Appointment form. Note that you can also open an appointment by right-clicking it and choosing <u>O</u>pen from the shortcut menu, or you can select the appointment and press Ctrl + O.

5. Change the **End <u>tim</u>e** so that the appointment is 1 hour in length.

6. Click the <u>S</u>ave and Close button. The Appointments Calendar now shows that the appointment is one hour in length. You can also make changes to an appointment in the Appointments Calendar.

7. Click anywhere in the Appointments Calendar to deselect the "Weekly meeting with Will" appointment.

8. Select the "Weekly meeting with Will" appointment again. A blue border surrounds the appointment when it is selected. The location is dropped from the appointment when it is selected, and an insertion point appears at the beginning of the subject.

9. Use Delete to remove "Weekly" from the subject, and edit the remaining text so that the subject now reads "Meeting with Will."

10. Click anywhere in the Appointments Calendar to deselect the appointment. The "Meeting with Will" appointment shows the location again.

11. Select the "Meeting with Will" appointment, position the pointer on the bottom border, and drag the border down one-half hour so that the end time of the meeting is 12:30.

12. Click anywhere in the Appointments Calendar to deselect the appointment. The appointment is scheduled from 11:00 to 12:30.

NOTE: You can delete an appointment from your Calendar like any other item by simply selecting it and clicking the Delete button X on the Standard toolbar.

EXERCISE **2-4** **Schedule a Recurring Appointment**

Appointments that occur repeatedly are *recurring* appointments. Examples of recurring appointments are a weekly status meeting or a monthly haircut.

You can specify a new appointment as a recurring appointment, or you can edit an existing appointment to make it recurring. When you create a recurring appointment, you define:

- The recurrence pattern, which specifies when the recurrence takes place (such as monthly or every Friday).
- The range of recurrence, which specifies how long or for how many times the recurrence takes place.

You can also mark appointments as private so that the subject of the appointment is hidden from individuals who have access to your Calendar. The word "Private" appears instead of the actual subject. You mark appointments as private by selecting the Private option on the Appointment form.

1. Click the next business day from the current date on the Date Navigator.
2. Click the New button [icon] (or press Ctrl + N) to create a new appointment. The Appointment form appears.
3. In the Subject text box, key **Dr. Johnson**
4. In the Location text box, key **2 Belmont St., Suite 200**
5. Set the Start time: as **1:00 PM** and the End time as **1:30 PM**
6. Deselect Reminder.
7. Select the Private option, which is located in the lower right corner of the Appointment form.
8. Click the down arrow next to the Show time as text box and choose Out of Office. Outlook classifies your appointments in different ways, using color codes for the appointment type in the various views. Out of Office displays with a purple border.

[Recurrence...]

9. Click the Recurrence button on the Appointment form toolbar (or press Ctrl + G). The Appointment Recurrence dialog box appears.

FIGURE 2-3
Appointment
Recurrence
dialog box

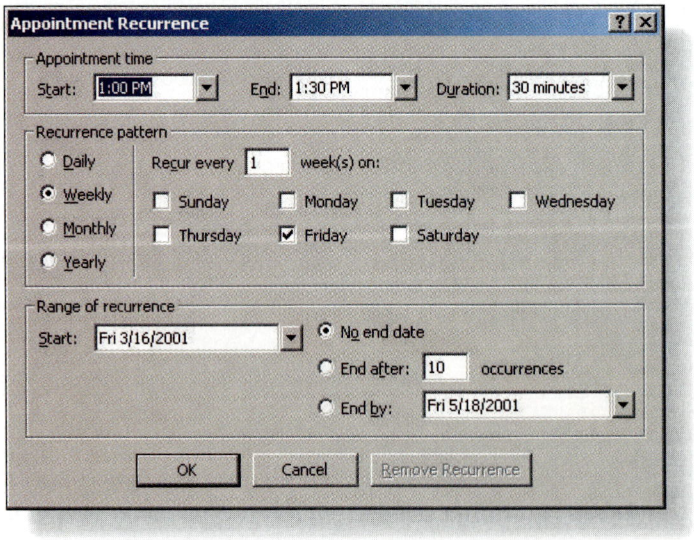

10. Under Recurrence pattern, select the Monthly option, and select options so that it occurs the **second Friday** of every month ("of every **1** month(s)").

11. Under Range of recurrence, select End after, and key **6** for the number of occurrences.

12. Click OK. A description of the recurrence appears under the Location text box. Notice that the Start time: text boxes are no longer displayed.

> **NOTE:** If you want to change the date and/or time of an appointment that has been designated as a recurring appointment, you must first remove the recurrence designation. You do this by clicking the Recurrence button on the Appointment form toolbar and then clicking Remove Recurrence.

13. Click the Save and Close button. The new appointment is scheduled as a monthly recurring appointment.

14. Select the date in the Date Navigator of the first occurrence of this appointment. The appointment in the Appointments Calendar displays a recurrence icon, and the second Fridays in the successive months appear in bold. The key icon indicates that the appointment is private.

EXERCISE   **2-5**   **Print an Appointment**

Printing an individual appointment is easy. You might want to print an appointment when you need a hard copy to remind yourself of details that don't appear in the Calendar.

1. Locate the date in the Date Navigator for the "Meet with Valerie" appointment, which should be roughly three weeks from the current week.

2. Double-click the "Meet with Valerie" appointment to open it. The Appointment form appears.

3. Choose File, Print from the Appointment form menu. The Print dialog box appears.

4. Click OK. The appointment prints.

5. Close the appointment without saving.

> **NOTE:** When an appointment is printed, the name that appears above the appointment is the user name for your e-mail account.

Using Reminders

You can have Outlook remind you of appointments, events, and tasks. Outlook reminds you of an activity by displaying a reminder box. For appointments, the reminder appears 15 minutes before the appointment is set to begin. This is the default setting for appointment reminders. Reminders can be quite useful when your day is filled with many appointments and activities. You'll want to use the reminder option for those activities that are most important.

EXERCISE **2-6** **Set a Reminder**

You can set a reminder to appear a certain time in advance of an appointment. The time period can range between five minutes and two weeks. The longer-term intervals are useful for activities you've scheduled at some distance in the future, such as a dentist's or doctor's appointment. By default, reminders also are accompanied by a tone, which you can change or disable.

1. Display the Appointments Calendar for the first Friday in which there is an appointment to see Dr. Johnson, which you scheduled in the Exercise 2-1.

2. Double-click the Dr. Johnson appointment. The Open Recurring Item dialog box appears. When you're changing events in a series, Outlook gives you the choice of changing an individual event or all the events in the series.

FIGURE 2-4
Open Recurring
Item dialog box

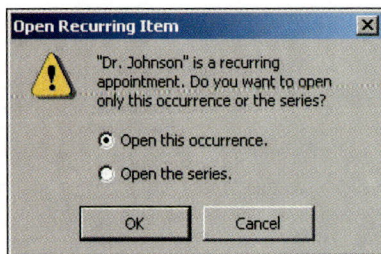

3. Select the **Open the series** option. This will let you set a reminder for every appointment.

4. Click **OK**. The Appointment form for the Dr. Johnson appointment appears.

5. Select the **Reminder** option. The default time for the reminder is 15 minutes.

6. Click the down arrow next to the reminder time and select **1 day** from the drop-down list. You can also control whether Outlook plays a sound with the reminder.

7. Click the loudspeaker icon at the right of the **Reminder** time. The Reminder Sound dialog box appears. Notice that the default is to play a sound. You can choose a different sound if you prefer, or none at all. Click **Cancel** to leave the sound unchanged.

8. Click the **Save and Close** button. A bell icon appears in the Dr. Johnson appointment, which indicates that Outlook will remind you of the appointment. When your computer's clock reaches the specified date and time, a reminder will sound and a message will appear on the screen. Figure 2-5 on the next page shows this message.

FIGURE 2-5
Reminder box for
appointments using
the reminder option

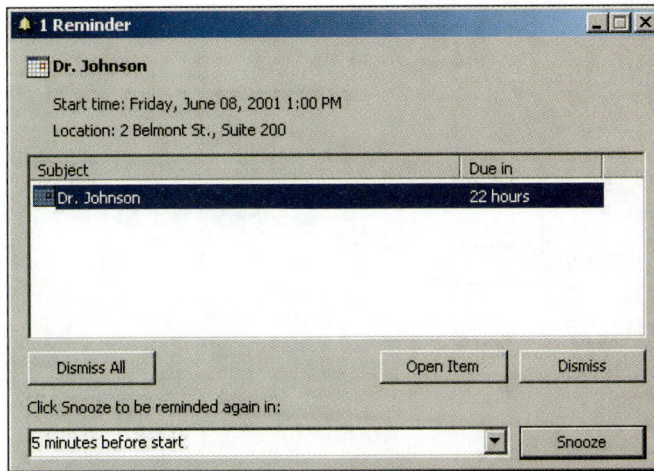

TIP: Use the Snooze button on the Reminder dialog box to make sure you don't forget a meeting or an appointment. The Snooze button works like an alarm-clock snooze button, redisplaying the message at intervals you specify, from 5 minutes to 1 day.

Scheduling Events

An *event* is an activity that lasts an entire day or longer, without any times being specified. Events do not occupy blocks of time in your Appointments Calendar, but instead appear as banners at the top of your Calendar. The banner can occupy multiple days. Because events do not occupy blocks of time in your Calendar, that time appears as free when others view your Calendar. In contrast, an all-day appointment will show you as busy.

EXERCISE **2-7** **Schedule an Annual Event**

Birthdays, anniversaries, or holidays are typical events. Like appointments, they can be recurring events.

1. From the Actions menu, choose New All Day Event. The Event form appears. The Event form is similar to the Appointment form, except that the start and end times show only dates, not times. The default settings for other options are also different. (See Figure 2-6 on the next page.)

NOTE: You can also display the Event form by double-clicking the date at the top of the Appointments Calendar or by right-clicking the date and choosing New All Day Event from the shortcut menu.

FIGURE 2-6
Event form

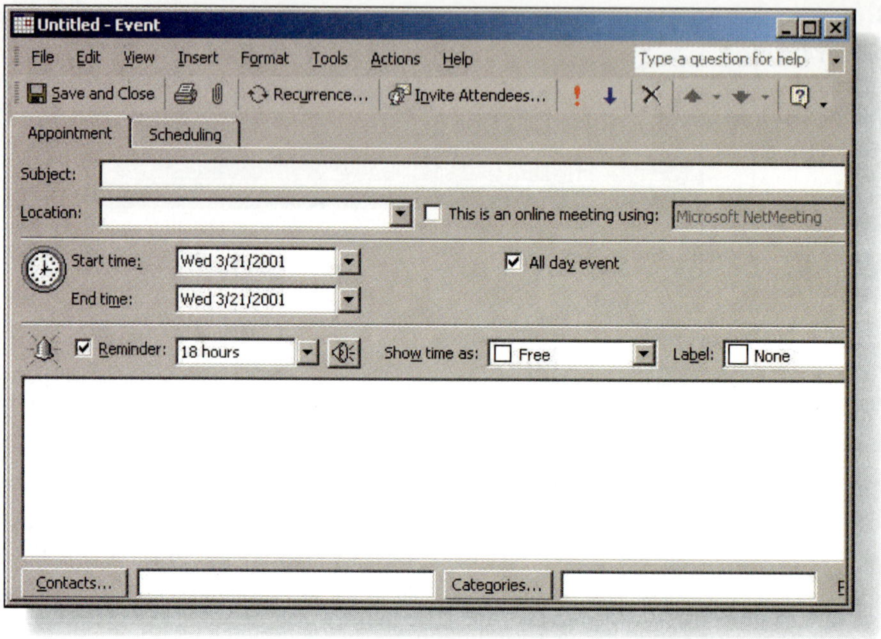

2. In the Subject text box, key **Angelica's birthday**

3. Press ⎡Tab⎤ until the Start time: is selected. Instead of keying the exact date in the text box or using the drop-down list box, delete the existing date and key **next Tuesday**. This uses Outlook's Autodate feature. Outlook will display the precise date, based on the text you keyed.

> **TIP:** You can use the Autodate feature to set start times for meetings and appointments as well as events. You can key text such as "tomorrow" or "noon" instead of keying the exact date or time.

4. Click the down arrow next to the Reminder text box, and choose **1 day** from the drop-down list. Outlook will remind you the day before Angelica's birthday.

5. Click the Recurrence button on the Event form toolbar. The Appointment Recurrence dialog box appears.

6. Under Recurrence pattern, select Yearly.

7. Under Range of recurrence, select No end date, if it is not already selected.

8. Click OK. The Event window is redisplayed, and the details of the appointment recurrence appear under the Location text box.

9. Click the Save and Close button. Outlook saves the event and closes the Event window.

10. Select the date in the Date Navigator for Angelica's birthday. The banner is displayed under the date in the Appointments Calendar. Icons indicate that a reminder will appear and that this is a recurring event. However,

the Date Navigator does not show the date in bold unless there is another appointment scheduled for that day.

FIGURE 2-7
Appointments Calendar for a date with an annual event

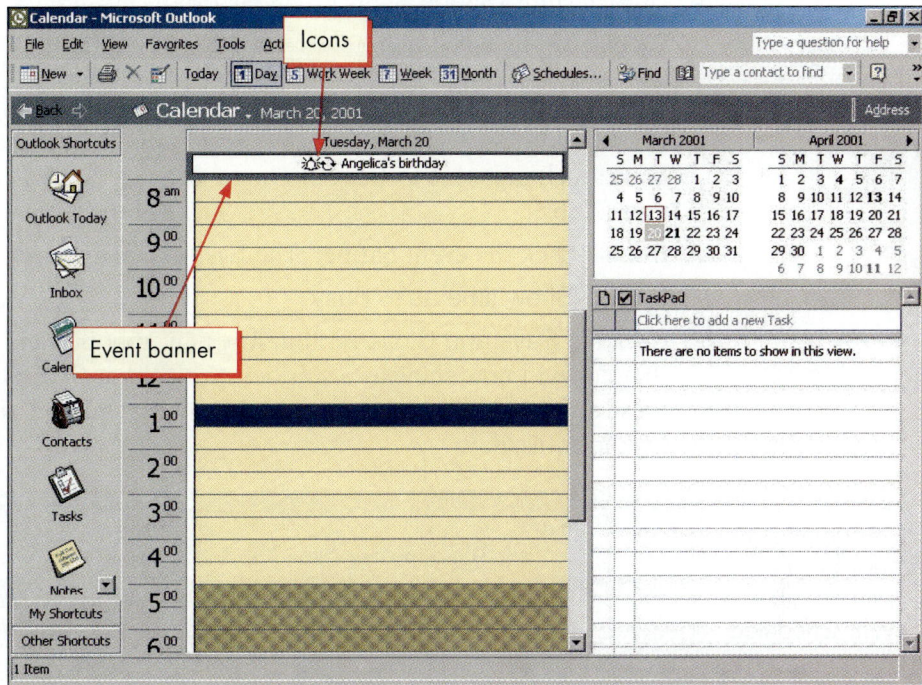

EXERCISE   2-8   Schedule a Multi-Day Event

Events can be scheduled over several days. A conference or a training course might be a multi-day event.

1. Chose <u>A</u>ctions, New All Day <u>E</u>vent from the menu. The Event window appears.

2. In the Subject text box, key **Store Managers Conference**

3. In the <u>L</u>ocation text box, key **Lodging International Hotel**

4. Click the down arrow next to the Start time: text box. A drop-down calendar for the current month appears.

5. Select a date on a Monday, Tuesday, or Wednesday, roughly two weeks from the current date. The date appears in the Start time: text box

6. Click the down arrow next to the End ti<u>m</u>e text box, and select a date two days later. This makes the event a three-day event. Events are considered to run from midnight to midnight.

7. Deselect <u>R</u>eminder. Notice the setting for Sho<u>w</u> time as. The default for events is to show this time as Free when others view your Calendar.

8. Click the <u>S</u>ave and Close button. The new event is saved and the Event window closes.

9. Display your Appointments Calendar for the event date, which should be roughly two weeks from today. Notice the banner under the date. This indicates that an all-day event is scheduled for that day. You can still schedule an appointment or meeting for that day, because the time is considered free. The Date Navigator does not show these dates in bold. You can change this to Busy or Out of Office if you wish this time to be unavailable.

10. Double-click the event banner. The Event form appears.

11. Change Sho<u>w</u> time as to Busy.

12. Click the <u>S</u>ave and Close button. Any new appointment you schedule for that day will now show as a conflict. Notice that the Date Navigator displays these dates in bold, and the Appointments Calendar displays a blue border for the entire day.

FIGURE 2-8
Appointments Calendar for a date with an all-day event scheduled

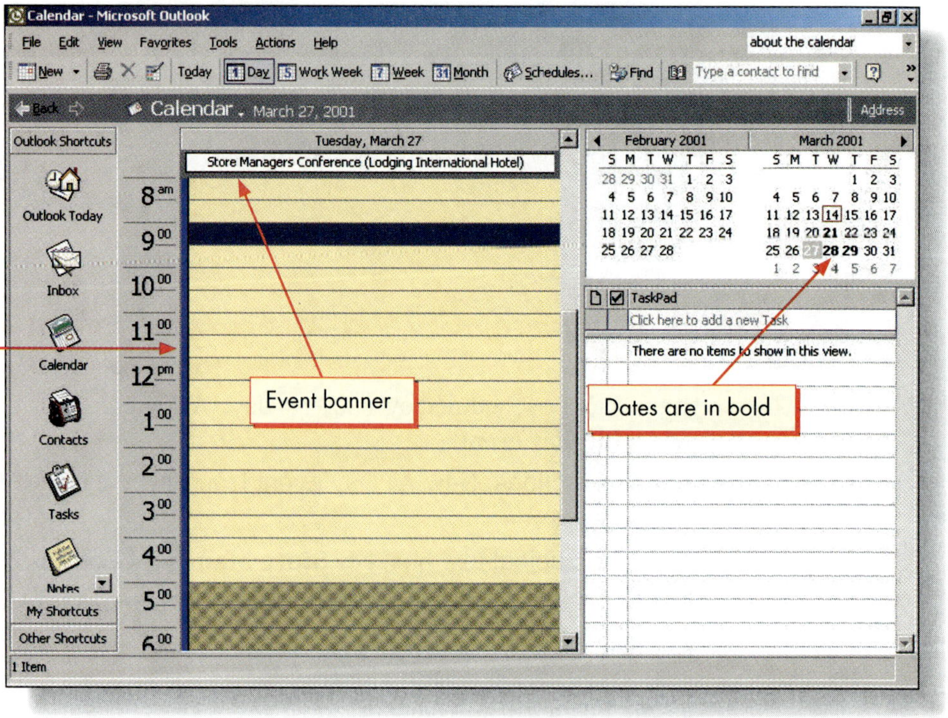

Border shows time as busy

Event banner

Dates are in bold

Printing the Calendar

You've seen how you can print an individual appointment. You might find that when your schedule becomes especially busy, you need to print your entire Calendar. The basic procedures for printing and setting print options in Outlook's Calendar are similar to other areas of Outlook. You can use several methods to print:

- Click the Print button 🖨 on the Standard toolbar.
- Choose File, Print from the menu.
- Press Ctrl + P.

EXERCISE **2-9** **Configure Calendar Print Options**

Outlook lets you print individual appointments or a range of hours from the Appointments Calendar. You also can print an entire week or month. Depending on what you are printing, you can use one of several different print styles.

1. Click a week in the Date Navigator that has more than one appointment, if you have one.

2. Choose File, Page Setup from the menu. The submenu shows choices for six built-in print styles.

3. Choose **Weekly Style**. The Page Setup: Weekly Style dialog box appears.

FIGURE 2-9
Page Setup:
Weekly Style
dialog box

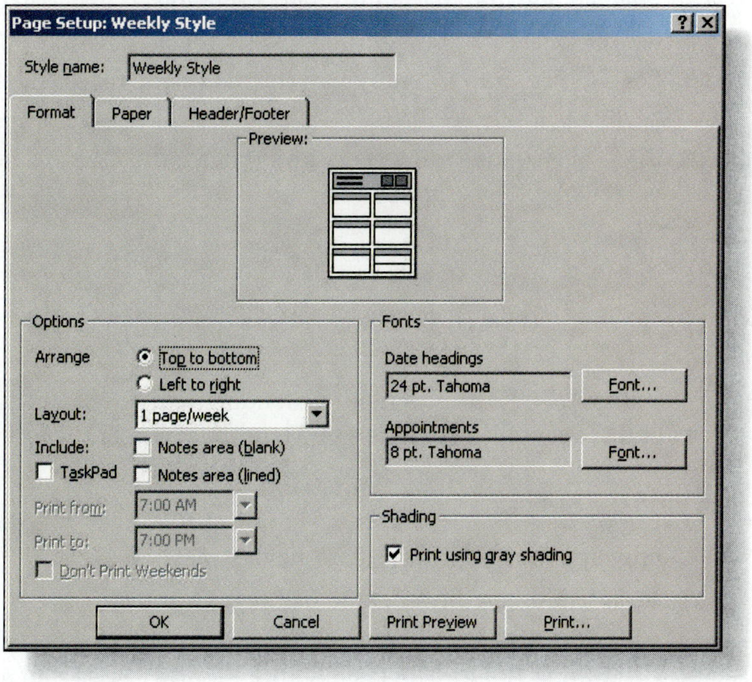

4. Click the **Format** tab, if it is not already displayed. You can control the size and font of the date headings and appointments on this tab.

5. Click the **Paper** tab. Page orientation is set on this tab.

6. Click the **Header/Footer** tab. The default is for a footer that includes the User Name, the page number, and the date. The User Name on your computer is the same name that appears in the "From" fields when you send an e-mail message from Outlook.

7. Replace the User Name in the footer with your name.

8. Click **Print Preview**. Outlook displays the Appointments Calendar as it appears when it is printed. If necessary, zoom in to see the details of the preview, and then click **Close**. The Calendar reappears.

9. Display a date in the Appointments Calendar that has at least one appointment scheduled.

10. Choose **File, Page Setup** from the menu once again, and select **Daily Style**. The Page Setup: Daily Style dialog box appears.

11. Click the **Format** tab if it is not already displayed. Under **Options**, you can include the **TaskPad** and the **Notes area** in the printout.

12. Deselect **TaskPad** and the **Notes area (blank)**.

13. Click the **Header/Footer** tab, and replace the User Name in the footer with your name.

14. Click **Print Preview**. This shows a preview of the appointments for the selected day in the Appointments Calendar. If necessary, zoom in to view the details of the preview, and then click **Close**.

15. Choose **File, Page Setup** from the menu one more time, and select **Monthly Style**.

16. Click the **Header/Footer** tab, and replace the User Name in the footer with your name. Click **OK**.

EXERCISE 2-10 Print a Calendar

When you print an individual Calendar item, a Memo Style print style shows you all the details of the item. A Monthly Style shows your Calendar as a single page.

1. Choose **File, Print** from the menu or press Ctrl+P. The Print dialog box appears. (See Figure 2-10 on the next page.)

2. Choose **Monthly Style** as the print style. You can also access Page Setup from this dialog box.

3. Click **Page Setup**. The Page Setup: Monthly Style dialog box appears.

4. Click the **Paper** tab, and change the **Orientation** option to **Portrait**.

5. Click **OK**, and then click **OK** again. Outlook prints the currently displayed month.

FIGURE 2-10
Print dialog box

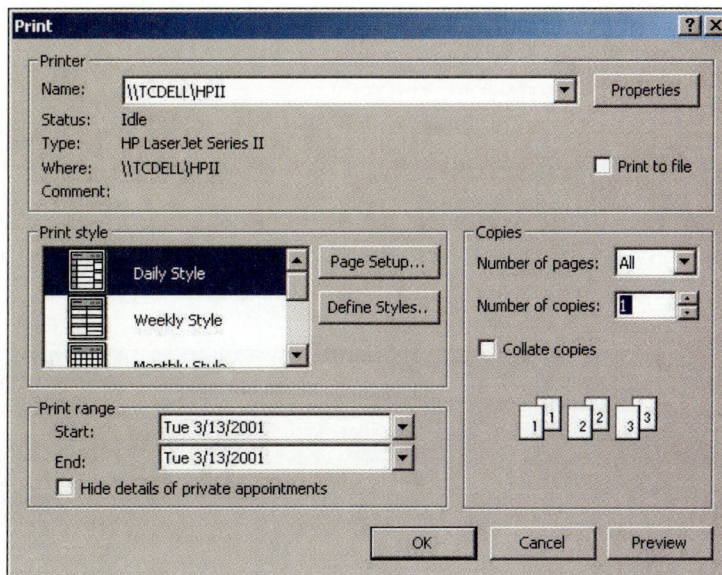

6. Locate and select the Dr. Johnson appointment.

7. Click the Print button 🖨 on the Standard toolbar. The Print dialog box appears. It defaults to the Daily Style.

8. Select the Memo Style.

9. Click Page Setup. Then click the Header/Footer tab. Key your name as a centered header if it is not already entered.

10. Click OK, and then click OK again. Outlook prints the individual appointment.

Creating and Updating Tasks

A *task* is a personal or work-related activity that you want to track to completion. A task can occur once or repeatedly. When you create a task, it appears in the *task list*, which is the list of these tracked activities that appears in the Tasks folder or in the TaskPad. Tasks are added to the task list as you create them.

After you've created a task, you can update it in various ways, such as marking it completed, changing the due date, or making it a recurring task. Recurring tasks can occur at regular intervals or at a date you set for completion. Examples of recurring tasks are weekly status reports to your supervisor or the monthly updating of your computer's anti-virus program.

You can delete a task from the task list just as you delete other items in Outlook—by selecting it and clicking the Delete button ✕ on the Standard toolbar.

You can create new tasks in two different ways. You can create tasks by using the Task form, or you can enter tasks directly into the task list.

1. Click the Tasks shortcut 📋 on the Outlook Bar. The Tasks folder appears. By default, the Tasks folder shows the current tasks in Table view, with four columns (fields) in the table: Icon, Complete, Subject, and Due Date.

FIGURE 2-11
Tasks folder

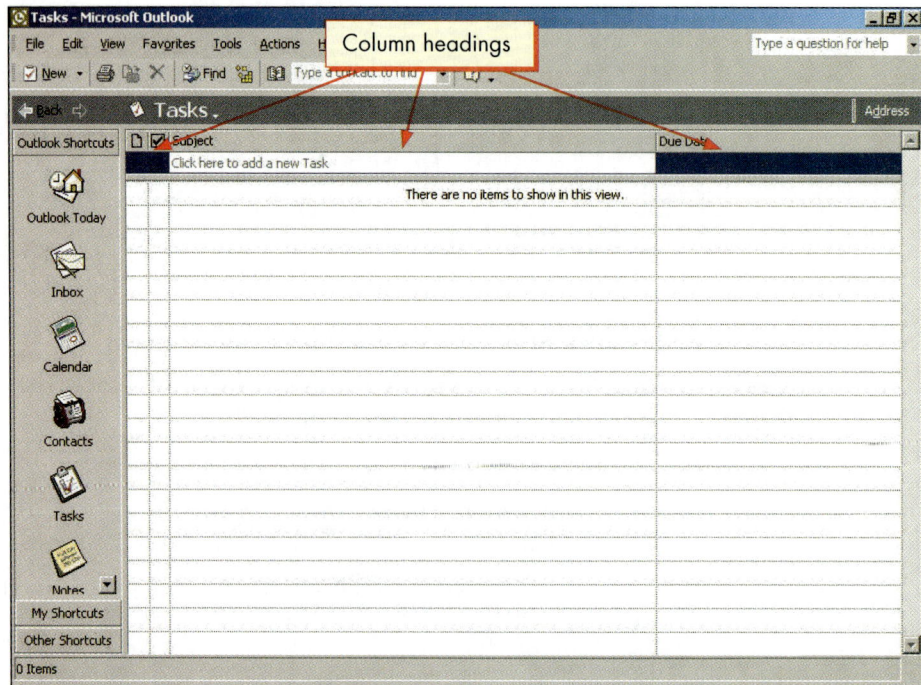

2. Click the <u>N</u>ew button 📋 New on the Standard toolbar (or choose <u>F</u>ile, <u>N</u>ew, <u>T</u>ask from the menu). The Task form appears. (See Figure 2-12 on the next page.)

3. In the Subject text box, key **Write up summary of store managers input.**

4. Click the <u>S</u>ave and Close button on the Task form toolbar. The task is added to the task list, and the Tasks folder reappears.

5. Click the box under the Subject column heading titled Click here to add a new Task.

6. Key **E-mail Shaker file to Connie** and press Enter. Another task is added to the task list. The Click here to add a new Task box is still selected, so you can create another task.

FIGURE 2-12
Task form

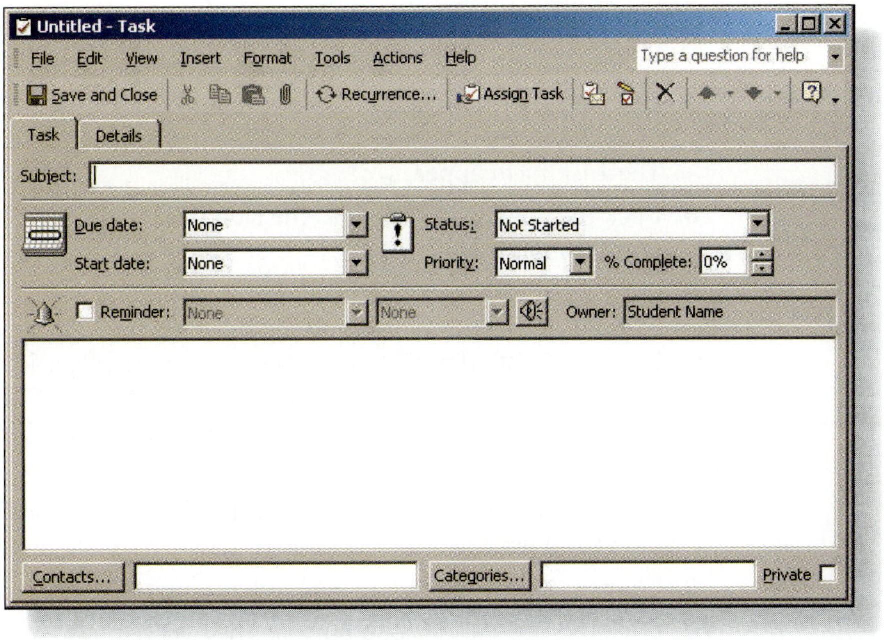

7. In the Click here to add a new Task box, key **Make travel arrangements for trip**, and press Enter. Another task is added to the task list. The Click here to add a new Task box is still selected.

8. Key **Call Bill about Mission chair backorder problem** and press Enter. Another task appears in the task list. Click anywhere in Tasks to deselect the Click here to add a new Task box.

EXERCISE 2-12 Change and Open Tasks

You can change a task in the task list, or you can open it and add more options in the Task form. You might want to change the subject of the task, set a due date, or add a reminder.

1. Click the "Write up summary" task in the task list. The task is selected. You will add some text to the Subject of this task.

2. Position the insertion point in the Subject column so it appears just before the word "input."

3. Key **new collections**. The text of the subject is changed. You can change other columns in a task in the same way.

4. Click the Due Date field for the "Call Bill" task, key **today**, and press Enter. Outlook's Autodate feature converts this to the current date. Next you'll open a task to add other options and make more extensive changes.

> 🔴 **NOTE:** Tasks that are overdue appear in red in the task list.

5. Open the "Write up summary" task by double-clicking it in the task list (or by selecting it and choosing <u>F</u>ile, <u>O</u>pen, <u>S</u>elected Items from the menu). The Task form appears.

6. Click the down arrow next to the <u>D</u>ue date text box. A calendar for the current month appears.

7. Click the date on the Calendar that is seven business days from the current date. The Calendar closes and the selected date appears in the <u>D</u>ue date text box. The Re<u>m</u>inder option has been automatically selected because there is now a due date associated with this task. A banner also appears above the **Subject** text box, indicating the number of calendar days until the task is due.

8. Click the down arrow next to the Sta<u>r</u>t date text box, and select a date three days from now.

9. Change the date shown in Re<u>m</u>inder to match the date in Sta<u>r</u>t date.

10. Click the <u>S</u>ave and Close button. The task list now shows that a due date has been added to the task.

> ✖ 🔴 **NOTE:** You can delete a task from the task list by simply selecting it and clicking the Delete button ✖.

FIGURE 2-13
Tasks with due dates

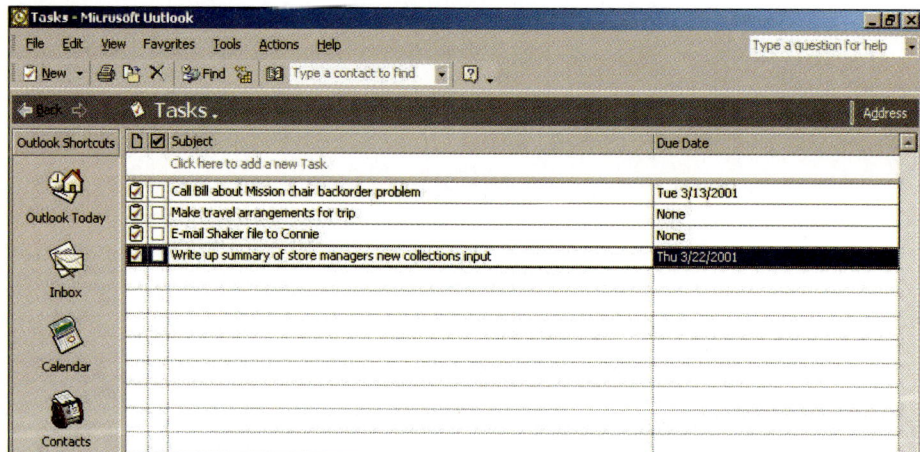

EXERCISE 2-13 Update Tasks

You can update the status of tasks as they progress. You might want to show tasks as completed or in progress.

1. Double-click the "Call Bill" task. The Task form opens.

2. Click the down arrow next to the **Status:** text box, and select **Completed**. (You can also mark a task as completed by clicking the Mark Complete button on the Task form toolbar.)

3. Click the **Save and Close** button. The task list shows the updated task as crossed out, with a check mark under the Complete column heading.

> **TIP:** You can change the status of a task in the task list to "Complete" without opening the task by clicking the Complete box next to the task subject.

FIGURE 2-14
Updated task list
with a
completed task

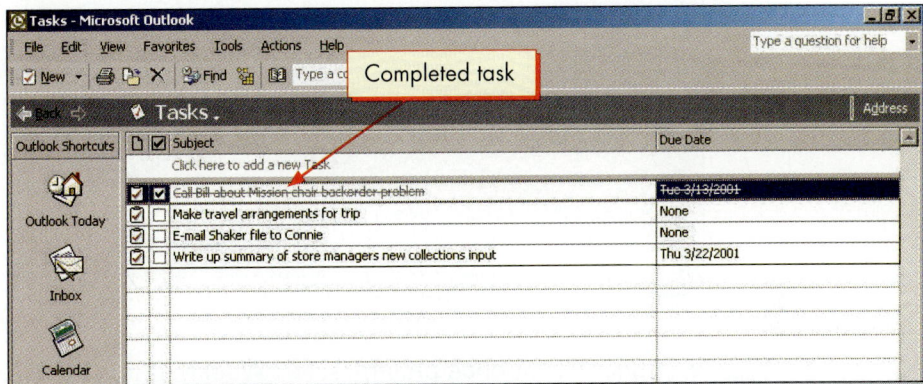

4. Double-click the "Make travel arrangements" task. The Task form opens.

5. Change the **Status:** to **In Progress**.

6. Click the Next Item button on the Task form toolbar. A confirmation dialog box appears.

7. Click **Yes** to save the changes. The Task form displays the next task in the task list, "E-mail Shaker file to Connie."

8. Change the **Status:** to **In Progress**.

9. Click the **Save and Close** button.

10. Click the Calendar shortcut in the Outlook Bar. Tasks are displayed in the TaskPad in the Calendar. Only tasks due for the current date, as well as tasks with no specified date, appear in the TaskPad.

11. Click the Tasks shortcut in the Outlook Bar to return to Tasks.

EXERCISE **2-14** **Create a Recurring Task**

A recurring task can be any task that occurs more than once on a regular basis. Examples of recurring tasks are a weekly status report and a monthly homework assignment.

1. Click the <u>N</u>ew button ☑ New (or press Ctrl + N). The Task form appears.

2. In the Subject text box, key **Weekly status report**

↻ Recurrence...

3. Click the Rec<u>u</u>rrence button on the Task form toolbar. The Task Recurrence dialog box appears.

FIGURE 2-15
Task Recurrence dialog box

Task Recurrence	? ✕
Recurrence pattern	
○ Daily ◉ Recur every [1] week(s) on	
◉ Weekly ☐ Sunday ☐ Monday ☑ Tuesday ☐ Wednesday	
○ Monthly ☐ Thursday ☐ Friday ☐ Saturday	
○ Yearly ○ Regenerate new task [1] week(s) after each task is completed	
Range of recurrence	
Start: [Tue 3/13/2001 ▼] ◉ No end date	
○ End after: [10] occurrences	
○ End by: [Tue 5/15/2001 ▼]	
[OK] [Cancel] [Remove Recurrence]	

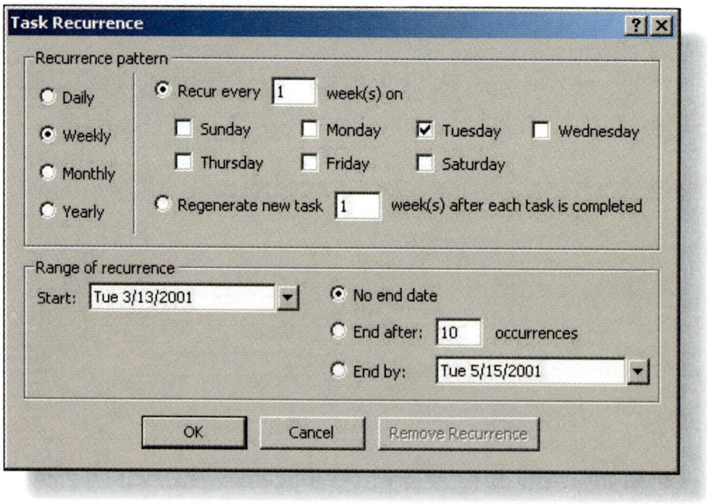

4. Under Recurrence pattern, select <u>W</u>eekly, if it is not already selected. Then select Wednesday. Deselect any other days.

5. Select Re<u>g</u>enerate new task. This option repeats a task at the specified interval after the original task is marked completed. Leave the specified interval at **1 week**.

6. Under Range of recurrence, select <u>N</u>o end date, if it is not already selected.

7. Click OK. The Task form reappears. A banner above the Subject text box specifies when the next occurrence of the task is due.

8. Click the <u>S</u>ave and Close button. The task list shows the new task. This task has an icon under the Icon column heading that indicates this is a recurring task.

EXERCISE 2-15 **Print a Task and the Task List**

You might wish to print an individual task to see details of the task. You might also want to print the entire task list to use as a "to-do" list when you're not at your computer.

1. Select the "Make travel arrangements" task on the task list.

2. Chose <u>F</u>ile, <u>P</u>rint from the menu. The Print dialog box appears. There are two available print styles, Table and Memo. The Table Style prints the entire task list, and the Memo Style prints the currently selected task.

3. Select **Memo Style**.

4. Click **Page Setup**. The Page Setup: Memo Style dialog box appears.

5. Click the **Header/Footer** tab and add your name as a centered header if it does not already appear. Then click **OK**. The Print dialog box reappears.

6. Click **OK**. The "Make travel arrangements" task prints.

7. Press Ctrl + P. The Print dialog box appears.

8. Select **Table Style**. This is the print style used to print the entire task list.

9. Click **Page Setup**. The Page Setup: Table Style dialog box appears.

10. Click the **Header/Footer** tab and add your name as a centered header. Then click **OK**. The Print dialog box reappears.

11. Under **Print range**, make sure **All rows** is selected. Note that you can use this option to print only selected rows (tasks) in your task list.

12. Print **OK** to print the entire task list.

USING HELP

If you're involved in a group project or activity that has a number of important dates and meetings, you can develop a Calendar for everyone in the group and save it as a Web page. You might then post it on your company's intranet or on a personal Web site. You can give everyone the URL (the address of the page on the intranet or the World Wide Web), and they can refer to it as needed.

Outlook has a number of useful features specifically tailored to Calendars saved as Web pages. For example, you can specify the start and end dates of the Calendar when you save it as a Web page. You can also specify whether appointment details entered in the text section of an appointment should be included.

Use Microsoft Outlook Help to learn how to save a calendar as a Web page:

1. Click the Microsoft Outlook Help button [?] on the Standard toolbar and then click the **Answer Wizard** tab, if it is not already displayed.

2. In the **What would you like to do?** text box, key **Save a calendar as a web page** in the text box and click **Search**. A list of related topics appears under Select **topic** to display.

3. Click **About saving a personal calendar as a Web page**. Microsoft Outlook Help displays information about saving calendars as Web pages in the right pane of the Help window.

4. In the left pane of the Help window, click **Save a personal calendar as a Web page**. The steps for saving a calendar as a Web page appear in the right pane of the Help window.

FIGURE 2-16
Help screen for saving a personal calendar as a Web page

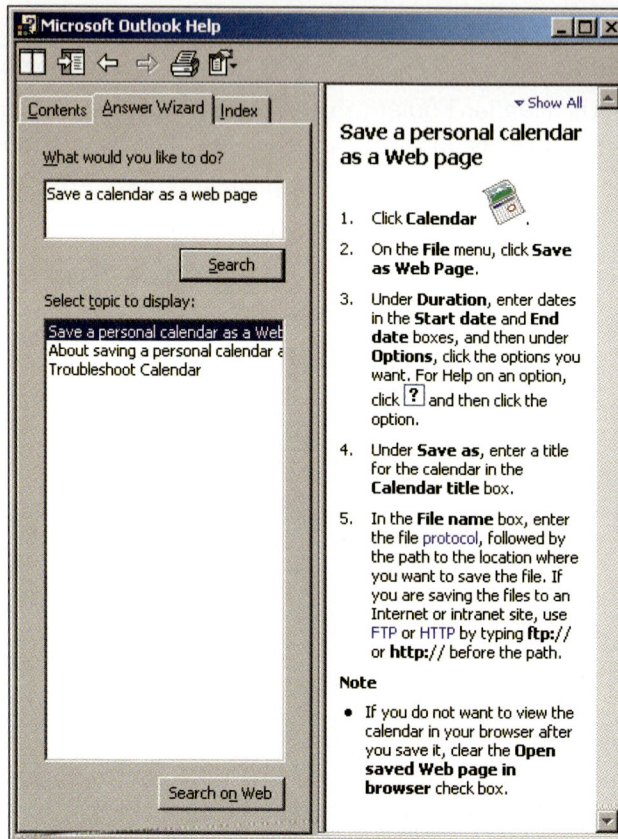

Microsoft Outlook Help

Contents | Answer Wizard | Index

What would you like to do?

Save a calendar as a web page

Search

Select topic to display:

Save a personal calendar as a Web
About saving a personal calendar a
Troubleshoot Calendar

Search on Web

▼ Show All

**Save a personal calendar
as a Web page**

1. Click **Calendar**.

2. On the **File** menu, click **Save as Web Page**.

3. Under **Duration**, enter dates in the **Start date** and **End date** boxes, and then under **Options**, click the options you want. For Help on an option, click [?] and then click the option.

4. Under **Save as**, enter a title for the calendar in the **Calendar title** box.

5. In the **File name** box, enter the file protocol, followed by the path to the location where you want to save the file. If you are saving the files to an Internet or intranet site, use FTP or HTTP by typing **ftp://** or **http://** before the path.

Note

• If you do not want to view the calendar in your browser after you save it, clear the **Open saved Web page in browser** check box.

5. Read the information and close Microsoft Outlook Help when you have finished.

LESSON 2 Summary

➤ Outlook's Calendar is accessed from the Outlook Bar or the folder list.

➤ The TaskPad is an abbreviated list of current tasks. The Date Navigator displays dates in the Appointments Calendar, and the toolbar buttons control Calendar views.

➤ Appointments do not require inviting people or reserving resources. Outlook gives you the option of letting others see your Calendar.

➤ You can add new appointments by using the Appointment form or by entering them directly in the Appointments Calendar. Appointment dates appear in bold in the Date Navigator.

➤ You can move an appointment to another time in the Appointments Calendar by dragging the move handle. Existing appointments can be edited or deleted.

➤ Appointments that occur repeatedly are recurring appointments. Recurrence options define when the appointment takes place and how many times it occurs.

➤ Appointment reminders are set in the Appointment form. A bell icon appears in the Appointments Calendar next to appointments with reminders.

➤ Events last an entire day or longer without any times being specified and appear as banners at the top of the Appointments Calendar.

➤ Events can be scheduled over several days. The default for events is to show this time as Free when others view your Calendar.

➤ Outlook can print individual appointments or a range of hours from the Appointments Calendar. Entire weeks or months also can be printed.

➤ There are different print styles for Calendar printing. Dialog boxes for each print style control the font, page orientation, and headers and footers. The TaskPad can be included in a printout.

➤ A task is a work-related activity that can be traced to completion. It appears on the task list or the TaskPad.

➤ The task list is accessed from the Outlook Bar or the Tasks folder in the folder list and is displayed in Table view. You can create new tasks directly in the task list or by using the Task form.

➤ You can change tasks in the task list, or you can open and change them in the Task form. The Task form displays a banner that indicates when a task is due, and you can add a reminder to a task.

➤ You can update the status of a task as it progresses.

➤ A recurring task can be any task that occurs more than once on a regular basis.

➤ You can print an individual task, selected tasks, or the entire task list. Two different print styles are available for printing tasks, Table Style and Memo Style.

LESSON 2 **Command Summary**

FEATURE	BUTTON	MENU	KEYBOARD	SPEECH
Day View	1 Day	View, Day	Alt + Y	✓
Work Week View	5 Work Week	View, Work Week	Alt + R	✓

continues

LESSON 2 Command Summary *continued*

FEATURE	BUTTON	MENU	KEYBOARD	SPEECH
Week View	7 Week	View, Week	Alt + W	✓
Month View	31 Month	View, Month	Alt + M	✓
New Appointment	New	File, New, Appointment	Ctrl + N	✓
New Task	New	File, New, Task	Ctrl + N	✓
Open Appointment/ Task		File, Open, Selected Items	Ctrl + O	✓

Concepts Review

TRUE/FALSE QUESTIONS

Each of the following statements is either true or false. Indicate your choice by circling **T** or **F**.

T F   **1.** By default, the Appointments Calendar divides the workday into one-hour segments.

T F   **2.** The Week view displays weekends in the Appointments Calendar.

T F   **3.** The pointer changes to a two-pointed arrow when it is placed over the move handle of a selected appointment in the Appointments Calendar.

T F   **4.** The date of a scheduled appointment appears in bold in the Date Navigator.

T F   **5.** By default, the reminder option is selected in a new appointment.

T F   **6.** You must open a task before you can change it.

T F   **7.** Events can last only one day.

T F   **8.** The TaskPad is displayed in the Inbox.

SHORT ANSWER QUESTIONS

Write the correct answer in the space provided.

1. Which keystroke command displays the Day view in the Appointments Calendar?

_____

2. What do you call an activity you schedule in your Calendar that does not involve inviting others or reserving resources?

_____

3. What surrounds an appointment when you select it in your Appointments Calendar?

_____

4. What do you call appointments that occur repeatedly?

_____

5. When scheduling a new appointment, what keystroke command displays the Appointment Recurrence dialog box?

_____

6. When specifying a Start time for an appointment, what is the Calendar feature that lets you key text such as "next Tuesday" instead of the precise date?

_____

7. How is an annual event displayed in the Appointments Calendar?

_____

8. What does Outlook call a personal or work-related activity that you want to track to completion?

_____

CRITICAL THINKING

Answer these questions on a separate page. There are no right or wrong answers. Support your answers with examples from your own experience, if possible.

1. The reminder feature in Calendar can be a useful way to ensure that you don't miss important appointments. What kind of appointments would you use it for? Can you imagine instances when it might be more of a nuisance than a help? Why or why not?

2. When you have many activities you need to get done during the course of a day or week, using Tasks can be a great way to keep track of all of them. Describe activities in your own personal, academic, and/or work life that might be useful for tracking with Tasks.

Skills Review

EXERCISE 2-16

Navigate in the Calendar, schedule an appointment, and print an appointment.

1. Open the Calendar by clicking the Calendar shortcut 🗐 in the Outlook Bar.
2. Change Calendar viewing options by following these steps:
   a. To display the Week view, click the **Week** button on the Standard toolbar (or press Alt + W).
   b. Display the Work Week view by clicking the **Work Week** button on the Standard toolbar.

c. Display the Day view by clicking the Day button on the Standard toolbar.

d. Click the date in the Date Navigator that is one week from the current date.

3. Schedule an appointment by following these steps:

   a. Choose File, New, Appointment from the menu, or press Ctrl + N.

   b. In the Subject text box, key **Discuss presentation slide show**

   c. In the Location text box, key **My office** (or use the down arrow next to the Location text box to select it from the drop-down list).

   d. Set the date for the Start time: by clicking the down arrow next to the date text box. Select a date from the drop-down calendar roughly one week from the current date, if that date is not already selected.

   e. Set the time for the Start time: by clicking the down arrow next to the time text box and choosing 1:00 PM.

   f. Deselect Reminder.

   g. Click the Save and Close button on the Appointment form toolbar.

4. Print the appointment by following these steps.

   a. Click the date in the Date Navigator of the appointment you scheduled in the previous step.

   b. In the Appointments Calendar, select the "Discuss presentation slide show" appointment.

   c. Choose File, Open, Selected Items from the menu.

   d. In the Appointment form, choose File, Print from the menu.

   e. Click OK.

   f. Close the appointment without saving.

EXERCISE 2-17

Schedule an appointment, add a reminder, and print the appointment.

1. Click the Calendar shortcut 📇 in the Outlook Bar to display the Calendar if it is not already displayed.

2. Click the Date Navigator to display the Appointments Calendar for the next business day.

3. Press Ctrl + N to create a new appointment.

4. In the Subject text box, key **Meet with Personnel**

5. In the Location text box, key **Susan Delaney's office**

6. Set the Start time: to 3:30 PM, and set the End time: to 4:00 PM.

7. Set a reminder for the appointment by following these steps:

   a. Select the Reminder option, if it is not already selected.

   b. Click the down arrow next to the Reminder text box, and select 30 minutes.

8. In the text area of the Appointment form, key **Go over new 401K options for next year**

9. Print the appointment.

10. Click the <u>S</u>ave and Close button on the Appointment form toolbar.

EXERCISE 2-18

Schedule an event, add a reminder, and print the Calendar.

1. Click the Calendar shortcut in the Outlook Bar to display the Calendar, if it is not already displayed.

2. Display the Calendar in Work Week view by clicking the **Wo<u>r</u>k Week** button on the Standard toolbar.

3. Delete any existing appointments or events for this work week by following these steps:

    a. Select the appointment or event.

    b. Delete the appointment or event by clicking the Delete button on the Standard toolbar.

> **NOTE:** Your Calendar might not contain appointments or events for this week.

4. Create a new event by following these steps:

    a. Choose **<u>A</u>ctions, New All Day <u>E</u>vent** from the menu.

    b. In the **Subject** text box, key **John's birthday**

    c. Set the date of the **Start time:** as two business days from the current date.

    d. Select the <u>R</u>eminder option if it is not already selected, and select a reminder time of **1 day.**

    e. Click the <u>S</u>ave and Close button on the Event form toolbar.

5. Print a Calendar by following these steps:

    a. Choose **<u>F</u>ile, <u>P</u>rint** from the menu.

    b. Under Print style, choose **Weekly Style.**

    c. Click Page Setup.

    d. Click the **Header/Footer** tab, and replace the User Name in the footer with your name if it is not already displayed.

    e. Click OK to return to the Print dialog box.

    f. Click OK again.

6. Display the Calendar in Day view.

EXERCISE 2-19

Create a task, change a task, update a task, and print the task list.

1. Click the Tasks shortcut in the Outlook Bar to display the task list, if it is not already displayed.

2. Delete any existing tasks in your task list by following these steps:

    a. Select the task in the task list.

b. Delete the task by clicking the Delete button ⊠ on the Standard toolbar.

NOTE: Your task list might already be empty.

3. Create a new task by following these steps:

    a. Click the New button 🗹 New on the Standard toolbar or choose File, New, Task from the menu.

    b. In the Subject text box, key **Revise shipping costs worksheet**

    c. Click the down arrow next to the Due date text box, and select the next business day.

    d. Click the Save and Close button on the Task form toolbar.

4. Change a task by following these steps:

    a. Select the task you created in the previous step.

    b. Move the insertion point to the end of the subject text.

    c. Key the text **for Maria**. The subject of the task should read "Revise shipping costs worksheet for Maria."

    d. Click anywhere in the task list to deselect the "Revise shipping costs" task.

5. Update a task by following these steps:

    a. Double-click the "Revise shipping costs" task to open it.

    b. Click the Mark Complete button 🗹 on the Task form toolbar.

6. Print the task list by following these steps:

    a. Choose File, Print from the menu.

    b. Choose Table Style.

    c. Click Page Setup.

    d. Click the Header/Footer tab and enter your name as a centered header if it is not already displayed.

    e. Click OK to return to the Print dialog box.

    f. Under Print range, select All rows, if it is not already selected.

    g. Click OK.

Lesson Applications

Change the Calendar view, schedule appointments, set reminders, and print the Calendar.

Will McCarthy has asked you to schedule time to work on the feedback he's received from store managers on a new line of furniture. You want to be sure you keep track of the appointments.

1. Display the Calendar folder if it is not already displayed, and change the view to Work Week view.

2. Create a new appointment with the subject **Go over sales managers input**. Schedule it roughly two weeks from the current date, but do not schedule the meeting on a Monday. Make it an hour-long appointment, starting at 3 p.m. (Ignore any banners that might appear, informing you of conflicts with other appointments.)

3. Key the location of the appointment as **Will's office**. In the text area of the Appointment form, key **Find out which suggestions Will thinks most important**

4. Set a reminder to go off 1 hour before the appointment.

5. Schedule a half-hour appointment at 10 a.m. the day before the appointment you just scheduled with Will McCarthy.

6. Make the subject of the appointment **Get final input data from Jasmine**, key the location as **Jasmine's office**, and set a reminder to go off 1 hour before the appointment.

7. Display the week for the appointments you created in the previous steps. Delete any other appointments or events for this week not entered in this exercise, and then print the Calendar in Weekly Style. Include your name as a centered header.

8. Display the Calendar in Day view.

Schedule an event, use reminders, create tasks, and print the Calendar and tasks.

You've decided to organize a surprise birthday party for one of your coworkers. You'll be in charge of buying the present and reserving a restaurant. You need to keep track of the activities and tasks.

1. Schedule an event one month from the current month, keying as the subject **Joan's birthday**. Set a reminder the day before. In the text area, key

Surprise party after work. Mark the event as private, and have the time shown as free.

2. Make the event a recurring event, with a yearly recurrence pattern. Don't put an end date in the range of recurrence.

3. Display the Tasks folder, and add a new task with the subject **Get birthday present for Joan**. Make the due date roughly one week before the birthday party you scheduled in the previous steps.

4. Set a reminder for the task for two days before the due date.

5. In the text area for the task, key **Bill says she hates candy and flowers.**

6. Create another task with the subject **Find restaurant for Joan's birthday party**, with the due date roughly one week from the current date. Do not use a reminder.

7. Display the date of the event in the Appointments Calendar, and then print the Calendar, using a Daily Style. Change Page Setup so that the TaskPad and Note area are not included in the printing. Add your name as a centered header.

8. Display Tasks, and select the two tasks you created in the previous steps. (*Hint*: Press Ctrl while you click an item to select multiple items in the task list.)

9. Print the selected tasks in Table Style, using the Print range option of Only selected rows. Add your name as a centered header, if it is not already present in the page setup.

10. Print the "Get birthday present for Joan" task. Use a Memo print style with your name as centered header.

EXERCISE 2-22

Schedule a recurring appointment and an event, use reminders, create a task, and print the task and Calendar.

Your manager has asked you to coordinate the annual departmental staff meeting. You'll need to schedule the event and time in your Calendar for preparations.

1. Using the Date Navigator, find a week in the coming month in which there are no appointments or events scheduled, or select a week and delete any existing appointments and events for that week. Schedule an appointment on the Monday of that week.

2. Key the subject for the appointment **Preparation time for annual staff meeting**, and start the appointment at 2 p.m. and end it at 5 p.m. Specify the location as **My office**. (*Hint*: Remember to use the down arrow next to the Location text box to use previously entered text.)

3. Deselect the reminder, and in the text area of the appointment, key **Do not schedule any other appointments for this time!**

4. Make this a recurring appointment, using a daily recurrence pattern, with a range of recurrence that is to end after four occurrences.

5. On the Friday of that same week, schedule an all-day event. For the subject of the event, key **Annual staff meeting**. For the location, key **Conference center**.

6. Deselect the reminder, but set the Show time as option as Busy.

7. Add a new task to the task list with the subject **Complete departmental budget**. Set the due date as Thursday of the week you used in the previous steps, and set the start date as the Monday before. Deselect the reminder.

8. Print the Calendar for the week you scheduled the appointment and event, using a Weekly Style. Add your name as a centered header, if it does not appear in the header already.

9. Print the "Complete departmental budget" task, using a Memo Style and adding your name as a centered header.

EXERCISE 2-23 ➕ *Challenge Yourself*

Schedule an appointment, schedule an event, add reminders, create tasks, and print the tasks and Calendar.

You've been asked to accompany the staff of the Design Department to a furniture manufacturers' conference. You need to schedule tasks and calendar time in preparation for the trip.

1. Use the Date Navigator to find a week roughly two months from the current month, in which there are no appointments or events scheduled, or select a week and delete any existing appointments and events for that week.

2. On Monday of that week, schedule an appointment, keying the subject **Discuss conference travel arrangements**. Make the location of the appointment as **Maria's office**, starting at 10 a.m. and ending at 10:30 a.m. Have the reminder go off 30 minutes before the appointment.

3. Schedule an event for Friday of that week, keying the subject as **Midwestern Furniture Manufacturers Association meeting**. Specify the location as **Chicago**. Set a 1-day reminder for the event, and show the time as Out of Office.

4. Create a task with the subject **Work out travel budget**, with a due date of Monday of that same week. In the text area of the task, key the text **Maria needs this budget before she will authorize the expenses.** Set a reminder for the preceding Friday. Set the status as In Progress.

5. Create a new e-mail message, addressing the message to your instructor. Key the subject of the message as **Travel budget**. For the text of the message, key the material shown in Figure 1-17, using a Plain Text message format.

NOTE: Your instructor will provide you with an appropriate e-mail address.

FIGURE 2-17

```
Maria:

This is just to let you know that I am scheduling a time for us to
meet a few days before the Midwestern Furniture Manufacturers Association
conference in Chicago. I would like to discuss my projected expenses.
```

6. Connect to the Internet and send the message.

7. Log off the Internet if your instructor tells you to do so.

8. Locate the message you just sent in the Sent Items folder and print it. Use a Memo Style print style, with your name as a centered header.

9. Display the date for Monday of the week that you scheduled the appointment and the event in the previous steps.

10. Print the Calendar, using Weekly Style. Add your name as a centered header and the date as a centered footer.

11. Print the task you created in step 4. Use a Memo Style print style, with your name as a centered header.

On Your Own

In these exercises you work on your own, as you would in a real-life work environment. Use the skills you've learned to accomplish the task—and be creative.

EXERCISE 2-24

Plan an elaborate, catered surprise birthday party for a friend or relative. Schedule meetings and tasks for the event. Consider all elements for the party, such as food, entertainment, and invitations. Print the Calendar and task list.

EXERCISE 2-25

Use the Internet to research a destination to which you'd like to travel for two days. Set up a detailed itinerary in your Calendar, and develop a task list to prepare for the trip. Print the Calendar and the task list.

EXERCISE 2-26

Document your week. Use the Calendar and task list to show all your work- and school-related tasks, activities, and personal chores. Print the Calendar and task list.

Unit 1 Applications

UNIT APPLICATION 1-1

Create and send a new e-mail message with a file attachment, add an appointment to the Calendar, and print the e-mail message and Calendar item.

Rob Connelly, AllWood's president, needs some information e-mailed to him quickly. He wants a list of all the living-room pieces in this year's Mission collection, plus the Excel file of Mission sales data for the 4th quarter. He also wants to schedule two meetings with you next week to work on this project with him.

1. Create a new e-mail message, addressing it to your instructor.

NOTE: Your instructor will provide you with an appropriate e-mail address.

2. For the subject of the message, key **Mission collection information**

3. Change the message format to Plain Text. In the message text area, key the material shown in Figure U1-1.

FIGURE U1-1

> Rob:
>
> Here is a list of ^Mission^ living ^—^ room pieces for the ~~2000~~ *2001* season. Note that it includes the three new items. I am set ting aside time in my calendar next week to me^e^t with you. Attached you will find the sales figures for the 4th quarter.

4. Open the Word file **Mission1** and copy the list of the living-room pieces to the Clipboard. Close the Word file and Word, and paste the contents of the Clipboard into the text area of the Message form, under the text you keyed in step 3.

5. Add the following items to the list:

Computer workstation

CD storage rack

Writing desk

6. Attach the Excel file **MSalesQ4**.

7. Connect to the Internet and send the message.

8. Display the Sent Items folder, and select the message you just sent. Restore the line breaks and print out the message, using a Memo Style as the print style. Add your name as a centered header.

9. Log off the Internet if your instructor tells you to do so.

10. Delete any Calendar items for next week, including all recurrences of any appointment or event. Enter a new appointment at 10 a.m. on a day in the beginning of next week. The subject of the appointment is **Meeting with Rob, discuss 4th Q sales figures**. Set the location of the meeting as **Rob's office**.

11. Make the meeting 1 hour in length, and set a reminder for 30 minutes before the meeting. In the text area of the Appointment form, key **Go over Excel MSalesQ4 worksheet with him.**

12. Print the appointment, using Calendar Details Style as the print style. Add your name as a centered header. Delete any existing footer information.

13. Hand in all printouts to your instructor.

UNIT APPLICATION 1-2

Schedule an event, create tasks, create a contact, send a new e-mail message using the contact in the Cc field, and print the Calendar, task list, contact information, and e-mail message.

The office staff wants to stage a birthday party for Maria Lopez, Allwood's VP of Administration. They've asked you to organize a surprise party after work on the day of her birthday.

1. Schedule the birthday as a new, all-day event in your Calendar, choosing a date several months after the current date. The subject of the event is **Maria's birthday**. In the text area of the Event form, key **Surprise party at Marty's Grill**. Have a reminder set two days before the event. Mark the event as private.

2. On the day of the event, schedule the party as an appointment in your Calendar, from 4:30–6:00 p.m., with the subject of the appointment **Surprise birthday party**. Specify the location as **Marty's Grill**. Set a reminder for one hour before the appointment. Mark the appointment as private. In the text area of the Appointment form, key **Guests are scheduled to arrive at 4:45 p.m. Maria to arrive at 5:00 p.m.**

3. Delete any existing tasks in the task list. Create a new task titled **Shop for birthday present**. Make the due date the week before the party, and deselect the reminder. Create a second task titled **Invite guests for birthday party**. Make the due date two weeks before the party, deselect the reminder, and make the status of the task In Progress. Create a third task, titled **Shop for party food, make snacks and cake**. Make the due date the day before the party, and set a reminder for the day before.

4. Create a new contact, using a classmate's name and address. Use your classmate's home address and phone number, and make the home address the mailing address. Include an e-mail address for the contact.

5. Create a new e-mail message, addressing it to your instructor. Cc the classmate you added as a contact in step 4. Use the **Cc** button to add the classmate's e-mail address to the Cc field from the Contact list. Make the subject of the message **Come to a surprise party!** Change the message format to Plain Text. In the message text area, key the material shown in Figure U1-2.

FIGURE U1-2

I'm planning a surprise birthday party for Maria, and I am hoping you can attend. Can you put it on your calendar? I realize it is some time away, but I will e-mail you a reminder a few days before.

NOTE: Your instructor will provide you with an appropriate e-mail address as well as the e-mail address of a classmate.

6. Connect to the Internet and send the message. Log off the Internet if your instructor tells you to do so.

7. Display the Sent Items folder, and select the message you just sent. Print the message, using a Memo Style as the print style. Add your name as a centered header, and delete any existing footer information.

8. Print the task list, using the Table Style as the print style. Make sure all rows are included in the task list. Add your name as a centered header, and delete any existing footer information.

9. Print your classmate's contact information, using the Memo Style as a print style. Add your name as a centered header, and delete any existing footer information.

10. Display the date of the event. Delete any Calendar items not entered in this exercise. Print the Calendar in Daily Style, adding your name as a centered header. Delete any existing footer information.

11. Select the birthday party item in the Calendar and print the Calendar again, this time using the Calendar Details Style as the print style and adding your name as a centered header.

12. Hand in all printouts to your instructor.

UNIT APPLICATION 1-3

Send new e-mail messages, forward a received e-mail message, and create contact information.

Rob Connelly, AllWood's president, has asked his VP of Design to create a line of office furniture. The line will use some existing pieces from each of the existing collections, as well as new pieces. You've been asked to join the team working on this project. Your initial tasks will be to exchange information with other team members, define responsibilities, and set up meeting times.

NOTE: This exercise is a team effort. Your instructor will assign a classmate to work with you as a team member. You will be required to exchange e-mail messages with your teammate to complete the exercise. Your instructor will provide e-mail addresses for your teammate.

1. Open your task list and delete any existing tasks.

2. Add a new task to your task list with the subject **Send my contact information**. Make the due date the current date. Add a second task with the subject **Print completed e-mail message**, also due today. Add a third task to your task list, containing the subject **Forward all received contact information to Rob**, without specifying a due date. Add one more task to the task list, containing the subject **Meet with _____** (substitute your teammate's name in the blank). Do not specify a due date.

3. Create a new e-mail message, addressing it to your teammate. The subject of the message is **My contact information**.

4. Change the message format to Plain Text. In the message text area, key the material shown in Figure U1-3, substituting your name and address information where appropriate (do not key comments in red).

FIGURE U1-3

Here is my contact information for your contact list. I've included my home address and phone number.

Name:

Address: *(Home)*

Phone: *(Home)*

Phone: *(Work, if applicable)*

5. Connect to the Internet and send the message. Log off the Internet if your instructor tells you to do so.

6. Display the Sent Items folder, and select the message you just sent. Restore the line breaks, if they have been placed in the message. Print the message, using a Memo Style as the print style. Add your name as a centered header.

7. Display your contact list and delete any existing contacts in the list.

8. After you've received your teammate's e-mail message, including contact information, enter that information in your contact list. Include the e-mail address as well.

9. Create a new contact for Rob Connelly, the President of AllWood Mills, Inc., keying the information shown in Figure U1-4, which is a business address and phone number. Include his job title and company name.

NOTE: Your instructor will supply you with an appropriate e-mail address to use for the contact's e-mail address.

FIGURE U1-4

```
Rob Connelly

3100 Jackson Street

Dubuque, IA 52004

Phone: (319) 555-4400

E-mail: instructor's.name@ISP.isp
```

10. Open the contact information e-mail message you received from your teammate. Restore any line breaks that have been placed in the message. Forward the message to Rob Connelly (your instructor). Use the **To** button to address the message from your contact list.

11. Above the original message, key the material shown in Figure U1-5, substituting the name of your teammate in the blank.

FIGURE U1-5

```
For your records, here is the contact information I received from _____.
```

12. Connect to the Internet and send the message. Log off the Internet if your instructor tells you to do so.

13. Display the Sent Items folder, and select the message you just sent. Restore the line breaks, if they have been placed in the message. Print the message, using a Memo Style as the print style. Add your name as a centered header.

14. Display the Calendar for the beginning of next month. Delete any appointments and events that appear in your schedule for the entire month.

15. Display a day in the first week of the next month. Schedule a new appointment titled **Office furniture project**, which will meet for 1 hour beginning at 10 a.m. Specify the location as **My office**. In the text area of the Appointment form, key **Meet with** _____ (substitute your teammate's name in the blank). Deselect the reminder.

16. Make the appointment a recurring appointment, meeting weekly on the same day every week. Have the range of recurrences end after three occurrences.

17. Display the day of the first appointment for the next month and print the Calendar, using the Monthly Style print style. Add your name as a centered header, delete any footer information, and set the page orientation to Portrait.

18. Select the first appointment for the next month. Change the end time of the appointment to 11:30 a.m. Do not change the remaining appointments in the month. With the first appointment selected, print the Calendar, using the Daily Style print style. Add your name as a centered header, and delete any footer information.

19. Display your task list. Mark the following tasks as completed: "Send my contact information," "Print completed e-mail message," and "Forward all received contact information to Rob."

20. Print the task list, using the Table Style as the print style. Add your name as a centered header. Make sure all rows are selected in the print range.

21. Hand in all printouts to your instructor.

UNIT APPLICATION 1-4   *Using the Internet*

Pick a friend or relative to whom you'd like to give a gift. The occasion could be a holiday or a birthday. Think of that person's hobbies or interests and locate Web sites that specialize in those products. For example, the gifts might be music CDs, computer games, jewelry, specialty coffees and teas, hard-to-find books, sporting goods, and so on.

Choose at least three products, preferably in different price ranges. Do comparison shopping on at least four different Web sites selling the same or similar product. If possible, note the shipping costs associated with each online retailer.

After you've obtained your information, use Outlook to create the following:

● Compose an e-mail message describing the information you've obtained, addressing it to your instructor. Include the address of the Web site for each of the online retailers. Send the message and print a copy of the message from the Sent Items folder.

- Pick a date in your Calendar to give your gift, choosing either a holiday or the individual's birthday. Make that date an event, and set a reminder for the day before. Delete any other appointments or events for that day and print the Calendar for that day, using a Daily Style print style.

- Create a task list with at least four tasks associated with this project. You may mark any or all of them completed, if you wish. Delete any other tasks in the task list and print out the task list, using a Table Style for the print style.

- Hand in all printouts to your instructor.

NOTE: Your instructor will provide you with an appropriate e-mail address.

Managing E-Mail Efficiently

Working with Contacts

OBJECTIVES

**MOUS
ACTIVITIES**
In this lesson:
OL2002 **4-1**
OL2002 **4-2**
OL2002 **4-3**
See Appendix E.

After completing this lesson, you will be able to:

1. **Edit contacts.**
2. **Categorize contacts.**
3. **Work with distribution lists.**
4. **View, sort, and print contacts.**

Estimated Time: 1 hour

Y ou've seen how you can use Contacts to keep track of people and organizations with whom you communicate. But you can use Outlook's Contacts for much more than simply storing a name, address, phone number, and e-mail address. There are many other details about a contact that you might wish to store, and you can also categorize contacts and link them with one another.

If you have an extensive contact list, you can organize and display various contacts by category. Outlook enables you to develop distribution lists from your contacts. A *distribution list* is a set of contacts to whom you send e-mail messages. Outlook also gives you many different ways to view and print your contact list.

Editing Contacts

Outlook lets you change and delete items stored in the Contacts folder as needed. You can add details, change addresses and phone numbers, and flag items to remind yourself of birthdays and anniversaries. If a contact is associated with one or more other items in your contact list, you can make note of the other contacts.

EXERCISE 3-1 Edit a Contact

You can edit an existing contact either directly in the contact list or by opening the contact and editing it in the Contact form. You can open a contact by:

- Double-clicking the contact.
- Selecting the contact and then choosing File, Open, Select Items from the menu.
- Selecting the contact and pressing Ctrl + O.
- Selecting the contact and pressing Enter.
- Right-clicking the contact and choosing Open from the shortcut menu.

1. Click the Contacts shortcut 📇 in the Outlook Bar. The Contacts folder appears.

2. Make sure the contact list in displayed in Address Cards view. (If it is not, choose View, Current View, Address Cards from the menu.)

3. Add the contacts shown in Figure 3-1. Specify all addresses as the mailing addresses. Do not key the red text; this only shows the information as home or business data. Make sure you enter the MediaArt name in the **Company** field, not the Full **Name** field.

REVIEW: When creating multiple new contacts, use the Save and New button 📇 on the Contact form toolbar to save a newly created contact and display a new, blank Contact form. Also, remember that you do not need to supply the parentheses, hyphens, or spaces when keying phone numbers. Outlook automatically formats the number for you.

FIGURE 3-1

```
Mr. Tom Smith                 MediaArt (Company)

22 Elm Street (Home)          125 Main Street

East Dubuque, IL 61025        Dubuque, IA 52001

(815) 555-1111 (Home)         (319) 555-1199

E-mail: tsmith@ISP.isp        E-mail: art@ISP.isp
```

continues

FIGURE 3-1   *continued*

Ms. Doris Jones   Dr. Henry Williams, Jr.

240 Cedar Avenue *(Business)*   1200 Sunset Road *(Home)*

Dubuque, IA 52002   Dubuque, IA 52003

(319) 555-1231 *(Business)*   (319) 555-1119 *(Home)*

Mrs. Janet K. Woo   Julio Alvarez

111 Third Ave. *(Home)*   1800 Main St. *(Business)*

New York, NY 10011   Dubuque, IA 52001

(212) 555-8881 *(Home)*   (319) 555-1199 *(Business)*

                                   E-mail: jalvarez@ISP.isp

4. Double-click the Tom Smith contact to open it. The Contact form for Tom Smith appears.

5. Click the down arrow under A**d**dress and select **Business**.

6. Key the following business address:

   1200 Main Street

   Dubuque, IA 52001

7. Make the new address the mailing address.

8. Key the following business phone:

   (319) 555-1299

9. Click the **S**ave and Close button to save the new information. The new address now appears under the name. Outlook always displays the mailing address in this view.

10. Click the address portion of the Doris Jones contact. Notice that the insertion point is located within the text of the address. You can edit the text directly in the contact list.

11. Select the Tom Smith contact and press [Enter]. The Contact form for Tom Smith appears again.

12. Click the down arrow under A**d**dress and select **Home** to display the home address. Select **This is the mailing add**r**ess**.

13. Click the **S**ave and Close button. The address for Tom Smith now displays his home address.

> ⭐ **TIP:** When entering multiple contacts from the same company, you can use the Contact form menu command <u>A</u>ctions, New <u>C</u>ontact from Same Company. After entering the data for the first contact, this command repeats the same address and phone number data for subsequent contacts.

EXERCISE | **3-2** | **Add Detail to a Contact**

In addition to name and phone information, you can store more detailed information about a contact, such as the contact's manager, birthday, anniversary, or spouse's name. You can also add a flag to a contact, reminding you of a follow-up action associated with that contact.

1. Select the Tom Smith contact and press ⌷Enter⌷. The Contact form for Tom Smith appears.

2. Click the **Details** tab. The Details portion of the Contact form appears. You can include information about a contact, such as the contact's manager or assistant.

FIGURE 3-2
Details tab of Contact form

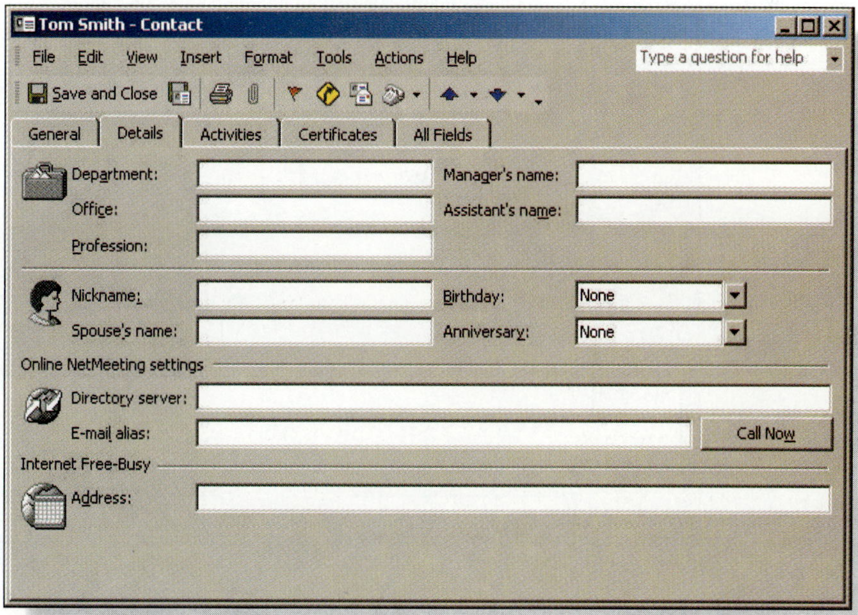

3. Click the down arrow next to the <u>B</u>irthday text box. Click Today to set the birthday to the current date.

> ⭐ **TIP:** You can use the arrows at the top of the drop-down calendar to advance months or years into the future.

4. To flag this date so you'll be reminded to call Tom Smith on his birthday, click the Follow Up button on the Contact form toolbar. The Flag for Follow Up dialog box appears.

5. Click the down arrow next to the Flag to box, and select Call. Leave the Due by date and time as None. (A reminder appears when you specify a date and time.)

6. Click OK, and then click the Save and Close button. Under Tom Smith's name, notice the words "Follow Up Flag: Call."

7. Open the Contact form for Tom Smith. A banner appears above Tom Smith's name and a birthday icon appears in the Notes area of the form.

NOTE: The Notes area might be compressed too much for you to see the birthday icon. If this is the case, drag the bottom border of the Contact form to enlarge the viewing area.

FIGURE 3-3
Contact form with flag banner and birthday icon

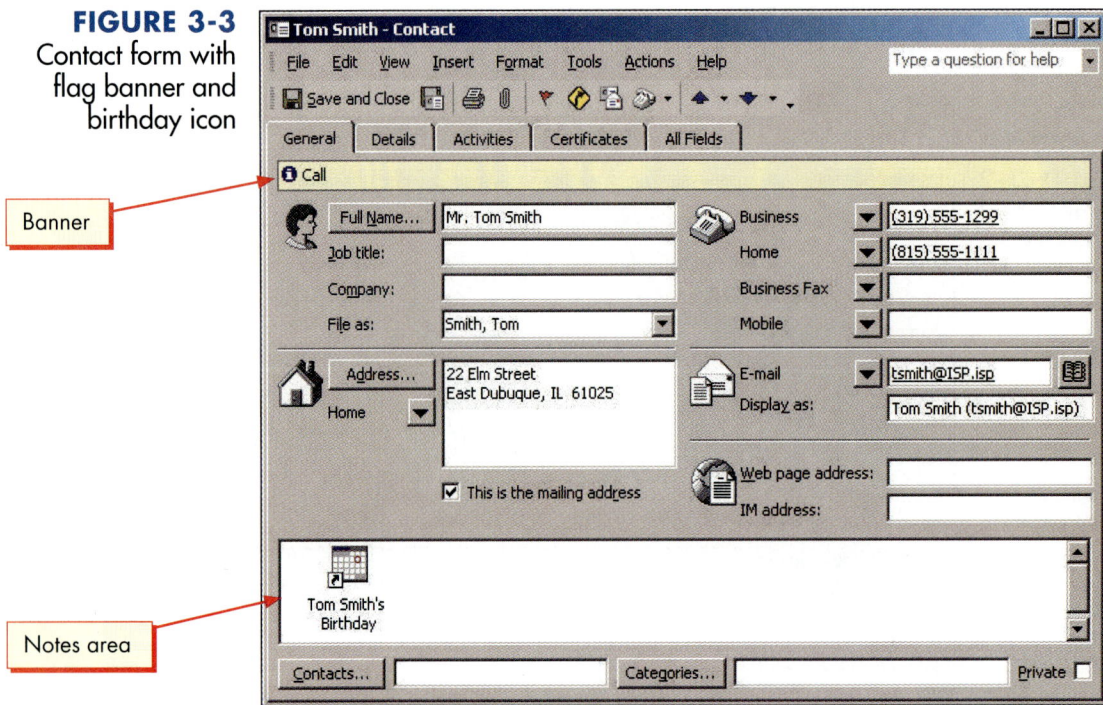

Banner

Notes area

8. Close the Contact form for Tom Smith.

EXERCISE 3-3 Link a Contact with Another Contact

Outlook lets you link contacts. You can link any entry in your contact list with another contact. You might use this feature to link contacts who work at the same company, or you might link a subordinate and supervisor. Links help you keep track of what contacts belong together.

1. Open the Contact form for Tom Smith.

2. In the Company text box, key **MediaArt**

3. Click Contacts, which is located at the bottom of the Contact form. The Select Contacts dialog box appears. The lower pane of this dialog box lists Contact items in your default Contacts folder. If you have more than one Contacts folder, you can select one in the upper pane.

FIGURE 3-4
Select Contacts
dialog box

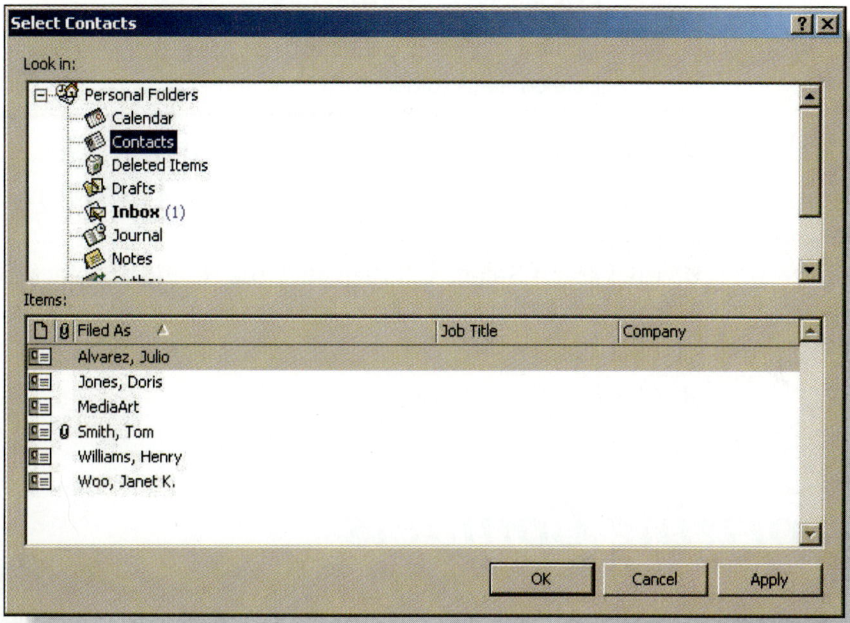

4. Select the MediaArt contact, and then click Apply.

5. Click OK. The Contact form for Tom Smith reappears. Notice in the Contacts text box that there is now an entry for MediaArt. You can use this feature to link business contacts with one another.

6. Click the Save and Close button. The Contacts folder is redisplayed.

EXERCISE   3-4   Delete and Print a Contact

You can delete contacts like any other Outlook item. There are various ways to delete a contact. You can:

● Select the contact and click the Delete button ☒ on the Standard toolbar.

● Right-click the contact and choose Delete from the shortcut menu.

- Select the contact and choose Edit, Delete from the menu.
- Select the contact and press Ctrl + D.

1. Select Doris Jones in the contact list.

2. Click the Delete button ✕ on the Standard toolbar (or press Ctrl + D). Outlook deletes the Doris Jones contact.

3. To restore the deleted contact, choose Edit, Undo Delete from the menu (or press Ctrl + Z). The Doris Jones contact is restored to the contact list.

NOTE: After you leave the Contacts folder, you cannot restore a deleted item from the Edit menu. However, you can restore the contact from the Deleted Items folder.

4. Select Tom Smith in the contact list and press Enter.

5. Choose File, Print from the menu (or press Ctrl + P). The Print dialog box appears.

6. Click Page Setup, and then click the Header/Footer tab if it is not already displayed. Add your name as a centered header.

7. Click OK, and then click OK once again. The Tom Smith contact is printed.

8. Close the Contact form.

Categorizing Contacts

Contacts can be assigned to categories. This enables you to sort and organize your contacts by categories. For example, you can assign all your friends and family members to a Personal category. Contacts can be assigned to one or more predefined categories. Assigning categories to your contacts helps you keep a large contact list organized.

EXERCISE **3-5** **Assign Individual Contact Items to Categories**

You can assign categories to individual contacts. You can assign a contact to as many categories as you wish.

1. Select the Henry Williams contact and press Enter. The Contact form for Henry Williams appears.

2. Click Categories (located at the bottom of the form). The Categories dialog box appears. (See Figure 3-5 on the next page.)

FIGURE 3-5
Categories
dialog box

3. Select **Gifts** and **Personal**. Click **OK**. The text box adjacent to **Categories** now shows your selections. You can also assign categories to contacts as you create them.

4. Click the **Save and Close** button. Another way to assign categories to contact items is with the shortcut menu.

5. Right-click the Henry Williams contact. The shortcut menu appears.

6. Select **Categories** from the shortcut menu. The Categories dialog box appears. Notice under **Available categories** that Gifts and Personal are already selected.

7. Select **Favorites** and click **OK**. Henry Williams has been added to the Favorites category.

EXERCISE 3-6 Assign Multiple Contacts to Categories

Sometimes you might want to assign a group of contacts to a category all at one time. A quick way to do this is to use the Ways to Organize pane.

1. Select the Tom Smith contact.

2. Click the Organize button ![icon] on the Standard toolbar. The Ways to Organize Contacts pane appears.

FIGURE 3-6
Ways to Organize
Contacts pane

3. Choose **Using Categories**, if it is not already selected.

4. Click the down arrow next to **Add contacts selected below to** text box. Use the scroll bar to scroll down the drop-down list, and select **Suppliers**.

5. Press and hold [Ctrl], and then select the contacts Julio Alvarez and MediaArt. (Tom Smith should already be selected.)

6. Click **Add**. The three contacts are assigned to the Suppliers category.

7. Click the down arrow next to **Add contacts selected below to** text box once again, and select **Business**.

8. Click **Add**. The three contacts are also assigned to the Business category. You can assign a contact to as many categories as you wish.

9. Click the Organize button 🔳. The Ways to Organize Categories pane closes.

10. Open the Contact form for Julio Alvarez. Notice that the **Categories** text box shows Suppliers and Business.

11. Close the Julio Alvarez Contact form.

12. Open the Contact form for Janet Woo and add it to the Personal category.

13. Click the **S**ave and Close button to save the change and redisplay the Contacts folder.

Working with Distribution Lists

After you've created some contacts, you can select items from your contact list to create an e-mail distribution list. Think of a distribution list as a collection of contacts. You use a distribution list as an address to send e-mail messages to everyone on the list. For example, if you frequently send messages to a group of people who are members of a marketing team, you can create a distribution list named Marketing that contains the addresses of everyone on the list.

E X E R C I S E   **3-7**   **Create a Distribution List**

You can create a new distribution list in one of several different ways. You can:

- Choose **A**ctions, New **D**istribution List from the menu.
- Click the down arrow next to the **N**ew button 🔳 and choose **Distribution List** from the drop-down menu.
- Press [Ctrl]+[Shift]+[L].

1. Display the Contacts folder, if it is not already displayed.

2. Choose **A**ctions, New **D**istribution List from the menu (or press [Ctrl]+[Shift]+[L]). The Distribution List form appears. (See Figure 3-7 on the next page.)

FIGURE 3-7
Distribution List form

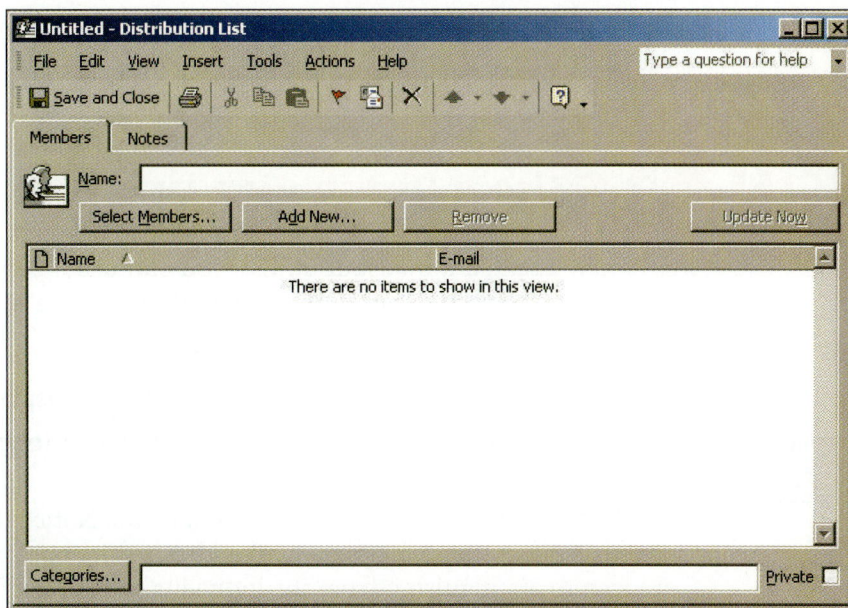

3. In the **N**ame text box, key **MediaArtList**. This is the name of your e-mail distribution list. Next, you'll add the e-mail addresses of the members of the list.

4. Click **Select M**embers. The Select Members dialog box appears.

5. If Contacts is not displayed in the **Sh**ow Names from the text box, click the down arrow next to that box and select **Contacts**. Notice that not all of the names in your contact list are displayed. Outlook only lists contacts containing e-mail addresses.

6. Under **Name**, select **MediaArt** and click **Mem**bers. The MediaArt e-mail address is placed under **Add to distribution list**.

7. Select **Julio Alvarez**, and click **Mem**bers. The distribution list now has two names.

> **TIP:** You can double-click a name when you want to place a new name under Add to distribution list, instead of selecting the name and clicking Mem**b**ers.

8. Click **OK**. The Distribution List form reappears. Both names are shown as members of the MediaArtList distribution list. Notice that you can use **Categories** to assign categories to the distribution list just as with any other contact.

9. Click the **S**ave and Close button on the Distribution List form toolbar. The new distribution list is saved and the contact list reappears. The distribution

list is shown as an item in the contact list. The icon after the listing indicates it is a distribution list.

EXERCISE **3-8** **Use a Distribution List**

After you've created a distribution list, you can use it as you would any other e-mail address. Every name in the distribution list is a recipient of the e-mail message.

1. Click the Inbox shortcut in the Outlook Bar to display the Inbox folder.

2. Click the **New** button on the Standard toolbar (or press Ctrl + N). The Message form appears.

3. Click To. The Select Names dialog box appears. Notice that MediaArtList is listed as one of the available e-mail addresses. It appears in bold and with an icon to distinguish it from the individual e-mail addresses.

FIGURE 3-8
Select Names
dialog box

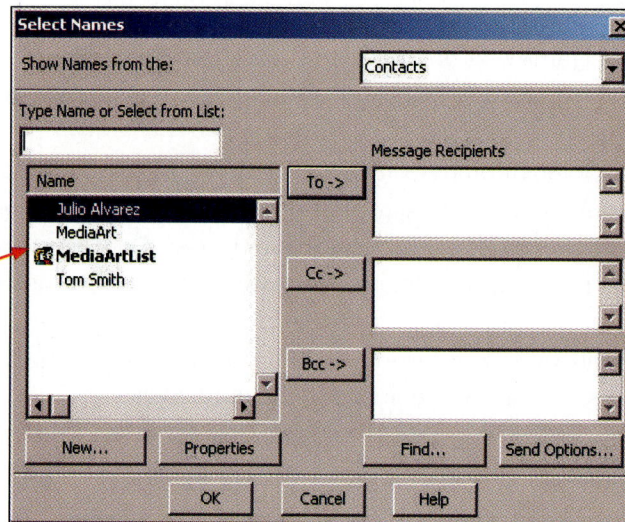

Distribution list

4. Under **Name**, select MediaArtList, click **To**, and then click **OK**. The Message form reappears with MediaArtList in the **To** text box. Any e-mail message you compose and send will be sent to all members of the list. You might wish to see the names on the list before you send the message.

5. To see the members of the distribution list, double-click MediaArtList in the **To** text box. The Distribution List form shows the members of the list.

6. Close the Distribution List form, and then close the Message form without saving or sending the message.

EXERCISE **3-9** **Modify a Distribution List**

You can add and delete names in a distribution list. For lengthy and frequently used distribution lists, this enables you to keep your lists up-to-date.

1. Click the Contacts shortcut ▨ in the Outlook Bar to display the Contacts folder.

2. Double-click the MediaArtList contact. The Distribution List form opens.

3. Click Select Members. The Select Members dialog box appears. As before, the names that appear under **Name** are the items in your contact list that contain e-mail addresses.

4. Select Tom Smith and click **Members**. The selection appears under **Add to distribution list**.

5. Click OK. The Distribution List form reappears, showing Tom Smith's name as one of the members of the list. You can also add new names to your distribution list that are not on your contact list.

6. Click Add New. The Add New Member dialog box appears.

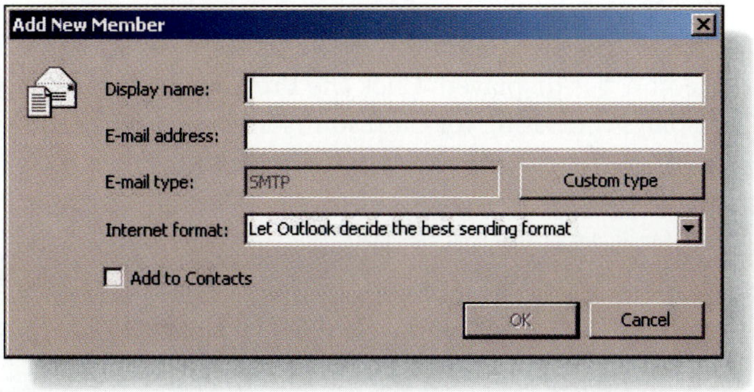

FIGURE 3-9
Add New Member
dialog box

7. In the Display name text box, key **Sam Johnson**

8. In the E-mail address text box, key **sjohnson@ISP.isp**. You can add the new distribution list member to your contact list.

9. Select Add to Contacts and click OK. The new name is added to your distribution list and your contact list. To delete a name from the distribution list, you would simply select the name and click **Remove**.

10. Click the Save and Close button. The MediaArtList has been modified, and Sam Johnson now appears in your contact list.

⭐ **TIP:** If you've removed names from your contact list and would also like them removed from your distribution lists, you can use the Update No_w_ option on the Distribution List form. Outlook will scan the names in the selected distribution list and give you the option of removing any name on the list that has been removed from your contact list.

Viewing, Sorting, and Printing Contacts

Outlook provides many ways to view your contacts. This makes it easy to find the information you want in a hurry. You can change the view of the contact list, displaying more details or arranging the contacts by flagged items. If you've assigned your contacts to different categories, you can sort the contact list according to these categories. And when you need to print portions of your contact list, you can use Outlook's printing features.

E X E R C I S E `3-10` **View Contacts**

You can cycle through the contact list while viewing an individual contact in the Contact form, or you can use the letter tabs on the right side of the Contacts folder.

1. Make sure the Contacts folder is displayed, and open the listing for Doris Jones.

2. Click the Next Item button ⬇ on the Contact form toolbar. The listing for MediaArt is displayed. Click the Previous Item button ⬆ twice. Outlook displays the listing for Sam Johnson. You can use the small arrows next to these toolbar buttons to skip to the beginning or end of the folder.

3. Close the Contact form to redisplay the Contacts folder. Notice the letter tabs on the right side of the Contacts folder.

4. Click the **s** tab. Outlook selects Tom Smith. Click the **w** tab. Outlook selects Henry Williams. Click the **ab** tab. Outlook selects Julio Alvarez.

> **NOTE:** Depending on the size of your screen, the letter tabs in the Contacts folder might display only single letters for some of the tabs. For example, the letters "i" and "j" might appear on separate tabs instead of a single tab for both letters.

5. Press Ⓦ. The listing for Henry Williams is selected. When you press a letter key, Outlook selects the first item in your contact list starting with that letter (or the item closest to the letter in the alphabet).

6. Choose <u>V</u>iew, Current <u>V</u>iew from the menu, and then choose **Detailed Address Cards**. Depending on the size of your screen, one or more listings move to a second column. Outlook truncates entries in the columns because the columns aren't wide enough for the individual items. For large contact lists, you can adjust the view with the scroll bar that appears at the bottom of the folder.

7. Position the pointer between the two columns until it displays a two-pointed horizontal arrow ↔ , and drag the column divider to the right so all

the information for the individual contacts appears. Repeat for the second column, if necessary.

FIGURE 3-10
Contacts folder in
Detailed Address
Cards view

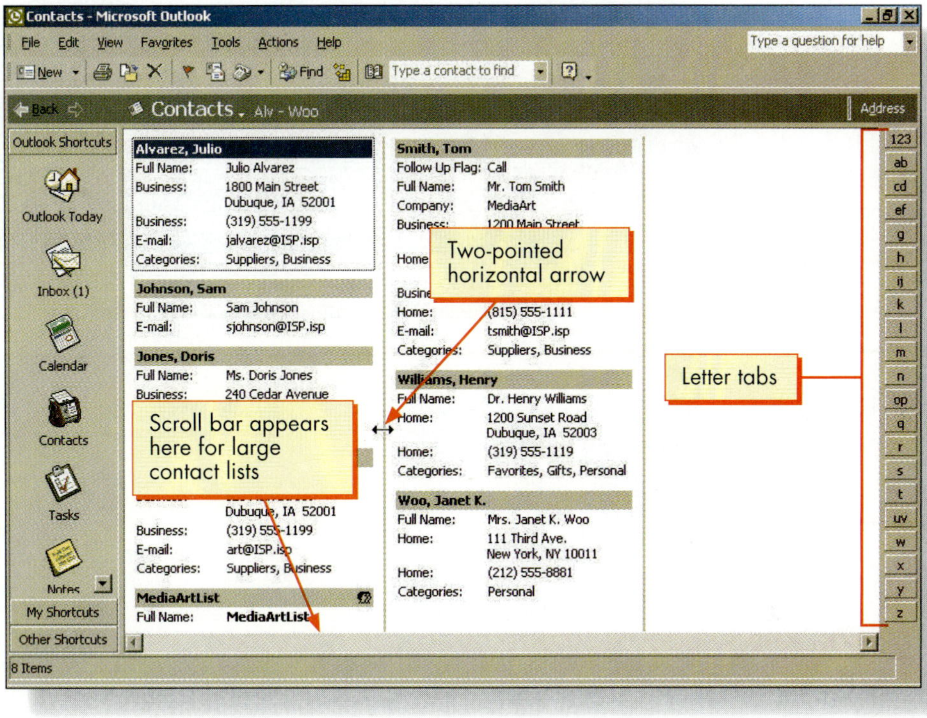

8. Choose **View**, **Current View**, and choose **By Follow-up Flag**. Outlook switches to a Table view, placing the contacts with flagged items at the top of the list.

9. Display the contacts in Detailed Address Card view.

EXERCISE 3-11 Sort Contacts by Category

If you assigned categories to your contacts, you can view them by category.

1. Choose **View**, **Current View** from the menu, and then choose **By Category**. Outlook switches to a Table view, grouping the contacts by categories. There are groups for every category you've assigned to your contacts, plus a group for contacts not assigned to any category. Notice the plus sign to the left of each category. They are used to display the details of each group.

2. Click the plus sign (+) next to the Business category. The details of the Business category are displayed, showing the contacts assigned to this group.

3. Click the plus sign next to the Personal category. The contacts for the Personal category appear. (See Figure 3-11 on the next page.)

FIGURE 3-11
Contacts folder in
By Category view

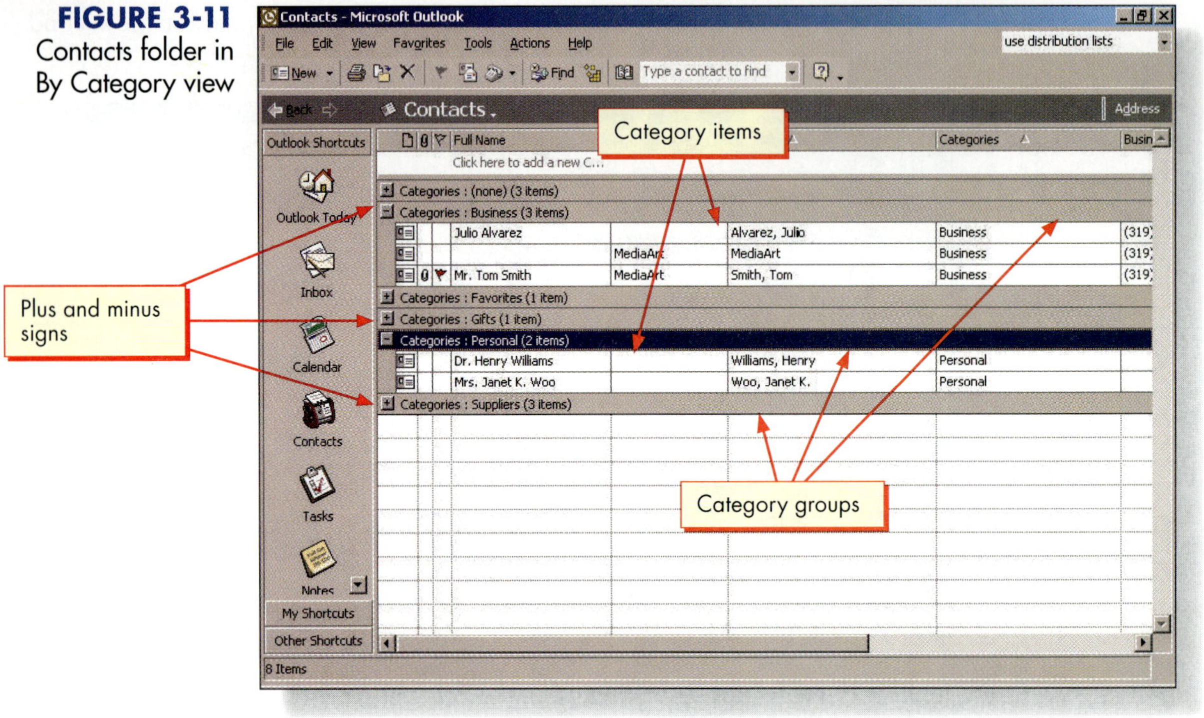

4. Display the items within each remaining group by clicking the plus signs.

5. Click the minus sign (–) next to the Business category to hide the group's details.

6. Hide the rest of the items within each group.

EXERCISE 3-12 Sort Contacts by Field

By default, Outlook sorts your contact list by using the **File as** text box in the Contact form as the sorting field. In most cases, this is the contact's last name. However, sometimes you might wish to have Outlook sort the list in a different way. For example, you might want your contacts displayed by using the **Company** field.

1. Choose **View**, Current **View**, Detailed Address Cards from the menu.

2. Choose **View**, Current **View** again from the menu. Then choose **Customize** Current View. The View Summary dialog box appears.

3. Click **Sort**. The Sort dialog box appears. (See Figure 3-12 on the next page.)

4. Click the down arrow in the **Sort items by** text box, and scroll through the list of sort options.

5. Select **Company** from the drop-down list, and then select **Descending**, if it is not already selected.

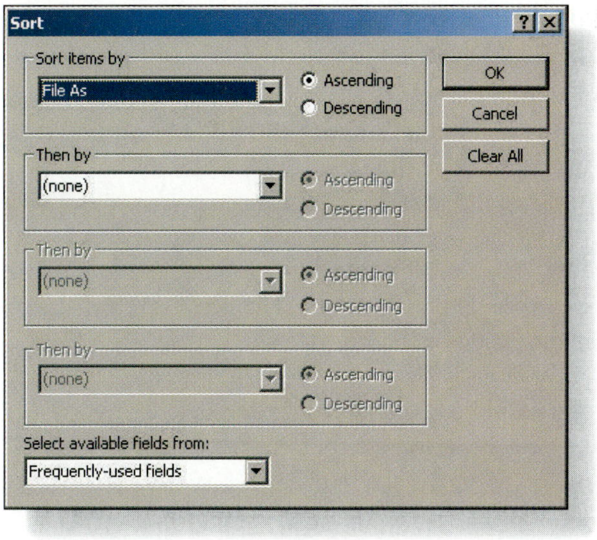

FIGURE 3-12
Sort dialog box

6. Click **OK** and click **OK** again. Outlook sorts the Contacts folder by the **Company** field. Only the listings for Tom Smith and MediaArt have any data entered into that field, so they are shown at the beginning of the contact list.

7. Open the listing for Sam Johnson. In the **Company** text box, key **AllWood Mills, Inc.**

8. Click the **Save and Close** button. Outlook moves the position of the Sam Johnson contact, using the company field to place it among the other items in the contact list with information entered in this field.

9. Return the sort order of the contact list to its default setting by choosing **View, Current View, Customize Current View** and then clicking **Sort**. Set **Sort items by** to **File As**, and select **Ascending**. Click **OK** twice. The contact list is restored to its default sort order. (Your contact list might be displayed in three columns because you have added new information to the Sam Johnson listing. Use the scroll bar at the bottom of the screen to adjust the display, if necessary.)

NOTE: Make sure you have completed the last step of this exercise. This step restores Outlook to its default setting. Always leave Outlook in its default state for the next class or student to use.

EXERCISE **3-13** **Print Items on the Contact List**

You can print one, several, or all the items in the Contacts folder, using various print styles.

1. To print all the contacts, choose **File, Print** from the menu (or press Ctrl + P). The Print dialog box appears.

2. Scroll down the list of available print styles. The Small Booklet Style and Medium Booklet Style require double-sided printing.

3. Choose **Phone Directory Style** and click **Preview**. Notice that this print style prints only the contact's name and phone number(s), and the contacts are arranged alphabetically.

4. Click **Page Setup** and make sure the **Header/Footer** tab is displayed.

> ⭐ **TIP:** You can eliminate the letter headings that appear above each group of items in the Phone Directory Style and Card Style by deselecting the **H**eadings for each letter option on the Format tab.

5. Add your name as a centered header, delete any existing footer, and click OK. The preview page reappears, showing the header.

6. Click **Print**, and then click **OK**. Outlook prints the contact list in Phone Directory Style.

7. To print two individual items, select MediaArt, press and hold Ctrl, and then select Julio Alvarez.

8. Press Ctrl + P. Select the **Memo Style** print style.

9. Click **Page Setup**, and add your name as a centered header, if it is not already displayed. Click **OK** to return to the Print dialog box.

10. Click **OK** to print the selected items. MediaArt appears at the top of the printout. The items are printed in the order of their selection, not the order in which they appear in the contact list. You can also print selected items in Card Style.

11. With MediaArt and Julio Alvarez still selected, click the Print button 🖨 on the Standard toolbar. The Print dialog box appears.

12. Select the **Card Style** print style, select **Only selected items**, and then click **Preview**. Note on the Preview toolbar that there is more than one page. Click the Page Down button 📥. The second page appears. When printing selected items from your contact list, the Card Style print style includes a page of blank forms at the end for you to add new contacts by hand. You may exclude this page from the printout if you wish.

> ↗ **NOTE:** Your preview might not show a second page if a printout has already been generated excluding the blank forms.

13. Click the **Page Setup** button on the Preview toolbar. The Page Setup: Card Style dialog box appears. Make sure the **Format** tab is displayed. Click the down arrow next to the **B**lank forms at end text box, and select **None**.

14. Click the **Header/Footer** tab, and add your name as a centered header. Click OK. The Print Preview reappears.

15. Click the Print button ![print icon] on the Preview toolbar. The Print dialog box is redisplayed. Click **OK**. The selected items print in Card Style.

16. Chose View, Current View, Address Cards to display the Contacts folder in the default view.

USING HELP

When you want to send items in your Contacts folder to someone, you can send these items via e-mail. Outlook supports a file format called *vCard*, which is the Internet standard for creating and sharing virtual business cards. You can save a contact as a vCard and send the information to someone. If you receive a vCard, you can add it to your own Contacts folder.

Use Microsoft Outlook Help to learn how to save a contact as a vCard:

1. In the Ask a Question box, key **Save a contact as a vCard** and press Enter. A list of related topics appears. The first topic describes how to create a vCard from a contact.

2. Click Create a vCard from a contact. A Help screen appears.

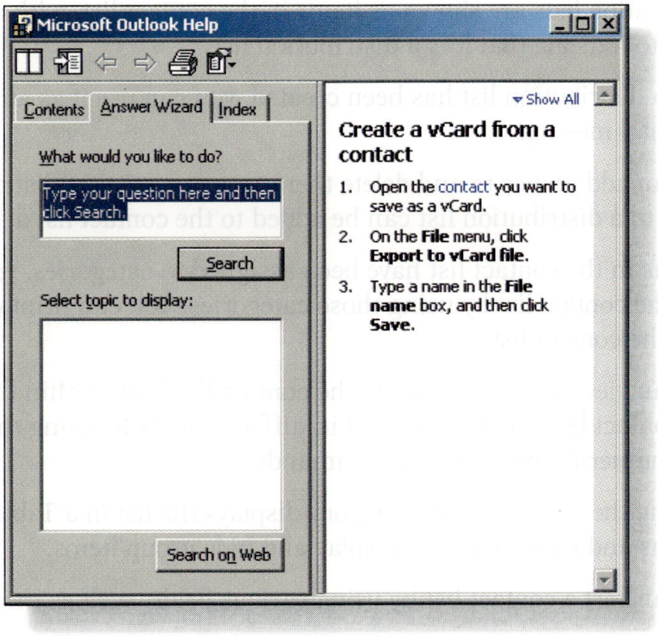

FIGURE 3-13
Help screen for saving contact as a vCard

3. Read the information. Then, on the left side of the screen in the What would you like to do? text box, key **Save a vCard attachment to Contacts** and click Search. This screen describes how you add a vCard attachment to your contact list when one is sent to you.

4. Read the information and then click the Close button ![X].

Concepts Review

TRUE/FALSE QUESTIONS

Each of the following statements is either true or false. Indicate your choice by circling T or F.

T F   *1.* Outlook always uses a contact's home address as the mailing address.

T F   *2.* Outlook lets you store multiple addresses for contacts.

T F   *3.* Outlook stores birthday and anniversary dates on the General tab of the Contact form.

T F   *4.* The Contacts folder is the only place where you can restore deleted contacts.

T F   *5.* You can assign a contact to as many categories as you like.

T F   *6.* You create a new distribution list by using the Contact form.

T F   *7.* To add to a distribution list new members whose names and e-mail addresses are on your contact list, you use the Add New Member dialog box.

T F   *8.* Pressing a letter key displays the first item in your contact list starting with that letter, or the item closest to it in the alphabet.

SHORT ANSWER QUESTIONS

Write the correct answer in the space provided.

1. Which toolbar button on the Contact form toolbar do you use to save changes to a contact?

_____

2. How do you restore a deleted item?

_____

3. What button on the Contact form toolbar do you click to skip to the listing immediately after the current contact?

_____

4. What button on the Contact form toolbar do you click to skip to the listing immediately preceding the current contact?

_____

5. What keystrokes do you use to display the Distribution List form?

_____

6. What button on the Standard toolbar do you use to assign items on your contact list to categories?

_____

7. Where do you enter the name of the distribution list in the Message form when you want to use it to send an e-mail message to the members of the distribution list?

_____

8. What command would you use to see all the address card details of the contact list?

_____

CRITICAL THINKING

Answer these questions on a separate page. There are no right or wrong answers. Support your answers with examples from your own experience, if possible.

1. Which do you prefer: a computerized contacts list or a paper phone and address book? Why?

2. What kinds of problems might arise if you have separate contact lists on a work computer and a home computer?

Skills Review

EXERCISE 3-14

Create and edit a contact, add details, link a contact with another contact, and print the contact.

NOTE: This exercise uses the MediaArt contact you created in Exercise 3-1. Add this contact first if you don't have it in your contact list.

1. Open the Contacts folder by clicking the Contacts shortcut 📇 in the Outlook Bar.

2. Add the contact shown in Figure 3-14, entering the address and phone number as business information. (See Figure 3-14 on the next page.)

FIGURE 3-14

```
Susan Epstein

333 Second Ave., #4

Dubuque, IA 52004

(319) 555-9876

E-mail: sepstein@ISP.isp
```

3. Add details to a contact by following these steps:
   a. Make sure the Susan Epstein contact you created in step 2 is open.
   b. Click the **Details** tab on the Contact form.
   c. Click the down arrow next to the **Birthday** text box. From the drop-down calendar, select a date two weeks from the current date.

4. Link a contact with another contact by following these steps:
   a. Click the **General** tab on the Contact form.
   b. Click **Contacts**.
   c. Under **Items**, select **MediaArt**.
   d. Click **Apply**, and then click **OK**.

5. Print the contact by following these steps:
   a. With the Susan Epstein contact still open, choose **File**, **Print** from the menu.
   b. Click **OK**.

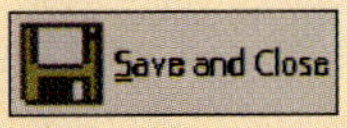

6. Click the **Save and Close** button.

EXERCISE 3-15

Assign a contact to categories.

NOTE: This exercise uses the Doris Jones contact you created in Exercise 3-1. Add this contact first if you don't have it in your contact list.

1. Click the Contacts shortcut in the Outlook Bar to display the Contacts folder if it is not already displayed.

2. Open the Doris Jones contact.

3. Assign the contact to several categories by following these steps:
   a. Click **Categories**.
   b. Under **Available categories**, select **Business** and **Suppliers**.
   c. Click **OK**.

4. Choose <u>F</u>ile, <u>P</u>rint from the menu.

5. Click OK.

6. Click the <u>S</u>ave and Close button on the Contact form toolbar.

EXERCISE 3-16

Create and modify a distribution list.

NOTE: This exercise uses the Julio Alvarez and Tom Smith contacts you created in Exercise 3-1. Add these contacts first if you don't have them in your contact list.

1. Click the Contacts shortcut 📇 in the Outlook Bar to display the Contacts folder if it is not already displayed.

2. Create a distribution list by following these steps:

a. Choose <u>A</u>ctions, New <u>D</u>istribution List from the menu.

b. In the <u>N</u>ame text box, key **Friends**

c. Click Select <u>M</u>embers.

d. Under Name, select Julio Alvarez and click Mem<u>b</u>ers.

e. Select Tom Smith and click Mem<u>b</u>ers.

f. Click OK.

g. Click the <u>S</u>ave and Close button on the Distribution List form toolbar.

3. Modify a distribution list, assigning it to a category, by following these steps:

a. Select the Friends item on your contact list, and press Enter.

b. Click Categories.

c. Under A<u>v</u>ailable categories, select Personal and then click OK.

d. Click the <u>S</u>ave and Close button.

4. Open the Friends distribution list.

5. Choose <u>F</u>ile, <u>P</u>rint from the menu, click OK, and then close the Distribution List form.

EXERCISE 3-17

Display contact list in Address Card view, sort contacts by category, print the contact list, and print several contacts together.

NOTE: This exercise uses the contacts you created in Exercises 3-1, 3-7, and 3-9. Complete these exercises if you don't have these contacts in your contact list.

1. Click the Contacts shortcut 📇 in the Outlook Bar to display the Contacts folder if it is not already displayed.

2. If the contact list is not already displayed in Address Card view, choose View, Current View, Address Card from the menu.

3. Delete Susan Epstein and the Friends distribution list if these items appear on your contact list. Your contact list should contain only the following items: Julio Alvarez, Sam Johnson, Doris Jones, MediaArt, MediaArtList, Tom Smith, Henry Williams, and Janet K. Woo.

4. Sort the contact list by following these steps:

   a. Choose View, Current View, Detailed Address Card from the menu.
   b. Choose View, Current View, Customize Current View.
   c. Click Sort.
   d. Under Sort items by, click the down arrow next to the text box and choose Company.
   e. Select Ascending, and then click OK.
   f. Click OK again.

5. Print the first two items in the contact list by following these steps:

   a. Click the first item in the contact list to select it.
   b. Press and hold Ctrl and click the next item in the contact list.
   c. Choose File, Print from the menu.
   d. Choose the Phone Directory print style.
   e. Click Page Setup, and click the Header/Footer tab. Add your name as a centered header, and then click OK.
   f. Select Only selected items.
   g. Click OK.

6. Restore the sort order of the contact list to its default setting by following these steps:

   a. Choose View, Current View, Customize Current View from the menu.
   b. Click Sort.
   c. Under Sort items by, click the down arrow next to the text box and choose File As.
   d. Select Ascending, and then click OK.
   e. Click OK once again.
   f. Choose View, Current View, Address Card.

NOTE: Make sure you have completed the last step of this exercise. This step restores Outlook to its default setting. Always leave Outlook in its default state for the next class or student to use.

Lesson Applications

Add details to a contact and assign it to several categories; create a distribution list; and print the contact and the distribution list.

NOTE: This exercise uses the Doris Jones, Tom Smith, and Henry Williams contacts you created in Exercise 3-1. Add these contacts first if you don't have them in your contact list.

Will McCarthy, AllWood's VP of Design, has assigned you to work with Doris Jones for the next six months. You need to add some information to her listing in your contact list. You also need to create a distribution list related to your work with her.

1. Display your Contacts folder and open the Doris Jones contact.
2. Key a job title of **Design Associate** and a home phone number of **(319) 555-0101**. Key an e-mail address of **djones@ISP.isp**
3. Set a birthday for the contact, choosing a date roughly a month from the current date.
4. Delete any existing categories that have been assigned to Doris Jones, and assign her to Goals/Objectives.
5. Link the contact with another contact, selecting Henry Williams from the Select Contacts dialog box.
6. Create a new distribution list entitled **Design List**. From your existing contact list, add Doris Jones and Tom Smith. Assign the distribution list to the Business category.
7. Select the Doris Jones and Design List contacts, and print both items together, using a Memo Style print style. Add your name as a centered header, and delete any existing footer information.

Create and edit contacts, categorize the contacts, create and modify a distribution list, sort the contact list, and print the new contacts.

NOTE: This exercise uses the contacts you created in Exercises 3-1 and 3-7. Add these contacts first if you don't have them in your contact list.

You've recently learned that a new employee at AllWood attended the same school you attended. You've decided to add entries for all your old school friends and create an e-mail distribution list.

1. Delete all contacts on the contact list except the following: Julio Alvarez, Doris Jones, MediaArt, MediaArtList, Tom Smith, Henry Williams, and Janet Woo.

2. Key the contacts shown in Figure 3-15, entering the phone and address information in the home fields for both contacts.

FIGURE 3-15

```
Dr. Phil Small              Laurie Delaney

311 Aspen St. (Home)        13 Bayou Lane (Home)

Denver, CO 80832            Houston, TX 77042

(303) 555-7722 (Home)       (713) 555-9945 (Home)

E-mail: small@ISP.isp       E-mail: delan@ISP.isp
```

3. For the Phil Small contact, add a suffix to his name of **Jr.**, using the Full Name dialog box. Key the spouse name as **Jade**, with an anniversary date two weeks from the current date. Add the following business information:

   1000 Cold Spring Road, Suite 666

   Denver, CO 80811

   (303) 555-2323

4. For the Laurie Delaney contact, add the title **Miss** to her name, key a spouse name of **Jordan**, and choose a birthday three weeks from the current date. Add the following business information:

   900 Milam St., Suite 1200

   Houston, TX 77001

   (713) 555-5550

5. Assign both contacts to the Personal category.

6. Create a new distribution list called **School Friends**, assign it to the Personal category, and add to the list the two new contacts you created in the previous steps.

7. Add the Tom Smith contact to the distribution list. Assign another category to the distribution list, using the Holiday Cards category.

8. Sort the contact list, specifying the Sort items by field as File As and using an Ascending order. (Your contact list might already be set to sort in this order.)

9. Display the contact list in Address Card view.

10. Print the contact list in a Card Style print style, adding your name as a centered header. Delete any existing footer information. Eliminate the blank form page at the end. (*Hint*: Use the <u>B</u>lank forms at end option on the **Format** tab of the Page Setup dialog box.)

11. Select the two new contacts and the distribution list you created in the previous steps, and print those three items, using a Memo Style print style. Add your name as a centered header, and delete any existing footer information.

EXERCISE 3-20

Create and edit contacts, assign categories to the contacts, create and use a distribution list, and print the new contacts and distribution list.

You've been asked by Rob Connelly, AllWood's president, to work on a special project with two other colleagues. The project involves researching online furniture sales. Rob has asked your team to provide him with regular e-mail updates. You need to create entries in your contact list for your teammates and Rob.

1. Using the names of two of your classmates, add two new contacts to your contact list. Information should include name, home address, home phone number, and e-mail address.

   NOTE: Your instructor will provide you with the names of the classmates you should use for your contacts.

2. Edit the contacts, assigning each to the Goals/Objectives category. Determine the birthday of one of the new contacts and record that information.

3. Create another new contact, using the information shown in Figure 3-16. For the e-mail address, you will use your instructor's e-mail address.

FIGURE 3-16

```
Mr. Rob Connelly

AllWood Mills, Inc.

3100 Jackson Street

Dubuque, IA 52004

(319) 555-4400

E-mail: Instructor@ISP.isp
```

NOTE: Your instructor will provide you with an appropriate e-mail address.

4. Edit the contact item for Rob Connelly, assigning it to the Goals/Objectives category. Link the contact with the contacts you created in step 1. For the e-mail address, make sure the Display as option is shown as Rob Connelly. Key a job title of **President**

5. Edit the contacts you created in step 1, linking them with each other as well as Rob Connelly.

6. Create a distribution list named **Team List**, and include the names of the two contacts you created in step 1. Assign the distribution list to the Goals/Objectives category.

7. Create a new e-mail message, using the Team List distribution list in the **To** text box. Cc the message to Rob Connelly (your instructor). Key the subject of the message as **Project update**.

8. For the text of the message, key the material shown in Figure 3-17 using a Plain Text message format.

FIGURE 3-17

I've come across a number of web sites that are appropriate outlets for Allwood's products. I am going to be collecting the names and Internet addresses of these sites, which I will shall summarize for you by the end of the week.

9. Connect to the Internet and send the message.

10. Log off the Internet if your instructor tells you to do so.

11. Display the contact list in Detailed Address Card view. Select the four additions you've made in this exercise (your two classmates, Rob Connelly, and the Team List distribution list). Print the four contacts, using a Card Style print style and printing only the selected items. Add your name as a centered header. Delete any existing footer information, and eliminate the blank-form page at the end. (*Hint*: Use the Blank forms at end option on the Format tab of the Page Setup dialog box.)

12. Print the four contacts again, using a Memo Style print style. Add your name as a centered header and the page number as a centered footer.

13. Display the Sent Items folder, and select the message you just sent. Print the message, using a Memo Style print style and adding your name as a centered header. Delete any existing footer information.

14. Display the contact list in Address Card view to return Outlook to its default setting.

EXERCISE 3-21　➕　*Callenge Yourself*

Create, edit, and categorize contacts; create a distribution list; schedule an event and add reminders; create tasks; and print the tasks, Calendar, and contact list.

You've been asked by Jasmine Jones, AllWood's VP of Sales, to help organize the annual sales conference. You'll be responsible for scheduling the event, notifying the sales managers of the details, and managing the team effort. Senior management wants regular updates. Your first tasks are to organize your contact list, define your immediate tasks, and set a schedule.

1. Add the contacts shown in Figure 3-18, entering the address and phone numbers as business information. (*Hint*: Use the Contact form menu command Actions, New Contact from Same Company after entering the first contact to redisplay the address and company name. Be sure to change the name and phone number.)

FIGURE 3-18

```
Mr. Will McCarthy            Ms. Jasmine Jones

AllWood Mills, Inc.          AllWood Mills, Inc.

3100 Jackson Street          3100 Jackson Street

Dubuque, IA 52004            Dubuque, IA 52004

(319) 555-4412               (319) 555-4402

E-mail: willm@ISP.isp        E-mail: jones@ISP.isp



Ms. Maria Lopez              Mr. John Yu

AllWood Mills, Inc.          AllWood Mills, Inc.

3100 Jackson Street          3100 Jackson Street

Dubuque, IA 52004            Dubuque, IA 52004

(319) 555-4406               (319) 555-4414

E-mail: lopez@ISP.isp        E-mail: jyu@ISP.isp
```

2. Add job titles as follows: Will McCarthy, **VP of Design**; Maria Lopez, **VP of Administration**; Jasmine Jones, **VP of Sales**; and John Yu, **VP of Marketing**

3. Assign each of the contacts you created in step 1 to the VIP category, and link all four contacts with each other.

4. Create a distribution list titled **Management**, with the contacts you created in step 1 as members of the list. Assign the distribution list to the VIP category.

5. Display a date in the Calendar approximately one month from the current date. Delete any existing appointments or events for that date, and then schedule an appointment on that day, keying the subject as **Annual Sales Conference**. Specify the location as **Chicago** and the duration of the appointment from 9 a.m. to 5 p.m. Set a 1-day reminder for the event, and show the time as Out of Office.

6. On the same date as the sales conference, schedule an appointment titled **Dinner with sales team**, starting at 6 p.m. and ending at 8 p.m., with the location as **TBA**. Deselect the reminder.

7. Edit the listing for Jasmine Jones in your contact list, changing her e-mail address to your instructor's e-mail address. (You will be sending an e-mail message to your instructor.)

NOTE: Your instructor will provide you with an appropriate e-mail address.

8. Create a new e-mail message, addressing the message to Jasmine Jones from your contact list.

REVIEW: To use an e-mail address from your contact list, click To in the Message form and then select the name from the Select Names dialog box.

9. Key the subject of the message as **Annual Sales Conference schedule**. For the text of the message, key the material shown in Figure 3-19, using a Plain Text message format.

FIGURE 3-19

```
I am tentatively scheduling the annual Sales Conference for roughly one
month from today in Chicago. I plan to book space in a hotel near our
Chicago store for our meetings. I will notify you when I have specific
dates.
```

10. Connect to the Internet and send the message.

11. Log off the Internet if your instructor tells you to do so.

12. Display the Tasks folder and delete any existing tasks on the task list. Add a new task, with the subject heading **Find hotel in Chicago for sales meetings** and with a due date two days from the current date. Add another task with the subject heading **Notify sales managers of meeting dates and details** and with a due date approximately one week from the current date.

Add yet another new task with the subject heading **E-mail managers to see if the tentative date is acceptable** and with a due date of the current date.

13. Print the task list in portrait orientation, using the Table Style print style. Add your name as a centered header. Delete any existing footer information.

14. Display the date for the appointment you scheduled in step 5. Print the Calendar, using the Calendar Details Style print style. Add a centered header with your name. Add a centered footer with the date, deleting existing footer information.

15. Display the Sent Items folder and select the message you sent in step 10. Print the message, using the Memo Style print style and adding your name as a centered header. Delete any existing footer information.

16. Display the contact list in Detailed Address Card view. Select the five additions you've made in this exercise (Jasmine Jones, Maria Lopez, Will McCarthy, John Yu, and the Management distribution list). Print only the selected contacts, using a Card Style print style and adding your name as a centered header. Eliminate the blank-forms page at the end. (*Hint*: Use the Blank forms at end option on the Format tab of the Page Setup dialog box.)

17. Display the contact list in Address Card view to return Outlook to its default setting.

On Your Own

In these exercises you work on your own, as you would in a real-life work environment. Use the skills you've learned to accomplish the task—and be creative.

EXERCISE 3-22
Create contacts for every member of your class, including address information and other relevant data. Use categories and create a distribution list for class members with their own e-mail accounts. Print the contact list for the class, showing all the details.

EXERCISE 3-23
Create a distribution list for your family members and friends with e-mail accounts. Use the distribution list to send a brief e-mail message. Print the distribution list and the sent message.

EXERCISE 3-24
Create contacts for every individual whose birthday or anniversary you wish to remember, including the dates of the events. Categorize them appropriately, and create a distribution list for the individuals with e-mail accounts. Print the contact list showing all the details.

Managing E-Mail

MOUS
ACTIVITIES
In this lesson:
OL2002 **1-2**
OL2002 **1-3**
OL2002 **1-4**
OL2002 **3-1**
OL2002 **3-2**
OL2002 **3-5**
See Appendix E.

OBJECTIVES

After completing this lesson, you will be able to:

1. **Use mail features.**
2. **Use signatures.**
3. **Sort and manage mail.**
4. **Manage mail folders.**

Estimated Time: 1¼ hours

After you've become familiar with the basics of sending and receiving e-mail messages, you'll want to start using some of Outlook's more advanced e-mail features. Outlook provides many ways to personalize, organize, and store your e-mail messages. When you have a large volume of e-mail, you'll find it helpful to create separate mail folders for various types of messages that you receive. And as you accumulate received messages that you want to retain, Outlook lets you move messages from one folder to another.

Using Mail Features

Among Outlook's extensive mail features, you can flag e-mail messages. The flags bring specific messages to your attention or to the attention of the recipient, with optional reminders. Another useful mail feature is the spell checker. Outlook can check every message you compose for typing and spelling errors before you send the message. You can also apply sensitivity and importance options to a message. And when your Inbox contains many messages, Outlook can help you find a specific message based on its content.

EXERCISE 4-1 Flag E-Mail Messages

You can flag an e-mail message to draw the recipient's attention to it. The flag icon appears in the Flag column of the Inbox, and a banner is displayed in the Message form. The banner can contain a variety of messages.

1. Click the Inbox shortcut in the Outlook Bar. The Inbox folder appears.

2. Choose File, New from the menu and choose Mail Message, or click the New button on the Standard toolbar. The Message form appears.

3. In the To text box, key *[recipient's name]@[ISP]*

> **NOTE:** Your instructor will provide you with a list of e-mail addresses to use for the To and Cc text boxes.

4. Enter a second address in the Cc text box, keying *[recipient's name]@[ISP]*

5. In the Subject text box, key **Traditional Homes photo shoot**

6. Change the Message format to Plain Text, and then key the text shown in Figure 4-1 for the body of the message.

FIGURE 4-1

Traditional Homes magazine is doing an article on AllWood for their
May issue. Two members of their staff are arriving next Thursday for a
photo shoot. Could you let Paul's staff know? They will want to have
the shop in order.

7. Click the Message Flag button on the Message form toolbar. The Flag for Follow Up dialog box appears.

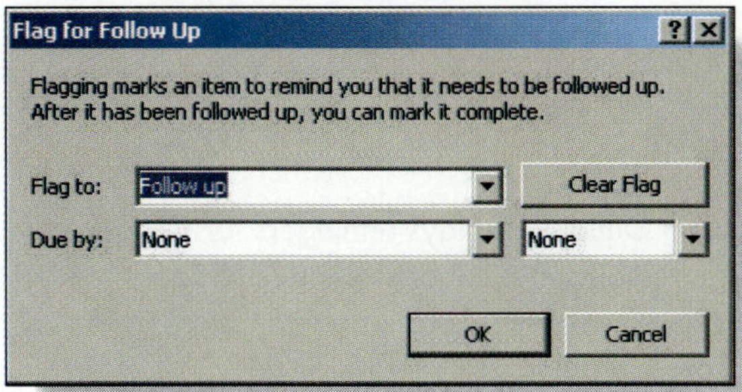

FIGURE 4-2
Flag for Follow Up
dialog box

8. Click the down arrow next to the Flag to text box. Scroll up the drop-down list and select Call.

9. Click the down arrow next to the Due by text box and select a date on the drop-down calendar roughly one week from the current date. In the adjacent text box, under the Clear Flag button, click the down arrow and set the time for 9:00 AM.

10. Click OK. The Message form reappears and now includes an information banner.

11. Connect to the Internet and send the message.

12. Click the Send/Receive button on the Standard toolbar to check for messages that have been sent to you. A flagged message appears in your Inbox, with a Flag Status symbol under the Flag column heading. If the flag includes a reminder, the reminder will be displayed at the specified time. An information banner is displayed in the preview pane and when the message is opened in the Message form.

13. Log off the Internet if your instructor tells you to do so.

FIGURE 4-3
Inbox with a
flagged message

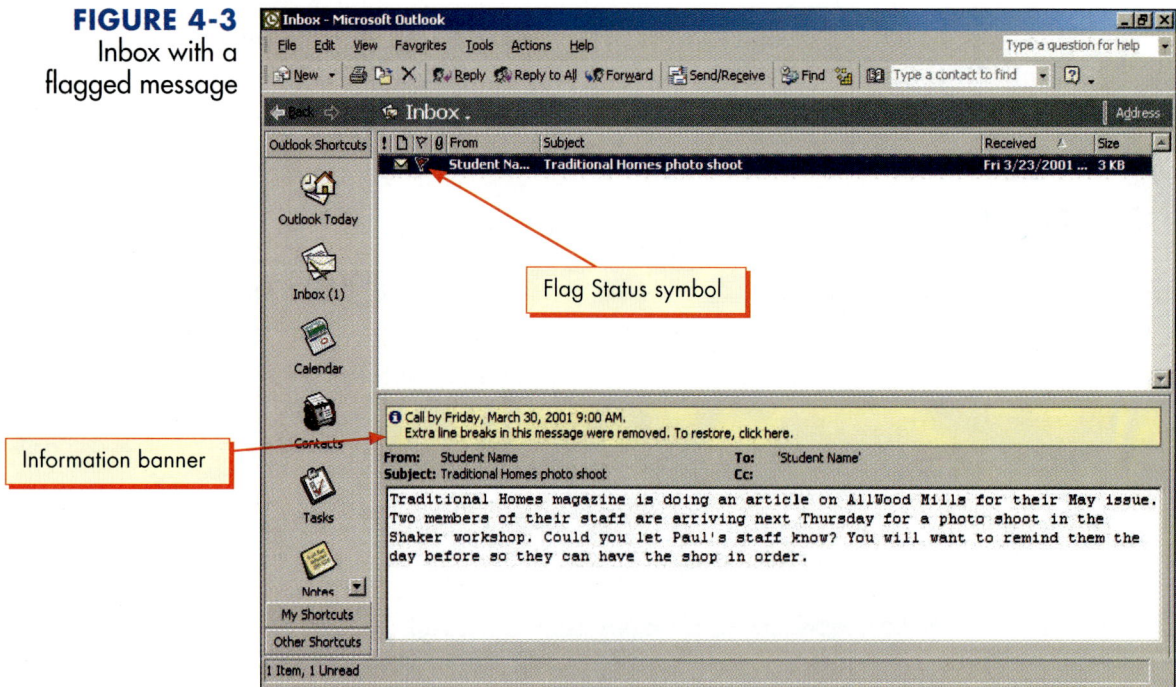

NOTE: Outlook displays reminders for flagged messages only when the message remains in the Inbox. If the message is moved to another folder, the reminder will not be displayed. Also, a flag can be removed by clicking Clear Flag in the Flag for Follow Up dialog box.

EXERCISE 4-2 Spell Check a Message

Outlook's automatic spell and grammar checker is turned on by default. You can control the spelling options, as well as manually spell-check a message. Taking extra time to spell- and grammar-check your work is worth the effort.

1. With the Inbox displayed, click the <u>N</u>ew button (or press Ctrl + N) to open the Message form for a new e-mail message.

2. In the To text box, key *[recipient's name]@[ISP]*

> **NOTE:** Your instructor will provide you with a list of e-mail addresses to use for the To and Cc text boxes.

3. Enter another address in the Cc text box, keying *[recipient's name]@[ISP]*

4. In the Subject text box, key **Offsite staff meeting**

5. Change the Message format to Plain Text. In the message text area, key the following text, typing it as written: **I have been looking into verious meeting locations**. Outlook automatically corrects "verious" to "various."

6. Position the pointer over "various" and notice after a moment that a blue underscore appears under the word. Move the pointer to the underscore, and the AutoCorrect Options button and a ScreenTip display under the word.

FIGURE 4-4
Displaying the AutoCorrect Options button

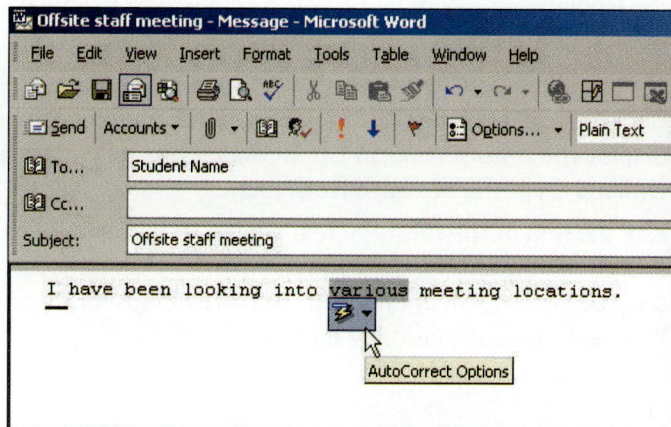

7. Click the down arrow on the button to display a shortcut menu. The menu options let you suppress the correction of this word if you don't need to change it.

8. Click <u>C</u>ontrol AutoCorrect Options. The AutoCorrect in Email: English (U.S.) dialog box appears. Click the **AutoCorrect** tab if it is not already displayed. Notice the corrections that Outlook makes automatically.

FIGURE 4-5
AutoCorrect in
Email dialog box

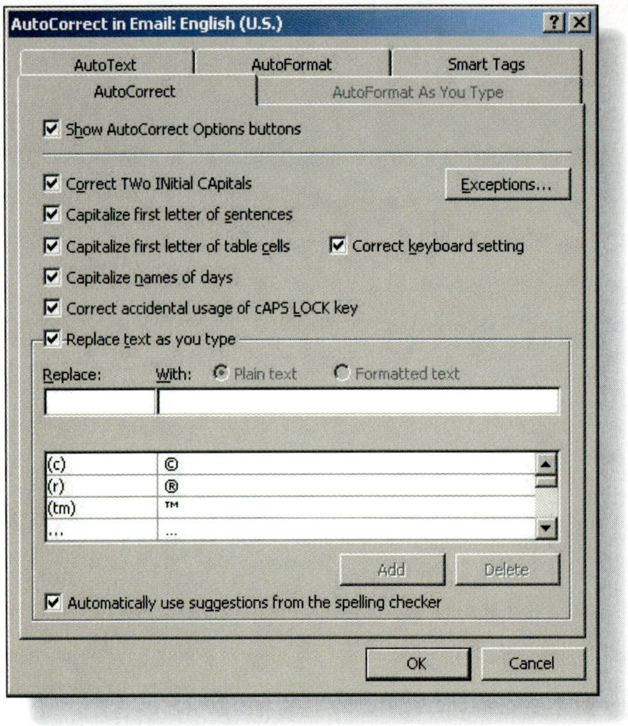

9. Scroll down the list of words in the lower portion of the dialog box. In the <u>R</u>eplace and <u>W</u>ith text boxes, you can add to this list any words you frequently misspell or mistype, and Outlook will automatically correct them as you type.

10. Click **Cancel** to close the AutoCorrect in Email dialog box. You can also display the AutoCorrect in Email dialog box by choosing <u>T</u>ools, <u>A</u>utoCorrect **Options** from the Message form menu.

11. Key the rest of the message text shown in Figure 4-6. Key the material exactly as it is shown. As you type, Outlook underscores text in red that it considers misspelled, and it underscores in green sentences or phrases that it considers grammatically incorrect.

FIGURE 4-6

> The hotel closest to AllWood's facilities are the most espensive. How far are we willing to travel? Let's discuss this at our next staff meeting.

12. Right-click the word "espensive." Outlook displays a shortcut menu. At the top of the menu are suggested corrections.

13. Click **expensive** at the top of the shortcut menu. Outlook replaces the misspelled word. You can also spell-check the entire message at once.

14. Click the Spelling and Grammar button 📧 on the Message form toolbar. The Spelling and Grammar: English (U.S.) dialog box appears, with the word "AllWood's" highlighted. Among spelling options, you can have Outlook ignore, correct, or add the word to the dictionary.

15. Click I̱gnore Once. Outlook next highlights the entire sentence. The sentence contains a grammatical error. The subject of the sentence ("hotel") is a singular noun, but the verb ("are") is plural.

16. Under Suggestio̱ns, select the second option, **hotels closest to AllWood's facilities are.**

17. Click C̱hange, and then click OK. The spelling and grammar check is completed.

18. Connect to the Internet and send the message.

> **TIP:** You can fine-tune how Outlook corrects spelling and grammar by choosing Ṯools, O̱ptions and clicking the Spelling & Grammar tab. You might wish to change certain items in this dialog box that spell-check ignores, such as the words in uppercase. You can also expand the grammar check under the W̱riting style option to include style as well as grammar. Clicking Se̱ttings displays the Grammar Settings dialog box. You can have Outlook check a wide variety of common grammatical and stylistic mistakes.

EXERCISE 4-3 Modify Message and Delivery Options, and Flag Received Messages

You can set message importance and sensitivity. If you need to call attention to a received message, you can add a flag to it.

1. Press Ctrl + N to open a new Message form.

2. In the To text box, key *[recipient's name]@[ISP]*

> **NOTE:** Your instructor will provide you with a list of e-mail addresses to use for the To and Cc text boxes.

3. Enter another address in the Cc text box, keying *[recipient's name]@[ISP]*

4. In the Subject text box, key **Manufacturing staff attire**

5. Change the Message format to Plain Text, and key the text shown in Figure 4-7 on the next page for the body of the message.

FIGURE 4-7

Rob brought up a delicate topic with regard to the photo shoot. As you know, we have no dress code at AllWood. We all dress in a professionally appropriate way. However, the manufacturing staff is extremely casual. Rob wants managers to tactfully ask their staff to "dress up" somewhat for the photo shoot. Let's discuss this.

6. Click the Importance High button [!] on the Message form toolbar. The importance for the message is set to High. You can set a message importance to Low by clicking the Importance Low button [↓] on the Message form toolbar.

7. Click the **Options** button on the Message form toolbar. The Message Options dialog box appears. Notice that the **Importance** option is already set to **High**. You can use this dialog box to control other aspects of the message, such as delivery and tracking options. For example, the **Request a read receipt for this message** option lets you determine if a message you've sent has been read by the recipient.

FIGURE 4-8
Message Options
dialog box

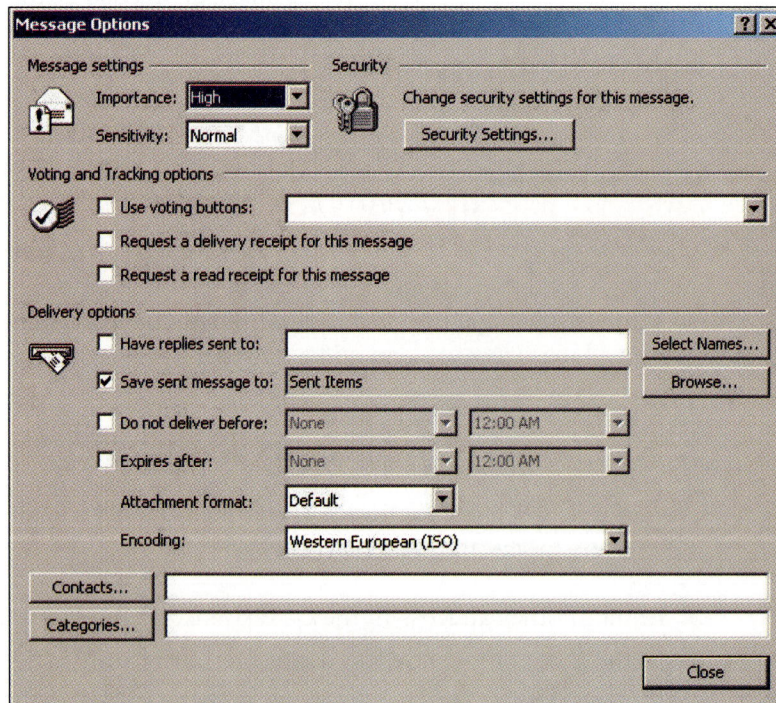

8. Click the down arrow next to Sensitivity and select Confidential.

9. Under Delivery options, select H̲ave replies sent to. Your return address automatically appears in the adjacent text box. You can delete or add to this address. You can use this feature when you want replies to your message sent to someone other than yourself. For example, you might want replies sent to your assistant.

10. In the H̲ave replies sent to text box, enter another address, keying *[recipient's name]@[ISP]* (Make sure you separate your address from the second address with a semicolon.) Replies to the message will be sent to both you and the specified recipient.

11. Click Close. The Message form reappears.

12. Connect to the Internet and send the message.

13. Click the Send/Rec̲eive button on the Standard toolbar to check for messages that have been sent to you. A message with a high message importance displays an Importance symbol (an exclamation point) under the Importance column heading.

14. Log off the Internet if your instructor tells you to do so.

15. Select the "Manufacturing staff attire" message if it is not already selected. Notice in the preview pane that the information banner indicates this is a confidential message.

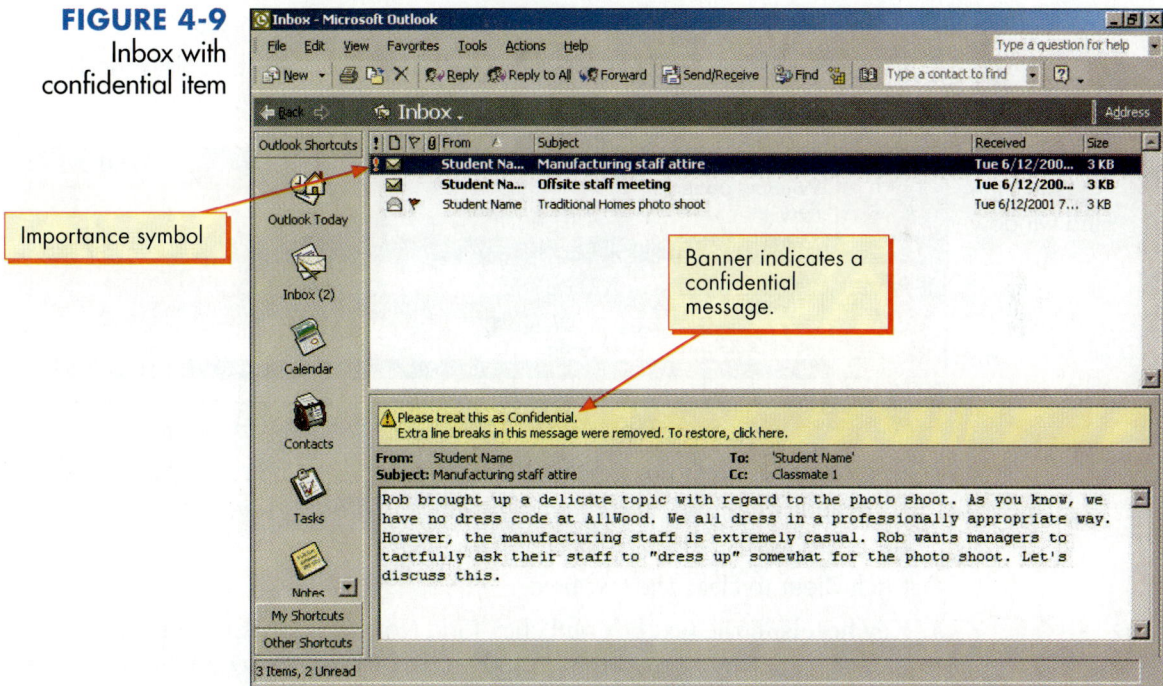

FIGURE 4-9
Inbox with confidential item

Importance symbol

Banner indicates a confidential message.

16. Press Enter to open the message. If you want to call attention to a message you've received, you can flag it just as you can flag a message you send.

17. Click the Message Flag button ⚑ on the Message form toolbar. The Flag for Follow Up dialog box appears.

18. Click the down arrow next to the <u>F</u>lag to text box, and select Call.

19. Click the down arrow next to the <u>D</u>ue by text box, and select None if it is not already displayed. No reminder will appear with this flag.

20. Click OK, and then close the message. The Inbox reappears with the "Manufacturing staff attire" message flagged.

TIP: If you want to see more listed items in your Inbox and less of the message preview, drag the divider that separates the two sections of the Inbox to reduce the preview area.

EXERCISE **4-4** **Find E-Mail Messages**

Outlook has several ways to help you locate specific data. This is particularly helpful if you have many messages. For example, you could search for all the messages sent to you by a particular individual. Or, you could search messages for all occurrences of a specific word or phrase.

1. If the Inbox is not already displayed, click the Inbox shortcut 📧.

2. Click the F<u>i</u>nd button on the Standard toolbar (or choose <u>T</u>ools, F<u>i</u>nd from the menu). A small Find window appears above the Inbox.

FIGURE 4-10
Using the
Find window

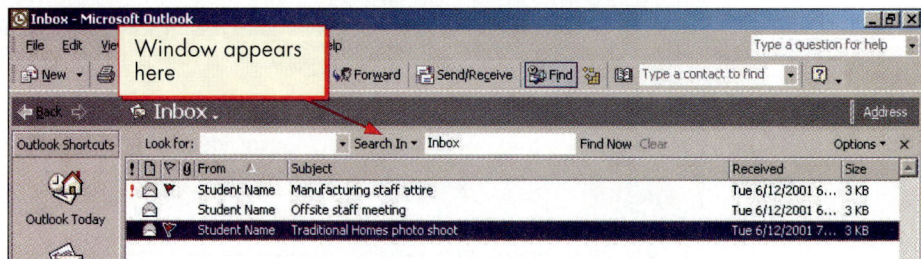

3. In the Look for text box, key **dress code** and click Find Now. The Inbox shows one item, the "Manufacturing staff attire" message. This item contains the words "dress code" in the message.

4. Click Clear to clear the text box.

5. Key **hotels** in the text box and click Find Now. The "Offsite staff meeting" message appears in the Inbox. You can perform more detailed searches by using Advanced Find.

NOTE: This search is not case-sensitive. You use Advanced Find to perform case-sensitive searches.

6. From the Tools menu, choose Advanced Find. The Advanced Find dialog box appears.

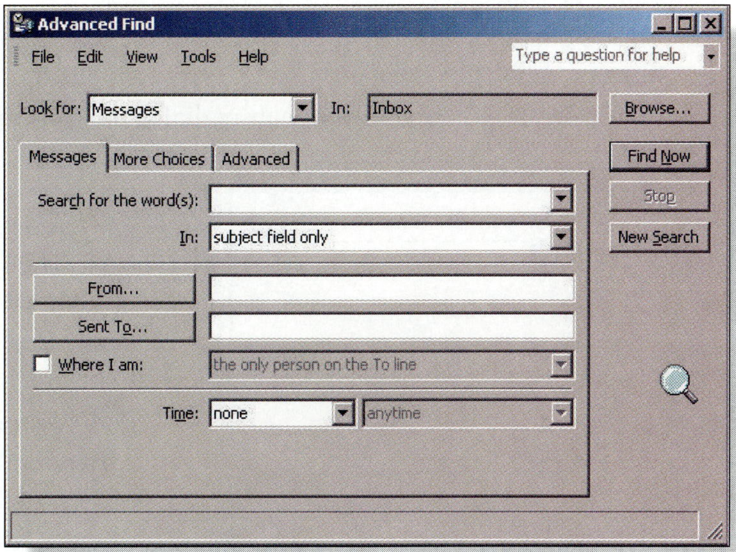

FIGURE 4-11
Advanced Find
dialog box

7. Click the Messages tab, if it is not already displayed. You'll be searching for text in the subject field and message body of messages.

8. Click the down arrow next to the In text box and choose **subject field and message body**.

9. Key **magazine** in the Search for word(s) text box and click Find Now. The results appear at the bottom of the dialog box and list the "Traditional Homes photo shoot" message.

10. Close the Advanced Find dialog box. Close the Find window by clicking the Find button.

Using Signatures

A *signature* is text automatically added to any message you send. For example, it can include your name, your job title, and your phone number. Signatures can also include paragraphs informing recipients how to respond to a message you send them or where to reach you.

EXERCISE **4-5** **Create and Add a Signature for Messages**

You must create a signature before you can apply it to your messages. You can create various signatures, inserting the one appropriate for the message.

1. With the Inbox displayed, choose **T**ools, **O**ptions from the menu, and then click the **Mail Format** tab if it is not already displayed. The Mail Format dialog box appears.

2. Click **Signatures** (located at the bottom of the dialog box). The Create Signature dialog box appears.

3. Click **N**ew. The Create New Signature dialog box appears.

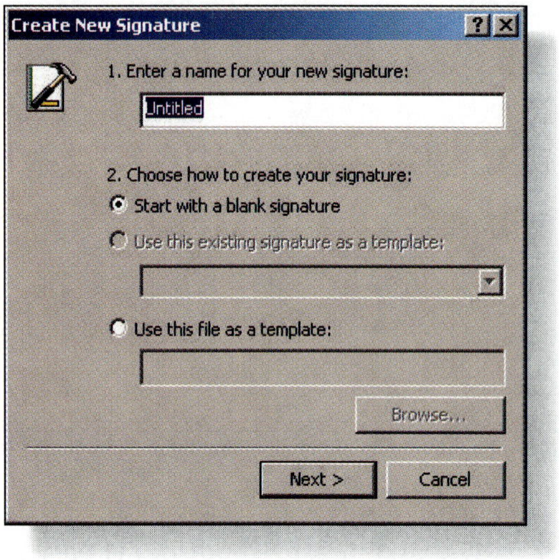

FIGURE 4-12
Create New Signature dialog box

4. In the text box under **Enter a name for your new signature**, key *[your initials]* and click **Next**. The Edit Signature dialog box appears.

5. Under **Signature text**, key the following text:

   [your name]

   AllWood Mills Intern

6. Click **Finish**. The Create Signature dialog box reappears. Your initials are now listed under **Signature**, and the content of the signature appears under **Preview**.

7. Click **OK**. The Options dialog box reappears. Now that you've created a signature, you can have it automatically applied to any new message you create.

8. If your initials do not appear in the **Signature for new messages** text box, click the down arrow next to the text box and select the signature you created in the previous steps.

9. Click **A**pply. The signature will be added to new messages. Notice that you can also specify a signature for replies and forwards.

10. Click **OK**. The Inbox reappears.

11. Click the **N**ew button [icon]. A Message form appears. Outlook adds the signature text to the text area of the Message form. You key text above the signature, just as you would with any new message.

NOTE: Microsoft Word might display an information box informing you that signature text will be reformatted to a Plain Text message format when you change the message format to Plain Text. You can proceed by simply clicking **C**ontinue.

12. Close the Message form without saving.

EXERCISE **4-6** **Edit a Signature**

You can make changes to any signature you've created. For example, if your signature includes your phone number or job title, you can edit your signature if this information changes.

1. Choose <u>T</u>ools, <u>O</u>ptions from the menu, and click the Mail Format tab if it is not already displayed.

2. Click Signatures. The Create Signature dialog box appears. The signature you created in the previous exercise is already selected.

3. Click <u>E</u>dit. The Edit Signature dialog box appears.

4. Delete "Intern" and key **Design Associate**

5. Click OK. The Create Signature dialog box reappears. In the Preview area, the signature shows the changed text.

6. Click OK and then click OK again.

EXERCISE **4-7** **Discontinue or Delete a Signature**

If you decide you no longer want signatures automatically added to your messages, you can instruct Outlook to stop applying them. You can also delete a signature if it is no longer needed.

1. Choose <u>T</u>ools, <u>O</u>ptions from the menu, and click the Mail Format tab.

2. Click the down arrow next to the Signature for n<u>e</u>w messages text box and select <None>.

3. Click <u>A</u>pply. Outlook will stop adding signatures to new messages. You can also delete a signature from the signature list completely.

4. Click Signatures. The Create Signature dialog box appears. Select the signature you created in the previous exercise, if it is not already selected.

5. Click <u>R</u>emove. Outlook asks if you want to permanently remove the signature.

6. Click <u>Y</u>es. The signature is deleted.

7. Click OK and then click OK again. The Inbox reappears.

NOTE: Outlook permanently saves any signature you create unless it is removed. Always leave Outlook in its default state for the next class or student to use.

Sorting and Managing Mail

After you start using Outlook on a regular basis, you'll probably find it necessary to organize your Inbox. Outlook makes it easy to keep track of your mail. You can sort mail and set various viewing options. If you delete an item from your Inbox that you later decide you'd like to keep, you can retrieve it from the Deleted Items folder.

EXERCISE **4-8** **Sort Inbox Messages**

There are various ways to sort your Inbox. You can sort it by:

- Clicking the Organize button 🗔 and using the Ways to Organize Inbox pane.
- Choosing <u>V</u>iew, Current <u>V</u>iew, <u>C</u>ustomize Current View from the menu, and then clicking <u>S</u>ort.
- Clicking the column headings in the Inbox.

1. Display the Inbox folder, if it is not already displayed.

2. Click the Organize button 🗔 on the Standard toolbar. The Ways to Organize Inbox pane appears above the Inbox.

FIGURE 4-13
Ways to Organize
Inbox pane

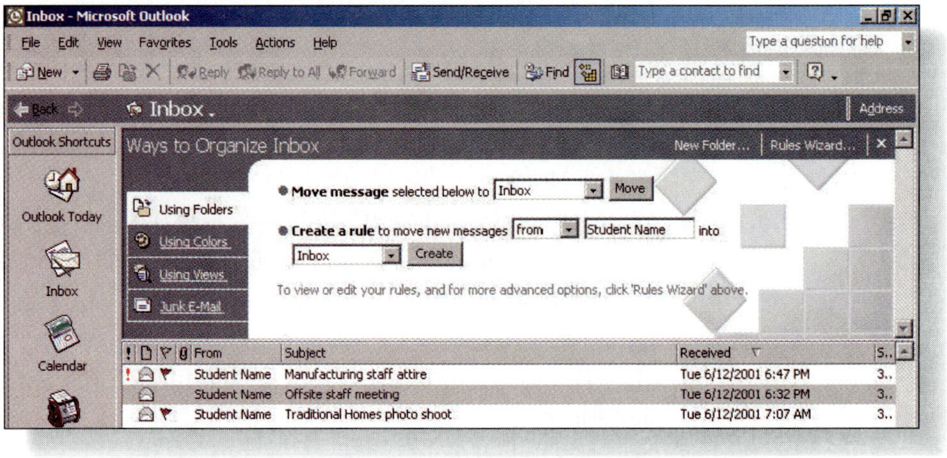

3. Click <u>Using Views</u>, and then click **Customize Current View** in the upper right corner of the Ways to Organize Inbox pane. The View Summary dialog box appears.

4. Click <u>S</u>ort. The Sort dialog box appears. In the <u>S</u>ort items by text box, notice that the current sort field is the date when you received the message.

5. Click the down arrow next to the <u>S</u>ort items by text box and scroll through the list of possible sort fields. Leave **Received** as the sort field.

6. To change the sort order, click the Ascending option, and then click OK. The View Summary dialog box appears.

7. Click OK once again. Outlook sorts the Inbox in ascending order. New messages appear at the bottom of the Inbox.

8. Click the Received column heading. The sort order in the Received column is changed from ascending to descending. You can use any column heading to sort the Inbox by simply clicking on the heading.

9. Click Customize Current View in the Ways to Organize Inbox pane once again. The View Summary dialog box appears.

10. Click Sort, and make sure Sort items by is set to Received with a Descending order.

11. Click OK, and then click OK again. The Inbox sort order is set to its default setting.

12. Click the Organize button 🔄 to close the Ways to Organize Inbox pane.

NOTE: Make sure you have completed the last four steps of this exercise. These steps restore Outlook to its default setting. Always leave Outlook in its default state for the next class or student to use.

EXERCISE 4-9 Set Viewing Options and Filter a View

You can display the contents of your Inbox in various ways. You can turn the preview pane and AutoPreview on and off. You can also use filters. A *filter* screens items in a folder based on conditions you define.

1. Turn off the preview pane by choosing View, Preview Pane from the menu. Outlook displays only message listings. This makes a larger area available for listing messages, which helps if you have a large number of Inbox items.

2. To display a few lines with each message, choose View, AutoPreview. Outlook displays the message list with the first few lines of each message in blue.

FIGURE 4-14
Inbox with preview pane turned off and AutoPreview turned on

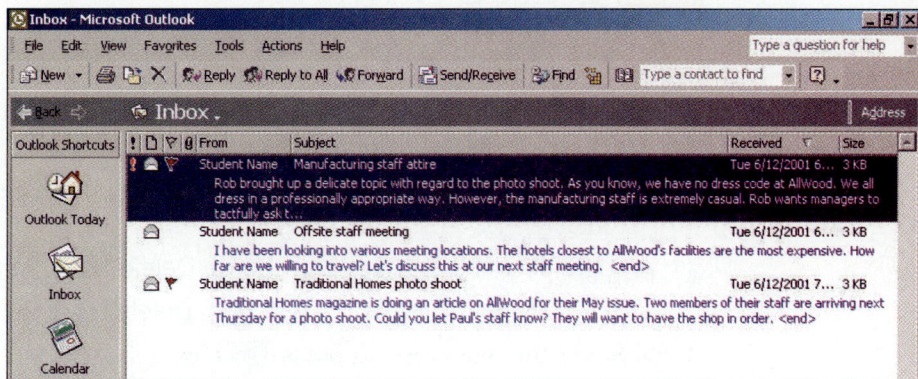

3. Click the Organize button on the Standard toolbar. The Ways to Organize Inbox pane appears.

4. Click Using Views.

5. Scroll through the list of viewing options under Change your view. The default is Messages. Select each option and notice how Outlook displays Inbox messages. When you finish, choose Messages.

NOTE: You can also use the menu command View, Current View to access the various viewing options found in the Ways to Organize Inbox pane.

6. Close the Ways to Organize Inbox pane by clicking the Organize button .

7. Choose View, Current View from the menu, and then click Customize Current View. The View Summary dialog box appears.

8. Click Filter. The Filter dialog box appears.

9. In the Search for the word(s) text box, key **attire**

10. Click the down arrow next to the In text box, and choose frequently-used text fields. Click OK. The View Summary dialog box appears again.

11. Click OK. Outlook filters the Inbox messages so only messages containing "attire" appear.

12. To clear the filter, choose View, Current View, Customize Current View, and click Filter. Click Clear All. Click OK twice. Outlook now displays all Inbox messages.

13. Click View, AutoPreview to turn off AutoPreview.

14. Click View, Preview Pane to redisplay the preview pane.

TIP: If you want to see more listed items in your Inbox and less of the message preview, drag the divider that separates the two sections of the Inbox to reduce the size of the preview area.

EXERCISE **4-10** **Delete a Message**

You can delete Inbox items the same way you delete items in any other folder. You can delete messages in one of four ways:

- Select the message and click the Delete button ⊠ on the Standard toolbar.
- Right-click the message and choose Delete from the shortcut menu.
- Select the message and choose Edit, Delete from the menu.
- Select the message and press Ctrl + D.

1. Select the "Manufacturing staff attire" message.

2. Click the Delete button ☒ on the Standard toolbar (or press Ctrl + D). The message is deleted from the Inbox and placed in the Deleted Items folder. You can restore a deleted message by using the menu if the Inbox is still displayed.

3. Choose Edit, Undo Delete from the menu (or press Ctrl + Z). The deleted message reappears in the Inbox. If you've deleted a message and have viewed other Outlook folders since the deletion, you can retrieve the deleted item from the Deleted Items folder.

4. Select the "Manufacturing staff attire" message and click the Delete button ☒. The message is deleted.

5. Click the Contacts shortcut 📇 on the Outlook Bar to display the Contacts folder.

6. Click the Inbox shortcut 📧 to redisplay the Inbox folder.

7. Choose Edit from the menu. The Undo command is unavailable This command is only available when you are still in the folder in which the deletion occurred. However, you can retrieve deleted items by using the Deleted Items folder.

EXERCISE 4-11 Retrieve Items from the Deleted Items Folder

There are several ways to locate and retrieve deleted items from the Deleted Items folder. You can sort the folder by using the column heading method, sorting by item type or by the date of the item.

1. Click **Inbox** on the folder banner and click **Deleted Items** on the folder list. The Deleted Items folder appears. The folder shows all items you've deleted in various Outlook folders. The type of item deleted is shown under the Icon column heading. Figure 4-15 shows how various deleted items appear in the folder.

FIGURE 4-15
Deleted Items folder

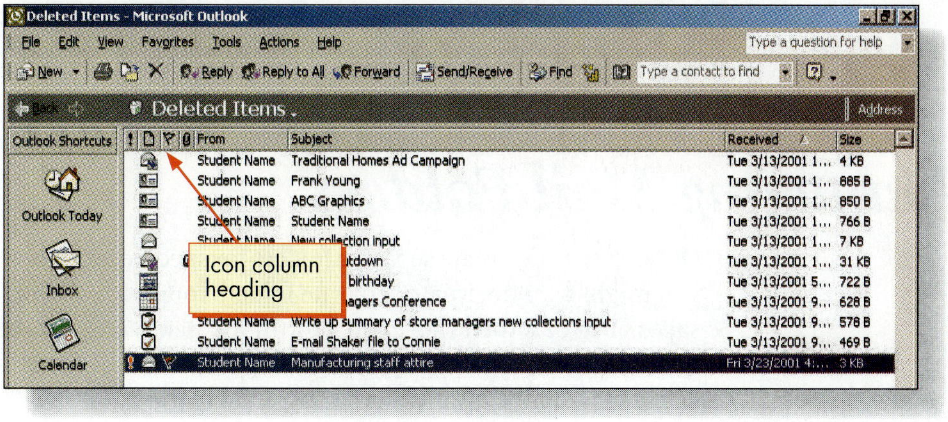

NOTE: The content of your Deleted Items folder might differ significantly from the items shown in Figure 4-15.

2. If your folder contains more items than can be displayed on the screen, use the vertical scroll bar to adjust the screen display. You can locate items by sorting them by type.

3. Click the Icon column heading. All the folder items are grouped by item type. (The screen adjusts to the position of the currently selected item, so you might need to use the vertical scroll bar to adjust the display to the top of the folder.)

4. Click the Received column heading to sort the items by date. You might want to use this column to locate the deleted item based on its date. Note that the date refers to an item's creation date, not the date it was deleted.

5. Locate the deleted message "Manufacturing staff attire" and select it.

6. Choose Edit, Move to Folder from the menu (or press Ctrl + Shift + V). The Move Items dialog box appears.

FIGURE 4-16
Move Items
dialog box

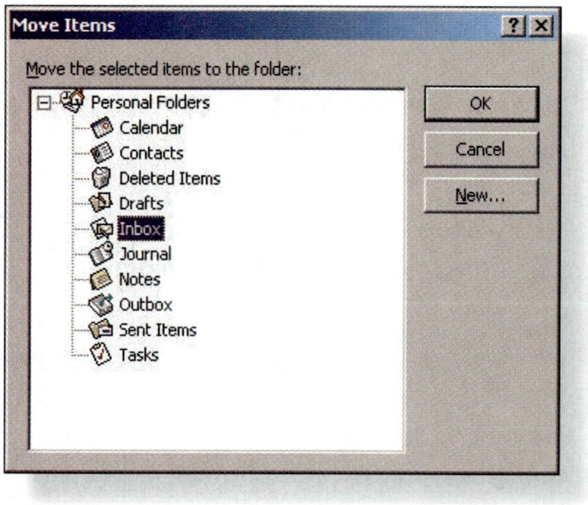

7. Select Inbox on the folder list if it is not already selected, and click OK. The deleted message moves from the Deleted Items folder to the Inbox folder.

8. Click the Inbox shortcut. The deleted item appears in the Inbox.

NOTE: Items deleted from the Deleted Items folder cannot be recovered. Outlook warns you that you are permanently deleting an item when you delete items from this folder.

Managing Mail Folders

Outlook lets you create separate folders for specific types of messages. For example, you might want to create separate folders for your personal or work-related messages. You can then move relevant Inbox items into those folders. You can also rename and move folders, placing them in various locations in the folder hierarchy. Older files can be archived for long-term storage.

EXERCISE 4-12 Create a Mail Folder

When you create a new mail folder, it is typically located under the Inbox folder in the folder list. You can view its contents with the View, Folder List command like any other Outlook folder.

1. Display the Inbox if it is not already displayed, and select the "Manufacturing staff attire" message. Press Ctrl and select the "Traditional Homes photo shoot" message (both are now selected).

2. Choose Edit, Move to Folder from the menu (or press Ctrl + Shift + V). The Move Items dialog box appears.

3. Click New. The Create New Folder dialog box appears.

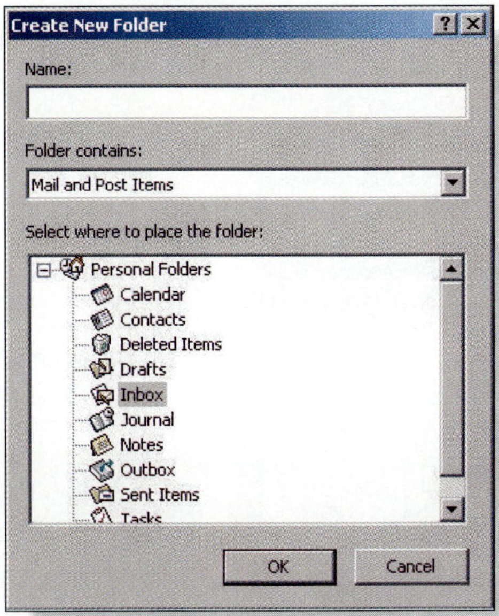

FIGURE 4-17
Create New Folder
dialog box

4. In the Name text box, key **Special**

5. Under Select where to place the folder, click Inbox, and then click OK. The Add shortcut to Outlook Bar? dialog box might appear. If so, click No. The Move Items dialog box now shows a new folder named "Special" under the Inbox folder.

6. Click OK. The Inbox shows your folder list. The two selected messages have been moved to the new folder.

7. To view the contents of the Special folder, double-click Inbox on the folder list and then click Special on the folder list.

8. To move the messages back to the Inbox, select the two photo-shoot messages and press Ctrl + Shift + V to display the Move Items dialog box. Click Inbox on the folder list and click OK. Outlook returns the photo-shoot messages to the Inbox.

9. Close the folder list.

TIP: By creating a rule with Outlook's Rules Wizard, you can automate processing messages. A *rule* is a set of conditions, actions, and exceptions that organizes messages. For example, you could create a rule to have Outlook automatically move all messages you receive from a particular individual to a specific folder. You can access the Rules Wizard by choosing Tools, Rules Wizard from the menu.

EXERCISE 4-13 **Rename a Folder**

You can rename a folder just as you can rename a file. Renaming can be useful when the contents of a folder change and you'd like the name of the folder to reflect the kinds of items stored in it.

1. Choose <u>V</u>iew, Fold<u>e</u>r List from the menu to open the folder list, if it is not already displayed.

2. Click the Inbox plus sign (+) to display the Special folder in the folder list, if it is not already displayed.

3. Click Special on the folder list to open it. The folder name should be highlighted in blue. (You might need to click the folder twice for the blue highlighting to appear.)

4. Press F2. An outline box surrounds the folder name, and the text of the name is in an editing mode.

FIGURE 4-18
Renaming a folder

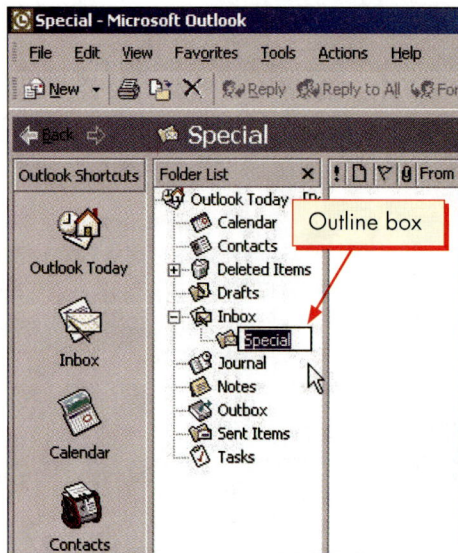

5. Key **Personal** and press Enter. The folder is renamed.

6. Close the folder list.

EXERCISE 4-14 **Delete a Folder and Restore Outlook Defaults**

You can delete any folder you no longer need. And it's always a good idea to make sure you've returned Outlook to its default settings.

1. Display the folder list if it is not already displayed.

2. Select **Personal** on the folder list and click the Delete button ☒. Outlook displays a confirmation prompt asking if you want to delete the selected folder.

3. Click **Yes**. The Personal folder is deleted. A folder does not have to be empty to be deleted, but the contents of a folder are deleted along with the folder when you delete a folder.

4. Close the folder list.

5. Choose **Tools**, **Options** from the menu, and click the **Mail Format** tab.

6. Click **Signatures**. If your initials appear as one of the options under **Signature**, select it, click **Remove**, and click **Yes** at the confirmation prompt.

7. Click **OK** twice.

8. Choose **View**, **Current View**, **Customize Current View** from the menu, and then click **Sort**.

9. Make sure **Sort items by** is set to **Received** in **Descending** order. Click **OK**. The View Summary screen reappears.

10. Click **Filter**. Click **Clear All**. Click **OK** twice. Outlook's default settings have been restored.

EXERCISE **4-15** **Manually Archive Mail Messages**

You can archive older messages you want to keep. When you *archive* an item, you move it to a location for storage and future access. Outlook automatically performs this task at regular intervals by using *AutoArchive*. This is an Outlook feature for automatically moving old items to an archive location and discarding expired items whose contents are no longer valid, such as a meeting that occurred months in the past and still appears on your Calendar.

You also can archive items manually. You might wish to manually archive folder items if a specific Outlook folder such as the Inbox is not set for AutoArchive. Archived messages can be stored in a separate folder on your computer, or in an external location, such as a network server.

You can restore archived files by displaying the folder list and dragging the archived items into their original folders or to a new folder.

1. Display the Inbox folder.

2. Choose **File**, **Archive** from the menu. The Archive dialog box appears. (See Figure 4-19 on the next page.)

3. Make sure **Archive this folder and all subfolders** is selected.

4. Click **Browse**. The Open Personal Folders dialog box appears. The file name shown in the **File name** box should be **archive.pst**. If a different name appears, key **archive** in this text box.

FIGURE 4-19
Archive dialog box

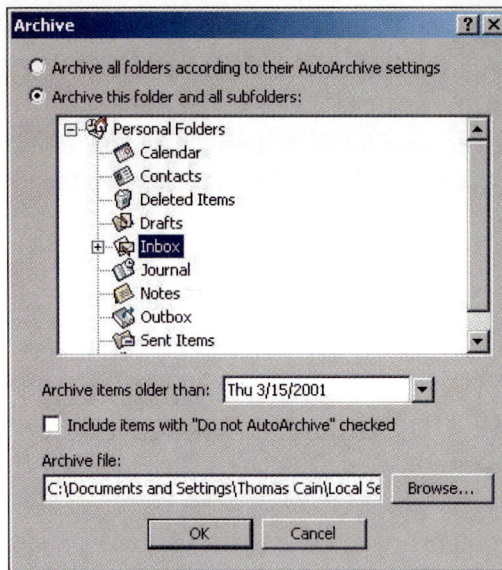

5. Click **OK**. The Archive dialog box appears. Next you'll specify a "cut-off" date for archiving messages.

6. Click the down arrow in the **Archive items o̲lder than** text box. A calendar appears. You can click the arrows at the top of the calendar to adjust the month. Typically you would select a date at some point in the past to archive older messages.

7. Click **Today**. Because all your Inbox messages are today's date, you'll need to select the current date to archive those messages.

8. Click **OK**. Outlook archives the Inbox messages. The Inbox is now empty. The folder list now includes a set of file folders called Archive Folders. These folders contain archived items from your Personal Folders. You can restore archived items to their original location.

NOTE: The Archive Folders might already be present in your folder list before you archive any files. Outlook creates these folders the first time a file is archived. They remain in the folder list even when they are empty. Also note that the listing in your folder list for Personal Folders might appear as Outlook Today – [Personal Folders].

9. In the folder list, click the plus sign (+) next to Archive Folders if the archive folders are not already displayed.

10. Click **Inbox** under the Archive Folders on the folder list. The contents of the Inbox Archive Folder appear. These are the items you just archived from your Personal Folders Inbox.

11. Select all three messages. (Remember to use Ctrl to select multiple messages.)

12. With the three messages selected, position the pointer over the selections, and then press and hold the mouse button. Drag the selections to the folder list, moving the pointer over Inbox under Personal Folders until it is highlighted.

FIGURE 4-20
Restoring
archived items

Archive Folders

Personal Folders

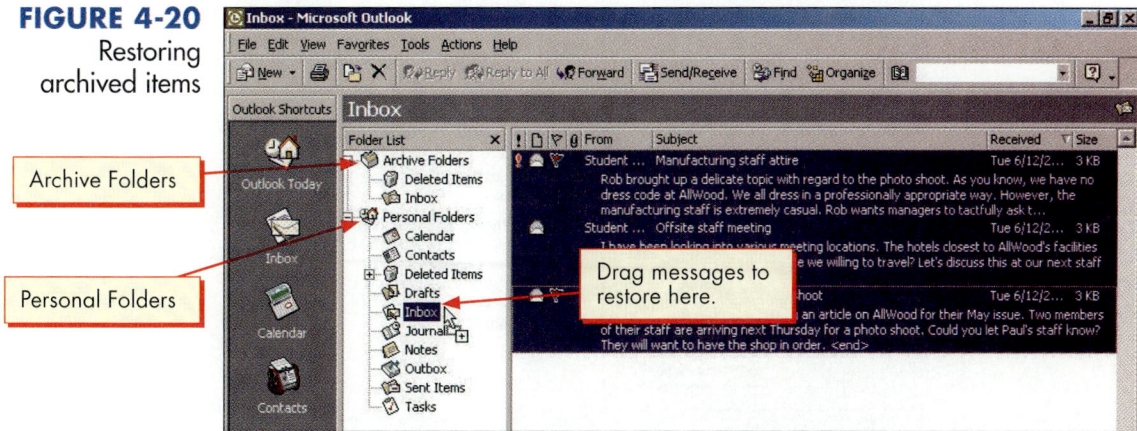

13. Release the mouse button while the Personal Folders Inbox is highlighted. The archived files are moved from the Archive Folders Inbox to the Personal Folders Inbox, which was their original location.

14. Click Inbox under the Archive Folders. Notice that it is now empty because you restored all the items to their original location.

15. Click Inbox under Personal Folders, and then close the folder list.

USING HELP

Outlook has various options for tracking your e-mail messages. You can control when a message is delivered, and you can receive a receipt for that message after it is delivered.

Use Microsoft Outlook Help to learn more about message tracking and delivery options:

1. In the Ask a Question box, key **track sent messages** in the text box and press Enter. A list of related topics appears.

2. Click Be notified when messages are delivered or read. The Help screen appears.

3. On the right side of the screen, click To be notified about a single message. (See Figure 4-21 on the next page.)

4. Read the information about how to receive notification for a sent message, and then click the Close button [X] when done.

FIGURE 4-21
Help screen on
message-tracking
options

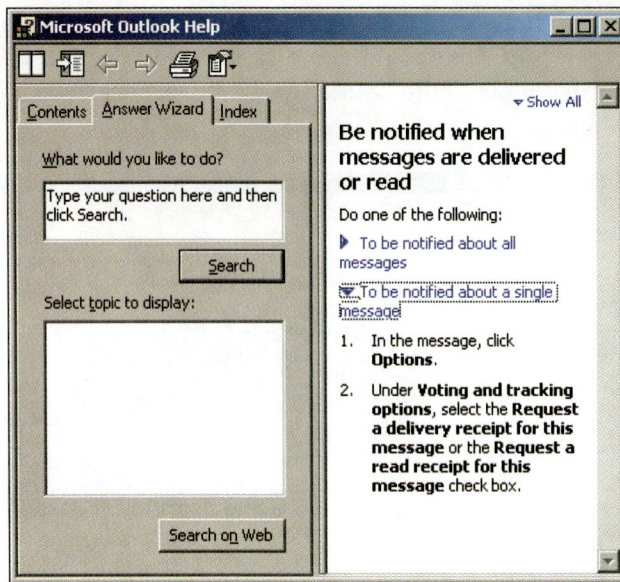

LESSON **4** **Summary**

➤ Received messages and sent messages can both be flagged.

➤ Options in the Flag for Follow Up dialog box are used to determine the type of flag and the reminder date and time, if any.

➤ Spell- and grammar-checking can be done both manually and automatically.

➤ You can set message sensitivity, delivery options, and message importance. Received messages are flagged in the same manner as sent messages.

➤ You use the Find button to search the Inbox for messages based on specific text.

➤ A signature is text added automatically to any message that is sent and might include information such as the sender's name, job title, and phone number.

➤ You can apply signatures to new messages as well as to replied and forwarded messages.

➤ You can edit an existing signature.

➤ You can discontinue or remove a signature.

➤ You use the Organize button 🗐 to sort the Inbox using various sort fields or sort orders.

➤ A filter can be used to screen items in the Inbox, and various viewing options are available by using the Organize button ▦.

➤ You can delete messages from the Inbox and then restore them if the Inbox remains displayed.

➤ The Deleted Items folder shows the items that have been deleted from all the Outlook folders. You can use the vertical scroll bar and the column headings to locate a deleted item.

➤ You can create new folders for messages as needed, and messages can be moved into new folders.

➤ You can rename a folder and delete folders no longer needed.

➤ Messages can be archived for storage and future access. You can do this either manually or automatically with AutoArchive. Archived items can be restored to their original locations.

LESSON 4 Command Summary

FEATURE	BUTTON	MENU	KEYBOARD	SPEECH
Delete Message	✕	Edit, Delete	Ctrl + D	✓
Undo Delete		Edit, Undo Delete	Ctrl + Z	✓
Move Item	📁	Edit, Move to Folder	Ctrl + Shift + V	✓
Find Item	Find	Tools, Find	Ctrl + E	✓
Organize Folder	▦	Tools, Organize		✓
Spelling and Grammar	ABC ✓	Tools, Spelling and Grammar	F7	✓

Concepts Review

Each of the following statements is either true or false. Indicate your choice by circling T or F.

T F **1.** You can flag both sent and received e-mail messages.

T F **2.** You can search for messages based on the content of the subject line.

T F **3.** You can create as many different signatures as you want.

T F **4.** You can sort messages only by using the options on the Ways to Organize Inbox pane.

T F **5.** You can use the filter feature only on the Subject field.

T F **6.** If you delete an Inbox message, you can restore the message while the Inbox is still displayed by pressing Ctrl + Z.

T F **7.** The Deleted Items file folder contains only deleted Inbox items.

T F **8.** A file folder does not have to be empty to be deleted.

SHORT ANSWER QUESTIONS

Write the correct answer in the space provided.

1. Which dialog box do you use to set message sensitivity?

_____

2. What is the name of text that is automatically added to any message you send?

_____

3. What button opens the Ways to Organize Inbox pane?

_____

4. What do you use to screen items in a folder based on conditions you define?

_____

5. What symbol appears under the Importance column heading for a message that has its importance set to High?

_____

6. What do you click when you want to sort or group items in the Deleted Items folder by item type?

_____

7. What keystrokes display the Move Items dialog box?

_____

8. What key do you use when renaming a folder?

_____

CRITICAL THINKING

Answer these questions on a separate page. There are no right or wrong answers. Support your answers with examples from your own experience, if possible.

1. You can send a message that includes both a flag and a reminder. Can you think of situations in which doing so might be inappropriate, unwise, or simply rude? List some examples when it would be appropriate and how you might use these features without offending the recipient.

2. Give some examples of signatures you might create, and explain why they would be useful.

Skills Review

EXERCISE 4-16

Flag a sent message, set message options, and manually spell-check it.

1. Open the Inbox by clicking the Inbox shortcut [icon] in the Outlook Bar.

2. Press `Ctrl`+`N` to open a new Message form.

3. In the **To** text box, key *[recipient's name]@[ISP]*

NOTE: Your instructor will provide you with an appropriate e-mail address.

4. In the **Subject** text box, key **Paul's presentation**

5. Change the Message format to Plain Text, and key the text shown in Figure 4-22 for the body of the message.

FIGURE 4-22

```
Paul will be unveiling the designs for the new collection of office
furniture next Tuesday at 11 a.m. His presentation will last roughly an
hour. Make sure you remind your staff to be on time.
```

6. Flag the message by following these steps:

    a. Click the Message Flag button 🚩 on the Message form toolbar.

    b. Click the down arrow next to the <u>F</u>lag to text box, and select **For Your Information** from the drop-down list.

    c. Click the down arrow next to the <u>D</u>ue by text box and select **None** on the drop-down calendar if it is not already selected.

    d. Click **OK**.

7. Set message options by following these steps:

    a. Click the Importance High button ❗ on the Message form toolbar.

    b. Click the **Op<u>t</u>ions** button on the Message form toolbar.

    c. Click the down arrow next to the **Sensitivit<u>y</u>** text box, and select Confidential.

    d. Click **Close**.

8. Manually spell-check the document by following these steps:

    a. Click the Spelling and Grammar button ✓ on the Message form toolbar.

    b. Make any necessary corrections and click **OK** when done.

9. Connect to the Internet and send the message.

10. Display the Sent Items folder and print the message, using Memo Style as the print style and using your name as a centered header. Delete any existing footer information.

EXERCISE 4-17

Create a signature, apply it to a message, and delete the signature.

1. Create a signature by following these steps:

    a. With the Inbox displayed, choose <u>T</u>ools, <u>O</u>ptions from the menu, and then click the **Mail Format** tab.

    b. Click **Signatures**.

    c. Click <u>N</u>ew.

    d. In the text box under **Enter a n<u>a</u>me for your new signature**, key *[your initials]* and then click **Next**.

    e. Under **Signature text**, key the following text:

    [your name]

    AllWood Mills Intern

    f. Click **Finish**.

    g. Click **OK**.

    h. Click <u>A</u>pply and then click **OK**.

2. Press Ctrl + N to open a new Message form.

3. In the To text box, key *[recipient's name]@[ISP]*

NOTE: Your instructor will provide you with an appropriate e-mail address.

4. In the Subject text box, key **Marketing information**

5. Change the Message format to Plain Text. If Microsoft Word displays an information box, click Continue to allow reformatting of the signature.

6. Key the text shown in Figure 4-23 for the body of the message.

FIGURE 4-23

```
I will be sending you the marketing information for the new line of office
furniture by the end of the week.
```

7. Connect to the Internet and send the message.

8. Display the Sent Items folder and print the message, using Memo Style as the print style and using your name as a centered header. Delete any existing footer information.

9. Delete a signature by following these steps:
    a. Choose Tools, Options from the menu, and then click the Mail Format tab.
    b. Click Signatures, and select the signature you created in step 1.
    c. Click Remove.
    d. Click Yes.
    e. Click OK and then click OK once again.

EXERCISE 4-18

Sort the Inbox, filter a view, and turn off filtering.

NOTE: This exercise uses the e-mail messages you received in Exercises 4-1, 4-2, and 4-3. If you do not have these messages in your Inbox, complete those exercises, addressing the messages to yourself.

1. Click the Inbox shortcut on the Outlook Bar to display the Inbox folder, if it is not already displayed.

2. Sort the Inbox by following these steps:
    a. Choose View, Current View, Customize Current View from the menu.
    b. Click Sort.
    c. Click the down arrow next to the Sort items by text box, and select Flag Status.
    d. Select Descending, and then click OK twice.

3. Print the Inbox, using a Table Style print style and adding your name as a centered header. Delete any existing footer information.

4. Sort the Inbox once again, selecting **Received** in the **Sort items by** text box, in a **Descending** sort order.

5. Filter a view by following these steps:
    a. Choose **V**iew, Current **V**iew, **C**ustomize Current View from the menu.
    b. Click Fi**l**ter.
    c. In the Sear**c**h for the word(s) text box, key **Traditional Homes**
    d. Click the down arrow next to the **I**n text box, and select subject field and message body.
    e. Click OK twice.

6. Print the Inbox, using a Table Style print style and adding your name as a centered header.

7. Turn off filtering by following these steps:
    a. Choose **V**iew, Current **V**iew, **C**ustomize Current View from the menu.
    b. Click Fi**l**ter.
    c. Click Clear **A**ll.
    d. Click OK twice.

EXERCISE 4-19

Create a new mail folder, move folder items, rename a folder, and delete a folder.

> **NOTE:** This exercise uses the e-mail messages you received in Exercises 4-1 and 4-3. If you do not have these messages in your Inbox, complete those exercises, addressing the messages to yourself.

1. Display the Inbox folder if it is not already displayed.

2. Create a mail folder and move items into it by following these steps:
    a. Select the "Manufacturing staff attire" message. Press Ctrl and select the "Traditional Homes photo shoot" message.
    b. Choose **E**dit, **M**ove to Folder from the menu.
    c. Click **N**ew.
    d. In the **N**ame text box, key **Photo Session**
    e. Under **S**elect where to place the folder, click Inbox under the Personal Folders.
    f. Click OK. The Add shortcut to Outlook Bar? dialog box might appear. If so, click No.
    g. Click OK.

3. Rename a folder by following these steps:
    a. Choose **V**iew, **F**older list to display the folder list, if it is not already displayed.

     b. Click the Inbox plus sign (+) to display the Photo Session folder on the folder list, if it is not already displayed.

     c. Click **Photo Session** on the folder list to open it. (The folder name should be highlighted in blue; you might need to click it again to highlight it.)

     d. Press F2.

     e. Key **Magazine** and press Enter.

4. Print the Magazine folder, using a Table Style print style and adding your name as a centered header. Delete any existing footer information.

5. Move the contents of the Magazine folder to the Inbox by following these steps:

     a. Display the Magazine folder, and select both items.

     b. Choose **E**dit, **M**ove to Folder from the menu.

     c. Under **M**ove the selected items to the folder, click Inbox.

     d. Click OK.

6. Delete a folder by following these steps:

     a. With the folder list still displayed, select the Magazine folder.

     b. Click the Delete button ☒ on the Standard toolbar.

     c. Click Yes.

7. Close the folder list.

Lesson Applications

Create a signature, apply the signature to a new message, add a flag, and delete the signature.

John Yu, AllWood's VP of Marketing, has asked you to help organize the marketing campaign for a new line of furniture the company will be offering in the coming months. Your first task is to notify the rest of the team that you'll be helping out.

1. Display your Inbox folder and create a signature. Use your initials as the name of the new signature, and key the following text for the signature:

   [your name]
   AllWood Mills Marketing Intern

2. Apply the new signature to new messages.

3. Compose a new e-mail message, addressing the message to your instructor's e-mail address. In the subject field, key **Joining marketing team**. Change the message format to Plain Text. Key an appropriate salutation, and then key the text shown in Figure 4-24 for the body of the message.

   NOTE: Your instructor will supply you with an appropriate e-mail address.

FIGURE 4-24

```
I have recently joined John Yu's marketing team. This is just to let
you know that I will be coordinating the marketing efforts for the new
collection in the coming months.
```

4. Flag the message for follow-up, with the flag text of For Your Information and no <u>D</u>ue by date.

5. Connect to the Internet and send the message.

6. Display the Sent Items folder. Print your message, using a Memo Style print style and adding your name as a centered header. Delete any existing footer information.

7. Remove your signature from the signature list.

   NOTE: Make sure you have completed the last step of this exercise. This step restores Outlook to its default setting. Always leave Outlook in its default state for the next class or student to use.

EXERCISE 4-21

Send a message by using various message options, create a new mailbox, and move messages into it.

NOTE: This exercise uses the e-mail message you received in Exercise 4-2. If you do not have this message in your Inbox, complete that exercise, addressing the message to yourself.

Rob Connelly, AllWood's president, has asked you to work with AllWood's VP of Administration, Maria Lopez. She has assigned you to work on compensation issues. Much of the work is highly confidential, so you need to keep track of all the e-mail correspondence.

1. Display your Inbox folder and compose a new e-mail message, addressing the message to your instructor's e-mail address. In the subject field, key **Year-end bonuses**. Change the message format to Plain Text. Key an appropriate salutation, and then key the text shown in Figure 4-25 for the body of the message.

NOTE: Your instructor will supply you with an appropriate e-mail address.

FIGURE 4-25

> Please provide me a list of employees on your staff eligible for a year-end bonus. I will forward the list to Rob for his review.

2. Set the message importance to High, and make the sensitivity level for the message Confidential. Flag the message for follow-up, with the text of Reply. Set a due date two business days from the current date, with a time of 10 a.m.
3. Connect to the Internet and send the message.
4. Display the Sent Items folder, select the message you just sent, and move that message to a new folder named **Compensation**, which should be located under the Personal Folders Inbox folder. (Do not add a shortcut to the Outlook Bar if you are asked.)
5. Display the Inbox, select the "Offsite staff meeting" message, and move the message to the Compensation folder.
6. Display the Compensation folder. Print the "Year-end bonuses" message, using a Memo Style print style and adding your name as a centered header. Delete any existing footer information.

7. Print the Compensation folder, using a Table Style print style and adding your name as a centered header. Add the date as a centered footer.

8. Move the "Offsite staff meeting" message back to the Personal Folders Inbox, and then delete the Compensation folder. Close the folder list if it is still displayed.

EXERCISE 4-22

Create a signature, send messages using various message options, and filter a folder view.

You've been assigned to work with Jasmine Jones, AllWood's VP of Sales. She would like you to help coordinate the sales conference for the store managers and company management. Your responsibilities will require a lot of e-mail correspondence.

1. Display your Inbox folder and create a signature. Use your initials as the name of the new signature, and key the following text for the signature:

   [your name]

   AllWood Mills Sales Intern

2. Apply the new signature to new messages.

3. Compose a new e-mail message, addressing the message to your instructor's e-mail address. In the subject field, key **Sales conference planning**. Change the message format to Plain Text. Key an appropriate salutation, and then key the text shown in Figure 4-26 for the body of the message (key the text exactly as shown).

   NOTE: Your instructor will supply you with an appropriate e-mail address.

FIGURE 4-26

```
I have located two sutable locations in Chicago for this year's sales
conforance. I will be sending information about the facilities by inter-
office mail later today.
```

4. Manually spell-check the message, making the necessary corrections.

5. Set the importance level to Low, and flag the message with the text For Your Information, but with no due date.

6. Connect to the Internet and send the message.

7. Edit the signature you created in step 1, changing the text as follows:

   [your name]

   AllWood Mills Sales Intern

   (319) 555-5500, ext. 4134

8. Compose another e-mail message, again addressing the message to your instructor's e-mail address. In the subject field, key **Your accommodations**. Change the message format to Plain Text. Key an appropriate salutation, and then key the text shown in Figure 4-27 for the body of the message (key the text exactly as shown).

FIGURE 4-27

```
Would you like me to include your wife in the hotel reservations I book
for you? You had mentioned domething aobut having her accompany you to
the sales conference.
```

9. Set the message sensitivity for the message to Personal.

10. Manually spell-check the message, making any necessary corrections.

11. Send the message.

12. Display the Sent Items folder, and filter the folder view, searching for the words "sales conference" in the subject field and message body.

13. Print the filtered Sent Items folder, using the Table Style print style. Add your name as a centered header, and delete any existing footer information. Print the two filtered messages separately, using the Memo Style print style for each message. Add your name as a centered header, and delete any existing footer information.

14. Remove the filter you applied to the Sent Items folder. Remove the signature you edited in step 7.

NOTE: Make sure you have completed the last step of this exercise. This step restores Outlook to its default settings. Always leave Outlook in its default state for the next class or student to use.

EXERCISE 4-23 ✚ *Challenge Yourself*

Create a new signature, send messages with various message options, manage file folders, create contacts and a distribution list, and schedule events in the Calendar.

AllWood is about to begin shipping a new line of office furniture. John Yu, AllWood's VP of Marketing, has asked you to help with their marketing efforts. The tasks he wants you to perform will require sending and receiving a lot of e-mail messages.

1. Display the contact list and delete any previously entered contacts or distribution lists. Add the contacts shown in Figure 4-28, entering the addresses and phone numbers as business information. (*Hint*: To save typing, use the Contact form menu command <u>A</u>ctions, New <u>C</u>ontact from Same Company after entering the first contact to redisplay the address and company name. Be sure to change the name, phone number, and e-mail address.)

FIGURE 4-28

Ms. Gloria Johnson	Mr. John Yu
AllWood Mills, Inc.	AllWood Mills, Inc.
3100 Jackson Street	3100 Jackson Street
Dubuque, IA 52004	Dubuque, IA 52004
(319) 555-4406	(319) 555-4414
E-mail: gjohnson@ISP.isp	E-mail: jyu@ISP.isp

2. Add job titles to the contacts you created in step 1 as follows: Gloria Johnson, **Marketing Associate**; and John Yu, **VP of Marketing**.

3. Assign each of the contacts you created in step 1 to the Goals/Objectives category, and link all of the contacts with each other.

4. Create a distribution list titled **Marketing** and containing the contacts you created in step 1 as members of the list. Assign the distribution list to the Goals/Objectives category.

5. Display a date in the Calendar approximately two months from the current date. Delete any existing appointments or events for that date, and then schedule an appointment on that day, keying the subject as **National Furniture Manufacturers Association Conference**. Specify the location as **St. Louis**, and the duration of the appointment from 9 a.m. to 5 p.m. Set a 1-day reminder for the event, and show the time as Out of Office.

6. On the same date as the sales conference, schedule an appointment titled **Dinner with marketing team** and starting at 6 p.m. and ending at 8 p.m., with the location as **TBA**. Deselect the reminder, and show the time as Out of Office.

7. Edit the listing for John Yu in your contact list, changing his e-mail address to your instructor's e-mail address. (You will be sending an e-mail message to your instructor.)

NOTE: Your instructor will provide you with an appropriate e-mail address.

8. Display your Inbox folder and create a signature. Use your initials as the name of the new signature, and key the following text for the signature:

    [your name]

    AllWood Mills Marketing Intern

9. Apply the new signature to new messages.

10. Create a new e-mail message, addressing the message to John Yu from your contact list.

    REVIEW: To use an e-mail address from your contact list, click To in the Message form and then select the name from the Select Names dialog box.

11. Key the subject of the message as **Trade show**. For the text of the message, key the material shown in Figure 4-29, using a Plain Text message format.

FIGURE 4-29

The National Furniture Manufacturers Association's annual meeting is being held next month in St. Louis. Rob suggested that the marketing team attend. He thought we might get some fresh ideas for the introduction of our new office line. I will take care of the arrangements.

12. Set the message importance to High, and set a flag to For Your Information with no due date. Manually spell-check the message

13. Connect to the Internet and send the message.

14. Display the Tasks folder and delete any existing items in the task list. Add a new task with the subject heading **Find hotel in St. Louis for trade show**, with the due date roughly two days from the current date. Add another task with the subject heading **Notify managers of travel arrangements**, with the due date approximately one week from the current date. Add another new task with the subject heading **Prepare trade show materials for John's review**, with a due date of the current date. Show the task as completed.

15. Display the Tasks folder, and filter the folder to show only those tasks with the text "trade show" in the subject field. Print the task list in portrait style, using the Table Style print style. Add your name as a centered header, and delete any existing footer information.

16. Display the date on which you scheduled the appointment in step 5. Print the Calendar, using the Calendar Details Style print style. Add a centered header with your name and a centered footer with the date.

17. Display the Sent Items folder, and select the "Trade show" message you sent in step 13. Print the message, using Memo Style as the print style. Add your name as a centered header, and delete any existing footer information.

18. Display the contact list in Detailed Address Cards view. Select the three additions you made in this exercise (the two individuals and the distribution list). Print the selected contacts, using a Card Style print style. Add your name as a centered header, and delete any existing footer information. Eliminate the blank form page at the end. (*Hint*: Use the <u>B</u>lank forms at end option on the Format tab of the Page Setup dialog box.)

19. Display the contact list in Address Cards view. Remove the filter for the Tasks folder that you applied in step 15. Remove the signature you created in step 8.

> **NOTE:** Make sure you have completed the last step of this exercise. This step restores Outlook to its default settings. Always leave Outlook in its default state for the next class or student to use.

On Your Own

In these exercises you work on your own, as you would in a real-life work environment. Use the skills you've learned to accomplish the task—and be creative.

EXERCISE 4-24

Use the Internet to search for local restaurants for a class party. Summarize the results in an e-mail to all your classmates, including your instructor. Use a signature, flag the message, and use message options. Place the responses in a separate mail folder and sort it. Print out the sent message. Print the folder containing your responses.

EXERCISE 4-25

Use the Internet to research a potential vacation location. Send an e-mail message to some family members and friends asking their opinion. Use a signature and message options. Place your sent message and the replies in a separate mail folder and sort it. Print your message and the folder containing the responses.

EXERCISE 4-26

Team up with a classmate to look for a job. Use the Internet to perform a search for your partner, and ask your partner to search for you. E-mail your results to each other, using a signature and message options. Place all your messages in a separate folder and print out both sent and received messages.

Working with Others and Using Notes

After completing this lesson, you will be able to:

1. Plan meetings.
2. Assign tasks to others.
3. Accept and decline tasks.
4. View, organize, and print tasks.
5. Create and edit notes.
6. View, organize, and print notes.

Estimated Time: 1¾ hours

With Outlook's Tasks and Calendar, you can schedule activities that involve others. Outlook lets you plan meetings in which you invite other people and reserve office resources. You can assign a task to someone and follow it until it is completed. Likewise, you can accept a task and let the individual who assigned it know when you've finished it. Outlook also lets you change the way tasks appear in the Tasks folder.

Outlook's Notes feature is an electronic version of the paper sticky notes that often fill the walls, desks, and computer screens of our work areas. You can use Notes to jot down reminders, ideas, questions, or anything else you might otherwise put on paper. As with Tasks, Outlook also lets you view and organize Notes in various ways.

Planning Meetings

A *meeting* is an activity that involves inviting other people or reserving resources. A *resource* might be a conference room, audio-visual equipment, or other shared organizational space or equipment used for meetings. You can use Outlook to plan your meetings and invite the meeting participants. Like appointments, meetings can be recurring.

In addition to inviting people to meetings, you can also use Outlook to reserve a resource. To do this, the resource must have a mailbox. An administrator in your organization must set up the mailbox for the resource, but thereafter, the resource can accept or reject the reservation request, depending on whether it is free or not.

EXERCISE **5-1** **Plan a Meeting Involving Others**

Planning a meeting involves finding an available time in your schedule for the meeting and inviting the meeting attendees. Outlook notifies the individuals via e-mail of your meeting request.

1. Click the Calendar shortcut 🖼 in the Outlook Bar to display the Calendar folder.

2. Display the Appointments Calendar for a business day your instructor has assigned for you within the next three weeks. Delete any previous appointments for that day.

> **NOTE:** You will be using the names and e-mail addresses of your class-mates to invite to your meeting. Your instructor will provide you with a list of names and e-mail addresses. Because you will be inviting each other to your meetings, you will need to select a day for your meeting that is not in conflict with other students. Your instructor will assign a date for you to use.

3. Choose Actions, Plan a Meeting from the menu. The Plan a Meeting dialog box appears. Appointments are color-coded. You can use the scroll bar under the time grid to adjust the times and days shown in the grid. (See Figure 5-1 on the next page.)

4. Click various time blocks on the time grid. The white column represents the selected meeting time for all attendees, and it moves in the time grid as you click a different block. The times shown in the Meeting start time and Meeting end time text boxes change as you click locations in the time grid. You can use these text boxes to manually specify the start and ending times of the meeting.

FIGURE 5-1
Plan a Meeting
dialog box

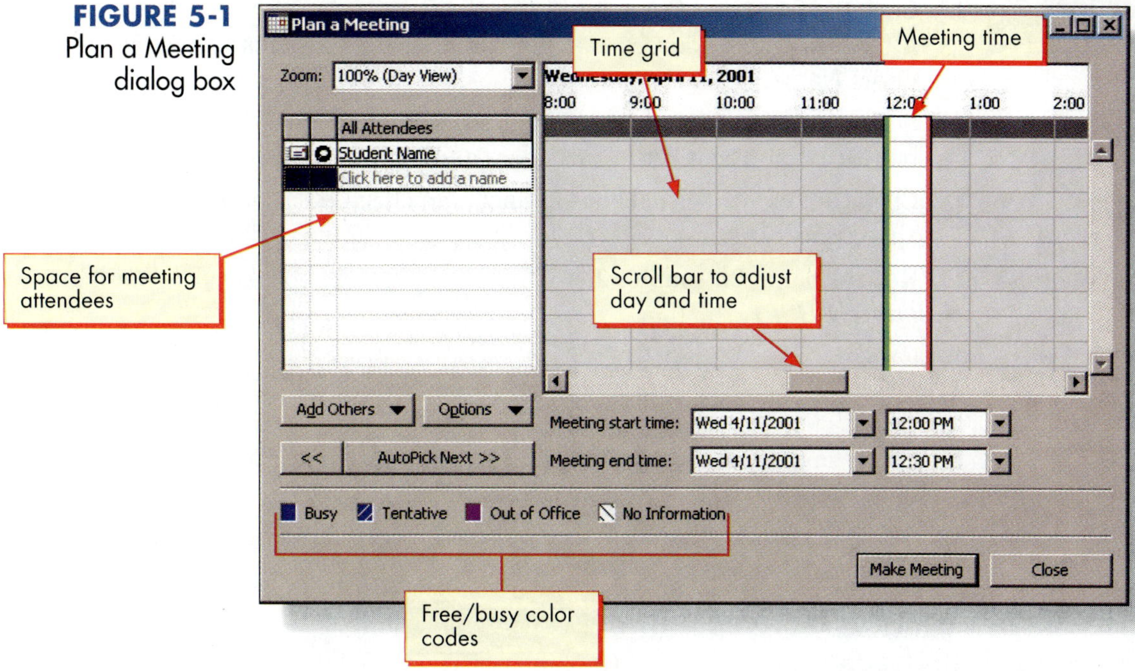

5. Click a time block under **2:00** so the meeting is set to run from **2:00 PM** to **2:30 PM**.

6. Position the pointer over the red border of the white column and drag the border to **3:00**. The meeting is now 1 hour long, from **2:00 PM** to **3:00 PM**.

7. Click **A**dd Others, and then choose **Add from A**ddress Book from the drop-down menu. The Select Attendees and Resources dialog box appears.

8. Click the down arrow next to the **Show Names from the** text box and select **Contacts** if it is not already displayed. The names shown are the names in your contact list. If a meeting attendee's name doesn't appear on the list, you must add the name as a new contact. Outlook notifies meeting attendees of the meeting via e-mail, so anyone you invite to a meeting must have an e-mail address.

9. Click **N**ew. The New Entry dialog box appears.

10. Under **S**elect the entry type, select **New Contact** and click OK. The Contact form appears.

11. Key the name as **Classmate 1**

12. In the **E-M**ail text box, key *[recipient's name]@[ISP]*

NOTE: Use the e-mail address from the list of valid e-mail addresses your instructor has provided you. You will send meeting requests to your classmates via e-mail.

![Save and Close button icon]

13. Click the **Save and Close** button on the Contact form toolbar. The Select Attendees and Resources dialog box reappears. Classmate 1's name appears under **Name**.

14. Select Classmate 1 and click **Required**. Note that you can distinguish between required meeting attendees and optional ones.

15. Click **New** again, select **New Contact**, and click **OK**. The Contact form appears as before.

16. Key the name **Classmate 2**, and in the **E-Mail** text box, key *[recipient's name]@[ISP]*

> **NOTE:** Use an e-mail address from the list of e-mail addresses your instructor has provided you.

17. Click the **Save and Close** button. The Select Attendees and Resources dialog box reappears.

18. Select Classmate 2, and click **Required**. The two names are added to the list of meeting attendees.

FIGURE 5-2
Select Attendees and Resources dialog box after new contacts have been added

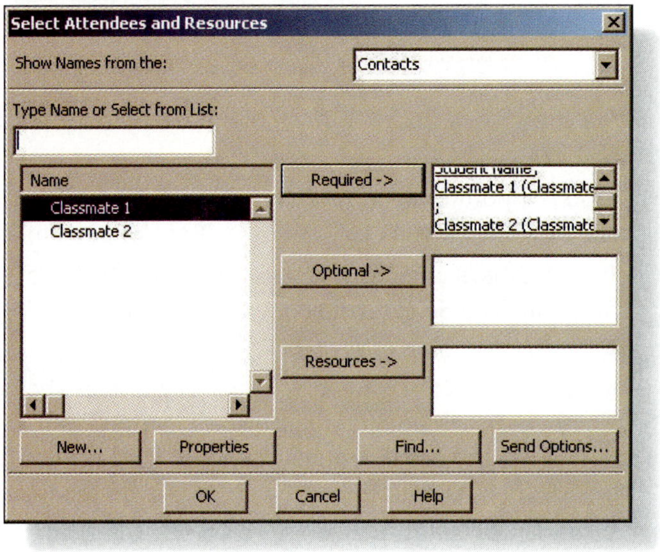

19. Click **OK**. The Plan a Meeting dialog box reappears, with Classmate 1 and Classmate 2 now shown under **All Attendees**. If you invite individuals who have made their Calendars available to others, you can see if they are free at the time you select. However, the individuals you've invited have not made their Calendars available, so their schedules show the No Information code.

> **NOTE:** Outlook might display a dialog box inviting you to sign up for the Microsoft Office Internet Free/Busy Service. If this dialog box appears, click Cancel. This is a Web-based service operated by Microsoft that stores your free and busy Calendar times. It enables people you designate to access this information and plan meetings around your availability.

20. Click Make Meeting. The Meeting form appears. The attendees' names appear in the To text box automatically.

21. In the Subject text box, key **Discuss conference topics**. In the Location text box, key **My office**. In the large text box in the lower half of the form, key **Go over major topics and discuss PowerPoint slide show material.**

REVIEW: You can click the down arrow next to the Location text box and select any location you've previously used, such as My Office.

22. Deselect the reminder.

23. Connect to the Internet and click the Send button on the Meeting form toolbar to send the invitation to the specified recipients.

24. Click Close to close the Plan a Meeting dialog box. The meeting is added to your Appointments Calendar.

EXERCISE **5-2** **Add and Remove Meeting Attendees**

Adding more people to a meeting you've already scheduled is easy. If you want to remove attendees from a meeting, Outlook will send them a notification that the meeting has been cancelled.

1. Display the date for the meeting in your Appointments Calendar, if it is not already displayed.

2. Open the meeting by double-clicking it (or select it and press Enter). The Meeting form appears. The meeting recipients' responses appear as a banner above the To text box. If none of the recipients have responded, the banner reads, "No responses have been received for this meeting." (See Figure 5-3 on the next page.)

3. Choose Actions, Add or Remove Attendees from the menu. The Select Attendees and Resources dialog box appears.

4. Click New. The New Entry dialog box appears.

5. Select New Contact and then click OK. The Contact form appears.

6. Key the name as **Classmate 3**

7. In the E-Mail text box, key *[recipient's name]@[ISP]*

NOTE: Use an e-mail address from the list of e-mail addresses your instructor has provided you.

8. Click the Save and Close button on the Contact form toolbar. The new contact is added to the list of names on the Select Attendees and Resources dialog box.

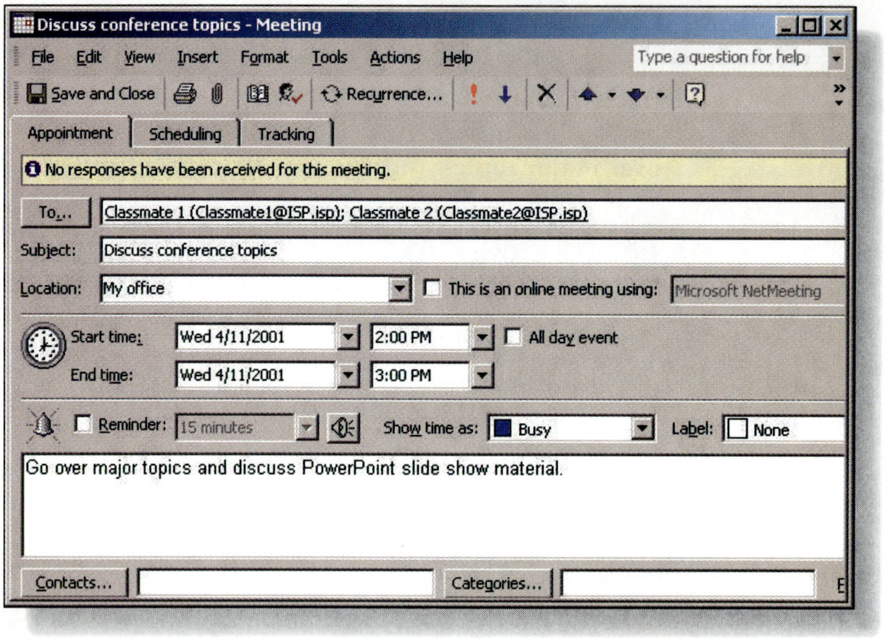

FIGURE 5-3
Meeting form for
scheduled meeting

9. Select Classmate 3, and click **Required**. The name is added to the list of meeting attendees.

10. Under the list of meeting attendees, select Classmate 1. (Use the vertical scroll bar to display Classmate 1's name if it is not visible.)

11. Press Delete. Classmate 1 is eliminated from the list of meeting attendees.

12. Click **OK**. The Meeting form reappears. Notice that Outlook has added Classmate 3 in the To text box and removed Classmate 1.

13. Make sure you are connected to the Internet.

14. Click the **Save and Close** button on the Meeting form toolbar. The Send Updates to Attendees dialog box appears. You can re-send the request to all attendees or only to the ones that have been added.

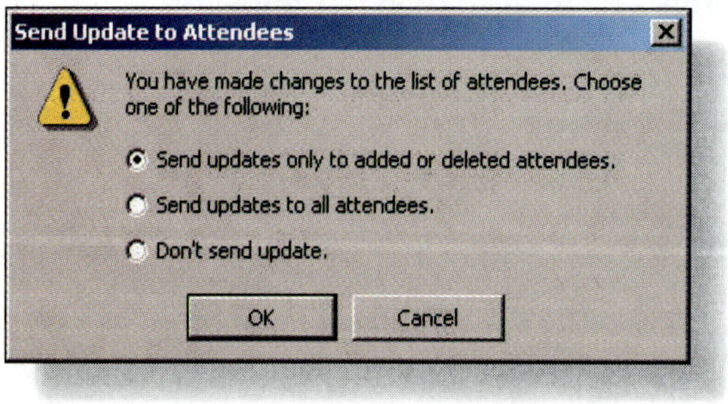

FIGURE 5-4
Send Update
to Attendees
dialog box

15. Select **Send updates only to added or deleted attendees** if it is not already selected, and then click **OK**. The Message form closes. Outlook sends a meeting request to Classmate 3 and notifies Classmate 1 that the meeting is

canceled. In the Meeting form for the recipient's e-mail, a toolbar button is available for removing the meeting from the Calendar.

EXERCISE 5-3 Book an Office Resource

If office resources are set up for reservations using Outlook, booking a resource is the same as requesting a meeting with an individual.

1. Select a day in your Appointments Calendar roughly two weeks in advance of the current date.

2. Select 4 p.m.

3. Choose Actions, Plan a Meeting from the menu. The Plan a Meeting dialog box appears.

4. Click Add Others and then select Add from Address Book from the drop-down menu. The Select Attendees and Resources dialog box appears.

5. Click New to add the name of the resource (conference room) to your contact list. The New Entry dialog box appears.

6. Select New Contact if it is not already selected, and then click OK. The Contact form appears. You'll add the resource to your contact list like any other contact, using a name for the resource (for example, "Conference Room 1") and an e-mail address.

> **NOTE:** Your instructor will provide you with the name and e-mail address of the resource.

7. After keying the name and e-mail address of your resource, click the Save and Close button on the Contact form toolbar. The Select Attendees and Resources dialog box reappears. The resource is shown as one of the available contacts.

8. Select the resource and click Resources. You could add attendees to your meeting at this time, if you wished; however, you'll only book the resource for now.

9. Click OK. The Plan a Meeting dialog box reappears. (Click Cancel if the Microsoft Office Internet Free/Busy dialog box appears.)

10. If necessary, set the Meeting start time as 4:00 PM and the Meeting end time as 4:30 PM, then click Make Meeting. The Meeting form appears. Notice that the Location text box automatically contains the name of the resource.

> **NOTE:** If you are actually reserving a time for an office resource, your instructor might have you use a different time to avoid conflicts in scheduling.

11. In the Subject text box, key **Conference presentation run-through**

12. Deselect the reminder option and make sure you're connected to the Internet.

13. Click the Send button and close the Plan a Meeting dialog box. The message is sent to the office resource. The office resource is now booked.

> **NOTE:** The administrator for your office resources might restrict who is allowed to reserve a given resource. For example, the administrator might allow only managers to reserve conference rooms. Invitations from managers might be accepted, and invitations from non-managers might be declined. If you are unable to reserve office resources, you might need to speak to your resource administrator about gaining permission. You access resource scheduling by choosing Tools, Options from the menu and clicking Calendar Options.

EXERCISE **5-4** **Accept or Decline a Meeting, or Propose a New Meeting Time**

Meeting invitations appear in the recipients' Inboxes. The symbol under the Icon heading indicates it as a meeting request. You can reply to a meeting request in one of four ways:

- **Accept:** Outlook creates an item on your Calendar and marks the time as busy.
- **Tentative:** Outlook creates an item on your Calendar and marks the time as tentative.
- **Propose New Time:** Outlook creates an item on your Calendar for the original time and sends a proposed new time to the meeting organizer.
- **Decline:** Outlook creates an item in your Deleted Items folder.

1. Display the Inbox folder.

2. Click the Send/Receive button on the Standard toolbar to get your messages from your mail server. Meeting invitations appear in the Inbox like other mail items, but the icon for the item shows it as a meeting. (You might receive more than one meeting invitation, depending on how many of your classmates invited you to their meetings.)

3. Open the message "Discuss conference topics." The Meeting form appears. You can use the toolbar buttons to accept an invitation, tentatively accept, propose a new time, or decline. (See Figure 5-5 on the next page.)

4. Click the Calendar button on the Meeting form toolbar. The Calendar for the meeting date appears. The color code for the meeting is tentative.

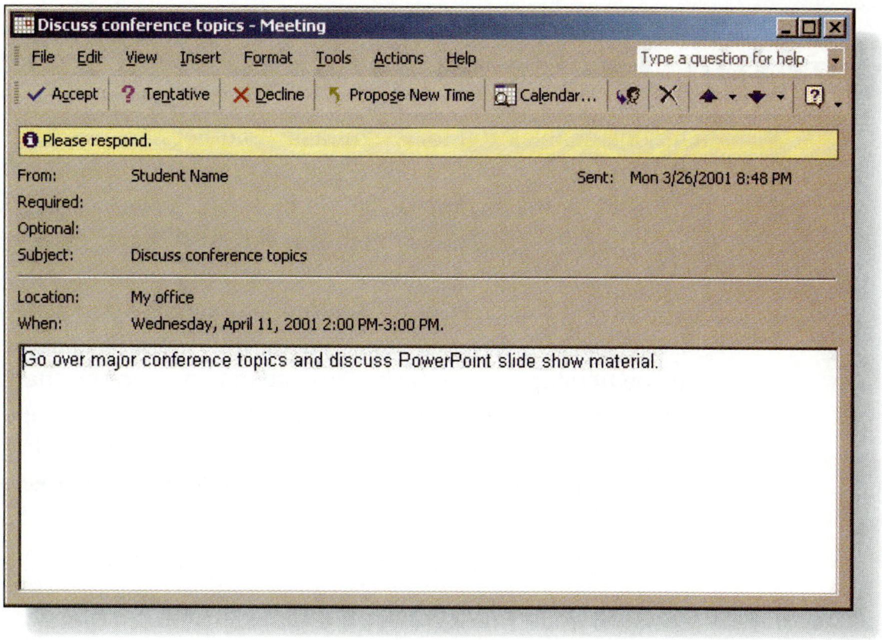

FIGURE 5-5
Meeting form for
meeting invitation

5. Click the Close button ☒ on the Calendar window to close the Calendar and redisplay the Meeting form. If you wish to propose a new meeting time, you can click the **Propose New Time** button on the Message form toolbar. You can also simply decline the invitation by clicking the **Decline** button. Otherwise, you can accept or tentatively accept the invitation.

NOTE: When you propose a new time by clicking the Propose New Time button, Outlook displays the Propose New Time dialog box, which is similar to the Plan A Meeting dialog box. You select a different time and/or date in the time grid and then click Propose Time. Outlook displays a Meeting Response form that is sent to the meeting organizer, suggesting the new meeting time.

6. Make sure you are connected to the Internet, and then click the **Accept** button on the Meeting form toolbar. Outlook places the meeting on your Calendar and displays an information dialog box asking if you want to include comments with your response.

7. Make sure **Send the response now** is selected, and then click **OK**. The meeting organizer is notified that you have accepted the meeting. The Inbox reappears. The meeting invitation is no longer in your Inbox, because you have accepted the invitation.

8. Click the **Send/Receive** button on the Standard toolbar to get responses from the meeting request you sent yourself. Responses to your meeting request appear in your Inbox.

9. Log off the Internet if your instructor tells you to do so.

Assigning Tasks to Others

Outlook enables you to assign tasks to others and to track their progress. If you are a supervisor, you could assign a task to a subordinate. Or, if you're working on a project with a group, you might assign a task to a coworker.

You assign a task to someone in the form of a *task request*, which is an e-mail message asking the message recipient to complete a specified activity. The recipient can either accept or decline the sender's request or delegate the task to someone else. When you *delegate* a task, you assign the task to someone else and you give up "ownership" of the task. This means you cannot change information in the task, such as the due date. However, you can keep an updated copy of the task in your task list, and you can receive status reports on its progress. You delegate tasks usually to a subordinate, occasionally to a coworker or equal, but never to a supervisor.

You can assign a task in various ways. You can:

- Create a new task request.
- Create a task request from a task that already exists in your task list.
- Delegate a task you received as a task request rather than accepting or declining it.
- Reassign a declined task request to someone else, or reclaim ownership yourself by adding it to your task list.
- Create an unassigned copy of a task request and reassign as needed.

Outlook keeps track of who owns an assigned task and when it is updated. When the owner of the task updates or completes the task, Outlook updates all copies of the task as well. When the task is completed, Outlook sends a status report to the owner of the task and everyone who requested a report.

EXERCISE **5-5** **Assign a Task to a Contact**

A task can be assigned to someone when it is created as a new task request. When you offer a task to someone else, you have the option of keeping a copy of the task in your task list. If the recipient of the task makes any changes, your version is updated.

1. Click the Tasks shortcut 📋 in the Outlook Bar to display the Tasks folder. Delete any existing tasks.

2. Click the down arrow next to the <u>N</u>ew button ☑ᴺᵉʷ and choose Task <u>R</u>equest from the menu (or press Ctrl + Shift + U). The Task form appears. (See Figure 5-6 on the next page.)

FIGURE 5-6
Task form for
new task request

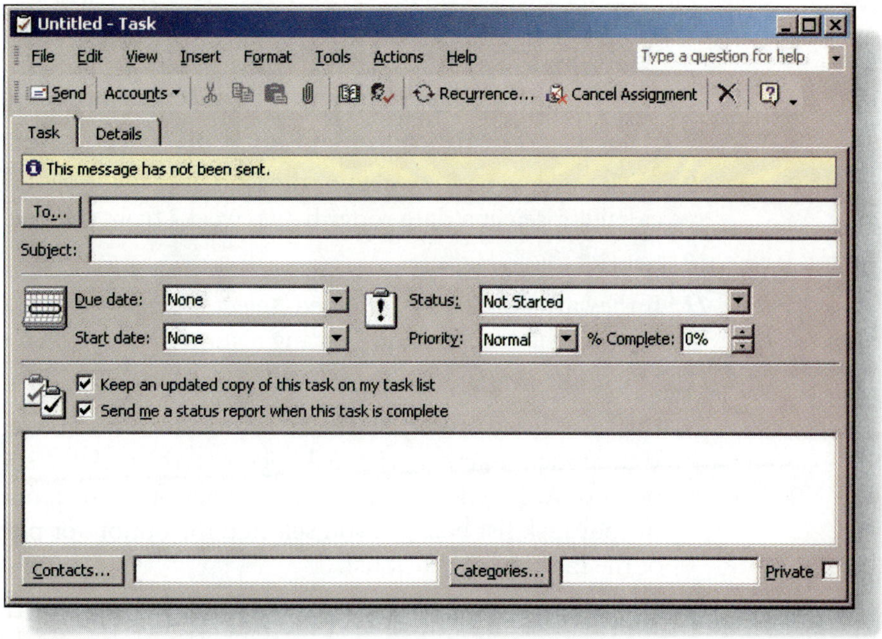

NOTE: Because this is a new task request rather than simply a new task, this form differs from the Task form you've seen previously. The toolbar includes some additional buttons and there are various text boxes that relate to the task assignment.

3. Click **To**. The Select Task Recipient dialog box appears. The list of names corresponds to the names in your contact list.

4. Click **New**. Under **Select the entry type**, make sure **New Contact** is selected, and then click **OK**. The Contact form appears.

NOTE: Your instructor will assign you a student partner for this and the next exercise. You will be assigning different tasks to each other. You and your partner will be referred to as "Student 1" and "Student 2" in the steps that follow. Decide which of you is Student 1 and which is Student 2. You and your partner will key different information for the task requests.

5. Key the name of your student partner and your partner's e-mail address in the **E-mail** text box.

6. Click the **Save and Close** button on the Contact form toolbar. The Select Task Recipient dialog box reappears. Your student partner's name appears under **Name**.

7. Select your student partner's name, click **To**, and then click **OK**. The Task form reappears, with your partner's name in the **To** text box.

8. In the Subject text box, key the following material for either Student 1 or Student 2, depending on which you have chosen:

Student 1: **Prepare handouts for conference presentation**

Student 2: **Locate equipment for conference presentation**

9. Click the down arrow next to the Due date text box. From the crop-down calendar, select a date roughly two weeks from the current date.

10. Set Priority to High.

11. If they are not already selected, select the options for keeping an updated copy on the task list and sending a status report when the task is completed.

12. Make sure you are connected to the Internet.

13. Click the Send button on the Task form toolbar. The task request is sent to your student partner. The task's icon on the task list shows this is a task request. Although you are not the owner of the task now, the task is listed in your task list because you selected the option for placing an updated copy of the task in your task list.

14. Open the "Prepare handouts" task if you are Student 1; open the "Locate equipment" task if you are Student 2. The Task form differs from the other tasks in the task list. This is a task request and you are not the owner of this task. You cannot change the details of the task, such as the status or the due date. Although your partner has not yet accepted the task assignment, your partner is the current owner of this task.

FIGURE 5-7
Task form for sent task request

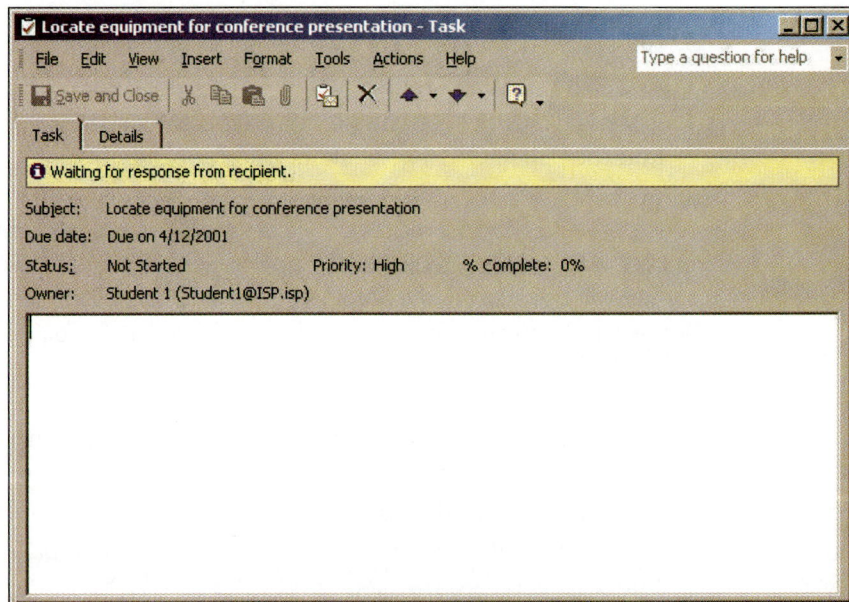

15. Close the Task form. The task list reappears.

EXERCISE **5-6** **Create a Task Request from an Existing Task**

An existing task in a task list can be assigned to someone else. When you offer an existing task to someone, Outlook modifies the Task form for the task assignment.

1. Create a new task by clicking the box titled "Click here to add a new Task" under the Subject column heading As in the previous exercise, you and your student partner will create different tasks.

2. Key the task subject for either Student 1 or Student 2, depending on which you have chosen, and then press Enter :

   Student 1: **Make travel arrangements for trip**

   Student 2: **Arrange car rental for trip**

3. Select "Make travel arrangements for trip" if you are Student 1; select "Arrange car rental for trip" if you are Student 2.

4. Press Enter to open the task. The Task form appears.

5. Click the A**ssign** Task button on the Task form toolbar. The Task form changes, now showing various options for assigning a task.

6. Click To. The Select Task Recipient dialog box appears.

7. Select your student partner's name, and then click To. Your partner's name now appears as the message recipient.

8. Click OK. The Task form reappears with your partner's name in the To text box.

9. In the text area of the Task window, key the following material for either Student 1 or Student 2, depending on which you have chosen:

   Student 1: **I've made airline reservations. Can you work out hotel accommodations?**

   Student 2: **I've made airline reservations. Can you work out the car rental?**

10. Make sure you are connected to the Internet and send the message. The task is sent to your partner. The task request is still listed as an item in the task list, but the icon under the Icon heading has changed to reflect that it is now a task request. (You might need to refresh the screen for your contact list before the icon will change.)

Accepting and Declining Tasks

Just as you can assign tasks to others, you can be the recipient of a task request. When you receive a task request, you become the temporary owner of the task. You can accept the task, decline the task, or assign the task to someone else.

If you accept the task, you assume ownership of the task and it is added to your task list. You are then the only person who can make changes to the task. When you decline a task, it is returned to the person who sent it to you. If you delegate the task to someone else, you can keep an updated copy of the task in the task list, but ownership and the ability to make changes are transferred to the person to whom you delegate it.

EXERCISE | **5-7** | **Accept a Task Request**

Task requests appear in your Inbox as e-mail items, identified by the words "Task Request" in the Subject field. You open them as you would open any e-mail message. They also appear in your task list.

1. Display the Inbox folder. Click the **Send/Receive** button on the Standard toolbar to retrieve the task requests sent to you, if you have not already received them.

2. Locate the task request items in your Inbox.

FIGURE 5-8
Inbox containing task requests

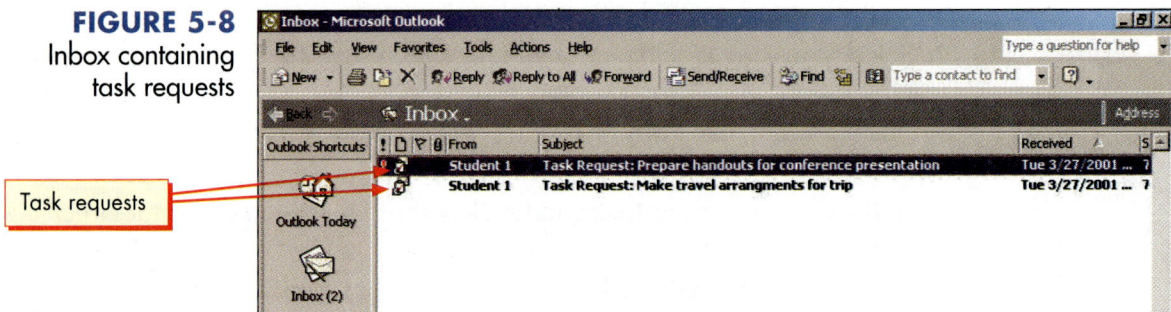

Task requests

3. Open the "Locate equipment" task if you are Student 1; open the "Prepare handouts" task if you are Student 2. The Task form appears. The toolbar for the Task window includes buttons for accepting or declining the task. (See Figure 5-9 on the next page.)

4. Click the **Accept** button on the Task form toolbar. The Accepting Task dialog box appears.

5. Select **E**dit the Response Before Sending, and click OK. The Task window reappears. Notice the change in the banner text.

6. In the text box at the bottom of the form, key **I'll get started on it right away.**

FIGURE 5-9
Task form for
received task
request

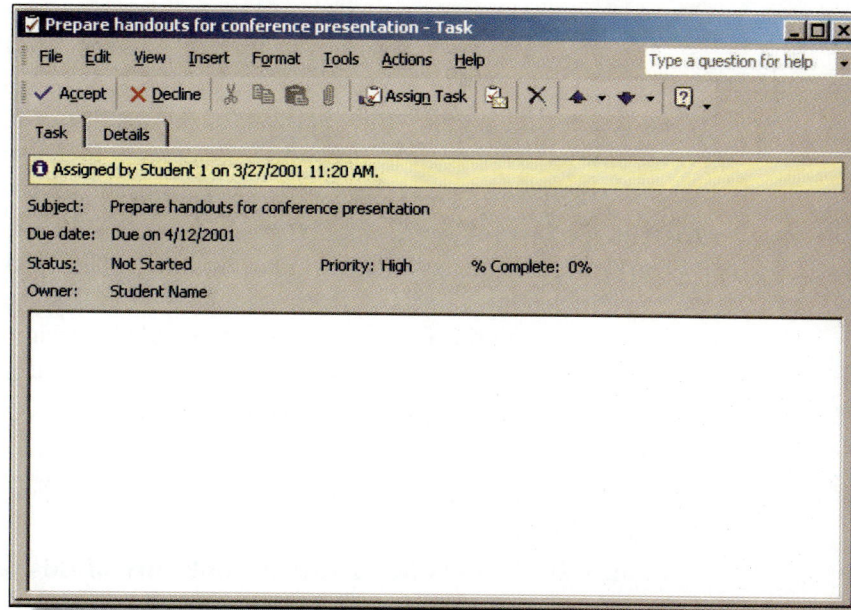

7. Make sure you are connected to the Internet, and click the **Send** button (or press Ctrl + Enter). The acceptance is sent to your partner, and the Inbox reappears. (If Outlook displays the next item in the message list, close the Message window to return to the Inbox.) The task request no longer appears in the Inbox. Because you have accepted the task, it has been moved to your task list.

8. Click the Tasks shortcut 📖 in the Outlook Bar to display the task list. The task you accepted (either "Locate equipment" or "Prepare handouts") appears in the task list. The other task request you received also appears in the task list, and it is shown in bold because you haven't opened it yet. Outlook places task requests in both your task list and your Inbox. You can open them in either location. Task requests appear in the task list whether or not you have accepted them. This is because you are the temporary owner of the task until you accept it, decline it, or assign it to someone else.

9. Open the task you accepted by double-clicking it. The banner indicates that you have accepted the task.

10. Click the **Details** tab. The task requester's name now appears in the **Update list** text box. Outlook notifies the requester of any changes you make to the task.

11. Close the Task form.

EXERCISE **5-8** **Decline or Delegate a Task Request**

When you decline a task, Outlook displays the Declining Task dialog box, which is the same as the Accepting Task dialog box except for the title. Delegating a task request to someone else is the same as assigning the task.

1. Open the "Arrange car rental" task if you are Student 1; open the "Make travel arrangements" task if you are Student 2. The Task form appears. You can decline a task by clicking either the <u>D</u>ecline button or the Assi<u>g</u>n Task button on the Task form toolbar. When you assign the task, you are delegating that task to someone else, usually a subordinate.

2. Click the <u>D</u>ecline button on the Task form toolbar. The Declining Task dialog box appears.

3. Select <u>E</u>dit the response before sending, and then click OK. Notice the change in the banner text.

4. In the text box, key **Cheryl already took care of this yesterday.**

5. Make sure you are connected to the Internet, and click the <u>S</u>end button. Your response declining the task is sent to your partner. (If Outlook displays the next item in your task list, close the Task window to return to the task list.) The task you declined no longer appears in your task list, because you have declined it. Your response appears as an item in the task requester's Inbox. After the requester opens it, that task in her task list is updated to show that you have declined it.

6. Log off the Internet if your instructor directs you to do so.

Viewing, Organizing, and Printing Tasks

You can change the look of the task list to reflect various levels of detail. If you have many types of tasks, expanding the Table view of the task list beyond the simple four-heading table can be helpful.

You can group tasks by using categories. Tasks can be assigned to pre-defined categories or you can create your own categories. After you've assigned tasks to categories, you can organize the task list by using those categories. You can also assign tasks to contacts.

There might be times when you'd like to see a printed copy of your tasks. As in other areas of Outlook, you can print either individual tasks or the entire task list.

EXERCISE **5-9** **Change the Tasks View**

You can add headings to the task list to show additional detail, such as Priority, % Completed, Status, and Date Completed. You can also arrange the view of the task list to show only tasks due in the next seven days.

1. Choose <u>V</u>iew, Preview Pa<u>n</u>e from the menu. The screen is split in two. The bottom half of the screen is the preview pane for the task list.

2. Select some tasks in the task list. Observe how the preview pane shows you details about a task.

FIGURE 5-10
Task list with
preview pane

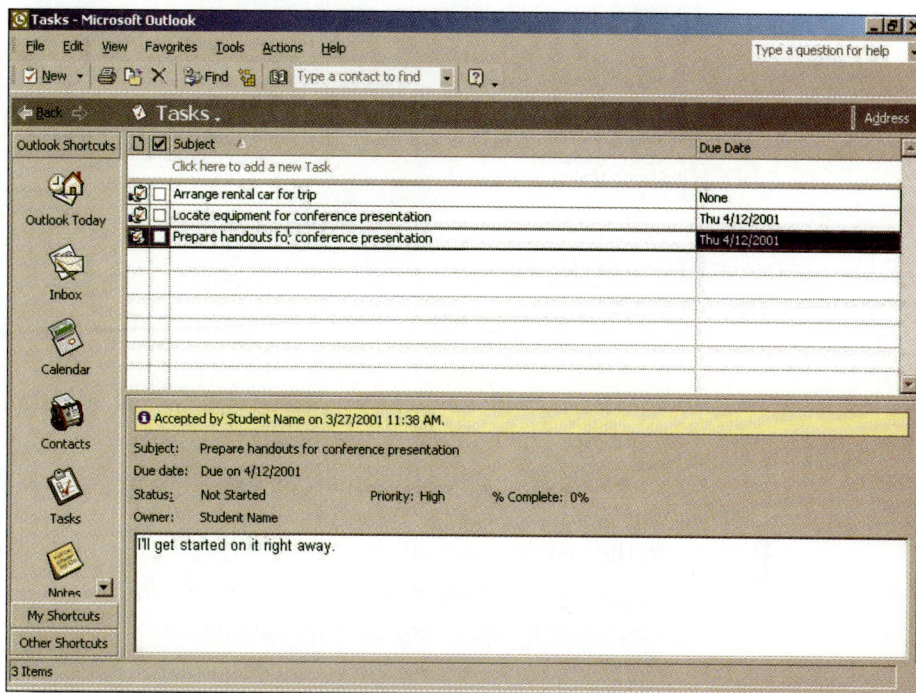

3. Choose <u>V</u>iew, Current <u>V</u>iew from the menu. A submenu appears. **Simple List** is the currently selected view. There are various ways to change the task view.

4. Select **Detailed List**. Outlook turns off the preview pane and displays the task list with five new fields in the Table view: Priority, Attachment, Status, % Complete, and Categories.

5. Choose <u>V</u>iew, Current <u>V</u>iew, and then choose **By Person Responsible**. The tasks are grouped by task owner. Notice that the number of tasks in each group appears after the group owner's name.

6. Click the plus sign for each group to see the individual tasks within the groups.

7. Use <u>V</u>iew, Current <u>V</u>iew to try out other available view options on the submenu. Then return the view to **Detailed List**. To control specific columns appearing in the Table view, you can create a customized view.

8. Choose <u>V</u>iew, Current <u>V</u>iew from the menu, and then choose <u>C</u>ustomize Current View from the submenu. The View Summary dialog box appears.

9. Click <u>F</u>ields. The Show Fields dialog box appears. You can use this dialog box to control the specific columns that appear in the Table view of the task list.

FIGURE 5-11
Show Fields
dialog box

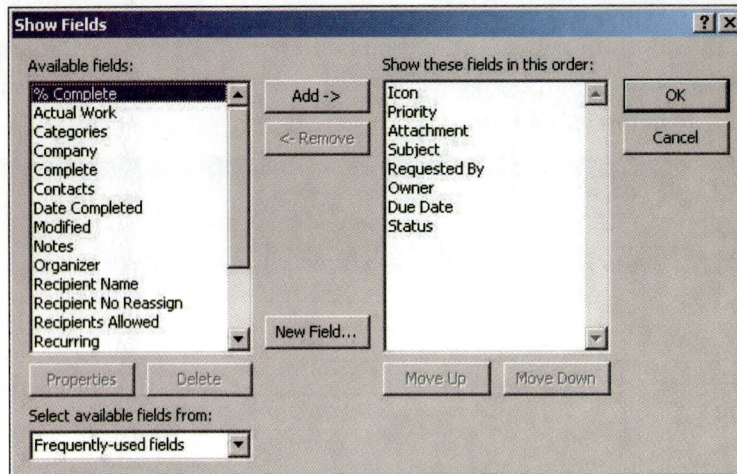

10. Under Sh<u>o</u>w these fields in this order, select **Attachment** and then click <u>R</u>emove. You will leave this field off of your task list.

11. Click **OK**. The View Summary dialog box reappears. Click **OK** again to return to the task list. The Attachment field is removed. You can add fields to the task list, as well.

12. Choose <u>V</u>iew, Current <u>V</u>iew, <u>C</u>ustomize Current View, and then click <u>F</u>ields. The Show Fields dialog box appears again.

13. Under A<u>v</u>ailable fields, select **Attachment**, and then click <u>A</u>dd. You can control the order of the fields in the task list by using Move <u>U</u>p and Move <u>D</u>own. The Attachment field is currently set to appear in the right-most column of the task list.

14. Click Move <u>U</u>p until **Attachment** appears just under **Priority**.

15. Click **OK**. The View Summary dialog box reappears. Click **OK** again to return to the task list. The Attachment field is restored to the task list.

16. Turn off the display of the preview pane.

NOTE: Make sure you have completed this exercise so that you return Outlook to its default setting. Outlook permanently saves any changes you make in the views. Always leave Outlook in its default state for the next class or student to use.

EXERCISE 5-10 Categorize and Organize Tasks

Every task can be assigned to a category. You can do this for both new and existing tasks.

1. Right-click the "Make travel arrangements" task if you are Student 1; right-click the "Arrange car rental" task if you are Student 2. The shortcut menu appears. When you display the shortcut menu for a selected task, the menu contains many of the buttons and options found on the Task form for that task.

FIGURE 5-12
Tasks shortcut menu

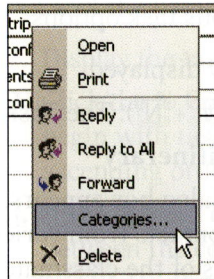

2. Choose **Categories** from the shortcut menu. The Categories dialog box appears.

3. Scroll down the **Available categories**, select **Phone Calls**, and then click **OK**. The task is assigned to the Phone Calls category.

4. Right-click the "Locate equipment" task if you are Student 1; right-click the "Prepare handouts" task if you are Student 2.

5. Choose **Categories** from the shortcut menu. The Categories dialog box appears again. Select **Status**, and click **OK**.

6. Open the "Prepare handout" task if you are Student 1; open the "Locate equipment" task if you are Student 2. The **Categories** option is not available in the Task form for a task if you are not the owner. You can, however, assign tasks you don't own to categories by using the shortcut menu.

7. Close the Task form for this task. Select the task again if it is not already selected, and right-click. Choose **Categories** from the shortcut menu and select **Phone Calls**. Click **OK**. Outlook displays an information box informing you that you are not the owner of this task and your changes might be overwritten by the owner. Click **OK**. The task is assigned to the Phone Calls category.

NOTE: A task can be assigned to more than one category.

8. Click the Organize button 🔲 on the Tasks toolbar. The Ways to Organize Tasks pane appears above the task list. As in other Outlook folders, this pane provides another way to access the functions on the shortcut menu or the **View**, **Current View** menu.

9. Click <u>Using Views</u>. Under **Change your view**, select **Simple List**. Outlook displays the task list in its default setting.

10. Close the Ways to Organize Tasks pane by clicking 🔲.

TIP: Another way to organize tasks is by sorting the fields in the table. Clicking a column heading sorts the task list, using the column to control sort order. For example, if you click the Date Due column heading, tasks are sorted by date due, in ascending order. Clicking the heading again re-sorts it in descending order. You can also sort tasks by using <u>V</u>iew, <u>C</u>urrent <u>V</u>iew, <u>C</u>ustomize Current View.

Concepts Review

Each of the following statements is either true or false. Indicate your choice by circling T or F.

T F *1.* When you schedule a meeting involving others, Outlook notifies the individuals you invite via e-mail.

T F *2.* Meeting attendees who are removed from a meeting receive e-mail notification informing them that they are no longer invited to the scheduled meeting.

T F *3.* The recipient of a task request does not need an e-mail address.

T F *4.* You can assign an existing task in your task list to someone if you are the owner of the task.

T F *5.* Any changes you make to a task of which you are not the owner might be overwritten by the task owner.

T F *6.* You must save any change you make to a note.

T F *7.* A note can remain open on the Windows desktop when other programs are minimized.

T F *8.* An office resource must have a mailbox in order to be reserved for a meeting in Outlook.

SHORT ANSWER QUESTIONS

Write the correct answer in the space provided.

1. Which menu commands open the Meeting form?

_____

2. When you invite people to a meeting, in which of their Outlook folders do their invitations appear?

_____

3. What button in the Meeting form would you use to reply to a meeting invitation that you cannot attend?

_____

4. What response options does the recipient of a task request have?

_____

5. When you receive a task request, in which Outlook folder(s) does it appear?

_____

6. Which <u>V</u>iew command enables you to see task details without actually opening the task?

_____

7. What command controls the fields displayed in the task list?

_____

8. What keystrokes open a selected note?

_____

CRITICAL THINKING

Answer these questions on a separate page. There are no right or wrong answers. Support your answers with examples from your own experience, if possible.

1. If you are a supervisor, the task assignment capabilities in Tasks can be an efficient way to assign tasks and keep track of when they get done. Can you think of situations when overuse of this feature might become counter-productive? What advice would you give to a supervisor about the best use of this component of Outlook?

2. The Notes component of Outlook is designed to replace the sticky paper notes that most of us use. What features would you use to make it best resemble your own work habits? List some examples of times when you'd use Outlook's Notes instead of paper notes.

Skills Review

EXERCISE 5-18

Add a contact to the contact list and schedule a meeting involving others.

1. Open the Contacts folder by clicking the Contacts shortcut 🗐 in the Outlook Bar.

2. Add your instructor's name and e-mail address to your contact list.

> **NOTE:** Your instructor will provide you with an appropriate e-mail address.

3. Open the Calendar folder by clicking the Calendar shortcut 🗐 in the Outlook Bar.

4. Plan a meeting by following these steps:

   a. Choose Actions, Plan a Meeting from the menu.

   b. Click the down arrow next to the Meeting start time text box for the date, and select a date roughly one week from the current date. Set the start time at 10 AM.

   c. Click Add Others, and select Add From Address Book.

   d. Click the down arrow next to the Show Names from the text box, and choose Contacts if it is not already displayed.

   e. Under Name, select your instructor's name, and then click Required.

   f. Click OK. (If you are asked to sign up for Microsoft Office Internet Free/Busy Service, click Cancel.)

   g. Click Make Meeting.

5. Complete the Meeting form and send the meeting notification by following these steps:

   a. In the Subject text box, key **Discuss new office furniture marketing plan**

   b. In the Location text box, key **Your office**

   c. Deselect Reminder.

   d. In the text area of the Meeting form, key **I'm following up on your request that we go over the marketing plan for the new line of office furniture.**

   e. Connect to the Internet and click the Send button on the Meeting form toolbar.

   f. Close the Plan a Meeting dialog box.

6. Display the Sent Items folder and print the message, using Memo Style as the print style. Add your name as a centered header and the date as a centered footer.

EXERCISE 5-19

Assign a new task to a contact and set the priority.

1. Display the Tasks folder by clicking the Tasks shortcut in the Outlook Bar.

2. Assign a new task by following these steps:

   a. Click the down arrow next to the New button and choose Task Request from the menu.

   b. Click To.

   c. If your instructor's name does not appear in the contact list, click New, select New Contact, click OK, and key your instructor's name and e-mail address as a new contact. Then click the Save and Close button on the Contact form.

> **NOTE:** Your instructor will provide you with an appropriate e-mail address.

     d. Under Name in the Select Task Recipient dialog box, select your instructor's name and click To.

     e. Click OK.

     f. Click the Subject text box and key **Review my assignment**

     g. Set the Due date for approximately one week from the current date and set the Priority as High.

     h. In the text area of the Task form, key **Please let me know if I have done everything correctly.**

     i. Connect to the Internet and click the Send button on the Task form toolbar.

3. Display the Sent Items folder and print the message. Use Memo Style as the print style, add your name as a centered header, and delete any existing footer information.

EXERCISE 5-20

Create a new task request, accept a task request, categorize tasks, change the Tasks view, and print the task list.

> **NOTE:** Your instructor will assign you a student partner for this exercise. You will be assigning different tasks to each other. You and your partner will be referred to as "Student 1" and "Student 2" in the steps that follow. Decide which of you is Student 1 and which is Student 2. You and your partner will key different information for the task requests.

1. Click the Contacts shortcut 🔲 in the Outlook Bar to display the Contacts folder.

2. Add your student partner's name and e-mail address to your contact list.

3. Display the Tasks folder, and delete any existing tasks.

4. Create a new task request. Assign the task to your student partner. If you are Student 1, key **Create marketing brochure for new office furniture** in the Subject text box; if you are Student 2, key **Write up schedule of activities for magazine crew** in the Subject text box.

5. Set the Due date for approximately one week from the current date, connect to the Internet, and send the message to your student partner.

6. Display the Sent Items folder and print the message you just sent. Use Memo Style as the print style and add your name as a centered header and the date as a centered footer.

NOTE: Your student partner will need to complete the above steps in this exercise before you can continue any further.

Send/Receive

7. Display the Inbox and click the Send/Re**c**eive button to receive the task assignment from your student partner.

8. Accept a task assignment by following these steps:

   a. If you are Student 1, open the "Write up schedule of activities for magazine crew" task assignment message; if you are Student 2, open the "Create marketing brochure for new office furniture" task assignment message.

   b. Click the A**c**cept button on the Task form toolbar.

   Accept

   c. Select **E**dit the Response Before Sending, and click OK.

   d. In the text box at the bottom of the form, key **I'll take care of it right away.**

   Send

   e. Connect to the Internet and click the **S**end button to send the message to your partner.

   NOTE: You will receive a message from your student partner, indicating his acceptance of the task assignment. You do not need to wait until you receive this response to complete this exercise.

9. Categorize tasks by following these steps:

   a. Display the task list if it is not already displayed.

   b. Select the "Create marketing brochure" task and the "Write up schedule of activities" task.

   c. Right-click one of the selected items and select Categor**i**es from the shortcut menu.

   d. Select Goals/Objectives and click OK.

10. Display the task list in detailed view by choosing **V**iew, Current **V**iew, Detailed List from the menu.

11. Print the task list in a Table Style print style, with your name as a centered header and the date as a centered footer.

12. Set the display of the task list to Simple List.

EXERCISE 5-21

Create notes, edit a note, categorize notes, and print notes.

1. Click the Notes shortcut in the Outlook Bar to display the Notes folder. Delete any existing notes.

2. Create a note by following these steps:

   a. Click the **N**ew button on the Standard toolbar.

   New

    b. For the text of the note, key **E-mail all store managers about the meeting time change**

    c. Click the note Close button ✖.

3. Create another new note, with the text **Call John**

4. Create another new note, with the text **Buy Dad a birthday gift**

5. Edit a note by following these steps:

    a. Select the "Call John" note.

    b. Press Ctrl + O .

    c. At the end of the existing text, key **and Robert**

    d. Click the note Close button ✖.

6. Categorize a note by following these steps:

    a. Right-click the "Buy Dad a birthday gift" note.

    b. Choose Categories from the shortcut menu.

    c. Select Personal, and then click OK.

7. Categorize the remaining two notes in the Business category.

8. Display the notes in Notes List view by choosing View, Current View, Notes List from the menu.

9. Print all three notes by choosing File, Print from the menu. Choose Table Style as the print style, and add your name as a centered header and the date as a centered footer.

10. Redisplay the notes in Icons view.

Lesson Applications

Plan a meeting, create new tasks and task assignments, organize the task list, and print it.

Rob Connelly, AllWood's president, has asked you to look into reducing the company's shipping costs. You've called a meeting with several key people in the company and assigned tasks to some people working with you on the project.

1. Display your Calendar folder and schedule a meeting. Plan the meeting for roughly one week from the current date from 1:00 p.m. to 2:00 p.m. Add your instructor as a required meeting attendee.

   NOTE: Your instructor will provide you with an appropriate e-mail address.

2. For the subject of the meeting, key **Discuss current freight charges** and make the location of the meeting **Your office**. Deselect the reminder option. Add the following text to the message: **Go over current freight charges from approved list of carriers.**

3. Connect to the Internet and send the message. Display the Sent Items folder and print the message you just sent, using a Memo Style print style. Add your name as a centered header and the date as a centered footer.

4. Display the Tasks folder and delete any existing tasks. Create a new task request. Send the task request to your instructor and make the subject of the task **Research alternative freight carriers**. Make the due date approximately one week from the current date. Add the following text to the message: **You asked me to remind you to do this.**

5. Create a second new task request to your instructor. Make the subject of the task **Suggest other team members**. Make the due date two business days from the current date and add the following text to the task: **I have already asked Joan to work with us. You need to assign other people to the project team.** Set % Complete to 25%.

6. Connect to the Internet and send the messages. Display the task list and print each task in a Memo Style print style. Add your name as a centered header and the date as a centered footer.

7. Create a new task with the subject **Call new team members**, and set % Complete to 50%.

8. Display the task list in Detailed List view, and sort the list by % Complete in ascending order. Print the task list in a Table Style print style, with your name as a centered header. Delete any existing footer information. Then redisplay the task list in Simple List view.

EXERCISE 5-23

Plan a meeting, create new tasks and task requests, organize the tasks, create and organize notes, and print notes.

Rob Connelly has asked you to work with Jasmine Jones on improving sales at the company's Web site. He's asked you to meet with the company's Web designers and salespeople to discuss which company products are the best for Web sales.

1. Display the Calendar folder and schedule a meeting. Plan the meeting for two weeks from the current date from 10:00 a.m. to 10:30 a.m. (Delete any existing appointments or meetings that might conflict with that time.) Add your instructor as a required meeting attendee. Add two classmates as optional meeting attendees.

NOTE: Your instructor will provide you with appropriate e-mail addresses.

2. For the subject of the meeting, key **Plan session with Web designers** and make the location of the meeting **My office**. Deselect the reminder. Add the following text to the message: **Discuss the changes we would like to see in the company Web site.**

3. Connect to the Internet and send the message. Close the Plan a Meeting form. Display the Sent Items folder and print the message you just sent, using a Memo Style print style. Add your name as a centered header and the date as a centered footer.

4. Display the Tasks folder and delete any existing tasks. Create a new task request. Send the task request to your instructor and make the subject of the task **Pricing for Web site items**. Make the due date two business days from the current date. Add the following text to the message: **I will send you the preliminary product list.** Set the Status: to In Progress, and set the Priority to High.

5. Create another new task request, sending it to your instructor. Make the subject of the task **Locate photographer for new Web site items**. Make the due date three business days from the current date and add the following text to the task: **Our usual photographer is away on assignment for the next three weeks**. Set % Complete to 25% and Priority to High.

6. Create a third new task request, sending the request to a classmate. Make the subject of the task **Analyze hit rates and page viewings of current Web site**. Make the due date one week from the current date and add the following text to the task: **Sean is preparing the numbers. He will send them directly to you.** Set the Status: to Waiting on someone else, and set the priority to Low.

7. Connect to the Internet and send the task request messages.

8. Display the task list in Detailed List view. Remove the Categories and Attachment fields and add the Notes field. Position the Notes field so that it is the right-most column. Adjust the column widths of the columns so that as much of the Notes field appears as possible. Sort the task list by Priority, with high-priority tasks first. Print the task list in landscape orientation with your name as a centered header. Delete any existing footer information.

9. Restore the Categories and Attachment fields to the Table view, and remove the Notes field. Make sure the Attachment field is positioned just before Subject, and Categories is positioned just after % Complete. Sort the table by Due Date, with the earliest dates first. Print the task list again, but use portrait orientation. Then display the task list in Simple List view.

10. Display the Notes folder and delete any existing notes. Create a new note with the following text: **Call Sean about Web site numbers**. Create a second note with the following text: **Call Personnel about 401K**. Create a third note with the following text: **Get stamps at Post Office**.

11. Display the Notes folder in Notes List view. Print the notes in a Table View print style with your name as a centered header. Delete any existing footer information. Then return the Notes folder to Icons view.

EXERCISE 5-24

Create a new task request, accept and decline task requests, and organize the task list; create, organize, and print notes.

Maria Lopez, AllWood's VP of Administration, has asked you to research customer satisfaction. She has suggested you contact various sales and marketing personnel to see if the company can create a method for tracking and cataloging customer feedback.

NOTE: Your instructor will assign you a student partner for this exercise. You will be assigning different tasks to each other. You and your partner will be referred to as "Student 1" and "Student 2" in the steps that follow. Decide which of you is Student 1 and which is Student 2. You and your partner will key different information for the task requests.

1. Add your student partner's name and e-mail address to your contact list.

2. Display the Tasks folder, and create a new task request. Assign the task to your student partner. If you are Student 1, key **Collect any customer complaint data** as the subject; if you are Student 2, key **Get returned merchandise records** as the subject. Set the due date for approximately one week from the current date, connect to the Internet, and send the message to your student partner.

3. Create a second task request, assigning it to your instructor, and make the subject of the task **Survey sales managers for customer comments**. Make the due date approximately three business days from the current date. Add the following text to the message: **I have done the Chicago and St. Louis stores. Can you do the rest?** Set the % Complete to 25% and the Priority to High.

4. Make sure you're connected to the Internet, and send the message to your instructor.

5. Display the Sent Items folder and print the messages you just sent, using Memo Style as the print style. Add your name as a centered header and the date as a centered footer.

> **NOTE:** Your student partner will need to complete the above steps in this exercise before you can continue any further.

6. Display the Inbox and open the task request you've received from your student partner. Accept the task, editing the response before sending. Add the text **I will contact Systems to see what data they may have. I already have gotten some information from John.** Set the % Completed to 25% and the Priority to High. Assign the task to the Goals/Objectives category, and link the task with your student partner as a contact.

7. Send the acceptance message. Display the Sent Items folder and print the messages you just sent, using Memo Style as the print style. Add your name as a centered header and the date as a centered footer.

8. Display the Notes folder and delete any existing notes. Create a new note with the following text: **Call John to see if he has any new data.** Create a second note with the following text: **Make doctor appointment.** Create a third note with the following text: **Fax status report to Maria.** Create a fourth note with the following text: **Get car serviced.**

9. Categorize the "Make doctor appointment" and "Get car serviced" notes as Personal. Categorize the remaining two notes you created in the previous step as Business.

10. Display the notes in Notes List view. Print the notes in a Table View print style, with your name as a centered header. Delete any existing footer information. Then return the notes display to Icons view.

EXERCISE 5-25 ➕ *Challenge Yourself*

Create a new signature, create contacts and a distribution list, schedule a meeting, compose and send a message, create new task requests and notes, and organize and print task list and notes.

In preparation for the rollout of the new line of office furniture, John Yu, AllWood's VP of Marketing, has asked you to help with the advertising campaign. You will be organizing meetings, tasks, and various other activities.

1. Create a listing in your contact list for an office resource. Identify the office resource as Conference Room 1. Create additional listings for two classmates and your instructor.

> **NOTE:** Your instructor will provide you with appropriate e-mail addresses.

2. Assign the contacts for your instructor and the classmates you created in step 1 to the Goals/Objectives category, and link these three contacts with each other.

3. Create a distribution list titled **Advertising**, with the contacts you created in step 1 as members of the list (do not include the resource). Assign the distribution list to the Goals/Objectives category.

4. Display your Inbox folder and create a signature. Use your initials as the name of the new signature, and key the following text for the signature:

   [your name]
   AllWood Mills Sales & Marketing Intern

5. Apply the new signature to new messages.

6. Create a new e-mail message, addressing the message to your instructor from your contact list. Key the subject of the message as **Advertising Team**. For the text of the message, key the material shown in Figure 5-19, using a Plain Text message format.

FIGURE 5-19

```
This is just to let you know that I will be working with John and
his team on the new advertising campaign. I will be sending you meeting
notifications shortly for our first Team Meeting.
```

7. Set the message importance to High, and set a flag to For Your Information with no due date. Manually spell-check the message. Send the message and then remove the signature.

8. Display the Calendar folder and schedule a meeting. Plan the meeting for two weeks from the current date from 8:30 a.m. to 9:30 a.m. (Delete any existing appointments or meetings that conflict with this time.) Add your instructor as a required meeting attendee. Add two classmates as optional meeting attendees. Use Conference Room 1 as the required resource.

9. For the subject of the meeting, key **First Ad Campaign Team Meeting**. Deselect the reminder option. Add the following text to the message: **Let's begin planning our ad campaign for the new office line.** Link the meet-

ing with your two classmates from your contact list. Send the message and close the Plan a Meeting form.

10. Display the Tasks folder and delete any existing tasks. Create a new task request. Send the task request to your instructor and make the subject of the task **Get data on past ad campaigns**. Make the due date two business days from the current date. Add the following text to the message: **I thought it would be good to review this.** Set the Status: to In Progress and the Priority to High.

11. Create a second new task request to your instructor. Make the subject of the task **Assign final team members**. Make the due date the next business day after the current date, and add the following text to the task: **You asked me to remind you. We already have nearly all we need.** Set % Complete to 75% and Priority to High.

12. Create a third new task request, sending the request to a classmate. Make the subject of the task **Contact our account rep at the ad agency**. Make the due date one week from the current date and add the following text to the task: **Let them know we are gearing up for a new campaign.** Set the Priority to Low. Link the task with your other classmate.

13. Display the task list in Detailed List view. Remove the Categories field and add the Contacts and Notes fields. Adjust column widths so that the Notes field shows as much as possible. Print the task list in landscape orientation, using the Table Style print style. Add your name as a centered header and delete any existing footer information. Then restore the fields to their default settings and set the view to Simple List view.

14. Display the Sent Items folder and select the "Advertising Team" message you sent in step 6. Print the message, using Memo Style as the print style. Add your name as a centered header and delete any existing footer information.

15. In the Sent Items folder, select the "First Ad Campaign Team Meeting" message you created in step 9. Print the message, using a Memo Style as the print style and your name as a centered header.

16. Display the contact list in Detailed Address Card view. Select the additions you've made in this exercise (the two individuals, your instructor, the distribution list, and the resource). Print the selected contacts, using a Card Style print style and adding your name as a centered header. Eliminate any existing footer information and the blank forms page at the end. (*Hint*: Use the Blank forms at end option on the Format tab of the Page Setup dialog box.). Display the contact list in Address Cards view.

17. Display the Notes folder and create a new note with the following text: **Call John to see if he has the new account information.** Categorize the note as Business. Print the note in a Memo Style print style with your name as a centered header. Delete any existing footer information.

On Your Own

In these exercises you work on your own, as you would in a real-life work environment. Use the skills you've learned to accomplish the task—and be creative.

EXERCISE 5-26

Plan a meeting with several of your classmates to explore interesting Outlook options. Assign as tasks to each team member a different component of Outlook to explore. Make notes of possible topics to discuss in the meeting. Print the sent messages, the task list, and the notes.

EXERCISE 5-27

Plan a meeting with several classmates to discuss a class picnic or similar outing. Assign each the task of researching a different aspect of the outing, such as food, location, and activities. Make notes of ideas you might have. Print the sent messages, the task list, and the notes.

EXERCISE 5-28

Team up with several classmates to search the Web for consumer items such as books, music, tools, or electronics at the best prices. Plan a meeting to decide the topics. Assign each team member a different content area. Make notes. Print the sent messages, the task list, and the notes.

Unit 2 Applications

UNIT APPLICATION 2-1

Create a new signature, create a contact, schedule a meeting, use message options for a new message, create a new task request, and print the task list

AllWood Mills has recently switched advertising agencies. Rob Connelly, AllWood's president, has asked you to work with the new agency's account executive, Brian Smith. You'll assist him in getting familiar with AllWood's products and personnel. You will also be organizing meetings and assigning tasks as part of your duties.

1. Create a new listing in your contact list, using the information shown in Figure U2-1. For the e-mail address, you will use your instructor's e-mail address.

FIGURE U2-1

```
Brian Smith, Account Executive

Jones, Underwood Media Inc.

711 Third Avenue, Suite 2300

New York, NY 10033

(212) 555-1200

E-mail: instructor@ISP.isp
```

NOTE: Your instructor will supply you with an appropriate e-mail address. If you've previously entered a different contact using your instructor's e-mail address, Outlook might display the Duplicate Contact Detected dialog box. If this dialog box appears, select Add this as a new contact anyway and click OK.

2. Assign the contact you created in step 1 to the Goals/Objectives category.

3. Display your Inbox folder and create a signature. Use your initials as the name of the new signature, and key the following text for the signature:

   [your name]
   AllWood Mills Sales Intern

4. Apply the new signature to new messages.

5. Create a new e-mail message, addressing the message to Brian Smith from your contact list. Key the subject of the message as **AllWood products and**

personnel. Key an appropriate salutation, and then key the material shown in Figure U2-2 for the text of the message. Use a Plain Text message format.

FIGURE U2-2

This is to let you know that I will be working as your liaison at AllWood while you are getting familiar with our firm. John Yu will be sending me some tasks that he would like you to complete before our next meeting. Please contact me if you have any questions.

6. Set the message importance to High, and set a For Your Information flag with no due date. Manually spell-check the message and then send the message.

7. Display the Calendar folder and schedule a meeting. Plan the meeting for one week from the current date, from 9:30 a.m. to 10:30 a.m. Add Brian Smith as a required meeting attendee.

8. For the subject of the meeting, key **New Ad Agency Meeting**. Deselect the reminder option. Add the following text to the message: **This is to introduce Brian Smith to AllWood management.** Specify the location as **Rob's office**. Send the message and close the Plan a Meeting dialog box.

9. Display the Tasks folder and delete any existing tasks. Create a new task request. Send the task request to Brian Smith and make the subject of the task **Develop plan for AllWood advertising**. Make the due date two business days from the current date. Add the following text to the message: **We will need this for your presentation to Rob next week.** Set the Status: to In Progress and the Priority to High. Send the task request.

10. Create a new task. Make the subject of the task **Notify remaining managers of meeting**. Make the due date the next business day from the current date. Set % Complete to 75% and the Priority to High. Deselect the reminder.

11. Create another new task. Make the subject of the task **Follow up task request to Brian with a phone call**. Make the due date the next business day. Set the Priority to Low. Link the task with Brian Smith. Deselect the reminder.

12. Display the task list in Detailed List view. Sort the list by % Complete in ascending order (0% complete at the beginning). Remove the Categories field and add the Contacts and Notes fields. Adjust column widths so that as much of the Notes field displays as possible. Print the task list in landscape orientation, using the Table Style print style. Add your name as a centered header. Add the date as a centered footer.

13. Restore the Detailed List view to its default setting by removing the Contacts and Notes fields from the Detailed List view and adding Categories. Restore the task list to Simple List view. Delete the signature you created in step 3.

NOTE: Make sure you have completed this step so that you return Outlook to its default setting. Outlook permanently saves any changes you make in the views and saves any signatures you create until they are removed. Always leave Outlook in its default state for the next class or student to use.

14. Display the Sent Items folder and select the "AllWood products and personnel" message you sent in step 6. Print the message, using Memo Style as the print style and your name as a centered header. Delete any existing footer information.

15. In the Sent Items folder, select the "New Ad Agency Meeting" message you created in step 8. Print the message, using a Memo Style as the print style and your name as a centered header.

16. Display the contact list in Detailed Address Card view. Select Brian Smith. Print the selected contact, using a Card Style print style and your name as a centered header. Delete any existing footer information and eliminate the blank-forms page at the end. (*Hint*: Use the <u>B</u>lank forms at end option on the Format tab of the Page Setup dialog box.) Restore the contact list to Address Cards view.

UNIT APPLICATION 2-2

Create new contact list items, create a distribution list, schedule appointments with a reminder, schedule a meeting, create tasks and a new task request, create a note, and print the Calendar, task list, note, contact, and message.

Jasmine Jones, AllWood's VP of Sales, has asked you to help organize the annual meeting for all the AllWood store managers. You will need to create a distribution list, organize meetings, and assign various tasks.

1. Create entries in your contact list for your instructor and two classmates. Assign them to the VIP category and link them with each other. Create a distribution list called **Sales** and include all three new contact items in the list. Assign it to the VIP category.

NOTE: Your instructor will provide you with an appropriate e-mail address and a list of addresses for your classmates.

2. Add a company name of **AllWood Mills, Inc.** for each of the contacts you created in step 1, with job titles as follows: Your instructor, **VP of Sales**; your classmates, **AllWood Sales Intern**.

3. Display a date in the Calendar approximately one month from the current date on any day except Monday. Delete any existing appointments or events for that date and the rest of that week. Schedule an appointment on that day, keying the subject as **Annual Sales Meeting**. Specify the location as

Dubuque and the duration of the appointment from 9 a.m. to 5 p.m. Set a 1-day reminder for the event and show the time as Out of Office.

4. On the same date as the sales meeting, schedule an appointment titled **Dinner with store managers**, starting at 6 p.m. and ending at 8 p.m., with the location as **TBA**. Deselect the reminder.

5. Display the date one business day before the sales meeting. Plan a meeting from 10:00 a.m. to 11:00 a.m. with your instructor as a required meeting attendee and your two classmates as optional attendees. Specify the subject of the meeting as **Prepare for sales meeting** and the meeting location as **My office**. Deselect the reminder and send the message.

6. Display the task list and delete any existing tasks. Create a new task titled **Put together list of possible restaurants**. Make the due date approximately one week from the current date. Set the % Complete to 25%. Deselect the reminder. Create a second task titled **Locate suitable hotel for meeting**. Make the due date two days from the current date, deselect the reminder, and set the % Complete to 50%. Create a third task titled **Write up tentative meeting agenda for Jasmine's review**. Make the due date five days from the current date, deselect the reminder, and set the % Complete to 75%.

7. Send a new task request to your instructor with the subject **Supply names of restaurants I should research** and a due date for the next business day. Send the message.

8. Display the Notes folder and create a new note with the following text: **Call Jasmine's office**. Categorize the note as Business. Print the note with your name as a centered header. Delete any existing footer information.

9. Display the task list in Detailed List view and sort the list by % Complete in descending order (largest to smallest). Print the task list in Table Style, in landscape orientation, and with your name as a centered header. Delete any existing footer information. Display the task list in Simple List view.

10. Display the Sent Items folder, locate the "Prepare for sales meeting" message invitation you sent in step 5, and print the message in Memo Style with your name as a centered header. Delete any existing footer information.

11. Display the date for the "Annual Sales Meeting" appointment, which is approximately one month from the current date and which you added to the Appointments Calendar in step 3. Display the Calendar in Work Week view, and print the Calendar in a Weekly Style print style with your name as a centered header and the date as a centered footer. Include the TaskPad in the printout. Redisplay the Appointments Calendar in Day view.

12. Display the contact list in Detailed Address Card view. Select the names and the distribution list you added in step 1 (your instructor, your two classmates, and the Sales distribution list). Print the selected contacts, using a Card Style print style and your name as a centered header. Delete any

existing footer information and eliminate the blank-forms page at the end. Display the contact list in Address Cards view.

UNIT APPLICATION 2-3

Create and categorize a contact, create a signature, send messages with various message options, schedule an event, schedule a meeting, create a new task request with a file attachment, create a note, and print the note, task list, Calendar, and message.

AllWood's VP of Design, Will McCarthy, has begun pricing the new line of office furniture. Will has asked you to work with his assistant in the project, Pamela Houston. Will also would like to see comparative data for competing office furniture and has suggested you attend a trade show next week.

1. Create a new listing in your contact list, using the information shown in Figure U2-3. For the e-mail address, you will use your instructor's e-mail address. Assign the contact to the VIP category.

FIGURE U2-3

```
Ms. Pamela Houston

Design Associate

AllWood Mills, Inc.

3100 Jackson Street

Dubuque, IA 52004

(319) 555-4002

E-mail: instructor@ISP.isp
```

NOTE: Your instructor will provide you with an appropriate e-mail address.

2. Display your Inbox folder and create a signature. Use your initials as the name of the new signature and key the following text for the signature:
   [your name]
   AllWood Mills Intern
   Ext. 4002

3. Apply the new signature to new messages.

4. Create a new e-mail message, addressing the message to Pamela Houston. Key the subject of the message as **Pricing information**. Set the message format to Plain Text. Open the Word file **Price1** and copy and paste the pricing information for the mission furniture to the text area of the message.

5. Set the message importance to High, the sensitivity level to Confidential, and set a flag to For Your Information with no due date. Send the message.

6. Display the date in your Appointments Calendar approximately one week from the current date. Delete any existing appointments or meetings. Schedule an event for that date with the subject **National Furniture Association Meeting** and a location of **Chicago**. Deselect the reminder.

7. Plan a meeting for that same date from 3:00 p.m. to 4:00 p.m. with Pamela Houston as a required meeting attendee. Make the subject **Caucus on trade show research** and the location **TBA**. Deselect the reminder. Set the importance to High. Send the message.

8. Create a new task request, assigning it to Pamela Houston from your contact list. Key the subject of the task as **Review proposed pricing**. Attach the Word file **Price1**. (*Hint:* Use the button on the Task form toolbar to attach the file.) Send the task-request message.

9. Display the Notes folder and create a new note with the text **Make Chicago hotel reservations.** Assign it to the Business category and link it to Pamela Houston. Print the note, using your name as a centered header.

10. Display your contact list and print the Pamela Houston contact in a Memo Style print style with your name as a centered header. Delete any existing footer information.

11. Display the Sent Items folder, locate the "Pricing information" message you sent in step 5, and print it in a Memo Style print style with your name as a centered header. Delete any existing footer information.

12. Display the date in your Appointments Calendar when you scheduled the "National Furniture Association Meeting" event in step 7 (approximately one week from the current date). Print the Calendar for that day in a Daily Style print style with your name as a centered header and the date as a centered footer.

13. Display the task list and print the "Review proposed pricing" task in a Memo Style print style with a header that includes your name on the left and the date on the right. Delete any existing footer information.

14. Remove the signature you created in step 2.

NOTE: Make sure you have completed the last step so that you return Outlook to its default setting. Outlook permanently saves any signature you create until it is removed. Always leave Outlook in its default state for the next class or student to use.

Imagine that you've just won the lottery. Plan an elaborate European vacation for yourself and three friends to celebrate. You'll be paying for all expenses yourself, but you'll want to be mindful of your costs. Although you're paying for your friends, you'll want to give them an idea of what everything is going to cost in case they would like to bring along a partner or spouse as well.

Plan your itinerary so that it includes at least three European cities. Make it at least a seven-day trip. Use the Internet to research airfares, hotel costs, meals, and other incidental expenses. For each city, select sights and points of interest and create a daily schedule of activities. Develop an alternate plan for inclement weather. Research the local currency and current exchange rates and include those currencies in your daily budget.

After you've obtained your information, use Outlook for the following activities:

- Add your instructor and your three traveling companions to your contact list. Create a distribution list with all four names. Create a signature for yourself that adequately describes your new-found financial status, such as "*[your name]*, Retired Food Service Employee." Print the new entries in your contact list in a Card Style print style.

NOTE: Your instructor will provide you with an appropriate e-mail address.

- Compose and send an e-mail message inviting your friends to join you in celebrating your good fortune, using the distribution list to address the message. Using the distribution list, send a second e-mail message describing the itinerary and the expenses associated with the trip. In both messages, use various message options. After you've sent the messages, locate them in the Sent Items folder and print them.

- Pick a date in your Calendar to schedule a pre-trip meeting. Make your traveling companions required meeting attendees and your instructor an optional attendee. Set a reminder for the day before. Delete any other appointments or events for the meeting day and print the Calendar for that day, using a Daily Style print style. Locate the meeting-invitation message in the Sent Items folder and print that out as well.

- Schedule the trip in your Calendar, filling in various time blocks as appointments. You do not have to account for an entire day, but show major activities. Display the Calendar in the most appropriate view to show the trip, and delete any other appointments or events that occur during that time period. Print the Calendar to show the trip.

- Create required tasks for each of your traveling companions. These might be such activities as getting a passport, buying traveling clothes, packing luggage, and so on. Assign a due date, a priority, and a reminder for each task, and include whatever task notes you think are appropriate. Create several tasks for yourself, as well. Display the task list and delete any existing tasks. Display the task list in Detailed List view, and include the Notes field. Print the task list in Table Style print style.

- Hand in all printouts to your instructor.

Advanced Topics

Customizing Outlook

After completing this lesson, you will be able to:

1. **Change the look of e-mail.**
2. **Modify the Master Category List.**
3. **Customize the Calendar.**
4. **Customize notes and tasks.**
5. **Use mail templates.**

Estimated Time: 1½ hours

After you've become familiar with Outlook's various components, you can customize it to conform to the way you work. Outlook enables you to change the format of messages and create mail templates. You can create your own categories to assign your tasks, messages, or Calendar appointments. And you can customize the Calendar, tasks, and notes.

Changing the Look of E-Mail

You can customize e-mail by changing message formats. Outlook supports three message formats: HTML, Microsoft Outlook Rich Text, and Plain Text. You can specify one format as the default and use other formats for individual messages.

There are many times when you will want to use formatting. If you know that the recipient also uses Outlook, you might want to use formatting to enhance the readability of your messages. Documents you create in Word are more attractive when formatting is applied. The same holds true with e-mail messages. You always want your work to look its best, even when you are composing an e-mail message.

EXERCISE 6-1 Use Alternate Message Formats

Each of Outlook's three message formats has different characteristics:

- HTML: Includes text formatting, numbering, bullets, alignment, horizontal lines, backgrounds, HTML styles, and Web pages. This is Outlook's default text format.
- Microsoft Outlook Rich Text (often abbreviated as "RTF," for "Rich Text Format"): Includes text formatting, bullets, and alignment.
- Plain Text: Has no text formatting. If you send most of your messages over the Internet, Plain Text might be the most appropriate. Otherwise, you might add formatting that recipients can't see.

1. Display the Inbox folder if it is not already displayed.

2. Click the **New** button [New]. The Message form appears. The default message format is HTML, which lets you apply the most extensive message formatting.

3. In the To text box, key *[recipient's name]@[ISP]*

   NOTE: You will be using an e-mail address of a classmate to send your e-mail message. Your instructor will assign you a student partner and provide you with an appropriate e-mail address.

4. In the Subject text box, key **New advertising campaign**

5. Place the insertion point in the text area of the Message form.

6. If the Formatting toolbar is displayed on one row, click the Toolbar Options button [»] and choose Show Buttons on Two Rows from the drop-down menu.

FIGURE 6-1
Formatting toolbars in Message form

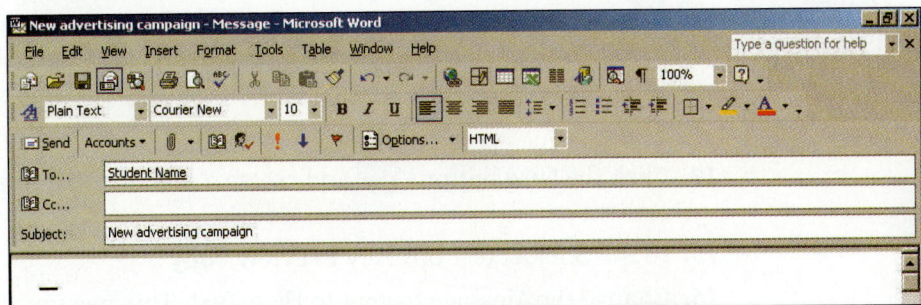

7. Change the message format to **Plain Text**. Text formatting is not available in Plain Text, so the formatting buttons on the two toolbars are shaded.

8. Change the message format to **HTML**. The formatting buttons are available again.

9. Make sure the font in the **Font** text box is Arial. (If it is not, click the down arrow next to the **Font** text box on the Formatting toolbar, and choose **Arial** from the drop-down menu.)

10. Key the text shown in Figure 6-2.

FIGURE 6-2

I was notified today by our advertising agency that their new campaign is
to begin in the coming months. The theme is "Traditional Style Follows
Contemporary Function." The focus is on AllWood's new line of office
furniture. Here's the list of magazines:

Traditional Homes – Holiday edition

New England Living – Winter, 2001

Fine Homes – January, 2002

Better Homes & Style – February, 2002

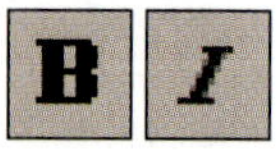

11. Change the campaign title, which is now in quotes, to italic by selecting the text and clicking the Italic button **I** on the Formatting toolbar. Remove the quotation marks. Make the magazine names bold by selecting the text and clicking the Bold button **B** on the Formatting toolbar.

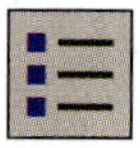

12. Format the last four lines as bulleted text by selecting the four lines and clicking the Bullets button on the Formatting toolbar.

13. Spell-check the message, connect to the Internet, and send the message.

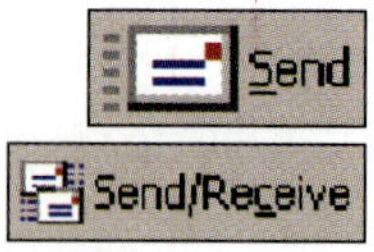

REVIEW: Clicking the Send button on the Message form toolbar immediately sends your message to the specified recipient when you connect to the Internet. If you are not connected, the message is sent to your Outbox. You must then click the Send/Receive button on the Standard toolbar to send your Outbox messages.

14. Click the **New** button and create a second e-mail message to your student partner.

15. In the **Subject** text box, key **Preview copy**

16. Change the Message format to **Rich Text**. This message format is similar to HTML but without HTML styles and Web pages.

17. Key the following text for the message: **I have received an advance copy of Traditional Homes magazine if you'd like to see the ad copy.**

18. Change the font style of the magazine title to italic. Spell-check the message, ignoring the grammatical suggestions. Make sure you are connected to the Internet and send the message.

19. Click the Send/Re<u>c</u>eive button on the Standard toolbar to retrieve messages sent to you.

20. Log off the Internet if your instructor tells you to do so.

> **NOTE:** By default, Outlook converts messages formatted in Rich Text to HTML for sent messages. To force Outlook to send messages formatted in Rich Text in that format, you must change the default setting. You do this by choosing <u>T</u>ools, <u>O</u>ptions from the menu, clicking the Mail Format tab, and then clicking I<u>n</u>ternet Format. You must change the setting under the Outlook Rich Text options to Send using Outlook Rich Text format.

EXERCISE 6-2 Save Messages as Text, Rich Text, and HTML Files

You can save messages in different file formats, depending on the message format of the message. This can be useful when you want to use a message in another program. For example, you might want to use the content of an Outlook message in a Word document. HTML and Rich Text Format are general-purpose formats that you can use in many other programs.

1. Display the Inbox if it is not already displayed, and open the "New advertising campaign" message you received from your student partner. All the formatting features appear in the message.

2. Choose <u>F</u>ile, Save <u>A</u>s from the menu. The Save As dialog box appears. Because this message is in HTML format, the default file type in the **Save as type** text box is **HTML**.

3. Click the down arrow next to the **Save as type** text box. The drop-down menu shows the other available file formats. (See Figure 6-3 on the next page.)

4. Select **Text Only (*.txt)**. You can save a message in a file format that is different from the message format.

> **NOTE:** Your instructor will tell you which file format to use if Text Only does not appear as one of the file-format options.

5. If your instructor tells you to do so, specify a location for your Lesson 6 files in the **Save** i<u>n</u> text box. For the File <u>n</u>ame, key *[your initials]***6-2a** and click <u>S</u>ave. Outlook saves the message as a text file. If the message is opened in Word, the text will appear without formatting.

FIGURE 6-3
Available file types
for saving messages
in HTML message
format

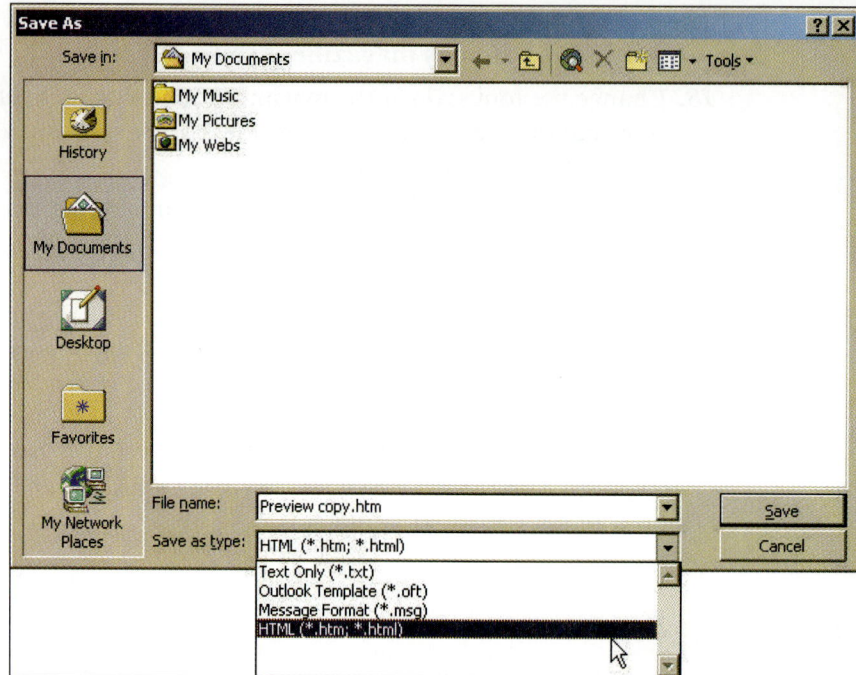

FIGURE 6-3
Available file types
for saving messages
in HTML message
format

6. Close the Message form.

7. To see the saved message in Word, click the **New** button [New], and choose **File**, **Open** from the Message form menu. The Open dialog box appears.

8. If the file type displayed in the **Files of type** box is not Text Files, click the down arrow next to **Files of type** and choose **Text Files (*.txt)** from the drop-down list.

9. Select *[your initials]*6-2a.txt and click **Open**. The "New advertising campaign" message appears. Notice that the magazine titles are no longer in bold and the font is Courier New. Outlook also has added the message header information at the beginning of the document.

10. Print the message by pressing Ctrl + P and clicking **OK**. Close the message and the blank Message form.

11. Open the "New advertising campaign" message again.

12. Choose **File**, **Save As** from the menu. The Save As dialog box appears. The **Save as type** is HTML because this message is in HTML message format.

13. Key the File **name** as *[your initials]*6-2b and click **Save**. The file is saved as an HTML file.

14. Close the Message form.

15. To see the saved message in Word in HTML format, click the **New** button [New], and choose **File**, **Open** from the menu. The Open dialog box appears.

16. Change the Files of type to Web Pages and Web Archives (*.htm; *.html; *.mht; *.mhtml).

17. Select *[your initials]***6-2b.htm** and click Open. The "New advertising campaign" message appears in the Message form. All the formatting features have been saved. As in the text file, Outlook has added the message header information to the beginning of the document.

18. Print the message. Close the message without saving any changes, and then close the blank Message form.

Modifying the Master Category List

When you assign categories to Outlook items such as tasks and appointments, you select from the *Master Category List*, which is the Outlook-supplied set of keywords for grouping, filtering, finding, or sorting items. You've used categories to organize items in various Outlook components, such as your tasks and notes. The categories in the Master Category list you've already used include Business, Phone Calls, VIP, and Personal. Outlook enables you to create your own categories that you can add to the Master Category List.

NOTE: Do not begin this objective unless you can complete Exercise 6-5. You will be changing the Outlook default setting in Exercise 6-3, and you restore Outlook to its default setting in Exercise 6-5. Always leave Outlook in its default state for the next class or student to use.

EXERCISE | **6-3** | **Add a New Category to the Master Category List**

The advantage of creating your own categories is that this lets you organize your tasks, appointments, and messages in ways that are most meaningful to you. For example, you might be assigned to a special project that lasts for a period of several months. You could create a category in your Master Category List that relates specifically to that project. You could then assign all relevant Outlook activities to that category as the project progresses.

1. Display the Inbox folder.

2. Choose Edit, Categories from the menu. The Categories dialog box appears.

3. Click Master Category List. The Master Category List dialog box appears. (See Figure 6-4 on the next page.)

4. In the New category text box, key **Advertising** and then click Add. The new category is added to the category list.

FIGURE 6-4
Master Category List
dialog box

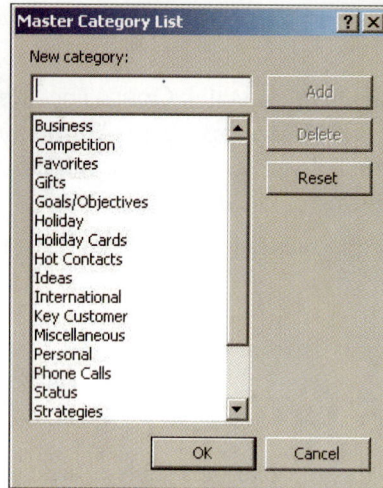

5. Click OK. The Categories dialog box reappears. Notice that Advertising is now listed under Available categories. You can also create a new category for selected items by simply keying the category name in the text box under Item(s) belong to these categories.

6. Click OK. The Inbox reappears.

EXERCISE **6-4** **Assign Messages to Categories**

You can assign messages to categories just as you can with contacts, tasks, and notes. When you have many messages in your Inbox, assigning them to categories is a good way to keep them organized.

1. With the Inbox folder displayed, select the "Preview copy" and "New advertising campaign" messages.

2. Right-click the selected messages. The shortcut menu appears.

3. Choose Categories from the shortcut menu. The Categories dialog box appears.

> **TIP:** If you had not already created the Advertising category, you could key it in the Item(s) belong to these categories text box in the Categories dialog box. Outlook would then automatically add it to the Master Category List.

4. Select Advertising and then click OK. The two messages are assigned to the Advertising category.

5. Open the "Preview copy" message. The description of this message in the title bar indicates it is in HTML format, even though it was sent in Rich Text format. By default, Outlook converts Rich Text messages to HTML format.

6. Choose View, Options from the menu. The Message Options dialog box appears. Notice in the Categories text box that this message is assigned to the Advertising category. You can use this command button to assign a message to additional categories, if necessary. You can also use this dialog box to categorize a message when you are creating the message. (See Figure 6-5 on the next page.)

FIGURE 6-5
Message Options
dialog box

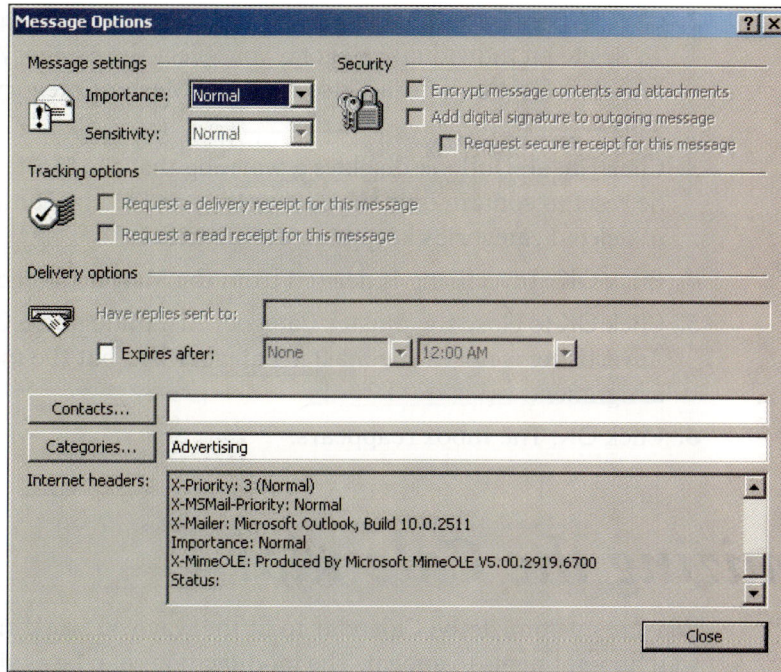

7. Close the Message Options dialog box.

8. Choose File, Page Setup, Memo Style from the menu. The Page Setup dialog box appears. To print messages formatted in HTML, you must set headers and footers in the Page Setup dialog box.

9. Key your name in the Header text box, and then click OK.

10. Choose File, Print from the menu. The Print dialog box for HTML messages is different from the Print dialog box for other Outlook items. Notice that you cannot access the Page Setup box from this dialog box, and Print Preview is not available.

11. Click Print. The message prints.

12. Close the message.

EXERCISE 6-5 Reset the Master Category List

You can delete any category in the Master Category List. You can also restore the Master Category List to its default state, removing any custom categories that have been created.

1. With the "Preview copy" message selected, choose Edit, Categories from the menu. The Categories dialog box appears.

15. Click **OK** twice to redisplay the Calendar. The font size of the Appointment Calendar is increased, the time scale is now in 15-minute intervals, and the boldface has been removed from the Date Navigator. You can also use the shortcut menu to change the time scale of the Appointments Calendar.

> **TIP:** You can change the font size of the Date Navigator by choosing <u>T</u>ools, <u>O</u>ptions from the menu, clicking the Other tab, and then clicking Advanced Options.

FIGURE 6-7
Calendar with new background color, font size, and time scale

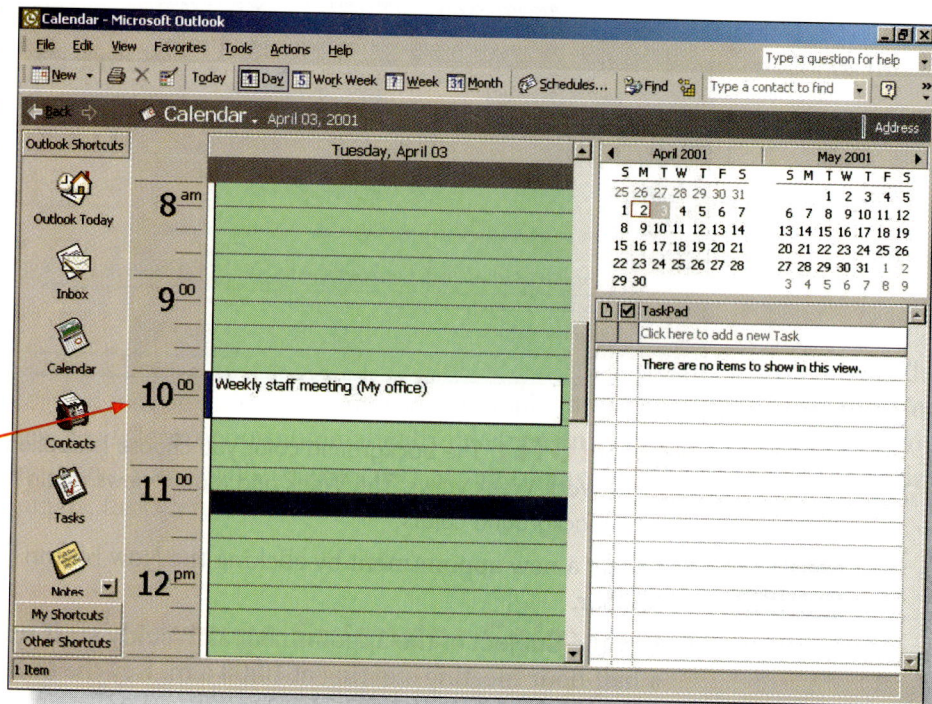

Right-click to change time scale.

16. Right-click any time along the left border of the Appointments Calendar and choose **30 Minutes** from the shortcut menu. The time scale is restored to 30-minute intervals.

17. Restore the default color of the Calendar background by choosing <u>T</u>ools, <u>O</u>ptions from the menu, clicking the **Preferences** tab, and then clicking <u>C</u>alendar Options. Change <u>B</u>ackground color to the first color on the drop-down palette (yellow). Click **OK** to return to the Options dialog box, and then click **OK** again to display the Calendar.

18. To restore the font size to its default setting, choose <u>V</u>iew, Current <u>V</u>iew, <u>C</u>ustomize Current View from the menu and click <u>O</u>ther Settings. Under Day, click <u>F</u>ont, change the <u>S</u>ize to 8, and then click OK. Under General settings, select <u>B</u>olded dates in Date Navigator represent days containing items.

19. Click **OK** twice to redisplay the Calendar.

NOTE: Make sure you have completed the last four steps of this exercise. These steps restore Outlook to its default settings. Always leave Outlook in its default state for the next class or student to use.

EXERCISE 6-7   Apply Conditional Formats to Appointments in the Calendar

You can have Outlook change the formatting of your Calendar items based on certain conditions, such as the subject of the appointment or who is in attendance.

1. With the Calendar folder still displayed, select a date roughly two weeks from the current date. Delete any existing items for that date.

2. Create a new appointment for that date by clicking the New button 🔲 on the Standard toolbar.

3. Key the Subject of the appointment as **Advertising discussion** and make it a half-hour meeting starting at 10:00 a.m. Click the down arrow next to the Location text box, and choose **My office** from the drop-down list. Deselect the reminder.

4. Click the Save and Close button on the Appointment form toolbar. Outlook adds the appointment to your Calendar.

5. To change the formatting of Calendar items based on certain conditions, choose View, Current View, Customize Current View from the menu. The View Summary dialog box appears.

6. Click Automatic Formatting. The Automatic Formatting dialog box appears. You'll use this dialog box to create a rule that controls how items in this view (the Calendar folder) are displayed. The area under Rules for this view is currently empty because there are no rules in effect now.

FIGURE 6-8
Automatic
Formatting
dialog box

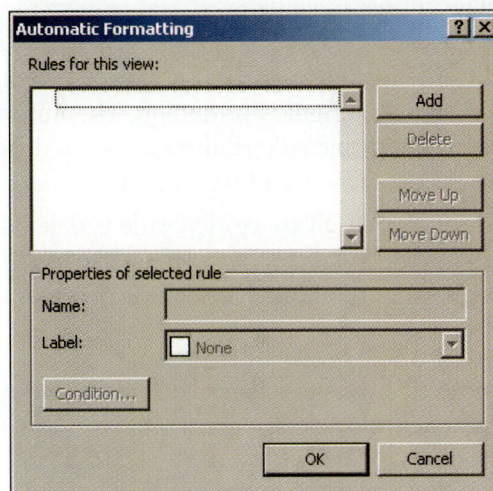

7. Click Add. A new rule called "Untitled" appears under Rules for this view.

8. Key **Topic** in the Name text box to name the rule for this view.

9. Click Condition. The Filter dialog box appears. You'll use this dialog box to specify when the formatting is to be applied to your Calendar items.

10. In the Search for the word(s) text box, key **Advertising**.

Click the down arrow in the <u>I</u>n text box and select **subject and notes fields.** This tells Outlook to apply the rule to items in which the word "Advertising" is found in either the subject or notes field of a Calendar item.

11. Click OK. The condition now has been defined and the Automatic Formatting dialog box reappears. Next you'll set the formatting you want applied when the condition has been met.

12. Click the down arrow next to the <u>L</u>abel text box, and select **Must Attend.** This label will apply the orange color to any item in your Calendar that meets the condition. Note that you can choose any label you wish.

13. Click OK twice. The Calendar folder reappears. The appointment you created in step 3 shows the new color because it meets the condition for applying the formatting.

14. Create a new appointment for 12:00–1:00 p.m. on that same day with a Subject of **Team Lunch** and a <u>L</u>ocation of **TBA.** Deselect the reminder and then save and close the appointment. Notice that its formatting is the default white because it does not meet the conditional formatting requirements. You can also manually format Calendar items.

15. Select the 4:30 p.m. time period in the Appointments Calendar, key **Get haircut**, and press Enter. The new appointment appears in the Calendar.

16. With the "Get haircut" appointment selected, click the Calendar Coloring button 📅 on the Standard toolbar. (If the Calendar Coloring button is not displayed on the Standard toolbar, click the Toolbar Options button ⏷ to access it.) Choose Personal from the Calendar Coloring drop-down menu. The "Get haircut" appointment is now green. (See Figure 6-9 on the next page.)

TIP: Conditional formatting also can be applied to other Outlook folders. For example, in the Inbox, you can apply various formats to messages based on a message subject, its sender, its importance, and so on.

17. To remove conditional formatting, choose <u>V</u>iew, Current <u>V</u>iew, <u>C</u>ustomize Current View and click <u>A</u>utomatic Formatting. The Automatic Formatting dialog box appears. The Topic rule is already selected. Note that you can deselect a rule to turn it off without deleting it.

18. Click <u>D</u>elete and then click OK twice. The rule is deleted, and the conditional formatting for the "Advertising discussion" appointment has been removed. The formatting remains in effect for the "Get haircut" appointment because it was applied manually.

NOTE: Make sure you have completed the last two steps of this exercise. These steps restore Outlook to its default settings. Always leave Outlook in its default state for the next class or student to use.

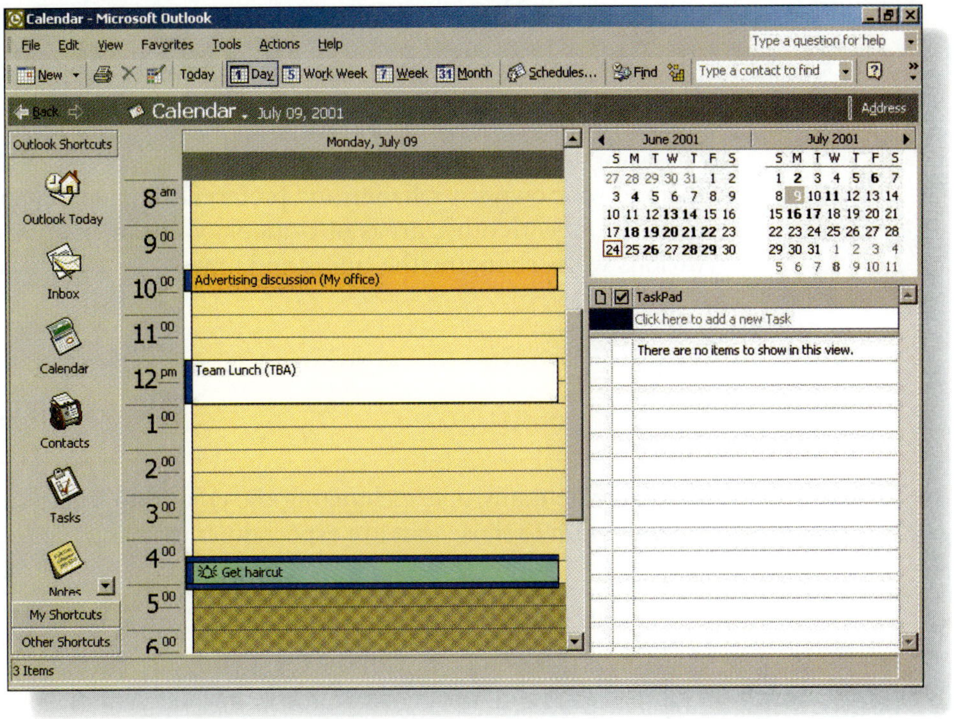

FIGURE 6-9
Calendar items with
conditional and
manual formatting
in effect

EXERCISE 6-8 Assign Categories to Appointments

You can assign categories to appointments just as you do for tasks and contacts. When you have many appointments, categories can help keep you organized.

1. Make sure the date in the Appointments Calendar with the "Advertising discussion" and the "Team Lunch" appointments is displayed.

2. Select both appointments. (Press Ctrl to select both items.)

3. Right-click one of the selected items and choose **Categories** from the short-cut menu. The Categories dialog box appears. Note that you can create your own categories for Calendar items just as you did for Inbox items.

4. Select **Business** and click **OK**. The two appointments are assigned to the Business category. You can see the categories assigned to the appointment by opening the appointment or by printing it in a Memo Style print format.

5. Open the "Advertising discussion" appointment. The **Categories** text box shows that the appointment is assigned to the Business category. You can click **Categories** to assign new categories.

6. Close the Appointment form without saving, and print the "Advertising discussion" appointment in a Memo Style print style with your name as a centered header. Delete any existing footer information.

Customizing Notes and Tasks

Notes are useful for jotting down reminders, ideas, questions, or any other thoughts you want to keep track of for a short time. Notes work best when you can adapt them to your own work habits and preferences. This is also true of tasks in your task list. As with other areas of Outlook, you can customize notes and tasks in various ways, changing the colors and fonts.

EXERCISE 6-9 Change the Color and Font of Notes

If you create many notes, changing the color and font of individual notes helps call attention to those that are especially important.

1. Display the Notes folder and delete any existing notes. Create a note with the text **Call plumber**

2. Create a second note with the text **Complete forms for 401K changes**

3. Make sure the notes are displayed as large icons in the Icons view. (If they are not, choose <u>V</u>iew, Current <u>V</u>iew, Icons from the menu, and then click the La<u>r</u>ge Icons button.)

4. Right-click the "Call plumber" note.

5. Choose <u>C</u>olor from the shortcut menu and choose <u>B</u>lue. The "Call plumber" note changes to blue. You can also change the default color of all new notes you create.

6. Choose <u>T</u>ools, <u>O</u>ptions from the menu. The Options dialog box appears. Make sure the Preferences tab is displayed.

7. Click <u>N</u>ote Options. The Note Options dialog box appears.

8. Click the arrow next to Co<u>l</u>or and choose Pink. Click the down arrow next to Si<u>z</u>e text box and choose Large.

9. Click <u>F</u>ont, change the <u>S</u>ize to 12 points, and click OK. Click OK to close the Note Options dialog box, and click OK again to close the Options dialog box.

10. Open the "Call plumber" note. The existing notes retain the same color but are given the new font size.

11. Create a new note with the text **Order new floppy disks**. The new note reflects both the changed color and the new font. (See Figure 6-10 on the next page.)

12. Close the note.

FIGURE 6-10
New note with changed color and font

13. Change the setting for notes back to its default by choosing Tools, Options, clicking the Preferences tab, and clicking Note Options. Set the Color to Yellow and the Size to Medium. Click Font and change the Size to 10 points. Click OK until the Notes folder is redisplayed. The appearance of new notes is restored to the default settings. The existing notes return to the default font size, but the color changes remain in effect.

NOTE: Make sure you have completed the last step of this exercise. This step restores Outlook to its default settings. Always leave Outlook in its default state for the next class or student to use.

EXERCISE 6-10 Change the Color of Tasks

Customizing tasks is helpful when your task list is long and complicated. For example, if your task list contains dozens of items, you might find it useful to differentiate certain tasks. Overdue tasks can be given one color and completed tasks a different color.

1. Display the Tasks folder and delete any existing tasks. Make sure the task list is displayed in Simple List view. (If it is not, choose View, Current View, Simple List from the menu.)

2. Click the box under the Subject column heading titled "Click here to add a new Task," key **Finish weekly status report**, and press Enter. A new task is added to the task list.

3. Add another new task to the task list, with the subject **Research new shipping costs**

4. Add a third new task to the task list, with the subject **Get updated price list of Shaker collection**

5. To change the color of tasks in the task list, choose Tools, Options. With the Preferences tab displayed, click Task Options. The Task Options dialog box appears. (See Figure 6-11 on the next page.)

FIGURE 6-11
Task Options
dialog box

6. Click the down arrow for <u>C</u>ompleted task color and select green. Click OK to close the Task Options dialog box, and click **OK** again to close the Options dialog box.

7. Mark the "Finish weekly status report" task as completed, and then select a different task in the task list. The completed task appears in green. You can change the font of tasks in the task list as well.

FIGURE 6-12
Task list with
changed color for
completed tasks

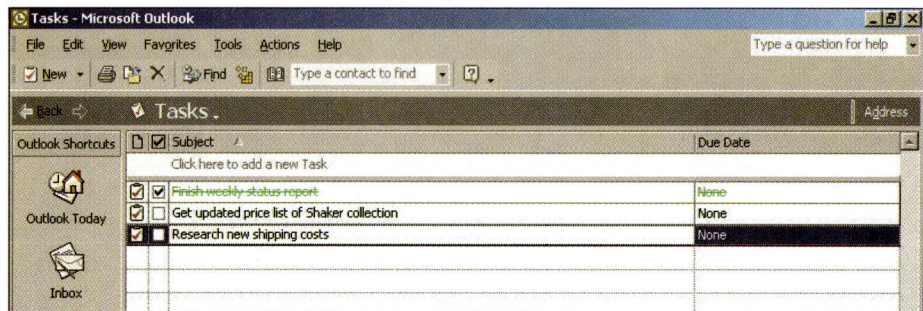

8. Choose <u>V</u>iew, Current <u>V</u>iew, <u>C</u>ustomize Current View from the menu and click <u>O</u>ther Settings. The Other Settings dialog box appears. Observe the various aspects of the task list that can be changed in this dialog box. For example, under **Rows**, you can click <u>F</u>ont to set the font size of the tasks.

9. Click Cancel to close the Other Settings dialog box without making any changes. The View Summary dialog box reappears.

10. Click <u>A</u>utomatic Formatting. The Automatic Formatting dialog box appears. You can use this dialog box to control the fonts of specific types of task list items. For example, you might wish to have completed tasks appear in bold or italic or in a different color.

11. Select **Completed and Read tasks** and click <u>F</u>ont. The Font dialog box appears. Note the various font options available.

12. Close the Font dialog box, and close the remaining dialog boxes without making any changes.

13. To restore the color of your task list to its default setting, choose Tools, Options from the menu, and make sure the Preferences tab is displayed. Click Task Options. Click the down arrow next to Completed task color and select the gray just above the red from the drop-down palette. Click OK to close the Task Options dialog box, and click OK again to close the Options dialog box. The default settings for the task list are restored.

> **NOTE:** Make sure you have completed the last step of this exercise. This step restores Outlook to its default settings. Always leave Outlook in its default state for the next class or student to use.

Using Mail Templates

Outlook enables you to create templates for e-mail messages. This can be a great time-saver when you send regular e-mail messages with large portions of text that don't change. Rather than creating text from scratch every time you compose the message, you can create and save a template. When you want to use the template, all you have to do is add the variable portions of the message.

EXERCISE 6-11 Create a Mail Template

You create a template for an e-mail message just as you create any other e-mail message. However, rather than sending the message, you save it in a special Outlook template file format.

1. Display the Inbox.

2. Choose Tools, Options from the menu and click the Mail Format tab.

3. Deselect the option Use Microsoft Word to edit e-mail messages. Outlook must be the editor for messages when you create a mail template.

4. Click Apply and then click OK.

5. Choose File, New, Mail Message from the menu (or click the New button 🔲New. The Message form appears.

6. In the Subject text box, key **Weekly Status Report**

7. In the text area of the Message window, key the text shown in Figure 6-13. Space the text appropriately in the text area so you can add items under the headings.

FIGURE 6-13

Below is a summary of my activities for this past week.
Activities are divided into the departments to which I have been
assigned for project work.

Marketing

Manager   Project Description

Administration

Manager   Project Description

Sales

Manager   Project Description

8. Choose <u>F</u>ile, Save <u>A</u>s from the menu. The Save As dialog box appears.

9. Click the down arrow next to the **Save as type** text box, and select **Outlook Template (*.oft)**. Notice that Outlook assigns the filename extension to templates of .oft.

10. If your instructor tells you to do so, specify the location for your Lesson 6 files in the **Save <u>i</u>n** text box. In the **File <u>n</u>ame** text box, key *[your initials]***6-11** and click <u>S</u>ave. The message is saved as a template.

11. Close the Message form without saving.

> ⭐ **TIP:** You can create templates for other Outlook items such as tasks, Calendar, and notes by using the <u>F</u>ile, Save <u>A</u>s command. For example, if you regularly send meeting requests to people, you can create a template for the meeting request in the Meeting form.

12. To restore Word as the message editor, choose <u>T</u>ools, <u>O</u>ptions from the menu, and click the **Mail Format** tab.

13. Select the option **Use Microsoft <u>W</u>ord to edit e-mail messages**. Click <u>A</u>pply and click OK. Word is restored as the editor for messages.

> ↗ **NOTE:** Make sure you have completed the last two steps of this exercise. These steps restore Outlook to its default settings. Always leave Outlook in its default state for the next class or student to use.

EXERCISE **6-12** **Use a Mail Template to Compose a Message**

1. Make sure the Inbox is displayed.

> **NOTE:** You must be in the specific component of Outlook to use a template created in that component.

2. Choose Tools, Forms, Choose Form from the menu. The Choose Form dialog box appears.

3. Click the down arrow next to the Look In text box, and select User Templates in File System or the location for your Lesson 6 files.

4. Select the template file *[your initials]*6-11 and click Open. The template appears in the Message form. You can use it as the basis for a new e-mail message, altering or adding to the existing text. After you make additions and specify the recipients in the To text box, you would click the Send button as you would with any new message. The original template file remains unchanged so you can use it again.

FIGURE 6-14
Message form
template

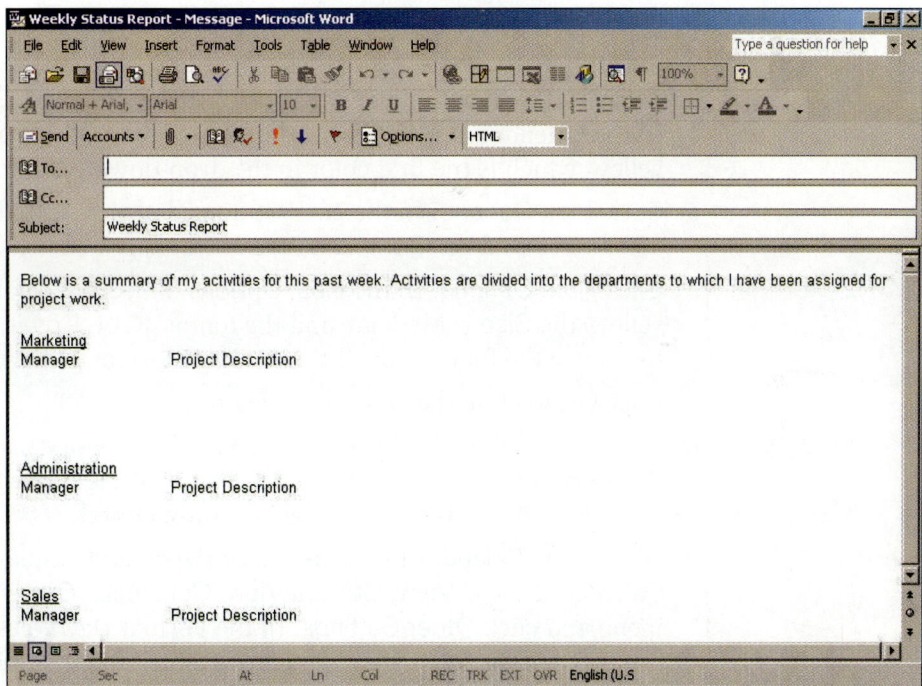

5. Place the insertion point in the text area and choose View, Header and Footer from the menu. Key your name as the header, and click Close on the Header and Footer toolbar.

6. Press Ctrl + P to display the Print dialog box and then click OK. Outlook prints the template. Close the Message form without saving or sending the message.

TIP: If you decide you want to edit a template, change the default message editor to the Outlook editor as you did in Exercise 6-11. Open the template, make the desired changes, and then choose File, Save As from the menu to save the modified template. Be sure to change the default message editor back to Word.

EXERCISE 6-13 Check System Defaults

It is always a good idea to make sure you've returned all aspects of Outlook to its default settings.

1. To check the default mail format settings, choose Tools, Options from the menu and click the Mail Format tab. Make sure the text box for Compose in this message format is set for HTML.

2. Select the option for Use Microsoft Word to edit e-mail messages if this option is not already selected.

3. Click the Preferences tab.

4. To check the default Calendar background color, click Calendar Options. In the Calendar Options dialog box, make sure Background color is set for yellow, which is the first color in the drop-down palette. Click OK.

5. Click Task Options. In the Task Options dialog box, make sure Overdue task color is red and the Completed task color is gray. Click OK.

6. Click Note Options. In the Note Options dialog box, make sure the Color is yellow, the Size is Medium, and the font is 10 pt. Comic Sans MS. Click Font to change the font setting if the font is incorrect. Otherwise, click OK.

7. Click OK to close the Options dialog box.

8. To check the default setting for the Master Category List, choose Edit, Categories from the menu, and then click Master Category List. Click Reset and click OK until all the dialog boxes are closed.

9. Display the Calendar folder. To check the default display format for the Calendar, choose View, Current View, Customize Current View from the menu and click Other Settings. In the Format Day/Week/Month View dialog box, under Day, make sure the Font is 8 pt. Tahoma and the Time scale is 30 minutes. Under General settings, make sure the option to have Date Navigator use bold for days with items is selected. Click OK.

10. Click Automatic Formatting. In the Automatic Formatting dialog box, delete any rules that might be in effect for this view and then click OK.

11. Click OK to close the View Summary dialog box.

USING HELP

Outlook enables you to apply formatting to mail messages as well as to Calendar items. You can use this feature to change the color of messages from specific individuals.

Use Microsoft Outlook Help to learn how to apply formatting to Inbox items:

1. Click the Microsoft Outlook Help button ? (or press F1). Make sure the Answer Wizard tab is displayed.

2. In the What would you like to do? text box, key **Automatically format Inbox messages**. Click Search. A list of related topics appears under Select topic to display:

3. Select Change how items are highlighted. Read the information on the right side of the screen to learn how to format messages from specific individuals.

FIGURE 6-15
Help screen on how to format Inbox messages

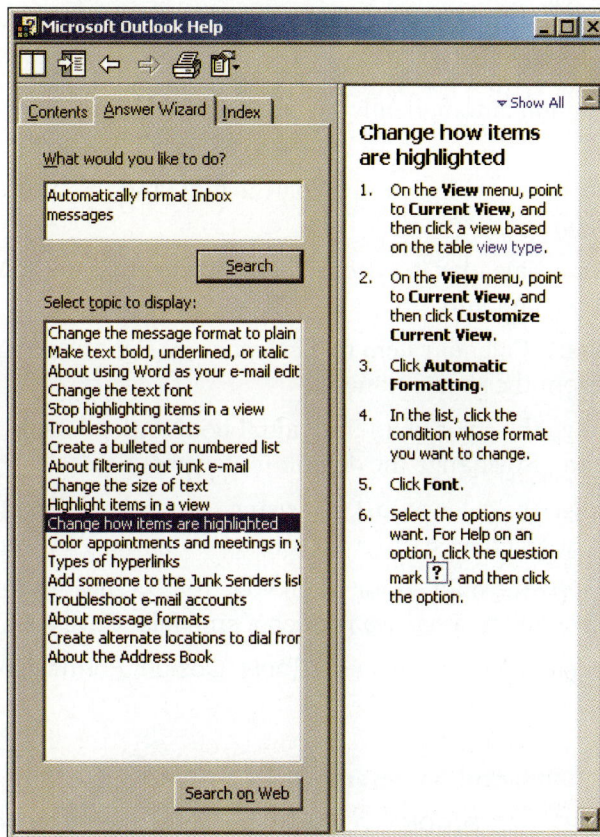

4. Click the Close button X when you have finished.

LESSON 6 Summary

➤ You can format messages in one of three different message formats: HTML, Microsoft Outlook Rich Text, and Plain Text.

➤ In the Message form, the formatting buttons are available when either HTML or Rich Text is selected as the message format.

➤ You can save messages in different file formats. You save a file in a file format different from the message format by choosing File, Save As.

➤ You can add new categories to the Master Category List.

➤ You add new categories to the Master Category List by choosing Edit, Categories from the menu.

➤ You can assign messages to categories by right-clicking the message and choosing Categories from the shortcut menu.

➤ You can delete a category from the Master Category List or restore it to its default state.

➤ A rule is an action automatically taken on an item in a folder under certain conditions.

➤ You can change the background color, the font, and the time scale of the Appointments Calendar.

➤ You can format Calendar items based on certain conditions. You can also format Calendar items manually.

➤ You can assign a Calendar item to a category by right-clicking it and choosing Categories from the shortcut menu.

➤ You can change the color of an individual note or the default color of all new notes. You can also change the default font size of notes.

➤ You can change the color of tasks by using the Options dialog box. You can give items in the Tasks folder a different font by using the View Summary dialog box.

➤ Outlook must be the mail editor when you create a message template. After you compose the template, you save it by choosing File, Save As.

➤ You can use a template by choosing Tools, Design, Forms, Choose Form from the menu.

LESSON 6 Command Summary

FEATURE	BUTTON	MENU	KEYBOARD	SPEECH
Color Appointments	🖼️	Edit, Label		✓

Concepts Review

TRUE/FALSE QUESTIONS

Each of the following statements is either true or false. Indicate your choice by circling **T** or **F**.

T F   **1.** You can change the color of a new or existing note.

T F   **2.** You create a template for an e-mail message in the same way you create any other e-mail message.

T F   **3.** You can change an e-mail template.

T F   **4.** Assigning messages and appointments to categories is the same as assigning tasks and contacts to categories.

T F   **5.** You can delete new categories added to the Master Category List.

T F   **6.** The bolding of dates in the Date Navigator can be turned on and off.

T F   **7.** You can customize your Calendar so that the color of an appointment changes based on the words in the subject field.

T F   **8.** You can change the color of tasks in your task list, but not the font.

SHORT ANSWER QUESTIONS

Write the correct answer in the space provided.

1. What menu command do you use to save a message as a template?

_____

2. What is the filename extension of an Outlook Template file?

_____

3. Which message format includes text formatting, bullets, and alignment but not Web pages?

_____

4. What command do you use to open a message template?

_____

5. What do you call an action automatically taken on an item in a folder under certain conditions?

_____

6. What dialog box enables you to create conditional formatting for Calendar items?

_____

7. What command on the Notes shortcut menu do you use to change the color of an individual note?

_____

8. What dialog box enables you to change the color of a task?

_____

CRITICAL THINKING

Answer these questions on a separate page. There are no right or wrong answers. Support your answers with examples from your own experience, if possible.

1. Outlook lets you change the color of your Inbox and Calendar items based on conditional formatting. When might you find this feature useful? What kind of conditions might you define to apply the formatting? Be specific.

2. Templates can be useful time-saving devices when you must frequently send e-mail messages with a lot of similar text. Describe some instances when you might find an e-mail message template useful.

Skills Review

EXERCISE 6-14

Send a message by using an alternate message format.

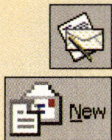

1. Open the Inbox by clicking the Inbox shortcut 📧 in the Outlook Bar.

2. Start a new message by clicking the <u>N</u>ew button 📋New on the Standard toolbar.

3. In the To text box, key *[recipient's name]@[ISP]*

> **NOTE:** Your instructor will provide you with an appropriate e-mail address.

4. In the Subject text box, key **Conference topics**

5. Change the Message format to Rich Text by clicking the down arrow next to the Message format box and choosing Rich Text.

6. Key an appropriate salutation in the message area, and then key the text shown in Figure 6-16 for the body of the message.

FIGURE 6-16

> I've begun working on the presentation we'll be giving next month at the
> National Furniture Manufacturers Conference. We are tentatively titling it
> "New Collection Rollout." Topics include:
>
> Sales and Marketing Preparation
>
> In-Store Displays
>
> Shipping Considerations
>
> Using Existing Collections

7. Change the conference title, which is now in quotes, to italic by selecting the text and clicking the Italic button *I* on the Formatting toolbar. Remove the quotes.

8. Format the last four lines as bulleted text by selecting the text and clicking the Bullets button on the Formatting toolbar.

9. Connect to the Internet and send the message.

10. Display the Sent Items folder and print the message, using Memo Style as the print style. Add your name as a centered header and delete any existing footer information.

EXERCISE 6-15

Add a new category to the Master Category List, assign a message to the category, and print an HTML message.

NOTE: This exercise uses the e-mail message you received in Exercise 6-1. If you do not have this message in your Inbox, complete Exercise 6-1, addressing the message to yourself.

1. Display the Inbox folder.

2. Add a new category to the Master Category List by following these steps:
   a. Choose Edit, Categories from the menu.
   b. Click Master Category List.
   c. In the New category text box, key **Magazine** and click Add.
   d. Click OK twice.

3. Locate the "Preview copy" message in the Inbox.

4. Delete a category and assign a message to a new category by following these steps:
   a. Right-click the "Preview copy" message.

   b. Choose Categories from the shortcut menu.

   c. Under Available categories, deselect Advertising if it is selected.

   d. Select Magazine.

   e. Click OK.

5. Print a message in HTML format by following these steps:

   a. Open the "Preview copy" message.

   b. Choose File, Page Setup, Memo Style from the menu.

   c. Add your name as a centered header.

   d. Click OK.

   e. Choose File, Print from the menu, and click Print.

   f. Close the message.

6. Delete a category from the Master Category List by following these steps:

   a. Choose Edit, Categories from the menu.

   b. Click Master Category List.

   c. Select Magazine and click Delete.

   d. Click OK twice.

NOTE: Make sure you have completed the last step of this exercise. This step restores Outlook to its default settings. Always leave Outlook in its default state for the next class or student to use.

EXERCISE 6-16

Assign an appointment to a category and customize a note.

1. Display the Calendar folder.

2. Display a date roughly two weeks from the current date, and delete any existing appointments in the Appointments Calendar.

3. Create a new appointment for that date by clicking the New button on the Standard toolbar.

4. Key the Subject of the appointment as **Get car inspected**, and make it a half-hour meeting starting at 12:30 p.m. Key the Location as **Dealer**. Deselect the reminder.

5. Click the Save and Close button on the Appointment form toolbar.

6. Assign the appointment to a category by following these steps:

   a. Make sure the date containing the appointment you created in step 3 is displayed.

   b. Right-click the appointment and choose Categories from the shortcut menu.

   c. Select Personal and click OK.

7. With the "Get car inspected" appointment selected, choose <u>F</u>ile, <u>P</u>rint from the menu, and print the appointment in a Memo Style print style. Add your name as a centered header and delete any existing footer information.

8. Click the Notes shortcut in the Outlook Bar to display the Notes folder.

9. Change the font size of a new note by following these steps:

   a. Choose <u>T</u>ools, <u>O</u>ptions from the menu.
   b. Click <u>N</u>ote Options.
   c. Click <u>F</u>ont.
   d. Under <u>S</u>ize, change the font size to 16 points, and then click OK three times.

10. Create a new note with the text **Get car inspected!** Close the note.

11. Select the note, choose <u>F</u>ile, <u>P</u>rint from the menu, and print the note in a Memo Style print style. Add your name as a centered header.

12. Restore the font size for new notes to the default setting by following these steps:

   a. Choose <u>T</u>ools, <u>O</u>ptions from the menu and click <u>N</u>ote Options.
   b. Click <u>F</u>ont.
   c. Under <u>S</u>ize, change the font size to 10 points.
   d. Click OK three times until the Calendar reappears.

   NOTE: Make sure you have completed the last step of this exercise. This step restores Outlook to its default settings. Always leave Outlook in its default state for the next class or student to use.

EXERCISE 6-17

Create and use a mail message template.

1. Display the Inbox folder if it is not already displayed.

2. Change the default message editor by following these steps:

   a. Choose <u>T</u>ools, <u>O</u>ptions from the menu and click the Mail Format tab.
   b. Deselect the option Use Microsoft <u>W</u>ord to edit e-mail messages.
   c. Click <u>A</u>pply and then click OK.

3. Click the <u>N</u>ew button.

4. In the Subject text box, key **Monthly Shipping Charges**

5. In the text area of the Message window, key the text shown in Figure 6-17 on the next page. Space the text appropriately in the text area so information can be added under the headings.

FIGURE 6-17

Below is a summary of shipping charges for our Chicago and St. Louis stores
for this month, showing number of items, weight, and total freight costs.

Chicago

Number of Items   Weight   Total Freight Costs

St. Louis

Number of Items   Weight   Total Freight Costs

6. Create a mail message template by following these steps:
   a. Choose File, Save As from the menu.
   b. Click the down arrow next to the Save as type text box and select Outlook
      Template (*.oft).
   c. In the File name text box, key *[your initials]*6-17 and click Save.
   d. Close the Message form without saving.

7. Restore the default message editor to Microsoft Word by following these
   steps:
   a. Choose Tools, Options from the menu and click the Mail Format tab.
   b. Select the option Use Microsoft Word to edit e-mail messages.
   c. Click Apply and then OK.

   NOTE: Make sure you have completed step 7 of this exercise. This step
   restores Outlook to its default settings. Always leave Outlook in its default state
   for the next class or student to use.

8. Use a mail message template by following these steps:
   a. Choose Tools, Forms, Choose Form from the menu.
   b. Click the down arrow next to the Look In text box, and select User
      Templates in File System or the location for your Lesson 6 files.
   c. Select the template file *[your initials]*6-17 and click Open.

9. Place the insertion point in the text area of the template, and choose View,
   Header and Footer from the menu. Key your name as the header and then
   click Close on the Header and Footer toolbar.

10. Press Ctrl + P to display the Print dialog box, and then click OK to print
    the message template.

11. Close the Message form without saving or sending the message.

Lesson Applications

EXERCISE 6-18

Create a new contact, send a message by using an alternate message format, categorize the message, use message options, and create a customized note.

Maria Lopez, AllWood's VP of Administration, has asked you to submit your status reports to her assistant, John Rosen, via e-mail messages. You would like to make the message appear as attractively formatted as the Word documents you usually submit. You also need to remind yourself to complete the reports on time!

1. Display the Contacts folder and delete any existing contacts. Add John Rosen to your contact list, using the information shown in Figure 6-18. For the e-mail address, you will use your instructor's e-mail address. Categorize the contact as Status.

FIGURE 6-18

```
Mr. John Rosen

Administrative Assistant

AllWood Mills, Inc.

3100 Jackson Street

Dubuque, IA 52004

(319) 555-4829

E-mail: Instructor@ISP.isp
```

NOTE: Your instructor will provide you with an appropriate e-mail address.

2. Create a new e-mail message, addressing the message to John Rosen from your contact list.

REVIEW: To use an e-mail address from your contact list, click To in the Message form and then select the name from the Select Names dialog box.

3. Key the subject of the message as **Weekly Status Report**. For the text of the message, key the material shown in Figure 6-19 on the next page, using a Rich Text message format.

FIGURE 6-19

Below is a summary of my project work this week ~~past~~ in each of the ~~different~~ areas to which I ~~had~~ have been assigned:

Marketing

Edited material for _Traditional Homes_ ad

Reviewed copy with agency account manager

Set up appointments for photography shoot

Sales

Worked on conference presentation slides

Arranged sales managers' meeting

4. Format the "Marketing" and "Sales" headings in bold. Change the entries under the headings to bulleted text. Space the text attractively.

5. Set the message importance to High. Assign the message to the Status category. Spell-check the message.

6. Connect to the Internet and send the message. Log off the Internet if your instructor tells you to do so.

7. Display the Sent Items folder and select the message you just sent. Print the message, using a Memo Style print style. Add your name as a centered header and delete any existing footer information.

8. Display the Notes folder and change the default font size for notes to 16 points. Create a new note with the text **Start next week's status report**. Print the note in a Memo Style print style, with your name as a centered header. Restore the default font size for notes to 10 points.

NOTE: Make sure you restore Outlook to its default settings. Always leave Outlook in its default state for the next class or student to use.

9. Display the Contacts folder in Detailed Address Cards view. Print the John Rosen contact, using a Memo Style print style. Add your name as a centered header and delete any existing footer information. Then display the contact list in Address Cards view.

EXERCISE 6-19

Schedule a meeting, add a new category to the Master Category List, customize the Calendar, send a task request, categorize an appointment, create a customized note, and customize the task list.

A local television station is doing a detailed story on AllWood Mills. Rob Connelly, AllWood's president, has asked you to work with Maria Lopez in coordinating their activities. Your tasks are quite different from your normal activities, so you'd like to call attention to them in Outlook wherever possible.

1. Display the Calendar folder and select a date roughly two weeks from the current date. Delete any existing appointments or meetings in the Appointments Calendar for that date. Schedule a meeting for that day from 10:00 a.m. to 11:00 a.m. Add your instructor as a required meeting attendee. Add two classmates as optional meeting attendees.

    NOTE: Your instructor will supply you with an appropriate e-mail address and the e-mail addresses of two classmates.

2. For the subject of the meeting, key **Plan TV crew visit** and make the location of the meeting **My office**. Deselect the reminder option. Add the following text to the message: **Discuss tour and company sites that the reporter visits, and what we want them to see**. Connect to the Internet and send the meeting request.

3. Display the Tasks folder and delete any existing tasks. Create a new task request. Send the task request to your instructor and make the subject of the task **Get contact person at TV station**. Make the due date two business days from the current date. Add the following text to the message: **I need the name of a contact person at the TV station to coordinate our plans.** Set Priority to High. Send the task request.

4. Create a task with the subject **Write up meeting agenda**. Deselect the reminder and make the due date three business days from the current date. Set % Complete to 25% and Priority to High.

5. Create a task with the subject **Find out from managers who is to do on-camera demonstrations**. Make the due date one week from the current date, and add the following text to the task: **Discuss who we want to demonstrate our production process.** Deselect the reminder, set Status: to Waiting on someone else, and set Priority to Low.

6. Display the Notes folder, change the default font size for notes to 14 points, and create a new note with the text **Call Will about interviews**. Create a second note with the text **Make dentist appointment**.

7. Add a new category to your Master Category List called Television. Assign the "Make dentist appointment" to the Personal category. Assign the "Call Will" note to the Television category. Display the task list and assign all tasks to the

Television category. Display the date in your Appointments Calendar of the "Plan TV crew visit" meeting that you scheduled two weeks from the current date in step 2. Assign the meeting to the Television category.

8. Customize the Calendar, changing the font size of the Day view to 10 points and the time scale to 15 minutes. Deselect the option that displays Date Navigator dates in bold for days containing Calendar items.

9. Print the Calendar for the day of the meeting date, using a Daily Style print style. Add your name as a centered header and the date as a centered footer.

10. Customize the task list by changing the font style of read and completed tasks to italic. Mark the "Find out from managers" task as completed. Display the task list in Detailed List view, adding the Notes field to the table. Sort the table by % Completed in ascending order. Print the task list in landscape orientation, adding your name as a centered header and the date as a centered footer.

11. Display the Notes folder. Print the "Make dentist appointment" and "Call Will about interviews" notes you created in step 6, adding your name as a centered header.

12. Display the Sent Items folder and print the message you sent in step 2, using a Memo Style print style. Add your name as a centered header and the date as a centered footer.

13. Restore the default settings for the Calendar by changing the font size of the Day view to 8 points, setting the time scale to 30 minutes, and selecting the Date Navigator option to display days with Calendar items in bold.

14. Restore the default settings for the task list by changing the font style of read and completed tasks from italic to regular. Remove the Notes field from the Detailed List view. Display the task list in Simple List view.

15. Restore the default settings for the Notes folder by changing the font size to 10 points.

16. Restore the Master Category List to its default setting by deleting the Television category from the list.

NOTE: Make sure you have completed the last four steps of this exercise. These steps restore Outlook to its default settings. Always leave Outlook in its default state for the next class or student to use.

EXERCISE 6-20

Add a contact to the contact list, create and use a message template, format the message, modify the Master Category List, categorize the message, and customize the Calendar.

John Yu, AllWood's VP of Marketing, has asked you to send out regular status reports concerning the rollout of the new line of office furniture. He wants you to send them to his assistant, Steve Harris. He also would like you to arrange regular meeting times with him and the rest of his staff to discuss the advertising campaign for the new line.

1. Display the Contacts folder and add Steve Harris to your contact list, using the information shown in Figure 6-20. For the e-mail address, you will use your instructor's e-mail address. Categorize the contact as Status. Create a new category in the Master Category list called Marketing, and assign this category to the new contact.

FIGURE 6-20

```
Mr. Steve Harris

Marketing Assistant

AllWood Mills, Inc.

3100 Jackson Street

Dubuque, IA 52004

(319) 555-4080

E-mail: Instructor@ISP.isp
```

NOTE: Your instructor will provide you with an appropriate e-mail address.

2. Change the default message editor to the Outlook editor (deselecting Word as the message editor), and compose a new message template with the subject **Marketing Status Report**. Use the text in Figure 6-21.

FIGURE 6-21

```
Below is a summary of Marketing activities related to the introduction of
the AllWood office furniture line:

Advertising


Direct Marketing Material


Sales Planning
```

3. Underline the heading for each section and provide enough space between headings for text. Save the message as a template, keying the filename as *[your initials]*6-20. Close the message without sending it.

4. Restore the default message editor to Word.

5. Open the message template you just created, add your name as a header, and print it.

6. Address the message to Steve Harris, using the contact list entry you made in step 1. Key the following text under the Advertising heading, using the same font as the existing text:

- **Reviewed magazine ad copy for agency**
- **Submitted ad budget for review**
- **Contacted editor at Home & Style magazine**

Under the Direct Marketing heading, key the following text:

- **Completed photography session**
- **Developed layout for in-store brochures**

Under the Sales Planning heading, key the following text:

- **Worked with Design on store displays**
- **Met with Sales to review sales training**

7. Make the text under each heading bulleted. Format "Home & Style" in italic. Make sure the message is spaced attractively and spell-check the document. Assign the message to the Status and Marketing categories, and set the message importance to High. Connect to the Internet and send the message.

8. Display the Sent Items folder and print the message you just sent, using Memo Style as the print style. Add your name as a centered header and delete any existing footer information.

9. Display the Calendar folder and customize the Calendar display so that the time scale is in 15-minute increments. Create a conditional format in which any appointment with the text "Marketing" in the subject field is displayed in red. (*Hint:* Use the Automatic Formatting dialog box to create a rule, name the rule with your initials, and set the Label at Important.)

10. Display the Appointments Calendar two business days from the current date. Delete any existing meetings or appointments, and key a new appointment with the subject **Marketing staff meeting** and a location of **TBA**. Make it a 45-minute appointment starting at 10:00 a.m. Deselect the reminder and assign the appointment to the Marketing category. Make it a recurring weekly appointment on the same day of the week for the next six weeks.

11. Print the Calendar for that day, using a Daily Style print style. Add your name as a centered header and delete any existing footer information. Select the appointment and print it, using a Memo Style print style. Add your name as a centered header and delete any existing footer information.

12. Display your contact list in Detailed Address Cards view. Select the entry for Steve Harris and print it, using a Memo Style print style. Add your name as a centered header and delete any existing footer information. Display the contact list in Address Cards view.

13. Restore the Master Category List to its default setting by resetting the list or by removing the Marketing category. Restore the Calendar to its default setting by deleting the rule you created for the conditional formatting and changing the time scale to 30-minute intervals.

NOTE: Make sure you have completed steps 4 and 13 of this exercise. These steps restore Outlook to its default settings. Always leave Outlook in its default state for the next class or student to use.

EXERCISE 6-21   Challenge Yourself

Create a new signature, create contacts and a distribution list, schedule a meeting, compose and send a formatted message, create new task requests and customized notes, customize the task list, and create a message template.

Rob Connelly has asked his senior managers to develop a cost-savings program. He has asked Paul Epstein, the VP of Manufacturing, to coordinate a team effort. You've been assigned to work with his team on this project. You will be organizing meetings, tasks, and various other activities.

1. Create a listing in your contact list for an office resource. Identify the office resource as Conference Room A. Create additional listings for two classmates and Paul Epstein, using the information shown in Figure 6-22. For the e-mail address of Paul Epstein, you will use your instructor's e-mail address.

FIGURE 6-22

```
Mr. Paul Epstein, VP of Manufacturing

AllWood Mills, Inc.

3100 Jackson Street

Dubuque, IA 52004

(319) 555-4401

E-mail: Instructor@ISP.isp
```

NOTE: Your instructor will supply you with appropriate e-mail addresses to use for your office resource and the contacts.

2. Assign the contacts for Paul Epstein and your classmates to a new category called **Costs**, added to the Master Category List. Link each of the contacts with each other.

3. Create a distribution list named **Costs Team** with the contacts you created in step 1 as members of the list (do not include the resource). Assign the distribution list to the Costs category.

4. Display your Inbox folder and create a signature. Use your initials as the name of the new signature, and key the following text for the signature:

   [your name]

   AllWood Mills Costs Savings Team

5. Format the "AllWood Cost Savings Team" portion of the signature in italic. Apply the new signature to new messages.

6. Create a new e-mail message, addressing the message to Paul Epstein from your contact list. Key the subject of the message as **Cost Savings Team Assignments**. For the text of the message, key the material shown in Figure 6-23, using a Rich Text message format.

FIGURE 6-23

```
This is just to confirm what we agreed I should be working on this week:

Create cost savings worksheets

Get cost savings targets from managers

Review shipping charges by all carriers
```

7. Format the last three lines as bulleted text. Set the message importance to Low, and set a flag to For Your Information with no due date. Manually spell-check the message. Assign the message to the Costs category. Connect to the Internet and send the message. Delete the signature.

8. Display the Calendar folder and customize the Calendar display to show time intervals in 15-minute increments. Schedule a meeting for two weeks from the current date and delete any existing appointments for that date. Schedule the meeting time from 8:45 a.m. to 10:15 a.m. Add Paul Epstein as a required meeting attendee. Add two classmates as optional meeting attendees. Use Conference Room A as the required resource.

9. For the subject of the meeting, key **Cost Savings Team Meeting**. Deselect the reminder option and add the following text to the message: **Develop**

plan for measuring cost savings by department. Link the meeting with your two classmates from your contact list. Assign the meeting to the Costs category and send the message.

10. Display the Tasks folder and delete any existing tasks. Display the task list in Detailed List view, and add the Contacts and Notes fields to the table. Customize the task list by changing the font style of read and completed tasks to italic. Create a new task request. Send the task request to Paul Epstein, and make the subject of the task **Get percentage savings value by department**. Make the due date two business days from the current date. Add the following text to the message: **I need this number from you to create the spreadsheet.** Set the Status: to In Progress, % Complete to 25%, and the Priority to High. Categorize it under Costs and send the task request.

11. Create a new task and make the subject of the task **Finish contacting all store managers**. Make the due date the next business day from the current date, and add the following text to the task: **Remind them that they will be expected to look for cost savings**. Set % Complete to 75% and the Priority to High. Categorize it under Costs. Deselect the reminder and link the task with both your classmates from their contact list entries.

12. Create another new task and make the subject of the task **Contact our shippers**. Make the due date one week from the current date, and add the following text to the task: **Ask what reduced-rate options are available**. Deselect the reminder, set the Priority to Low, and assign it to the Costs category.

13. Mark the "Contact our shippers" task as completed. Sort the task list by % Complete in ascending order. Adjust column widths so that as much of the Notes field prints as possible. Print the task list in landscape orientation, using the Table Style print style. Add your name as a centered header and the date as a centered footer. When you have finished, remove the Contacts and Notes fields from the Table view, restore the display of completed and read items to regular font style, and set the view to Simple List view.

14. Display the Sent Items folder and select the "Cost Savings Team Assignments" message you sent in step 6. Print the message, using Memo Style as the print style. Add your name as a centered header and delete any existing footer information.

15. In the Sent Items folder, select the "Cost Savings Team Meeting" message you created in step 9. Print the message, using a Memo Style as the print style and add your name as a centered header.

16. Display the contact list in Detailed Address Cards view. Select the additions you've made in this exercise (the two classmates, Paul Epstein, the Cost Team distribution list, and the resource). Print the selected contacts, using a Card Style print style and adding your name as a centered header. Eliminate the blank-forms page at the end and the headings for each letter. (*Hint*:

Headings can be eliminated on the **Format** tab of the Page Setup dialog box.) Then display the contact list in Address Cards view.

17. Display the Notes folder and customize the display of new notes by increasing the font size to 16 points. Create a new note with the text **Finish spreadsheet**. Assign the note to the Costs category. Print the note in a Memo Style print style and add your name as a centered header. Restore the default font size for notes to 10 points.

18. Display the Appointments Calendar date of the meeting two weeks from the current date that you created in step 8. Print the Calendar in a Daily Style print style, and add a header with your name on the left and the date on the right. Delete any existing footer information. When you have finished, restore the Calendar default to show time intervals in 30-minute increments.

19. Change the default message editor to the Outlook editor (deselect Word as the message editor). Create a message template with the subject as **Weekly Cost Savings Report**. Use the text in Figure 6-24.

FIGURE 6-24

```
Below find a summary of cost savings implemented for the past week. The
report shows savings by department, item, and estimated annualized savings.
The Total reflects only new totals implemented this week.


Dept.    Item      Annualized Savings


Total New Cost Savings Implemented:
```

20. Apply attractive formatting to the headings and total. Space the text so that data can be added to the template as needed. Spell-check the document. Save the message as a template and key the filename as *[your initials]*6-21. Close the message without sending it.

21. Restore the default message editor to Word. Open the message template, add your name as the header, and print the template. Close the template without saving.

22. Restore the Master Category List to its default setting by either deleting the Costs category or resetting the list.

NOTE: Make sure you have restored system defaults in all steps where indicated. Always leave Outlook in its default state for the next class or student to use.

On Your Own

In these exercises you work on your own, as you would in a real-life work environment. Use the skills you've learned to accomplish the task—and be creative.

EXERCISE 6-22

Prepare for a vacation by creating tasks, notes, and Calendar items in anticipation of it. Assign each item to a new category and customize each in various ways. Send a formatted e-mail message to family, friends, or employers indicating when you will be away. Print the message, task list, Calendar, and notes.

EXERCISE 6-23

Plan your taxes by using tasks, Calendar items, and notes. Customize the items in various ways and assign all items to a new category. Send a formatted e-mail message to someone, describing how well organized you are this tax year. Print sent messages, the task list, Calendar items, and notes.

EXERCISE 6-24

Research the purchase of a new computer on the Web with a classmate. Use tasks and notes to divide the effort. Customize the items in various ways and create a new category for the items. Report your results to each other in formatted e-mail messages. Print sent messages, the task list, and notes.

Integrating Outlook Features

OBJECTIVES

After completing this lesson, you will be able to:

1. Use e-mail with other Outlook components.
2. Link contacts.
3. Use the Journal.
4. Integrate tasks, Calendar, and contacts.
5. Create Office documents from within Outlook.

MOUS ACTIVITIES

In this lesson:

OL2002 **1-2**
OL2002 **1-3**
OL2002 **2-1**
OL2002 **3-1**
OL2002 **4-1**
OL2002 **4-3**
OL2002 **5-1**
OL2002 **5-2**

See Appendix E.

Estimated Time: 1½ hours

Now that you've become acquainted with each of Outlook's components, you can begin using them together. Outlook's e-mail, Calendar, contacts, and tasks components all work together. You'll also find that it's easy to use Outlook with other Microsoft Office programs such as Word and Excel.

Using E-Mail with Other Outlook Components

You've used Outlook to schedule meetings and assign tasks, so you've already seen how the Inbox is integrated with Calendar and Tasks. Meeting attendees receive meeting requests as e-mail messages. You assign tasks to others via e-mail. You can also use e-mail with contacts and notes. For example, you might want to create an e-mail message from a contact or forward a note to someone in an e-mail message. You can also move e-mail messages to other Outlook folders.

EXERCISE **7-1** **Save an E-Mail Sender as a Contact**

Many times you'll receive e-mail messages from individuals whose name and address you want to add to your contact list. You can make the addition while you're reading the message or in the preview pane.

1. Display the Inbox.

2. Choose File, New, Mail Message from the menu (or click the New button). Change the message format to Plain Text.

3. In the To text box, key *[recipient's name]@[ISP]*

> **NOTE:** You will be using an e-mail address of a classmate to send your message. Your instructor will provide you with a list of e-mail addresses.

4. In the Subject text box, key **New facilities team**

5. Key an appropriate salutation and then key the text shown in Figure 7-1.

FIGURE 7-1

```
Rob has asked me to join the team working on the new facilities for the
Manufacturing department. I understand this is for the production of the
new line of office furniture. Could you send me whatever information I
should have to get up to speed on the project? Thanks!
```

6. Spell-check the message, connect to the Internet, and send the message.

7. Press Ctrl + N to open the Message form to create another message.

8. In the To text box, key *[recipient's name]@[ISP]*

> **NOTE:** Use a classmate's address from the list of e-mail addresses your instructor has provided you.

9. In the Subject text box, key **Traditional Homes magazine**

10. Change the message format to Rich Text. For the text of the message, key an appropriate salutation and then key **Could I borrow your copy of Traditional Homes magazine? I need the one with our ad in it. Thanks!**

11. Change the magazine title to italic, and spell-check the message, ignoring the grammatical suggestion. Send the message.

12. Click the Send/Receive button on the Standard toolbar to get your messages from your mail server.

13. Open the new mail item "New facilities team."

14. Position the pointer over the address in the "From:" field and right-click. A shortcut menu appears.

FIGURE 7-2
Shortcut menu for adding e-mail address to Contacts

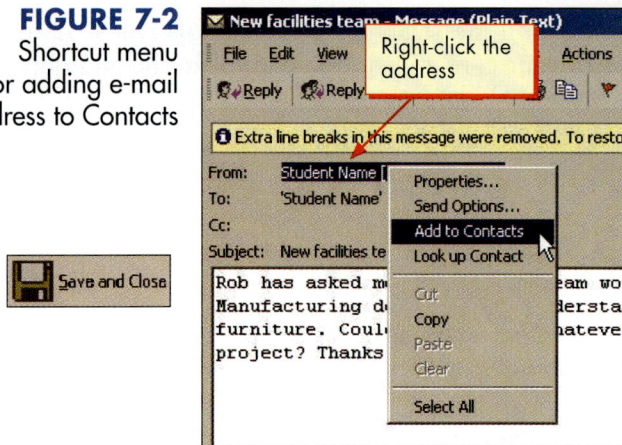

15. Select Add to Contacts from the shortcut menu. The Contact form appears. Outlook automatically supplies the name and e-mail address in the appropriate fields.

16. Add any other information about your classmate that is appropriate.

17. Click the Save and Close button on the Contact form toolbar. The e-mail sender is added to your contact list.

18. Close the Message form. The Inbox reappears.

19. Make sure the preview pane is displayed. Notice that a sender's address for an Inbox item also appears in the preview pane header. You can add the address to the contact list by right-clicking it.

EXERCISE **7-2** **Insert a Note as a Message Attachment**

You can send a note as an attachment to an e-mail message. When the recipient opens the note, it is displayed like any other Outlook note. This can be a handy way to put a reminder on someone's desktop.

1. Display the Notes folder and create a new note with the text **Update project timetable.** Create another note with the text **Get blueprints from Rob.**

2. Display the Inbox and click the New button on the Standard toolbar to compose a new e-mail message. The Message form appears.

3. In the To text box, key *[recipient's name]@[ISP]*

NOTE: Your instructor will provide you with a list of e-mail addresses.

4. In the Subject text box, key **Just a reminder**

5. Set the message format to Rich Text, key an appropriate salutation, and then key the text shown in Figure 7-3.

FIGURE 7-3

    I need to get this from you as soon as possible.

6. Click the down arrow next to the Insert File button [📎] on the Message form toolbar and click It<u>e</u>m. The Insert Item dialog box appears.

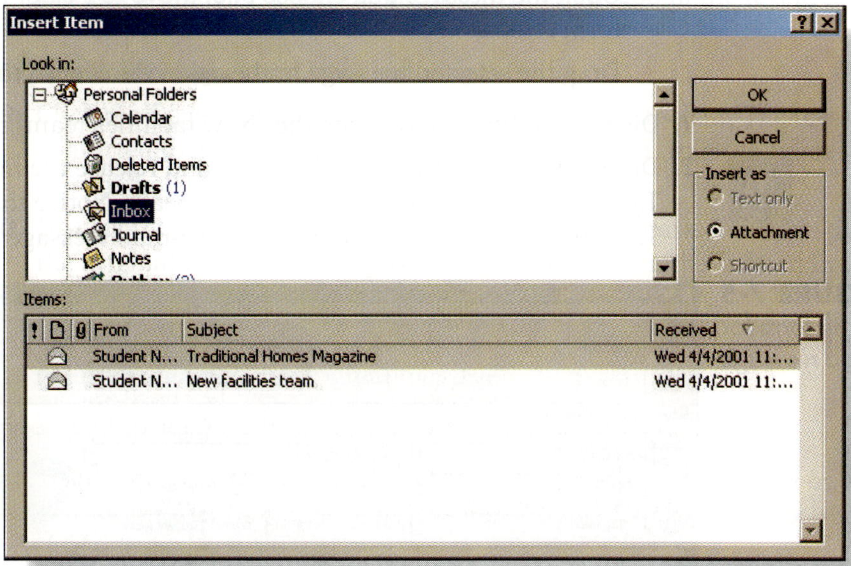

FIGURE 7-4
Insert Item
dialog box

7. Under <u>L</u>ook in, scroll down to the Notes folder and select it.

8. Locate the "Update project timetable" note, select it, and then click **OK**. The note appears as an icon in the message area. (The location of the insertion point when the item is inserted determines where the icon appears in the message.)

9. Send the message. The message will appear in the recipient's Inbox. When a message recipient opens an attachment, it is displayed like any other Outlook note.

> **NOTE:** You can also send a note via an e-mail message by right-clicking the note in the Notes folder and selecting For<u>w</u>ard from the shortcut menu.

EXERCISE **7-3** **Move Messages Among Folders**

You can move messages into other Outlook folders. For example, you might want to move a message into your Tasks folder. This action turns the message into a task. There are various ways to move messages to other Outlook folders. You can:

- Drag the selected Inbox message to a shortcut icon in the Outlook Bar.
- Right-click the Inbox item and select <u>M</u>ove to Folder on the shortcut menu.

3. Click the **Activities** tab. Outlook searches through your folders for items relating to the contact.

FIGURE 7-6
Activities tab for a contact

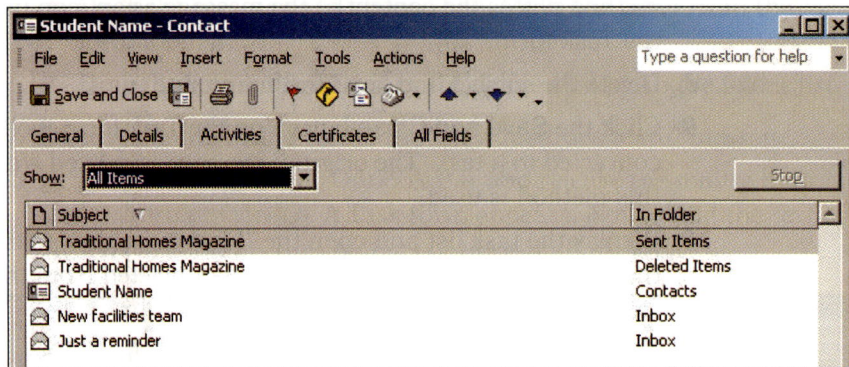

4. Click the down arrow next to the **Show** text box. Notice that you can have Outlook search for different types of items. This is useful when there are many activities related to a specific contact.

5. Close the Contact form. Outlook can also track other contacts associated with a contact.

6. Select and open another contact from the contact list, or create a new one if there are no other contacts (add a friend or a relative, if you wish).

7. Click **Contacts**. The Select Contacts dialog box appears. Select your classmate's name from the contact list. Click **Apply** and then click **OK**. The contact is linked to your classmate.

8. Close the Contact form, saving the changes.

9. Open the contact for your classmate and click the **Activities** tab on the Contact form. Outlook now includes the contact you linked with your classmate in steps 6 and 7. The icon and folder show that it is a contact.

FIGURE 7-7
Another contact as a contact's activity

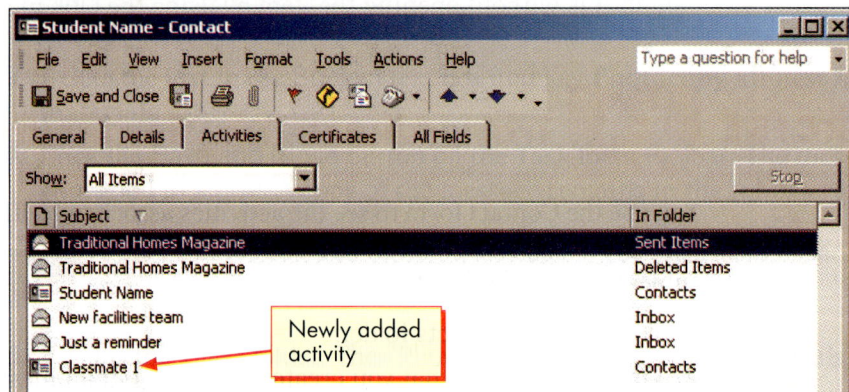

10. Close the Contact form.

EXERCISE   **7-5**   **Link a Contact to Activities**

You can select individual items in your Outlook folders and link them to a specific contact.

1. Make sure the Contacts folder is displayed.

2. Locate the contact for the classmate you created from the e-mail message in Exercise 7-1.

3. Select the contact and choose **Actions**, **Link** from the menu (or right-click the contact and select **Link** from the shortcut menu). Choose **Items** from the submenu. The Link Items to Contact dialog box appears. The upper half of the dialog box shows all your folders in Personal Folders. The lower half shows the individual items within each folder. The default selection is the Inbox folder.

FIGURE 7-8
Link Items to
Contact dialog box

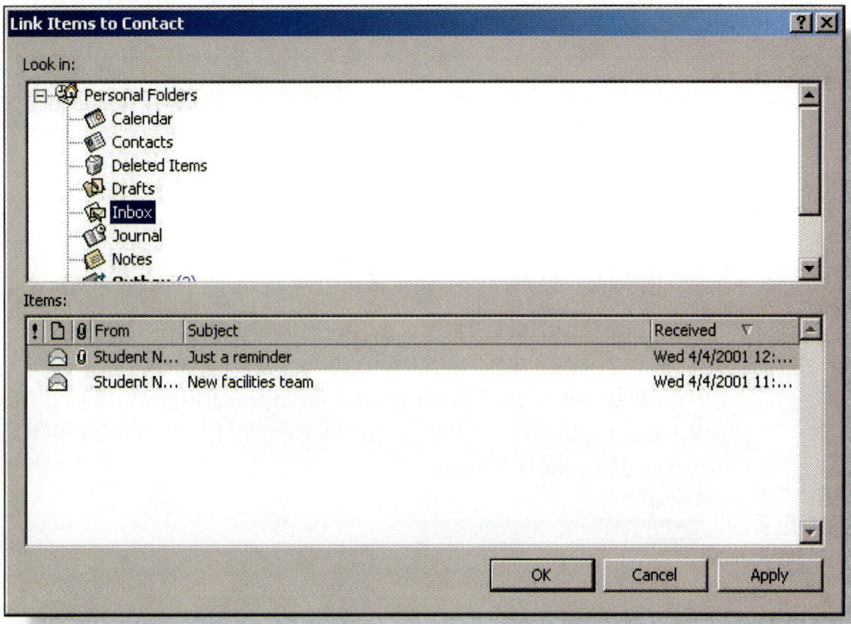

4. Under **Look in**, select **Notes**. The items in the Notes folder appear in the lower half of the dialog box.

5. Select the "Get blueprints from Rob" note, which you created in Exercise 7-2.

6. Click **Apply** and then click **OK**. The note is linked to the contact. If you display the Activities tab for the contact, the note will appear as one of the contact's activities.

7. Open the Contact form for your classmate and click the Activities tab.

8. Click the down arrow next to the **Show** text box and select **Notes**. The "Get blueprints from Rob" note appears as one of the activities.

9. Close the Contact form.

Using the Journal

Outlook's Journal is a more systematic way to track your daily activities. You can use it to automatically record e-mail messages you receive from specific contacts, including appointments, meeting invitations, and task requests. You can have the Journal log each time you work on an Office document. You can use the Journal to manually record letters, telephone calls, conversations, or anything else you consider important.

The default display of information in the Journal is in a timeline. A *timeline* is a view type that displays items from left to right on a time scale, typically a day, week, or month. A Timeline view shows when items occur in time.

EXERCISE 7-6 Use Automatic Journaling

You can use Outlook's Journal to make a record of each activity in the Journal folder in your Personal Folders file. When you turn on automatic journaling, you choose what types of activities you want saved as Journal items. The Journal is most useful when you're tracking more than e-mail, such as meeting invitations, task assignments, and activities with other Office applications.

1. Choose **Tools, Options** from the menu. The Options dialog box appears.

2. Click **Journal Options**. The Journal Options dialog box appears. You must specify the type of activity you wish to record, as well as the contact related to the activity. You can also have the Journal record the date and time when you create, open, close, and save any file in various Office programs, such as Microsoft Word.

FIGURE 7-9
Journal Options
dialog box

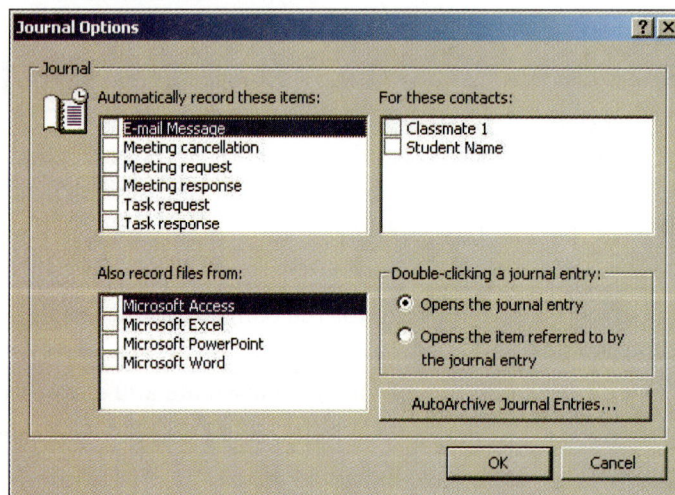

3. Under **Automatically record these items,** select **E-mail Message, Meeting request,** and **Task request.** These are the activities you will have Outlook record in the Journal.

4. Under **For these contacts,** select the classmate whose name you added to your contact list in Exercise 7-1. Outlook will track e-mail messages, meeting invitations, and task requests for this contact in the Journal.

5. Click **OK** twice. Automatic journaling is now in effect. To see how it works, you will need to send an e-mail message, task request, or meeting invitation to the specified contact.

NOTE: If automatic journaling has not been turned on—that is, if nothing has been selected in the Journal Options dialog box—Outlook might display a message box when you click the Journal shortcut 📇 in the Outlook Bar or select the Journal folder from the folder list. This message box asks if you wish to turn on automatic journaling. Clicking Yes displays the Journal Options dialog box. Clicking No simply displays the Journal without displaying the Journal Options dialog box.

6. Display the Inbox. Create a message to the contact you added to your contact list in Exercise 7-1 with a subject of **Photocopy request.** Key the text shown in Figure 7-10, using a Plain Text message format.

FIGURE 7-10

I will be sending you a task request to photocopy the materials for the new facilities project. I think you have the only complete set.

7. Connect to the Internet and send the message.

8. Display the Tasks folder and create a new task request to the same contact with the subject **Photocopy new facilities materials**

9. Send the request. Outlook records the activities in the Journal.

10. To see recorded Journal activities, click **My Shortcuts** in the Outlook Bar and then click Journal 📇. (You can also display the Journal folder by selecting it from the folder list.) The Journal folder appears, showing recorded items in a timeline. The default view for Journal entries is By Type. This means that items are categorized by entry type. You can use the right and left arrow keys to adjust the dates shown in the timeline. (See Figure 7-11 on the next page.)

11. Click the plus sign (+) next to the E-mail Message entry type to see the individual items within the group.

12. To see details of a Journal item, double-click **Photocopy request (sent)** under E-mail Message. A Journal Entry form appears, displaying the details of the Journal item.

FIGURE 7-11
Displaying
Journal items

13. Close the Journal Entry form.

14. To turn off automatic journaling, choose **T**ools, **O**ptions from the menu and click **J**ournal Options. Deselect all the items under **Automatically record these items** and the contacts under **For these contacts**. No options should be selected. Then click **OK** twice.

NOTE: Make sure you have completed the last step of this exercise. This step restores Outlook to its default settings. Always leave Outlook in its default state for the next class or student to use.

TIP: You can change the time scale of the Journal from a weekly timeline to either a monthly or a daily timeline by clicking the **Da**y button or the **M**onth button on the Standard toolbar. You can also adjust the days shown by using the left and right arrow keys.

EXERCISE **7-7** **Create Journal Items Manually**

In addition to automatic journaling, you can manually record activities in the Journal. This can be useful when you'd like to selectively record activities instead of having all items associated with a contact recorded in the Journal automatically.

You might want to do this when you need to track the amount of time you spend on specific projects.

1. With the Journal folder still displayed, click the **New** button on the Standard toolbar. The Journal Entry form appears. In addition to the subject and entry type, you can record the duration of an activity, associated contacts, and categories. You can use the timer to record the precise amount of time in an activity, such as a face-to-face conversation.

FIGURE 7-12
Journal Entry form
for manual
Journal items

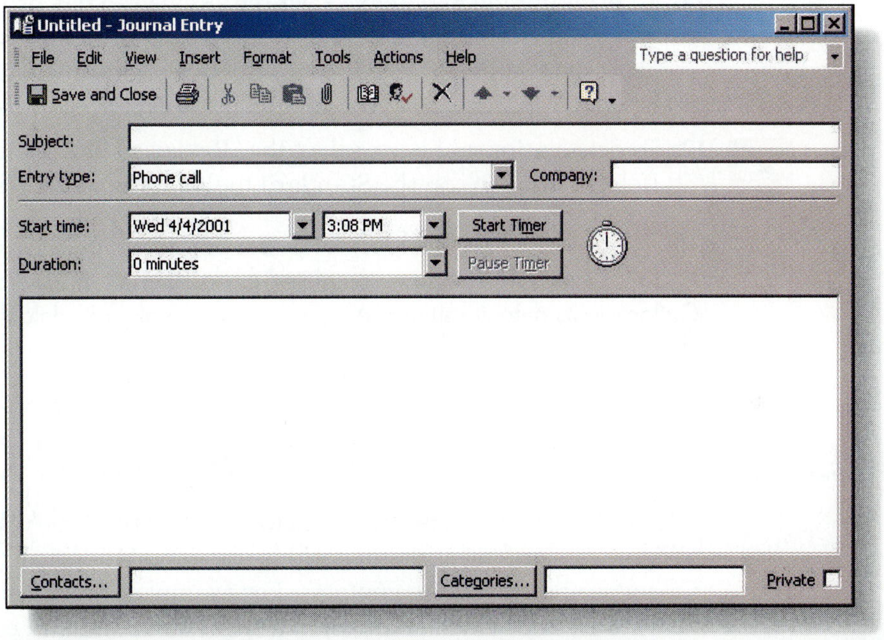

2. In the **Subject** text box, key **Reviewed blueprints**

3. Click the down arrow next to the **Entry type** text box and scroll down the available entry types. You can record faxes, letters, conversations, and other types of activities.

4. Select **Conversation** from the **Entry type** drop-down list (the first item on the drop-down list).

NOTE: You must choose an entry type from the Entry type drop-down list. Outlook will not let you specify your own entry types.

5. Click the **Save and Close** button on the Journal Entry form toolbar. The activity is recorded in the Journal.

6. Make sure the Journal folder is displayed. (Outlook might display a message asking if you wish to turn on automatic journaling. If this message appears, click **No**.)

7. Click the plus sign (+) for the Conversation entry type. The Journal item appears, which is the conversation you recorded in step 5. You can open and edit the item.

8. Double-click the "Reviewed blueprints" Journal item. The Journal Entry form appears.

9. Click the down arrow next to the <u>D</u>uration text box and select **30 minutes**.

10. Click the <u>S</u>ave and Close button on the Journal Entry form toolbar.

11. To print the Journal item, select the "Reviewed blueprints" item and choose <u>F</u>ile, <u>P</u>rint from the menu. The Print dialog box appears. The Memo Style print style is the only available print style. Add your name as a centered header and delete any existing footer information. Click **OK**.

12. To delete a Journal item, select the "Reviewed blueprints" item and click the Delete button ⊠ on the Standard toolbar. The item is deleted.

> **NOTE:** Manual Journal entries are stored in Outlook until they are deleted. Make sure you have completed the last step of this exercise. This step restores Outlook to its default settings. Always leave Outlook in its default state for the next class or student to use.

Integrating Tasks, Calendar, and Contacts

Outlook's components are designed to work together. You've already seen how task assignments and meeting invitations use e-mail messages. You can also use the Calendar and tasks with contacts. For example, you can select an entry in your contact list and schedule an appointment. You can use a contact to make a task request. You can also drag items to and from the TaskPad.

EXERCISE **7-8** **Create a Task from a Contact**

A quick way to create a task assignment is to drag an entry from your contact list to the Outlook Bar.

1. Click **Outlook Shortcuts** in the Outlook Bar if the Outlook shortcuts are not already displayed.

2. Display the Contacts folder and create an entry in your contact list for your instructor. Be sure to include the mailing address as well as the e-mail address.

> **NOTE:** Your instructor will supply you with an appropriate e-mail address.

3. Select the entry in your contact list for your instructor.

4. Drag the selection to the Outlook Bar and release it over the Tasks shortcut ⬛. Outlook displays the Task form. The presence of a **To** text box indicates that this is a task assignment. Outlook assumes you wish to assign a task to this individual when you create the task from Contacts. Outlook has placed the contact's e-mail address in the **To** text box and the contact's name in the **Contacts** text box.

FIGURE 7-13
Creating a task
from a contact

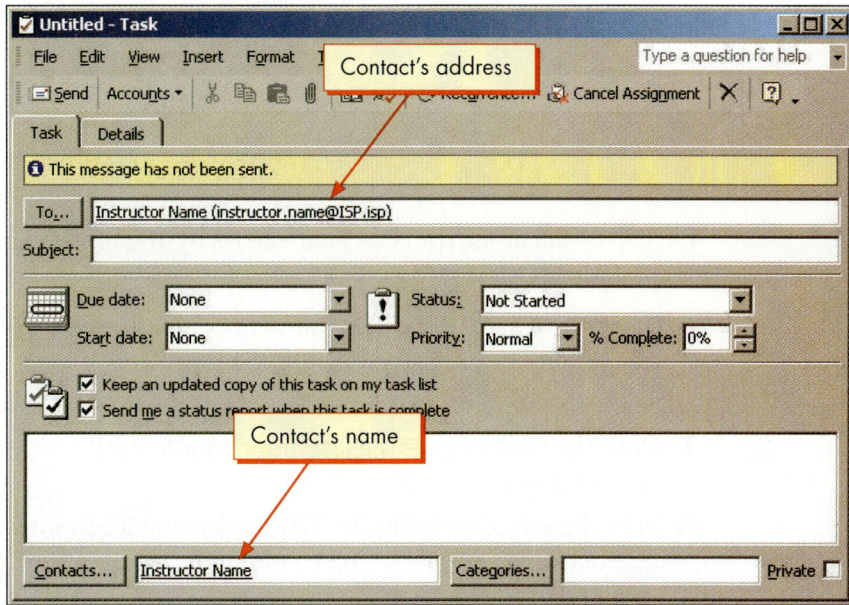

5. In the Subject text box, key **Write up request for proposal**

6. Make the Due date the next business day and set the Status: to In Progress.

7. Make sure you are connected to the Internet and send the message.

> **NOTE:** You can also create a new task request with a contact by using the menu bar or the shortcut menu. However, these methods do not place the contact's address in the To text box as the dragging method does.

EXERCISE **7-9** **Use Contacts to Schedule a Meeting**

The contact list can also be used as a quick way to send a meeting invitation to someone.

1. With the contact list still displayed, select the entry for your instructor.

2. Right-click the selection and choose New Meeting Request to Contact from the shortcut menu, or drag the selection to the Outlook Bar and release it over the Calendar shortcut 🖼. The Meeting form appears. Outlook places the contact's e-mail address in the To text box and the contact's name in the Contacts text box.

3. Key the Subject of the meeting as **Blueprint discussion** and make it a half-hour meeting on the next business day, starting at 10:00 a.m. Key the Location as **My office**. Deselect the reminder.

4. Make sure you are connected to the Internet and send the message.

EXERCISE 7-10 Drag a Calendar Item to the TaskPad

You can create tasks from Calendar entries by dragging an item from your Appointments Calendar to the TaskPad.

1. Display the date in the Appointments Calendar with the "Blueprint discussion" appointment you created in Exercise 7-9.

2. Select the appointment.

3. Move the pointer over the left move handle until the pointer changes to a four-pointed arrow ✛.

4. Drag the selection to the TaskPad, releasing it anywhere in the TaskPad. The Task form appears. The text area of the form shows the information about the Calendar item.

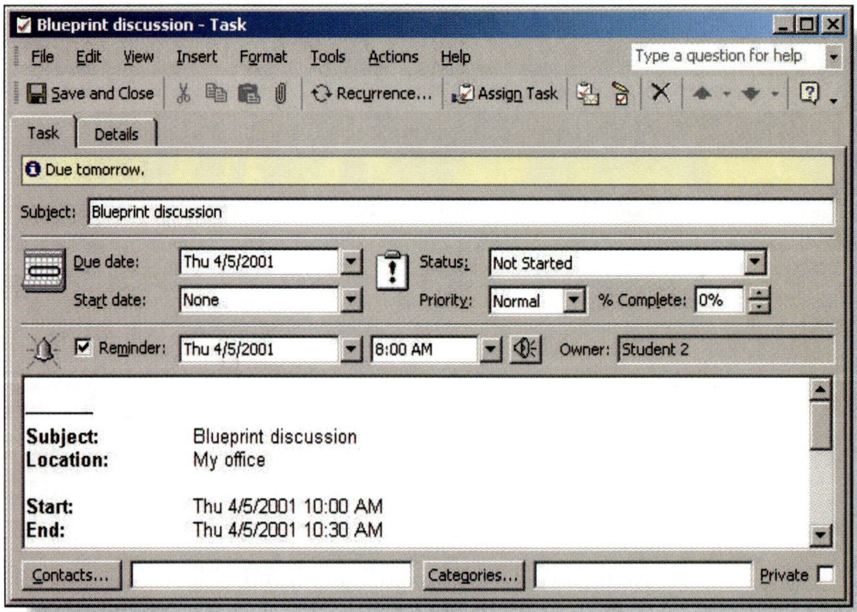

FIGURE 7-14
Task form for
Calendar item
dragged to TaskPad

5. Delete the existing text in the Subject text box and key **Prepare list of questions**

6. Change the Start date to the current date, and then click the Save and Close button on the Task form toolbar. The new task appears in the TaskPad. The Calendar item is unchanged.

Creating Office Documents from Within Outlook

There are many ways to use other Microsoft Office programs inside Outlook. You are already familiar with using Microsoft Word as your default e-mail editor. You can create other Word documents from within Outlook. For example, you might want to create a letter to individuals on your contact list. You can also create Excel worksheets and PowerPoint presentations from within Outlook. You can attach these files to messages, tasks, or Calendar items.

EXERCISE 7-11 Create a Letter to a Contact in Word

You can select a contact and use Outlook's Letter Wizard to create a letter template in Word that is addressed to the contact.

1. Display the contact list and select the entry for your instructor.

2. Choose Actions, New Letter to Contact. The Letter Wizard - Step 1 of 4 dialog box appears. (See Figure 7-15 on the next page.)

3. Select Date line to place the current date in the body of the text.

4. Click the Recipient Info tab or Next. The Letter Wizard - Step 2 of 4 dialog box appears. Notice that the letter recipient contains the address of the selected contact (your instructor).

5. Under Salutation, select Formal.

6. Click Next to display the Letter Wizard - Step 3 of 4 dialog box. You can use this box to include other elements in the letter such as Cc, Attention, or Subject.

7. Click Next again. The Letter Wizard - Step 4 of 4 dialog box appears.

8. In the Sender's name text box, key your name.

9. Under Closing, click the down arrow next to Complimentary closing and choose Sincerely.

10. In the Job title text box, key **Intern**, and in the Company text box, key **AllWood Mills, Inc.**

FIGURE 7-15
Letter Wizard - Step
1 of 4 dialog box

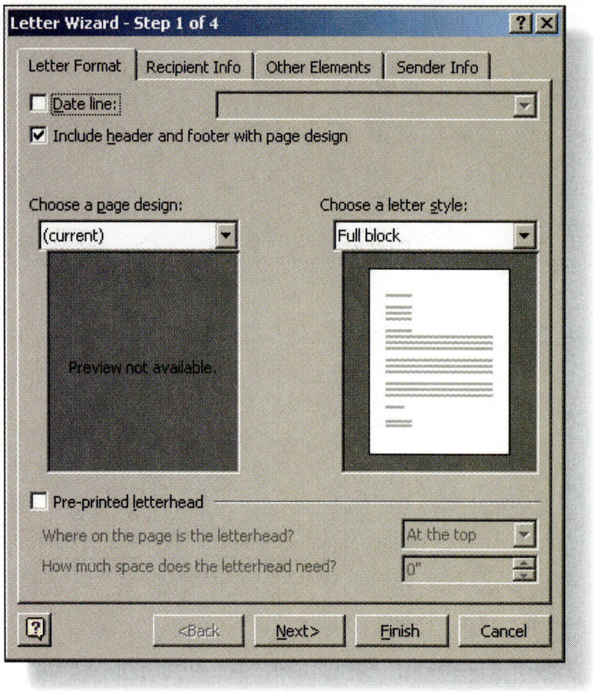

11. Select <u>E</u>nclosures and click <u>F</u>inish. A Word letter template appears. It is based on the information you provided in the Letter Wizard.

12. In the area marked "Type your text here," key **Enclosed you will find Rob's comments and corrections for the upcoming magazine ad campaign.**

13. To add the filename as a header, choose <u>V</u>iew, <u>H</u>eader and Footer from the menu. The Header and Footer toolbar appears. Click the In<u>s</u>ert AutoText button, and then click **Filename** from the drop-down menu. Click <u>C</u>lose on the Header and Footer toolbar.

14. Insert lines for appropriate spacing between the date, inside address, salutation, closing, your name, and enclosure line.

15. Save the file as *[your initials]***7-11** in your Lesson 7 folder.

16. Click the Print button 🖨 to print the letter.

17. Close the Word window and click **Yes** to save the changes. The Contacts folder reappears.

EXERCISE **7-12** **Start a New Office File in Outlook**

Outlook provides two ways to create a new Office file. You can use the <u>F</u>ile menu in any Outlook folder, or you can click **Other Shortcuts** in the Outlook Bar and use **My Computer** 🖥 to access other Office programs. After you've created the Office file, you can attach it to a task or an e-mail message.

NOTE: To open an Office file created in Outlook, you must be in Outlook.

1. Display the Tasks folder.
2. Choose File, New, Office Document from the menu (or press Ctrl + Shift + H). The New Office Document dialog box appears.

FIGURE 7-16

New Office Document dialog box

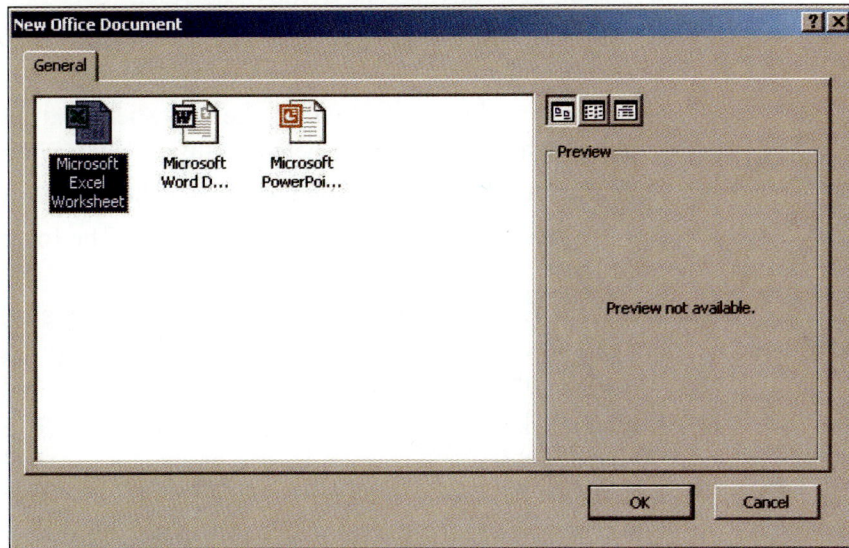

3. Make sure Microsoft Excel Worksheet is selected and then click OK. An Excel spreadsheet appears.
4. Create a spreadsheet, using the data shown in Figure 7-17.

FIGURE 7-17

New Facilities Project	
Areas of Responsibility	
Task	Manager
Develop project work plan	Paul
Write up RFP	John
Review bids	Maria
Supervise architect	Will
Supervise construction	Will
Oversee budget	Maria

5. To add a header with your name and the filename, choose <u>F</u>ile, Page Set<u>u</u>p from the menu. The Page Setup dialog box appears. Click the **Header/Footer** tab and then click <u>C</u>ustom Header. The Header dialog box appears. Key your name in the <u>L</u>eft section. Place the insertion point in the <u>R</u>ight section and click the Filename button 🔲 on the Header toolbar. Click OK, and then click OK again to close the Page Setup dialog box.

6. Format the worksheet attractively and save it as *[your initials]*7-12 in your Lesson 7 folder.

7. Click the Print button 🖨 to print the worksheet and then close Excel. Next, you'll attach the Excel worksheet to a task.

8. Open the task "Prepare list of questions." The Task form appears.

9. Choose <u>I</u>nsert, <u>F</u>ile from the Task form menu. The Insert File dialog box appears.

10. Select the Excel file *[your initials]*7-12 and click In<u>s</u>ert. An Excel icon appears in the text area of the Task form. You might want to view the worksheet after you've attached it to the task.

11. Double-click the Excel icon to open the worksheet. (If Excel displays an information dialog box warning you of viruses in attachments, select **Open** it and click **OK**.) You could make changes in the worksheet if you wished; however, you'll leave the worksheet unchanged for now.

12. Close the Excel worksheet.

13. Change the **Status:** of the task to **Completed**.

14. Click the <u>S</u>ave and Close button.

15. Print the task, using a Memo Style print style. Add your name as a centered header and delete any existing footer information.

USING HELP

The Office Clipboard is a useful way to copy data to Outlook from other Office programs. For example, you can use the Clipboard to copy data from an Excel worksheet to an Outlook e-mail message. You can copy multiple items from different programs and paste them at one time. Items collected on the Clipboard remain there until the last Office program is closed.

Use Microsoft Outlook Help to learn how to use the Office Clipboard:

1. Click the Microsoft Outlook Help button 🔲 and click the <u>A</u>nswer Wizard tab, if it is not displayed.

2. Key **Learn about the Office Clipboard** in the text box and click <u>S</u>earch. A list of related topics appears under Select <u>t</u>opic to display.

3. Select the topic About collecting and pasting multiple items. It contains a general description of how to use the Clipboard. Read the information on the right side of the screen.

FIGURE 7-18
Help screen on using the Office Clipboard

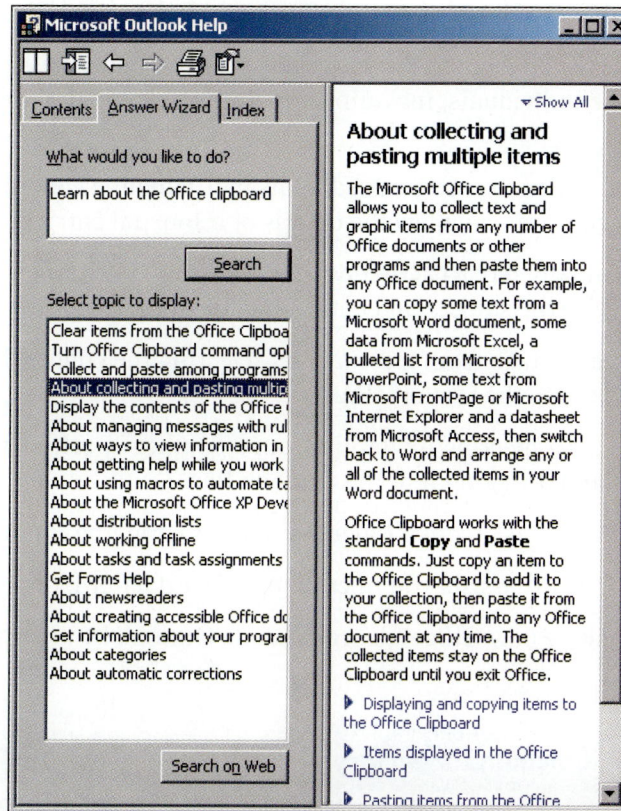

4. Click the topic Collect and paste among programs and read the information on the right side of the screen.

5. Close the Help screen.

LESSON 7 Summary

➤ When you receive an e-mail message, you can add the sender's address to your contact list. You can do this in either the message or the preview pane.

➤ You can send a note as an attachment with an e-mail message.

➤ You can move an Inbox message to other Outlook folders by dragging the message to an Outlook Bar shortcut or by using the shortcut menu.

➤ You can track activities for a contact by opening the contact and clicking the **Activities** tab of the Contact form.

➤ When a contact is selected in the contact list, you can link it to other Outlook items by using the shortcut menu command <u>L</u>ink.

➤ You can use the Journal to automatically record e-mail messages received from specific individuals, including appointments, meeting invitations, and task requests.

➤ The Journal folder shows recorded items in a Timeline view, categorized by the type of activity. You can view the details of a Journal entry by double-clicking it.

➤ You can manually record activities in the Journal. You can use the Journal Entry form to specify the subject and entry type for the activity.

➤ You can create a task from a contact by selecting the contact in the contact list and dragging it to the Outlook Bar.

➤ You can create a meeting invitation from a contact by selecting the contact in the contact list and dragging it to the Outlook Bar.

➤ You can create a task from a Calendar item by dragging it to the TaskPad.

➤ The Letter Wizard assists you in creating a Word letter from a contact.

➤ You can create a new Office file from inside Outlook by using the <u>F</u>ile command.

LESSON 7 Command Summary

FEATURE	BUTTON	MENU	KEYBOARD	SPEECH
New Office Document		<u>F</u>ile, <u>N</u>ew, Office <u>D</u>ocument	Ctrl + Shift + H	✓

Concepts Review

TRUE/FALSE QUESTIONS

Each of the following statements is either true or false. Indicate your choice by circling T or F.

T F **1.** You can add a sender's address to your contact list by using information in the preview pane header.

T F **2.** You can convert a message into a task by dragging it from the Inbox to the Outlook Bar.

T F **3.** To see all the e-mail messages linked to a particular contact, you must click **Contacts** in the Contact form for that contact.

T F **4.** Automatic journaling is turned off when no options are selected in the Journal Options dialog box.

T F **5.** You can drag items from the Appointments Calendar to the TaskPad.

T F **6.** When you drag a contact from your contact list to the Tasks shortcut 🗐 in the Outlook Bar, Outlook assumes you wish to assign a task to the contact.

T F **7.** You must display the Journal folder to see recorded Journal activities.

T F **8.** You can start a new Office file only from the Inbox folder.

SHORT ANSWER QUESTIONS

Write the correct answer in the space provided.

1. What do you click in a message to add the sender to your contact list?

_____

2. When you create a task from a contact by dragging the contact to the Outlook Bar, where does Outlook place the contact's e-mail address in the Task form?

_____

3. What keystrokes do you press in the Journal folder to manually create a new Journal item?

_____

4. What type of view does the Journal use to present its information?

_____

5. What command on the menu bar opens the Link Items to Contact dialog box?

_____

6. What keystrokes open the New Office Document dialog box?

_____

7. What do you click to display the individual items for each Journal Entry type?

_____

8. Where is the Journal shortcut 📇 located in the Outlook Bar?

_____

CRITICAL THINKING

Answer these questions on a separate page. There are no right or wrong answers. Support your answers with examples from your own experience, if possible.

1. Think of a large project you are preparing to do in which you might use several components of Outlook or other Office programs. Would linking these activities and/or automatically recording them in the Journal help you manage the different activities? Explain why or why not.

2. Outlook is full of numerous shortcuts and tricks that let you move data around from one part of the program to another. Which of these are you most likely to use to improve your efficiency? Name several in each of the Outlook components that you find particularly useful.

Skills Review

EXERCISE 7-13

Insert a note as a message attachment and create a task from a message.

NOTE: This exercise uses the e-mail message you received in Exercise 7-1. If you do not have this message in your Inbox, complete Exercise 7-1, addressing the message to yourself. You can also use a different Inbox message if one is available.

1. Open the Notes folder and create a new note with the text **Recharge laptop battery**

2. Display the Inbox and start a new message, addressing it to your instructor.

NOTE: Your instructor will provide you with an appropriate e-mail address.

3. In the Subject text box, key **Don't forget**

4. Change the message format to Rich Text, key an appropriate salutation, and then key the text shown in Figure 7-19 for the body of the message.

FIGURE 7-19

Remember to charge up the battery before your trip tomorrow. I thought the note would help. Remember that you can leave the note open on your desktop even if you close Outlook.

5. Insert the note as a message attachment by following these steps:
   a. Click the down arrow next to the Insert File button [paperclip icon] on the Message form toolbar and click It**em**.
   b. Under **L**ook in, select the **Notes** folder.
   c. Select the "Recharge laptop battery" note.
   d. Click OK.

6. Connect to the Internet and send the message.

7. Display the Sent Items folder and print the message, using Memo Style as the print style. Add your name as a centered header and delete any existing footer information.

8. Display the Inbox and locate the "New facilities team" message, which you received from your classmate in Exercise 7-1.

9. Create a task from a message by following these steps:
   a. Select the "New facilities team" message. 
   b. Drag the message to the Outlook Bar and release the mouse button over the Tasks shortcut [icon].
   c. Delete the text in the Subject text box and key **Write up summary of project to date** 
   d. Click the **S**ave and Close button on the Task form toolbar.

10. Display the task list and print the "Write up summary of project to date" task. Use a Memo Style print style and add your name as a centered header.

EXERCISE 7-14

Create a note and link it to a contact.

1. Display the Notes folder and create a new note with the text **Make reservations for team lunch**

2. Display the Contacts folder and create a new contact for your instructor.

NOTE: Your instructor will supply you with an appropriate address.

3. Link the note to your instructor's listing in the contact list by following these steps:

    a. Make sure the Contacts folder is displayed.

    b. Locate the contact for your instructor, which you created in step 2.

    c. Right-click the contact and select **L**ink from the shortcut menu.

    d. Choose **I**tems from the submenu.

    e. Under **L**ook in, select the **Notes** folder. Select the "Make reservations for team lunch" note, which you created in step 1.

    f. Click **A**pply and then click **OK**.

4. Display the Notes folder, select the "Make reservations for team lunch" note, and print it. Add your name as a centered header and delete any existing footer information.

EXERCISE 7-15

Display the Journal, manually record a Journal item, open and edit the item, and print it.

1. Manually record a Journal item by following these steps:

    a. Display the folder list and select the Journal folder.

    b. If the Microsoft Outlook information box appears, click **No**.

    c. Click the **N**ew button on the Standard toolbar.

    d. In the **S**ubject text box, key **Reviewed new facilities activities to date**

    e. Click the down arrow next to the Entry type text box and select Document.

    f. Click the down arrow next to the **D**uration text box and select **2 hours.**

    g. Click the **S**ave and Close button.

2. Open and edit a Journal item by following these steps:

    a. With the Journal folder still displayed, click the plus sign (+) next to the Document entry type.

    b. Double-click the "Reviewed new facilities activities to date" item.

    c. Change the duration to **1 hour.**

    d. Click the **S**ave and Close button.

3. Print a Journal item by following these steps:

    a. Make sure the "Reviewed new facilities activities to date" item is selected.

    b. Choose **F**ile, **P**rint from the menu and print the item, using the Memo Style print style. Add your name as a centered header.

4. Delete a Journal item by following these steps:

a. Make sure the "Reviewed new facilities activities to date" item is selected.

b. Click the Delete button ☒ on the Standard toolbar.

EXERCISE 7-16

Add an appointment to the Calendar, create a task from it, and create a letter to a contact.

1. Display a date in the Appointments Calendar approximately two weeks from the current date. Delete any existing appointments for that day.

2. Add a new appointment with the subject **Presentation to Rob on new facilities work plan**. Make it a 1-hour appointment starting at 11 a.m. with the location **Rob's office**. Deselect the reminder. Save and close the appointment.

3. Create a task from a Calendar item by following these steps:

   a. Select the appointment you created in step 2.

   b. Move the pointer over the left move handle until the pointer changes to a four-pointed arrow ✛.

   c. Drag the selection to the TaskPad and release it anywhere in the TaskPad.

   d. Delete the existing text in the Subject text box and key **Prepare Power-Point presentation**

   e. Change the Start date to one week from the current date, deselect the reminder, and then click the Save and Close button on the Task form toolbar.

4. Display the Tasks folder, select the "Prepare PowerPoint presentation" task, and print it, using a Memo Style print style. Add your name as a centered header and the date as a centered footer.

5. Display the Contacts folder and create a new contact, using the information shown in Figure 7-20.

FIGURE 7-20

```
Media Graphics

1200 Main Street

Dubuque, IA 52001

(319) 555-1200

E-mail: mgraph@ISP.isp
```

6. Create a letter from a contact by following these steps:

    a. Make sure the contact list is displayed. Select the Media Graphics contact.

    b. Choose <u>A</u>ctions, New <u>L</u>etter to Contact.

    c. Select <u>D</u>ate line.

    d. Click <u>N</u>ext.

    e. Click the down arrow under the <u>S</u>alutation text box and select Dear Madam or Sir:

    f. Click <u>N</u>ext, and then click <u>N</u>ext again.

    g. In the <u>S</u>ender's name text box, key your name.

    h. Under Closing, click the down arrow next to Complimentar<u>y</u> closing and choose Sincerely.

    i. In the <u>J</u>ob title text box, key **Intern**. In the C<u>o</u>mpany text box, key **AllWood Mills, Inc.**

    j. Select <u>E</u>nclosures and then click <u>F</u>inish.

7. In the area of the document marked "Type your text here," key **I will need the presentation slides by next Wednesday. Enclosed you will find a purchase order.**

8. Choose <u>V</u>iew, <u>H</u>eader and Footer from the menu, click In<u>s</u>ert AutoText on the Header and Footer toolbar, and choose Filename from the drop-down list. Click <u>C</u>lose on the Header and Footer toolbar. Add appropriate spacing to the letter.

9. Save the file as *[your initials]*7-16

10. Click the Print button 🖨 to print the letter.

11. Close the Word document, save the changes, and close Word.

Lesson Applications

EXERCISE 7-17

Create a new contact, send a message using an alternate message format, move a sent message to the Task folder, attach a note to a message, link the note to a contact, and manually record a Journal item.

John Yu has asked you to work with Sean Anderson at Media Graphics, preparing in-store display materials for the new line of office furniture. John has asked you to document your time during the project, so you've decided to track all your activities.

1. Display the Contacts folder and add Sean Anderson to your contact list, using the information shown in Figure 7-21. (*Hint*: If you already have a listing for Media Graphics, you can edit that contact and use the <u>A</u>ctions, New <u>C</u>ontact from Same Company command.) For the e-mail address, you will use your instructor's e-mail address. Categorize the contact as Time & Expenses.

FIGURE 7-21

```
Mr. Sean Anderson, Account Manager

Media Graphics

1200 Main Street

Dubuque, IA 52001

(319) 555-1200

E-mail: Instructor@ISP.isp
```

NOTE: Your instructor will provide you with an appropriate e-mail address.

2. Create a new e-mail message, addressing the message to Sean Anderson from your contact list.

3. Key the subject of the message as **Activities this week**. For the text of the message, key the material shown in Figure 7-22, using a Rich Text message format.

FIGURE 7-22

```
John Yu has requested that I bill out my time to you for this project.
Below is a summary of my work for Media Graphics this past week:

Research

Collected all Traditional Homes ads

Located ad photography for last 2 years



Correspondence & Meetings

Called editor at Furniture Today magazine

Met with ad agency account manager
```

4. Format the "Research" and "Correspondence & Meetings" headings in bold-face. Make the entries under the headings bulleted text. Italicize the magazine titles. Space the text attractively.

5. Set the message importance to High. Assign the message to the Time & Expenses category. Spell-check the message.

6. Connect to the Internet and send the message.

7. Display the Sent Items folder and select the message you just sent. Print out the message, using a Memo Style print style. Add your name as a centered header and delete any existing footer information.

8. Create a task from the message, using the method that includes the content of the message in the Task form's text area. Make the subject **Start next week's activities report** with the due date approximately one week from the current date. Print the task from the task list, using a Memo Style print style. Add a header with your name on the left and the current date on the right.

9. Display the Notes folder and create a new note with the text **Call ad agency**. Display the contact list and link the note to Sean Anderson. Print the note with your name as a centered header.

10. Display the contact list in Detailed Address Cards view and print the Sean Anderson contact, using a Memo Style print style. Add your name as a centered header and delete any existing footer information. Display the contact list in Address Cards view.

11. Send a new e-mail message to Sean Anderson (your instructor) with the subject of **Reminder**. Set the message format to Plain Text and the message importance to Low. For the text of the message, key **You asked me to remind you to call the ad agency. I've attached a note to help. Remember you can leave the note open on your desktop even if you close Outlook.** Attach the "Call ad agency" note you created in step 9 to the message.

12. Make sure you are connected to the Internet, and then send the message.

13. Display the Sent Items folder and select the message you just sent. Print out the message, using a Memo Style print style. Add your name as a centered header and delete any existing footer information.

14. Create a manual Journal entry with the subject **Reviewed print ads with ad agency** and the entry type as a Meeting. Make the duration 1 hour and the start time as 11:00 a.m. one business day before the current date. Print the item and add a header with your name on the left and the current date on the right. Delete any existing footer information. Delete the item from the Journal when you are done printing.

EXERCISE 7-18

Send a message; add the recipient to the contact list, using the address; create a task from the sent message, link the task to the contact, create a task from a Calendar item, and make a manual Journal entry.

A national business magazine is profiling AllWood Mills in a story on small companies. Rob Connelly, AllWood's president, has asked you to work with the Marketing department in planning the magazine staff's visit.

1. Display the Contacts folder and delete any existing contacts.

2. Send an e-mail message to your instructor. Key the subject of the message as **Magazine staff visit**. For the text of the message, key an appropriate salutation and then key the material shown in Figure 7-23, using a Plain Text message format:

NOTE: Your instructor will provide you with an appropriate e-mail address.

FIGURE 7-23

```
I will be scheduling a meeting with you, Maria, and the visiting magazine
staff for two weeks from today. We'll meet in Conference Room 1. Who else
should be in attendance?
```

3. Set the message importance to High and the sensitivity to Confidential. Spell-check the message. Connect to the Internet and send the message.

4. Display the Sent Items folder and open the message you just sent. Using the To address in the opened message, add the address to your contact list. Include postal address information. Then close the Contact form and close the sent message.

> **NOTE:** Your instructor will supply you with appropriate postal address information.

5. With the Sent Items folder still displayed, create a task from the "Magazine staff visits" message you sent in step 3. Use the method that includes the content of the message in the text area of the Task form. Make the subject of the task **Plan meeting agenda**. Make the due date roughly one week from the current date. Set the start date as the current date and % Complete to 25%. Deselect the reminder.

6. Display the contact list. Using the contact you created in step 4 (your instructor), link the contact to the "Plan meeting agenda" task you created in step 5.

7. Display the contact list in Detailed Address Cards view and print the contact you created in step 4 (your instructor), using a Card Style print style. Add your name as a centered header and delete any existing footer information. Display the contact list in Address Cards view.

8. Display the task list and open the "Plan meeting agenda" task. Specify the actual work time spent for the task as 30 minutes. (*Hint*: Use the Details tab of the Task form to specify this information). Save the task and print it, using a Memo Style print style. Add a header with your name on the left and the current date on the right.

9. Display the Calendar folder and select a date roughly two weeks from the current date. Delete any existing appointments or meetings in the Appointments Calendar for that date. Add a new appointment from 10:00 to 11:45 a.m. with the subject **Meet with magazine staff**. Make the location **Conference Room 1** and set the importance to High. Deselect the reminder.

10. Add another appointment for that day from 1:00 to 4:00 p.m. with the subject **Magazine photography sessions**. Make the location **Manufacturing & Design**. Deselect the reminder.

11. Customize the Calendar by changing the font size of the Day view to 10 points and the time scale to 15 minutes. Deselect the option that displays Date Navigator dates in boldface for days containing Calendar items.

12. Print the Calendar for the day of the meeting date, using a Daily Style. Add a header with your name on the left and the current date on the right. Delete any existing footer information.

13. Drag the "Meet with magazine staff" appointment to the TaskPad, creating a task with the subject **Reserve audio/visual equipment**. Make the due date roughly one week from the current date. Deselect the reminder and set the Priority to Normal.

14. Display the task list and print the "Reserve audio/visual equipment" task you created in step 13, using a Memo Style print style. Add a header with your name on the left and the current date on the right. Delete any existing footer information.

15. Create a manual Journal entry with the subject **Sent meeting time and location to magazine staff** and the entry type as Document. Make the duration 30 minutes and the start time as 10:00 a.m. one business day before the current date. Print the item, adding a header with your name on the left and the current date on the right. Delete the item from the Journal when you have finished printing it.

16. Restore the default settings for the Calendar by changing the font size of the Day view to 8 points, setting the time scale to 30 minutes, and selecting the Date Navigator option to boldface days with Calendar items.

NOTE: Make sure you have completed the last step of this exercise. This step restores Outlook to its default settings. Always leave Outlook in its default state for the next class or student to use.

EXERCISE 7-19

Add a contact to the contact list, create and use a message template, format the message, create a task from a sent message, link the message to a contact, send a message with a note attachment, and create a letter from a contact listing.

Jasmine Jones, AllWood's VP of Sales, has asked you to help monitor the sales of the new line of office furniture. She also would like you to arrange regular meeting times with her and the store managers to discuss sales.

1. Display the Contacts folder and add Jasmine Jones to your contact list, using the information shown in Figure 7-24. For the e-mail address, you will use your instructor's e-mail address. Categorize the contact as Status. Create a new category in the Master Category list called **Sales** and assign the new contact to this category.

FIGURE 7-24

```
Ms. Jasmine Jones, VP of Sales

AllWood Mills, Inc.

3100 Jackson Street

Dubuque, IA 52004

(319) 555-4402

E-mail: Instructor@ISP.isp
```

NOTE: Your instructor will provide you with an appropriate e-mail address.

2. Change the default message editor to Outlook and compose a new message with the subject **Sales Status Report**. Use the text in Figure 7-25.

FIGURE 7-25

Below is a summary of the sales of the new office line for the preceding month for each of the stores:

Dubuque

Chicago

St. Louis

Kansas City

Minneapolis

Milwaukee

3. Underline the heading for each section and provide enough space between headings for text. Save the message as a template in your Lesson 7 folder, keying the filename as *[your initials]*7-19. Close the message without sending it.

4. Restore the default message editor to Word.

5. Open the message template and add your name as a header. (*Hint*: Place the insertion point in the message area and use the View, Header and Footer command). Print the template.

6. Address the message to Jasmine Jones, using the contact list entry you made in step 1. Change the message format to Rich Text. Key the following text for each city, using the same font as the existing text:

Dubuque:	$13,245
Chicago:	$ 24,540
St. Louis:	$5,650
Kansas City:	$15,450
Minneapolis:	$25,650
Milwaukee:	$0

7. Make sure the message is spaced attractively, and set the message importance to High. Connect to the Internet and send the message.

8. Display the Sent Items folder and create a task by using the method that includes the content of the "Sales Status Report" message in the text area of the Task form. Make the subject of the task **Call Milwaukee store again**. Make the due date the next business day and deselect the reminder.

9. Display the contact list. Link the Jasmine Jones contact to the "Call Milwaukee store again" task you created in step 8. Display the task list and print the "Call Milwaukee store again" task you created in step 8, using a Memo Style print style. Add a header with your name on the left and the current date on the right. Delete any existing footer information.

10. Display the Notes folder and create a new note with the text **Call Milwaukee for sales figures.**

11. Send a new message to Jasmine Jones (your instructor) with the subject **Call Milwaukee for sales figures**. Set the message format to Plain Text and key the text of the message as **The Milwaukee store manager said he would send the figures to you directly.** Attach the "Call Milwaukee for sales figures" note you created in step 10. Make sure you are connected to the Internet, and then send the message.

12. Display the Sent Items folder and print the "Call Milwaukee store for sales figures" message you just sent, using a Memo Style print style. Add your name as a centered header and delete any existing footer information.

13. Display the contact list, select the Jasmine Jones contact, and create a letter to the contact. Use a date line, an informal salutation, and an appropriate closing. Key your name as the sender's name with your title as **Intern, AllWood Mills, Inc.** Include the enclosures line. For the text of the letter, key **As you requested, I am sending you a hard copy of the sales figures for this month. Enclosed you will find a copy of the e-mail message I previously sent to you.**

14. Insert lines for appropriate spacing between the date, inside address, and so on. Save the file as *[your initials]*7-19 in your Lesson 7 folder. Print the letter and close Word.

15. Display the contact list in Detailed Address Cards view. Print the Jasmine Jones contact in Card Style. Add your name as a centered header and delete any existing footer information. Then display the contact list in Address Cards view.

16. Delete the Sales category from the Master Category List.

NOTE: Make sure you have completed the last step of this exercise. This step restores Outlook to its default settings. Always leave Outlook in its default state for the next class or student to use.

EXERCISE 7-20 ➕ *Challenge Yourself*

Create contacts and a distribution list, customize the Calendar, schedule a meeting from a contact, send a formatted message, create a new task request from a contact, create a task from a sent message, link items, customize the task list, make a manual Journal entry, and create an Office document.

Sales figures for the new line of office furniture have been excellent. Rob Connelly would like to implement a one-time bonus for all company employees. He has asked you to work with Maria Lopez on this highly confidential project.

1. Create an entry in your contact list for an office resource. Identify the office resource as Conference Room B. Create additional listings for two classmates and Rob Connelly, using the information shown in Figure 7-26. For the e-mail address of Rob Connelly, you will use your instructor's e-mail address. If any of these contacts already exist in your contact list, you can use them, but make sure the information is correct.

FIGURE 7-26

```
Mr. Rob Connelly, President

AllWood Mills, Inc.

3100 Jackson Street

Dubuque, IA 52004

(319) 555-4400

E-mail: Instructor@ISP.isp
```

NOTE: Your instructor will supply you with appropriate e-mail addresses for your office resource and contacts.

2. Assign the contacts for Rob Connelly and your classmates to a new category added to the Master Category List called **Bonus**. Associate each of the contacts with each other.

3. Create a distribution list entitled **Bonus Team** with the contacts you created in step 1 as members of the list (Rob Connelly and your two classmates; do not include the resource). Assign the distribution list to the Bonus category.

4. Display the task list and delete any existing tasks.

5. Create a new e-mail message and address the message to Rob Connelly from your contact list. Key the subject of the message as **Bonus project**. For the text of the message, key the material shown in Figure 7-27, using a Rich Text message format.

FIGURE 7-27

```
I will be delivering the following material to you by the end of this week:

Base salaries for senior managers

Sample letter to employees
```

6. Format the last two lines as bulleted text. Set the message importance to High and set the sensitivity to Confidential. Spell-check the message and assign it to the Bonus category. Connect to the Internet and send the message.

7. Display the Calendar folder and customize the Calendar display to show time intervals in 15-minute increments.

8. Display the date in the Appointments Calendar two weeks from the current date and delete any existing appointments or events. Schedule a meeting from 9:45 to 11:00 a.m. Add Rob Connelly as a required meeting attendee and add two classmates as optional meeting attendees. Use Conference Room B as the required resource.

9. For the subject of the meeting, key **Bonus Team Meeting**. Reserve the location Conference Room B. Deselect the reminder option. Add the following text to the message: **Review bonus figures for each employee.** Link the meeting with your two classmates from your contact list. Assign the meeting to the Bonus category and set the importance to High. Make sure you are connected to the Internet and send the message.

10. Display the contact list and create a task request from Rob Connelly's entry. Make the subject of the task **Get percentage bonus value by department**. Make the due date two business days from the current date. Add the following text to the message: **This number is necessary for the bonus spreadsheet.** Set the Status: to In Progress, set % Complete at 25%, and set the Priority to High. Assign it to the Bonus category and send the task request.

11. Create a new task with the subject **Get complete employee list**. Make the due date the next business day and add the following text to the task: **Get this from Maria.** Set % Complete to 75% and the Priority to High, and assign it to the Bonus category. Deselect the reminder.

12. Display the Sent Items folder and locate the "Bonus Team Meeting" message. Create a new task from this message by using the method that includes the message text in the Task form. Make the subject of the task **Develop meeting agenda**. Make the due date one week from the current date. Deselect the reminder and set the Priority to High.

13. Display the contact list and link all the tasks on the task list to Rob Connelly.

14. Display the task list and add the Contacts and Notes fields to the Detailed List view. Adjust column widths so that as much of the Notes field prints as possible. Print the task list in landscape orientation, using the Table Style print style. Add a header with your name on the left and the current date on the right. Delete any existing footer information. When you have finished, remove the Contacts and Notes fields from the Detailed List view, and display the contact list in Simple List view.

15. Display the Sent Items folder and select the "Bonus project" message you sent in step 5. Print the message, using Memo Style as the print style. Add your name as a centered header and delete any existing footer information.

16. In the Sent Items folder, select the "Bonus Team Meeting" invitation message you created in step 9. Print the message, using a Memo Style as the print style. Add your name as a centered header and delete any existing footer information.

17. Display the contact list in Detailed Address Card view. Select the additions you've made in this exercise (the two classmates, Rob Connelly, the distribution list, and the resource). Print the selected contacts, using a Card Style print style and adding your name as a centered header. Eliminate the blank-forms page at the end, but make sure the headings for each letter are included. Display the contact list in Address Cards view.

18. Display the date of the "Bonus Team Meeting" you created in step 9, which is two weeks from the current date. Print the Calendar in a Daily Style print style. Add your name as a centered header and the date as a centered footer. Restore the Calendar default to show time intervals in 30-minute increments.

19. Create a manual Journal entry with the subject **Worked on spreadsheet design** and the entry type as a Conversation. Make the duration 1 hour and the start time as 10:00 a.m. one business day before the current date. In the text area, key **John gave me a quick tutorial.** Print the item, adding your name as a centered header, and then delete the item from the Journal.

20. Create an Excel worksheet as a new Office document. For the worksheet data, use the data shown in Figure 7-28.

FIGURE 7-28

```
AllWood Mills, Inc.

Additional Compensation


Full Time Salaried

Employee            Dept.          Base Salary      Bonus Total


Full Time Hourly

Employee            Dept.          Base Salary      Bonus Total
```

21. Apply attractive formatting to the headings and total. Adjust column widths appropriately. Space the text so that data can be added. Add a header with your name, the filename, and the date. Save the worksheet as *[your initials]*7-20 in your Lesson 7 folder. Print the worksheet and then close it.

22. Create a new task with the subject **Update spreadsheet figures**. Attach the spreadsheet *[your initials]*7-20 that you created in step 21. Print the task in Memo Style with your name as a centered header.

23. Reset the Master Category List to its default setting by either deleting the Bonus category or resetting the list.

NOTE: Make sure you have restored system defaults in all steps where indicated. Always leave Outlook in its default state for the next class or student to use.

On Your Own

In these exercises you work on your own, as you would in a real-life work environment. Use the skills you've learned to accomplish the task—and be creative.

EXERCISE 7-21
Use the Internet to search for a new house or apartment. Research moving companies. Send messages, and create Calendar entries, contacts, tasks, and

notes. Integrate various Outlook components. Create Journal entries for your activities and a Word document related to the project. Print the messages, task list, Calendar, Journal entries, and notes.

EXERCISE 7-22

Plan a family reunion. Use the Internet to research the best location. Create a message template and send messages. Create contacts, Calendar items, tasks, Journal entries, and notes. Print the messages, task list, Calendar, Journal entries, and notes.

EXERCISE 7-23

Team up with a classmate to search for a new car by using the Internet. Send messages and create contacts, tasks, notes, Calendar items, and Journal entries. Create a Word document associated with a task and send it to your partner. Report your results to each other in formatted e-mail messages. Print sent messages, Calendar items, the task list, Journal entries, and notes.

Unit 3 Applications

UNIT APPLICATION 3-1

Create a new signature, create and edit a contact, send a formatted message by using various message options, schedule a meeting from a contact, create a task from a message, and print the task, message, and contact.

AllWood Mills has been doing quite well with their new line of office furniture, and they are expanding rapidly. Now they need to fill several key positions. Maria Lopez, AllWood's VP of Administration, has asked you to work with the executive recruiting firm that is handling the hiring.

1. Create a new listing in your contact list, using the information shown in Figure U3-1. For the e-mail address, you will use your instructor's e-mail address.

FIGURE U3-1

```
Sara Stevenson, Account Manager

Starr Executive Staffing, Inc.

211 Third Street

Dubuque, IA 52001

(319) 555-1900

E-mail: instructor@ISP.isp
```

NOTE: Your instructor will supply you with an appropriate e-mail address.

2. Assign the Sara Stevenson contact you created in step 1 to the Goals/Objectives category. Edit the contact to add an assistant's phone number of **(319) 555-1911** and a business FAX number of **(319) 555-1913**. Display the contact list in Detailed Address Cards view. Print the contact in Memo Style print style. Add your name as a centered header and delete any existing footer information. Display the contact list in Address Cards view.

3. Display your Inbox folder and create a signature. Use your initials as the name of the new signature, and key the following text for the signature:

   [your name]
   AllWood Mills Administrative Intern

4. Italicize the second line of the signature. Apply the new signature to new messages.

5. Create a new e-mail message, addressing the message to Sara Stevenson from your contact list. Key the subject of the message as **Recruiting focus**. For the text of the message, key an appropriate salutation, and then key the material shown in Figure U3-2, using a Rich Text message format.

FIGURE U3-2

```
Maria asked me to remind you again of the key qualities we're looking for
in our new hires:

Energy and high motivation

Relevant work experience

Good communication skills
```

6. Set the message importance to High, and set a For Your Information flag with no due date. Format the last three lines as bulleted text. Underline the word "Good." Set the sensitivity to Confidential. Spell-check the message and then send it.

7. Delete the signature you created in step 3.

8. Display the contact list, select the Sara Stevenson contact, and schedule a meeting from the contact. Plan the meeting for one week from the current date, from 9:30 a.m. to 10:30 a.m.

9. For the subject of the meeting, key **Review position ads**. Deselect the reminder option. Add the following text to the message: **We'd like to see the position descriptions before you run the ads.** Specify the location as **Maria's office**. Assign the meeting to the Status category and send the message.

10. Display the Sent Items folder, locate the "Recruiting focus" message you sent in step 6, and create a new task from it by using the method that includes the content of the message in the text area of the task. Make the subject of the task **Create more specific recruiting focus**. Make the due date two business days from the current date. Add the following text to the message above the existing text: **Maria wants more specifics to give to the recruiters.** Deselect the reminder. Set the Status: to In Progress, and set the Priority to Normal. Specify total work time as 1 hour.

11. Display the task list and print the "Create more specific recruiting focus" task you created in step 10, using a Memo Style print style. Add a header with your name on the left and the current date on the right. Delete any existing footer information.

12. Locate the "Review position ads" meeting invitation message in the Sent Items folder and print it, using a Memo Style print style. Add your name as a centered header and delete any existing footer information.

UNIT APPLICATION 3-2

Create and edit a new contact list item, create a category, customize the Calendar and schedule a meeting from a contact listing, create a task from a Calendar item, link items to a contact, create a document from a contact listing, and print the contact, the meeting invitation, the task, the Calendar, and the document.

AllWood is in the process of interviewing various candidates for the new positions they have created. You've been asked to help with the interviewing. As part of the hiring process, AllWood has the final candidates' references checked. You will need to coordinate this with the firm that AllWood uses to perform this check.

1. Display the contact list and delete any existing contacts. Create a new listing in your contact list, using the information shown in Figure U3-3. For the e-mail address, you will use your instructor's e-mail address.

FIGURE U3-3

```
Philip Small, Private Investigator

Employee Background Screening, Inc.

110 Main Street, Suite 300

Dubuque, IA 52001

(319) 555-4400

E-mail: instructor@ISP.isp
```

NOTE: Your instructor will provide you with an appropriate address.

2. Assign the contact you created in step 1 to a custom category called **Hiring**. Edit the contact to add an assistant's phone number of **(319) 555-1401** and a business FAX number of **(319) 555-1430**. Display the contact list in Detailed Address Cards view. Print the contact in a Memo Style print style with your name as a centered header. Delete any existing footer information.

3. Display a date in the Calendar two business days from the current date. Delete any existing appointments or events for that date. Customize the Calendar to show time intervals in 15-minute increments. Schedule a new appointment from 9:00 to 9:45 a.m. with the subject of **Interview:**

T. Jones and a location of **My office**. Deselect the reminder. Schedule another 45-minute appointment starting at 10:00 a.m. Use a subject of **Interview: R. Fanelli** and the same location, and deselect the reminder.

4. Display your contact list and select Philip Small. Schedule a meeting from the selected contact at 11:00 a.m. on the same day as the interviews you scheduled in step 3. Make the subject **Review credentials of final candidates** and a location of **Maria's office**. Make the meeting 1 hour long. Deselect the reminder and set the importance to High. Send the meeting invitation.

5. Display the Calendar for the date when you scheduled the meetings in steps 3 and 4. Create a task from the "Review credentials of final candidates" meeting, using a method that includes the content of the meeting in the text area of the task. Make the subject **Send resumes of final candidates**. Make the due date the next business day (the day before the interviews). Deselect the reminder and make sure the Priority is set to High.

6. Display the contact list and select Philip Small. Link this contact to the three Calendar items you created in steps 3 and 4 (the two interviews and the "Review credentials of final candidates" meeting), the sent meeting invitation (the "Review credentials of final candidates" message), and the "Send resumes of final candidates" task you created in step 5.

7. Display the Sent Items folder, locate the "Review credentials of final candidates" meeting invitation you sent in step 4, and print it in a Memo Style print style. Add your name as a centered header. Display the task list and print the "Send resumes of final candidates" task you created in step 5 in a Memo Style print style. Add your name as a centered header. Display the Appointments Calendar for the date with the three appointments you created in steps 3 and 4. Print the Calendar in a Daily Style print style with your name as a centered header and the date as a centered footer.

8. Display the contact list and create a letter from the Philip Small listing. Include the date line and use an informal salutation. For the closing, include your name, a job title of **Administrative Intern**, the company name, and an appropriate complimentary closing. The letter should show two enclosures. For the text of the letter, key the information in Figure U3-4.

FIGURE U3-4

```
Enclosed you will find the resumes of the two final candidates for the
positions we are currently filling in the Marketing and Sales departments.
Please call Maria Lopez if you have any questions.
```

9. Insert appropriate spacing in the document, including a 2-inch top margin and spacing between the date, inside address, salutation, closing, your

name, and the enclosures line. Save the file as *[your initials]*U3-2. Print the document and close Word.

10. Restore the default setting to the Calendar of 30-minute time increments. Delete the Hiring category or reset the Master Category List.

UNIT APPLICATION 3-3

Create new contacts, edit the contacts and assign them to customized categories, create letters from contact listings, create and send a formatted message from a contact listing, create a task from a sent message, link an item to a contact, create a manual Journal entry, and print the contacts, task, letters, and Journal entries.

AllWood has recently hired two new professionals. Rob Connelly, AllWood's president, has asked you to help orient the new employees while they get familiar with the company and their coworkers. You'll be scheduling them for orientation meetings and lunches with their new colleagues and assigning them tasks that will help get them acquainted with everyone.

1. Create two new listings in your contact list, using the information shown in Figure U3-5, but do not key the comments in red, which indicate if the information is home or business data. For one of the e-mail addresses, you will use your instructor's e-mail address.

FIGURE U3-5

Mr. Ray Fanelli	Ms. Tasha Jones
23 Pine Street *(Home)*	67 Oak Lane *(Home)*
Dubuque, IA 52004	Dubuque, IA 52001
(319) 555-4462 *(Home)*	(319) 555-5150 *(Home)*
E-mail: instructor@ISP.isp	E-mail: tjones@ISP.isp

NOTE: Your instructor will provide you with his or her e-mail address.

2. Create a new category in the Master Category List called **Sales** and assign the Ray Fanelli contact to it. Create another new category called **Marketing** and assign the Tasha Jones contact to it. Add the company name to both new contacts and add the following business address to both contacts:

3100 Jackson Street
Dubuque, IA 52004

3. Display the contact list and create a letter from the Ray Fanelli listing. (The mailing address should be the home address.) Include the date line and use an informal salutation. For the closing, include your name, a job title of **Administrative Intern**, the company name, and an appropriate complimentary closing. The letter should not show any enclosures. For the text of the letter, key the information in Figure U3-6.

FIGURE U3-6

Welcome to AllWood Mills! I have been assigned the very pleasant duty of helping you get acquainted with your coworkers here at AllWood when you start next week. We're all looking forward to meeting you. I will be sending you an orientation packet in a day or two. If you have any questions in the meantime, please call me.

4. Insert appropriate spacing in the document, including a 2-inch top margin and spacing between the date, inside address, salutation, closing, and your name. Save the file as *[your initials]*U3-3a. Print the document and close Word. Create a similar letter from the Tasha Jones contact and save the file as *[your initials]*U3-3b. Print the second letter and close Word.

5. Create a new e-mail message, addressing the message to Ray Fanelli from your contact list. Key the subject of the message as **Your first week**. For the text of the message, key an appropriate salutation and then key the material shown in Figure U3-7, using a Rich Text message format.

FIGURE U3-7

This is just to let you know what we're scheduling for you for the rest of your first week:

Tuesday - Lunch with the Marketing Team

Wednesday - AM tour of Manufacturing

Thursday - AM meeting with Design Team

Friday - Lunch with Sales and Administration

6. Set the message importance to High, and set a No Response Necessary flag with no due date. Format the last four lines as bulleted text. Spell-check the message and then send it.

7. Display the Sent Items folder and locate the "Your first week" message you just sent. Create a task from the message by using the method that includes the content of the message in the text area of the task. Specify the subject of the task as **Complete Ray's agenda**. Set the Status: to In Progress and % Complete to 50%. Set the Priority to Normal, with a due date of the current date.

8. Display the contact list and link the "Complete Ray's agenda" task you created in step 7 to the Ray Fanelli contact. Display the task list and print the "Complete Ray's agenda" task in a Memo Style print style. Add a header with your name on the left and the current date on the right. Delete any existing footer information.

9. Create a manual Journal entry with the subject **Worked on Ray's first week** and the entry type as a phone call. Make the duration 1 hour and the start time as 10:00 a.m. one business day before the current date. In the text area, key **Called the managers of the different departments and set up agenda**. Link it with the Ray Fanelli contact. Print the item, adding your name as a centered header. Delete it from the Journal when you have finished.

10. Display the contact list in Detailed Address Cards view. Print both contacts you created in step 1 in a Card Style print style. Add your name as a centered header and delete any existing footer information. Display the contact list in Address Cards view.

11. Delete the Sales and Marketing categories from the Master Category List or reset the Master Category List.

UNIT APPLICATION 3-4   *Using the Internet*

Pretend you are going to purchase an item from an online auction house. Work out a strategy to research and buy a snowboard, skateboard, or scooter for yourself, a friend, or a relative. The item you choose may be new or used. Although you won't actually buy the object, you should follow the entire process as if you would.

If you've never bought anything from an online auction house, you'll first need to research how it's done. After you've learned how the bidding process works, search for sales of the item you've chosen. If you find there are not many being offered for sale, switch to something else. You might need to do some research to evaluate different models of the same item. For example, if you're buying a snowboard, you'll want to decide what size board is appropriate for you or the person for whom you're buying it. Snowboard sizes are based on an individual's height and weight.

Bidding on an item generally occurs over a period of several days or more. Sometimes there are no bids on an item until the very end of the auction. You might wish to observe the bidding on an item as it expires to see how the price can rapidly escalate. Many successful buyers find it is best to wait until the last hour or half-hour of the auction to place their bids. Successful bidders are under contractual obligation to buy the objects on which they bid. Payment is often made by check, money order, or credit card.

Find at least three auctions of your chosen item that are expiring during a three-day time period. Decide the maximum amount you would be willing to pay for each of the three objects. Research the sellers. Online auction houses maintain a history of buyers' and sellers' sales, and each can post comments about how satisfied they have been with the other. See how many sales the seller has conducted at that auction house, and evaluate the buyer feedback that is posted on the seller.

After you've obtained your information, use Outlook to create the following:

- Add one seller to your contact list and e-mail the seller with a question about the item. Sellers will usually gladly answer legitimate questions about their merchandise before the conclusion of the auction. Forward the response you get from the seller to your instructor. Locate the message in the Sent Items folder and print it.

- Compose and send an e-mail message to your instructor describing each of the three auctions you have selected. Explain your logic in choosing the ones you chose. Copy and paste any relevant feedback about each of the sellers into your message. Make sure you note when each auction is expiring. Use Rich Text or HTML formatting in your message to enhance its appearance and readability. Use any other message options that are appropriate.

- Schedule appointments in your Calendar for the last hour of the auction. The appointment should end when the auction ends. Customize the time scale of the Appointments Calendar, if necessary. Set a reminder to go off an hour before each appointment. Delete any other appointments or events for the week and print the Calendar, using a Weekly Style print style. Be sure to change the customized Calendar settings back to the default when you have finished.

- Create notes to remind yourself about the expiring auction times. Print the notes.

- Assume that you are the successful bidder for your item. Create a task in your task list related to the payment of the item, such as buying a postal money order. Print the task.

- After the auction period expires, check back on the auction site and see what price was actually paid for your chosen items. Note the prices and send the information to your instructor in another e-mail message. Flag the message as For Your Information with no reminder, and set the importance to High. Locate the message in the Sent Items folder and print it.

- Hand in all printouts to your instructor.

NOTE: Your instructor will provide you an appropriate e-mail address.

Appendices

APPENDIX A

Windows Tutorial

If you're unfamiliar with Windows, review this Windows Tutorial carefully. You'll learn how to use a mouse; how to start Windows; how to use the taskbar, menus, and dialog boxes; and other important aspects of Windows.

If you're familiar with Windows but need help navigating Windows files and folders, refer to Appendix B: "File Management." There you'll find information on how Windows stores information and how to use Windows Explorer.

NOTE: All examples from this Tutorial refer specifically to Windows 2000. If you are using any other version of Windows, your screen might differ slightly from the images shown in this Tutorial. However, because most basic features are common to all versions of Windows, this Tutorial should be helpful to you no matter what version of Windows you use.

Using the Mouse

Although you can use the keyboard with Windows, you'll probably find yourself using the mouse most of the time. A *mouse* is a pointing device that is typically attached to your computer. You roll the mouse on any flat surface, or on a *mouse pad*, typically a smooth pad on which the mouse rests. The mouse is used to move a pointer on the computer screen. A *pointer* is typically a small arrow that you move on the computer screen to accomplish specific tasks.

As you roll the mouse (typically on a mouse pad), the pointer on the computer screen moves in the direction you move the mouse. Thus, when you roll the mouse to the left, the pointer on the screen moves to the left. When you roll the mouse to the right, the pointer on the screen moves to the right. By using the mouse you can position the pointer on objects on the computer screen.

TIP: When moving the mouse on the mouse pad, if you reach the edge of the pad, just pick up the mouse and place it in the center of the pad. This won't change the position of the pointer on the screen.

A mouse typically has two buttons at the front (the edge of the mouse where the cord attaches)—one on the left and one on the right. (A mouse might also have a center button or a wheel, but these are not typical; therefore, a center button or wheel isn't discussed in this Tutorial.)

To choose an item on the computer screen by using the mouse, roll the mouse until the pointer on the screen is over the desired item. Then press and release the left mouse button once. Pressing and releasing the mouse button is referred to as a *click*. Doing this twice is referred to as a *double-click*. Whenever you're told to "click" or "double-click" an item on the computer screen, use the left mouse button.

The right mouse button is used less frequently. Pressing and quickly releasing the right mouse button is referred to as a *right-click*.

You can use the mouse to *drag* an object to another location on-screen. To do this you position the pointer on the object you want to drag, hold down the left mouse button, and roll the mouse until the pointer is at the position where you want to drop the object. Then release the mouse button and the object is dropped at the specified location. (You can see why this type of mouse action is also referred to as *drag-and-drop*.)

You can also select an object by using the mouse. To do this you position the pointer on one side of the object, hold down the left mouse button, and roll the mouse until the pointer reaches the other side of the object. Then release the mouse button. The selected object is highlighted in some way. In Windows, you often need to select an object before you can perform some action on it. For example, you often need to select an object before you can copy it.

As you progress in this Tutorial you will become familiar with the terms in Table A-1 describing the actions you can take with a mouse.

TABLE A-1   Mouse Terms

TERM	DESCRIPTION
Point	Roll the mouse until the tip of the pointer is touching the desired item on the computer screen.
Click	Quickly press and release the left mouse button.
Double-click	Quickly press and release the left mouse button twice.
Drag (or drag-and-drop)	Point to an object on-screen, hold down the left mouse button, and roll the mouse until the pointer is in position. Then release the mouse button.
Right-click	Quickly press and release the right mouse button.
Select	Hold down the left mouse button; roll the mouse so the pointer moves from one side of an object to another. Then release the mouse button.

As you perform actions on-screen using the mouse, the on-screen pointer changes its appearance, depending on where it's located and what operation you are performing. Table A-2 shows the most common types of pointers.

TABLE A-2   Frequently Used Mouse Pointers

POINTER	DESCRIPTION
⬥ Pointer	Used to point to objects.
I I-Beam	Used in keying, inserting, and selecting text.

continues

TABLE A-2 **Frequently Used Mouse Pointers** *continued*

POINTER	DESCRIPTION
↙ 2-Headed Arrow	Used to change the size of objects or windows.
✛ 4-Headed Arrow	Used to move objects.
⧖ Hourglass	Indicates the computer is processing a command. While the hourglass is displayed, it is best to wait rather than try to continue working.
🖐 Hand	Used in Window's Help system to display additional information.

Starting Windows

All computers are not set up the same way. In most cases, however, when you turn on your computer, Windows loads automatically and the Windows desktop appears. The *desktop* is the area that first appears on the computer screen after you start Windows. The desktop is your on-screen work area. All the elements you need to start working with Windows appear on the desktop.

1. Turn on the computer. Windows begins loading, and a Windows log-on screen displays.

NOTE: On some computers, the log-on screen does not appear automatically. You might have to press the following keys, all at once, and then quickly release them: Ctrl, Alt and Delete. If your computer is on a network, your instructor might need to provide you with special start-up instructions.

2. You now need to log on to Windows, using your user name and password. To start this process, move the pointer to the <u>U</u>ser name box. The pointer turns into an I-beam. If someone else's name appears in the <u>U</u>ser name box, use Delete or Backspace to delete the name before keying yours. Key your user name. If you make a mistake, press Backspace to delete your mistakes and then key correctly.

NOTE: If you don't know your Windows user name and password, ask your instructor for help. If your computer is attached to a network, you also might be prompted to log on to the network before you log on to Windows.

3. When you finish keying your user name, move the pointer to the <u>P</u>assword box and key your password.

4. When your user name and password are correctly keyed, click OK. The Windows desktop appears.

The Windows Desktop

The left side of the Windows desktop contains *icons*, small pictures that represent programs, files, or folders. If you double-click an icon, the program, file, or folder represented by that icon opens. (Appendix B: "File Management" contains a complete discussion of files and folders.)

FIGURE A-1
Windows desktop

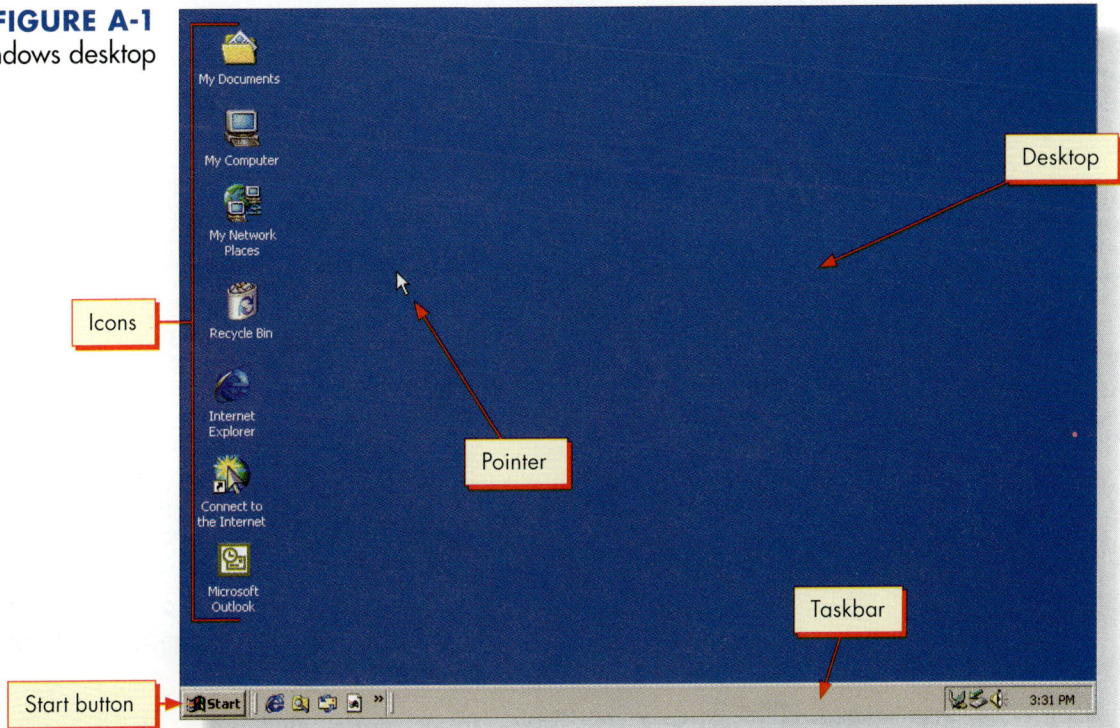

NOTE: Depending on how your computer is set up, your icons might be different from those shown in Figure A-1.

Two important icons are found on virtually all Windows desktops:

- **My Computer**
  When you double-click this icon, a new window opens showing icons representing the disk drives available on your computer (and on your network, if you are on one). Use My Computer when you want to view the contents of a hard disk or a floppy disk.

- **Recycle Bin**
  When you double-click this icon, a new window opens listing files you have deleted. Until you empty the Recycle bin, these files can be undeleted and used.

Another important component of the desktop is the *taskbar*. This bar usually appears at the bottom of the desktop. Buttons on the taskbar show which programs and windows are currently open.

Using the Start Menu

The taskbar contains the Start button , which is the most important button in Windows. Clicking the Start button causes the Start menu to appear. This menu provides a list of commands and shortcuts to files. From the Start menu you can perform many Windows tasks. Table A-3 describes the components of the Start menu.

FIGURE A-2
Start menu

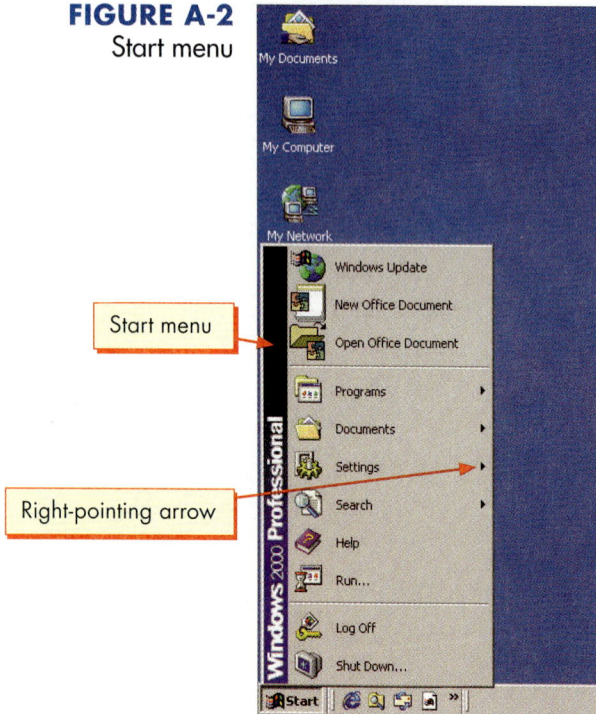

Start menu

Right-pointing arrow

Some items on the Start menu also show a right-pointing arrow. This means additional choices are available on a secondary menu, called a *submenu*. When you point to a menu item with a right-pointing arrow, the submenu appears.

1. Click the Start button on the Windows taskbar.

2. The Start menu appears.

NOTE: The Start menu can be customized. It might not show the Log Off command. It might show the Favorites command, which displays a list of favorite Internet addresses. It might also show the commands with individual letters underlined. You can use the underlined letters as an alternate method of executing a command. Instead of clicking the command, you key the letter that is underlined.

TABLE A-3	**Start Menu**
COMMAND	**USE**
Windows Update	Connects to the Microsoft Web site for Windows updates.
New Office Document	Starts a new Microsoft Office document of any type.
Open Office Document	Opens an existing Microsoft Office document.
Programs	Displays a submenu listing the programs on your computer. Clicking a program instructs Windows to start the program.
Documents	Displays a submenu listing recently opened documents.
Settings	Displays a submenu listing system components for which you can change settings.

continues

TABLE A-3	Start Menu *continued*
COMMAND	**USE**
Search	Displays a submenu listing commands that enable you to locate a file, folder, Internet address, or people.
Help	Starts the Windows Help function. Windows Help instructs you how to perform tasks in Windows.
Run	Allows you to type a command to start a program.
Log Off	Closes all programs, disconnects your computer from the network and Internet, and prepares your computer for someone else to use.
Shut Down	Shuts down, restarts, or places your computer in a stand-by mode.

Using the Programs Command

Most programs on your computer can be started from the **Programs** command on the **Start** menu. This is the easiest way to open a program.

The **Programs** menu normally uses the *Personalized Menus* feature in Windows. This feature keeps the menus relatively uncluttered by hiding items that have not been used recently. You expand the menu to its full size, showing all its options, by clicking the down arrow at the bottom of the menu.

1. With the Start menu open on your screen, point to **Programs**. (Or, you can click **Programs**.) The Programs submenu appears, listing the programs installed on your computer. Every computer has a different list of programs.

2. Point to the down arrow at the bottom of the **Programs** submenu (or click it). The Programs menu is expanded to its full size.

FIGURE A-3
Programs submenu

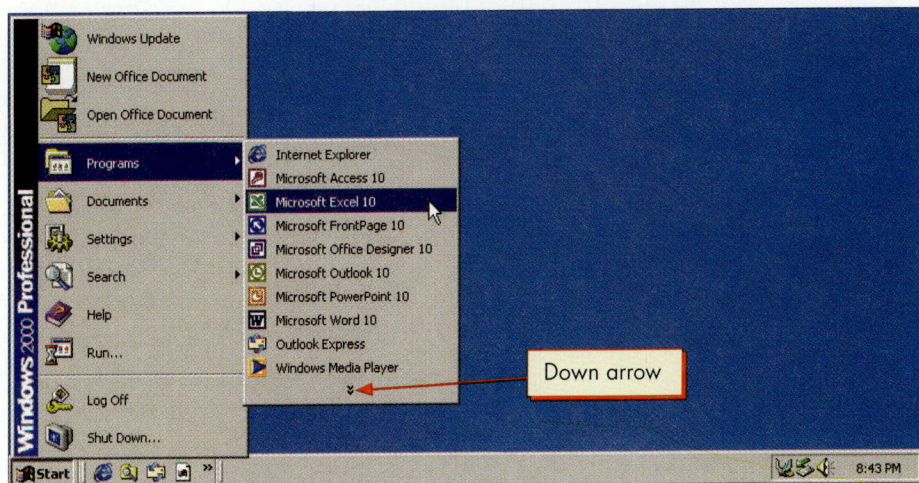

3. Point to the program you want to open and click. (For the purposes of this Tutorial, you can open Excel, a spreadsheet program in Microsoft Office.) In a few seconds, the program you selected loads and its first screen appears. Notice that a button for the program appears on the taskbar.

Using the Taskbar

Using the taskbar, you can switch between open programs and between open documents within a program. Windows displays a button on the taskbar for each program and document that is currently open.

The window in which you are working is called the *active* window. The title bar for the active window is highlighted, and its taskbar button is also highlighted.

1. The program window you opened in the previous procedure should still be open. To open a second program, click the Start button **Start**, choose **Programs** from the **Start** menu, and then choose an option from the **Programs** submenu. (For the purpose of this Tutorial, you can open Word, a word-processing program in Microsoft Office.) Notice how the second program covers the first. The window containing the second program is now active. Its title bar is highlighted, as is its button on the taskbar.

2. Click the button on the taskbar for the first program you opened. The first program (Excel) appears again.

3. Click the button on the taskbar for the second program (Word) to switch back to it.

4. Start a new blank document in Word by clicking the New Blank Document button on the Word toolbar. (Toolbars are usually located near the top of the screen. See Figure A-4 on the next page.) Notice that each open document has its own taskbar button so you can easily switch between documents.

5. Click the button on the taskbar for the first program you opened (Excel). Now practice using the taskbar to switch between program windows and between document windows until you feel comfortable.

6. Move the pointer to the top edge of the taskbar until it changes from a pointer to a two-headed arrow $\updownarrow$. Using the two-headed arrow, you can move the taskbar or change its size.

7. With the pointer displayed as a two-headed arrow, hold down the left mouse button and move the arrow up until the task bar moves up, changing position with the status bar at the bottom of the program window. (See Figure A-4 for the location of the status bar.)

8. Move the pointer to the top edge of the taskbar once again until the two-headed arrow displays. Hold down the left mouse button and move the arrow down to the bottom of the screen. The taskbar is restored to its original position.

FIGURE A-4
Excel is the
active window

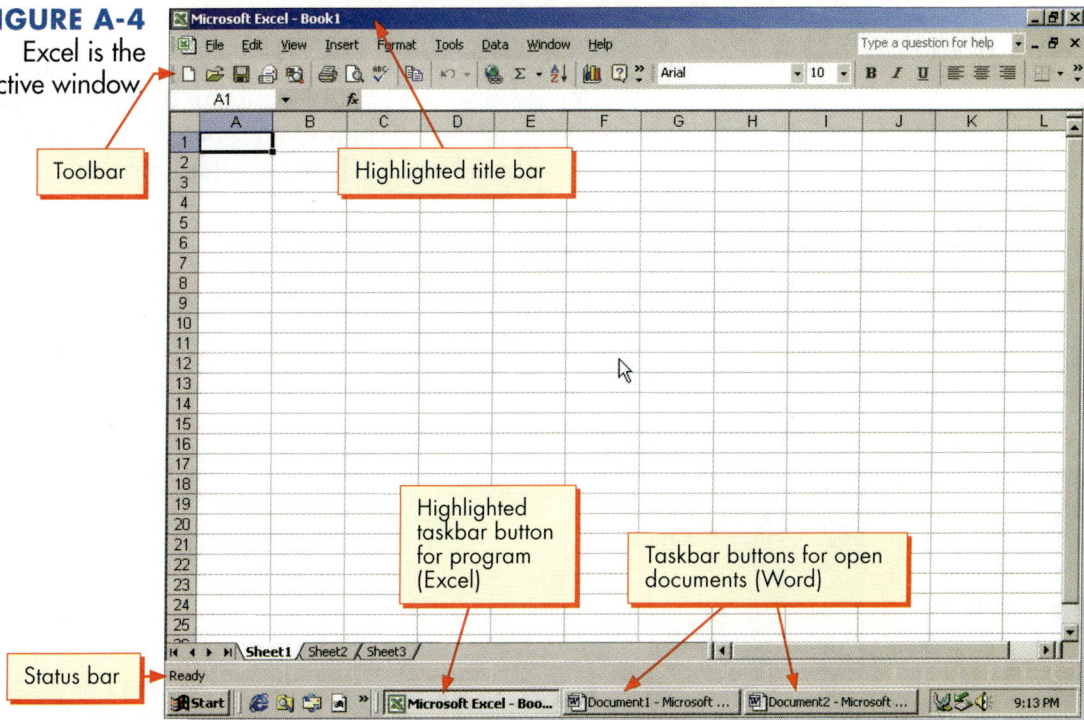

Toolbar

Highlighted title bar

Highlighted
taskbar button
for program
(Excel)

Taskbar buttons for open
documents (Word)

Status bar

NOTE: You might sometimes see the taskbar displayed along the sides or the top of the desktop. You can change the position of the taskbar on the desktop by dragging it. You do this by placing the pointer over the taskbar, holding down the left mouse button, moving the pointer to the new location, and then releasing the mouse button.

Using Menus

Most Windows applications use a similar menu structure. You use the mouse to open a menu containing various menu options (these are often called commands). You can open a menu by clicking the name of a menu from the *menu bar,* a row of menu names just below the title bar. Then you can click a menu option from the menu to execute that menu option.

Alternatively, you can use the keyboard to open menus and choose menu options. To open a menu, you press Alt and the underlined letter of the menu name at the same time. For example, to open the File menu, you hold down Alt and press F. You can use the keyboard again to choose a menu option. For example, with the File menu open, you use Alt + S (the underlined character from the Save command) to choose the Save command. Using a combination of Alt and a key underlined in the command you want to choose is a type of *keyboard shortcut.*

1. Make the Excel window the active window (if it is not already) by clicking its button on the taskbar.

2. Click **Edit** on the menu bar. The **Edit** menu appears.

Three dots following a menu option indicate that a dialog box is displayed when that menu option is chosen. (The next section of this Tutorial discusses dialog boxes.) Some commands also show toolbar buttons or keyboard shortcuts next to the command name. These are alternative ways to execute the command.

Notice that each of the menu names has an underlined character.

FIGURE A-5
Edit menu
from Excel

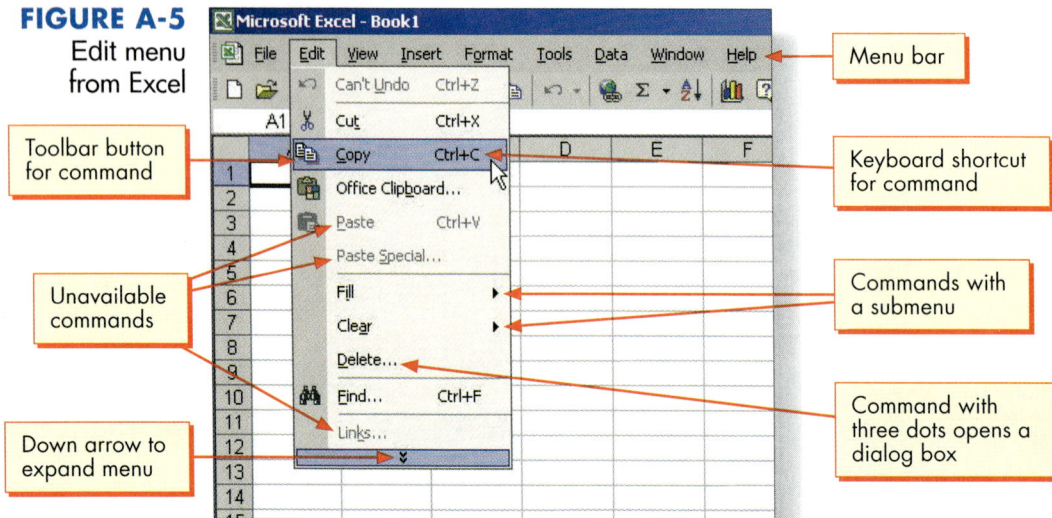

Menu bar

Toolbar button for command

Keyboard shortcut for command

Unavailable commands

Commands with a submenu

Command with three dots opens a dialog box

Down arrow to expand menu

3. Click **Edit** on the menu bar again. The menu closes.

4. Press [Alt]+[E], the keyboard shortcut for the Edit menu. The **Edit** menu appears again.

5. Click **Edit** on the menu bar again to close the Edit menu.

6. Press [Alt]+[V], the keyboard shortcut for the View menu. The **View** menu appears.

FIGURE A-6
View menu
expanded from
Excel

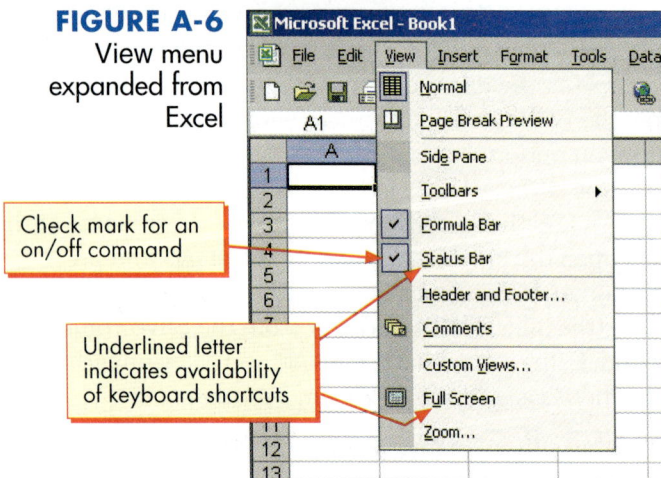

Check mark for an on/off command

Underlined letter indicates availability of keyboard shortcuts

7. Click the down arrow at the bottom of the menu to display the entire View menu. Some commands have check marks next to them. This means the command can be turned on or off.

Notice also that all the commands in the menu have an underlined letter, indicating that they, too, have keyboard shortcuts.

8. Click **View** to close the **View** menu.

Using Dialog Boxes

Windows applications make frequent use of dialog boxes. A *dialog box* is a window that requests input from you related to a command you have chosen. All Windows applications use a common dialog box structure.

1. Make the Word program the active window.

2. Choose File on the menu bar. The File menu appears.

3. Click the down arrow at the bottom of the menu to display the entire File menu. The three dots following the Print command indicate that when you choose Print, a dialog box will be displayed.

4. Choose Print. The Print dialog box appears. It contains some of the most common types of dialog box options.

FIGURE A-7
Print dialog box in Word

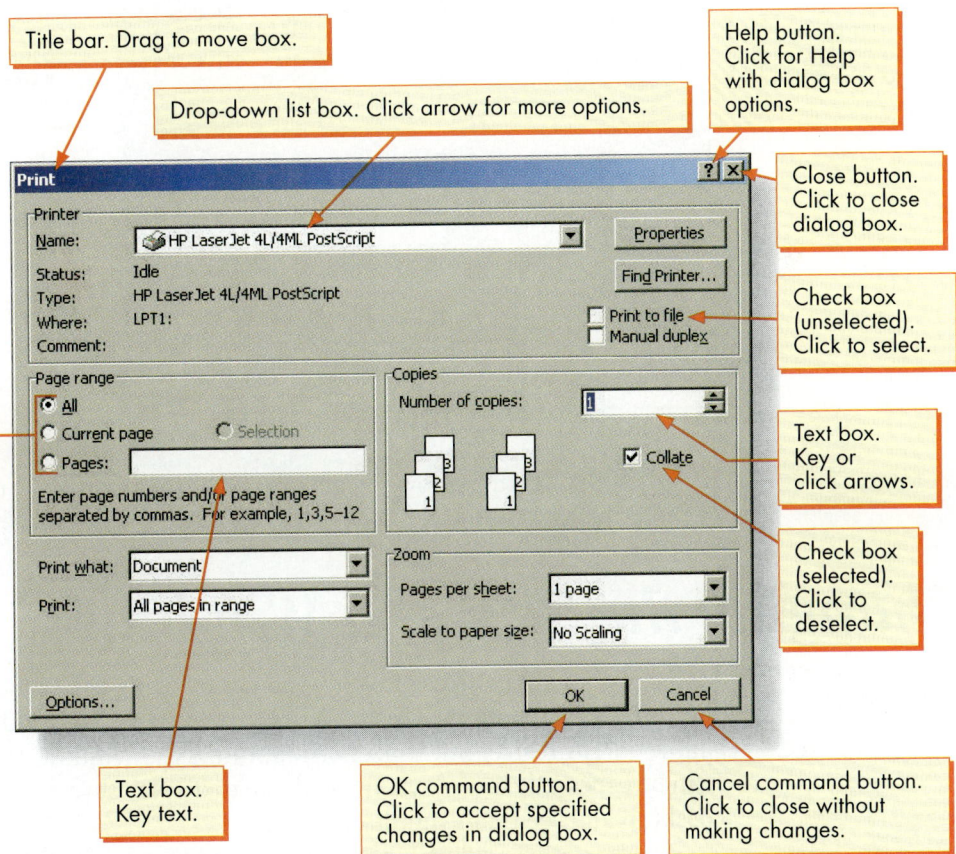

Title bar. Drag to move box.

Drop-down list box. Click arrow for more options.

Help button. Click for Help with dialog box options.

Close button. Click to close dialog box.

Option buttons. Only one in a group can be selected.

Check box (unselected). Click to select.

Text box. Key or click arrows.

Check box (selected). Click to deselect.

Text box. Key text.

OK command button. Click to accept specified changes in dialog box.

Cancel command button. Click to close without making changes.

NOTE: The underlined letters indicate the options that have keyboard shortcuts. For example, to choose All as the print range, you would key Alt + A.

5. Click Cancel, which is located in the lower right corner of the dialog box. The Print dialog box closes without making any changes.

6. Make Excel the active window.

7. Click **Format** on the menu bar. The **Format** menu appears.

8. Choose **Cells**. The Format Cells dialog box displays.

   The tabs under the title bar are the most significant feature of this type of dialog box. (See Figure A-8.)

9. Click the **Font** tab, if it is not already displayed.

   To use the scroll bar in the **Font**, **Font style**, or **Size** list boxes, you can click the vertical scroll arrows to scroll through the options. You can also drag the scroll box up or down to scroll through the options.

FIGURE A-8
Format Cells dialog box, Font tab, in Excel

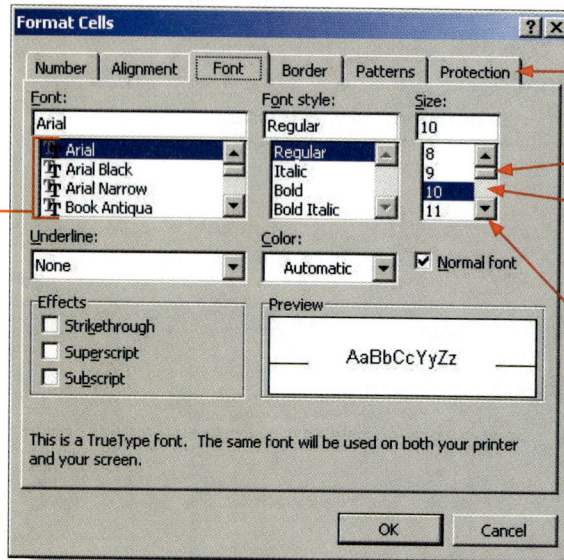

List box. Scroll to display; click to select.

Tabs. Click to display.

Scroll box. Drag to scroll.

Scroll bar. Use to move up or down in a list box.

Vertical scroll arrows: Click to scroll up or down.

10. Click **Cancel** in the lower right corner of the dialog box to close it without making any changes.

Changing the Size of a Window

You can change the sizes of your windows by using either the mouse or the sizing buttons. *Sizing buttons* are the small buttons on the right side of the title bar that allow you to resize, minimize, or maximize the window. (See Figure A-9.) This can be especially useful when you'd like to display several open windows on your desktop and see them simultaneously.

There are three sizing buttons that can appear on the title bar of every window: the Minimize button, the Maximize button, and the Restore Down button. Table A-4 (on the next page) describes each of these buttons.

1. Make Excel the active window, if it is not already. Click the Maximize button on the Excel title bar if the Excel window does not fill the entire desktop.

2. Click the Restore Down button on the Excel title bar. The Excel window reduces in size, and the Word window appears behind it. Notice that the highlighted title bar of the Excel window indicates it is the active window.

TABLE A-4　　　　**Sizing Buttons**

BUTTON	USE
▬ Minimize	Reduces the window to a button on the taskbar
▢ Maximize	Enlarges the window to fill the entire desktop (appears only when a window is reduced)
▦ Restore Down	Returns the window to its previous size and desktop position (appears only when a window is maximized)

3. Move the pointer to the border of the Excel window. The pointer changes to a two-headed arrow ↔ .

> **TIP:** Sometimes the borders of a window can move off the computer screen. If you're having trouble with one border of a window, try another border or drag the entire window onto the screen by using the title bar.

4. With the two-headed arrow displayed, drag the border to make the window smaller.

5. Click the title bar of one of the Word windows behind the Excel window. The Word window becomes the active window. The Excel window is still open, but it is now behind the Word window.

6. Click the Maximize button ▢ if the Word window does not fill the entire desktop.

7. Click the Minimize button ▬ on the title bar of the Word window. The Excel window becomes the active window. The second Word window appears behind the Excel window.

8. Click the Close button ☒ on the title bar of the second Word window. The Excel window is still the active window. Notice there are only two program buttons on the taskbar now.

9. Make the Word window the active window by clicking the Word button on the taskbar.

10. Click the Restore Down button ▦ on the Word window. The Word window reduces in size. The Excel window might be partially visible behind the Word window. You can drag the two reduced windows so parts of both can be seen simultaneously.

11. Drag the title bar of the Word window until you can see more of the Excel window. Use both title bars to reposition the windows.

   Some program windows, such as those for Excel and Word, contain two sets of sizing buttons. The upper set (on the title bar) controls the program window. The lower set controls the sizing of the document within the program window. See Figure A-9 (on the next page) for the location of the lower set in Word and Excel.

FIGURE A-9
Displaying two program windows simultaneously

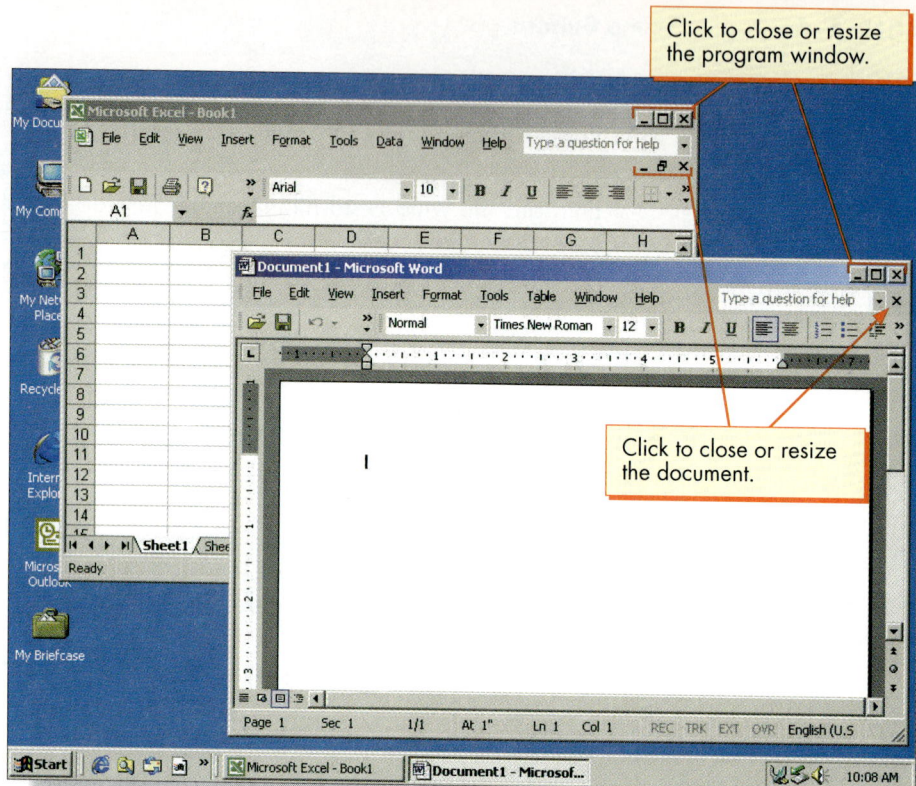

Click to close or resize the program window.

Click to close or resize the document.

12. Click the Close button ☒ on the title bars of each of the two program windows to close them. You have a clean desktop again.

Using the Documents Command

Windows lets you open an existing document by using the Documents command on the Start menu. This command allows you to open one of the last 15 documents previously opened on your computer.

1. Click the Start button ⊞Start on the taskbar to display the Start menu.

2. Choose Documents. The Documents submenu appears, showing you the last 15 documents that were opened.

3. Click a document. The program in which the document was created opens and the document displays. For example, if the document you chose is a Word document, Word opens and the document appears in a Word program window.

4. Click the program window's Close button ☒ (remember, it is the Close button on the title bar). The program window closes and the desktop is clear once again.

Using the Settings Command

The **Settings** command on the **Start** menu lets you change the way Windows looks and works. Because your computer in school is used by other students, you should be very careful when changing settings. Others might expect Windows to look and work the standard way. Having Windows look or work in a nonstandard way could easily confuse them.

FIGURE A-10
Settings submenu

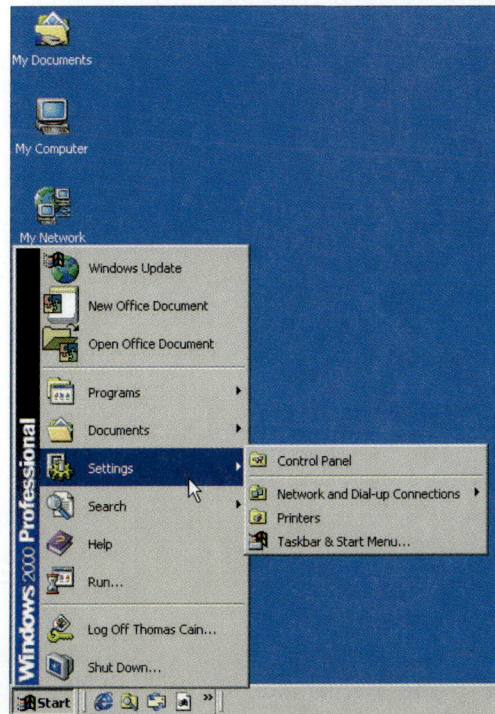

NOTE: Talk to your instructor before changing any settings on your computer.

1. Click the Start button [Start] on the taskbar.
2. Choose **Settings**. The **Settings** submenu displays.
3. Click anywhere on the desktop to close the **Settings** submenu without making any changes.

TABLE A-5	Settings Options
OPTION	**USE**
Control Panel	Displays the Control Panel window, which lets you change screen colors, add or remove programs, change the date and time, and change other settings for your hardware and software.
Network and Dial-up Connections	Displays a submenu that lets you make connections with other computers or a private network.
Printers	Displays the Printers window, which lets you add and remove printers, as well as modify your printer settings.
Taskbar & Start Menu	Displays the Taskbar and Start Menu Properties dialog box, which you use to customize the taskbar and add and remove programs on the Start menu.

Using the Search Command

If you don't know where a file or folder is located, you can use the **Search** command on the **Start** menu to help you find and open it.

1. Click the Start button [Start] on the taskbar.

2. Choose **Search**. The **Search** submenu appears.

3. Choose **For Files or Folders**. The **Search Results** dialog box appears.

FIGURE A-11
Search Results
dialog box

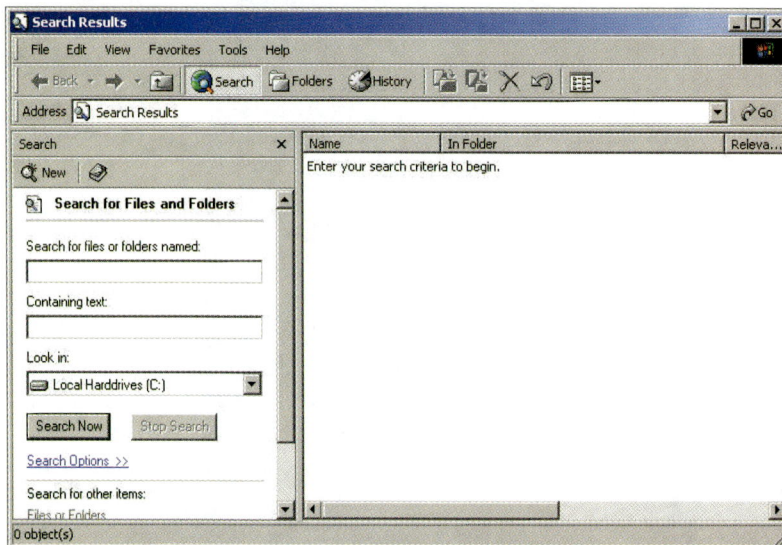

4. In the **Search for files or folders named** text box, key the name of the file or folder you want to find. Remember, you can use [Backspace] or [Delete] to delete any keying errors you make.

> **TIP:** To search files for specific text, use the Containing text text box. To search for files by date, size, type, or other attributes, click Search Options.

5. Click the down arrow next to the **Look in** text box to specify where you want Windows to search. The default location is the C drive.

6. Click **Search Now** to start the search. Any matches for the file are shown on the right side of the dialog box.

7. Double-click on any found item to open the program and view the file or folder Windows has located.

8. When you are finished with your search, close all open windows and clear your desktop.

Using the Run Command

Windows allows you to start a program by using the Run command and keying the program name. This command is often employed to run a "setup" or "install" program that installs a new program on your computer.

1. Click the Start button **Start** on the taskbar.

2. Choose Run. The Run dialog box appears.

FIGURE A-12
Run dialog box

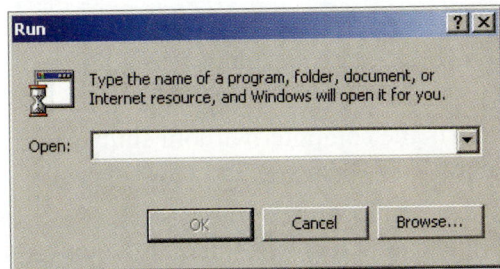

3. If you know the name of a program you want to run, key the name in the Open text box. Often you will need to click Browse to open a drop-down list of the disk drives, folders, and files available to you.

4. Click Cancel to close the Run dialog box.

Displaying a Shortcut Menu

When the mouse pointer is on an object or an area of the Windows desktop and you right-click, a shortcut menu appears. A *shortcut menu* typically contains commands that are useful in working with the object or area of the desktop to which you are currently pointing.

FIGURE A-13
Shortcut menu for the desktop

1. Position the mouse pointer on a blank area of the desktop and right-click. A shortcut menu appears with commands that relate to the desktop, including arranging icons and displaying properties.

2. Click outside the shortcut menu to close it.

3. Right-click the time in the bottom right corner of the taskbar. A shortcut menu appears with a command that relates to adjusting the time.

4. Click Adjust Date/Time. The Date/Time Properties dialog box appears. You can use this dialog box to adjust your computer's date and time.

5. Click Cancel.

6. Click outside the shortcut menu to close it.

7. Right-click an icon to display its shortcut menu, and then close the menu.

Exiting Windows

You should always exit any open applications and Windows before turning off the computer. This is the best way to be sure your work is saved. Windows also performs other "housekeeping" routines that ensure everything is ready for you when you next turn on your computer. Failure to shut down properly will often force Windows to perform time-consuming system checks the next time it is loaded.

To exit Windows, use the **Shut Down** command on the **Start** menu. This command has several shut-down options:

- **Log off.** Logs off the current Windows user and makes Windows available for another user to log on.
- **Restart.** Restarts the computer without shutting off the power. This is sometimes necessary when you add new software.
- **Shut down.** Closes all open programs and makes it safe to turn off the computer. Some computers will turn off the power automatically.
- **Stand by.** Places the computer in stand-by mode, which generally turns off the screen display and puts the computer in "hibernation." (This option is not available on all computers.)

1. Click the Start button ![Start] on the taskbar.

2. Choose **Shut Down** from the **Start** menu. The Shut Down Windows dialog box appears.

FIGURE A-14
Shut Down
Windows
dialog box

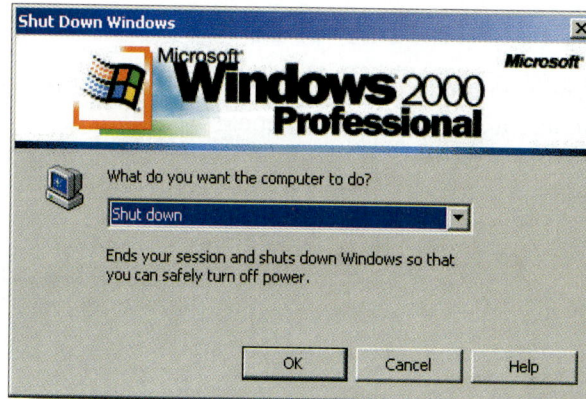

3. Click the down arrow next to the text box and select **Shut Down** if it is not already selected.

4. Click **OK**. Windows prompts you to save changes in any open documents. It then prepares the computer to be shut down. Windows will tell you when it is safe to turn off your computer.

5. When Windows tells you it is safe to turn off your computer, turn off your computer and your monitor.

APPENDIX B

File Management

Most of your tasks in Windows 2000 will involve working with information stored on your computer. This Appendix briefly explains how information is stored in Windows 2000.

It also introduces you to one of the most useful programs for managing information in Windows—the Windows Explorer. This program shows you how information is organized on your computer and provides you with the tools to manage it.

Files and Folders

The basic unit of storage in Windows is a *file*. The documents you create and use, as well as the programs you use, are all files. These files are stored in *folders*, which can contain other folders as well as files.

Filenames in Windows may be up to 255 characters, including spaces. A filename also has a three-letter extension, which identifies the type of file. For example, the extension "doc" identifies a file as a Word document. The extension is separated from the filename by a period (often called a "dot"), as in "Birthday.doc."

NOTE: By default, file extensions are not displayed. To display them in Windows Explorer, open the Tools menu, choose Folder Options, diplay the View tab, and then clear the Hide file extensions for known file types check box.

Opening Windows Explorer

One of the most useful tools in Windows 2000 for managing folders and files on your computer is *Windows Explorer*. This program displays folders and files in a hierarchical structure, similar to a family tree. It allows you to browse through all your computer's drives and folders in a single window. You can also use it to see the contents of other computers on your network.

To open Windows Explorer:

1. Click the Start button ![Start] on the taskbar.

2. Choose Programs.

3. From the Programs submenu, choose Accessories.

4. From the Accessories submenu, choose Windows Explorer. (If Windows Explorer does not appear on the Accessories menu, click the down arrow at the bottom of the menu to display the entire Accessories menu.). (See Figure B-1 on the next page.)

FIGURE B-1
Starting Windows
Explorer

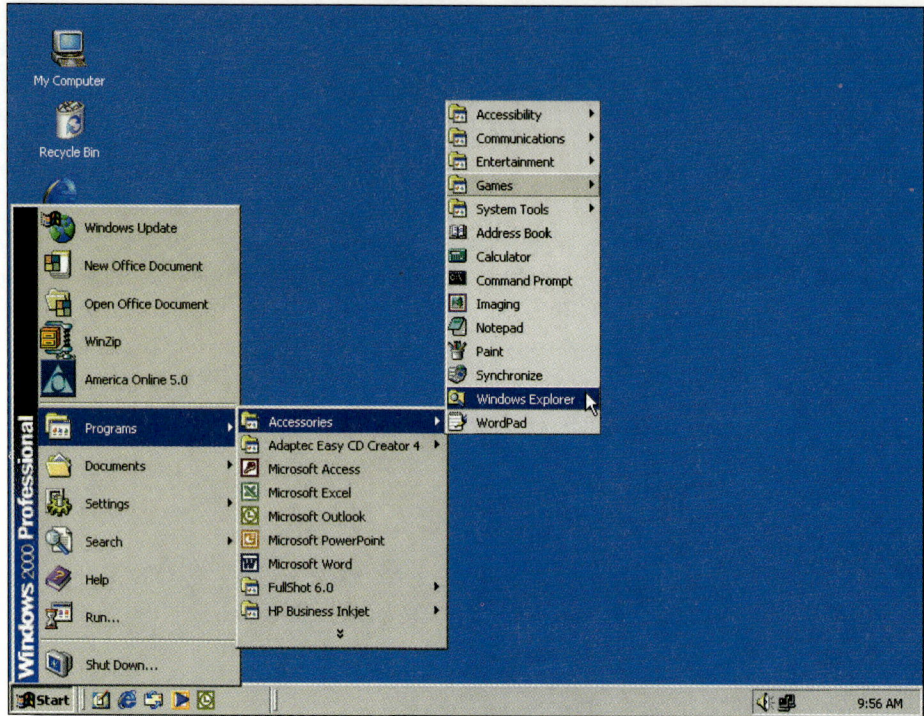

Windows Explorer appears. The window is divided into two panes: The left pane shows the network (if any) and the hierarchy of computers, drives, and folders. The right pane shows the contents of the item you click on the left pane. Various icons are used to represent folders, computers, drives, and networks. Notice the Plus symbols ⊞ and Minus symbols ⊟. These are used to navigate among the drives and folders on your computer.

FIGURE B-2
Windows Explorer

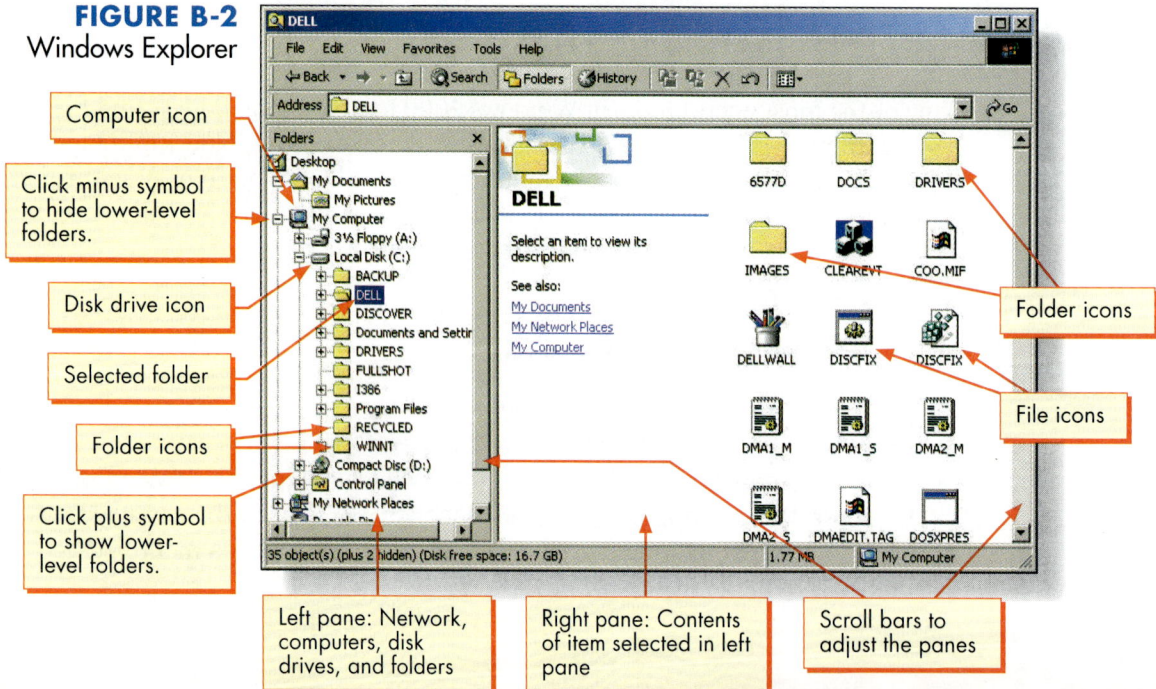

Computer icon

Click minus symbol to hide lower-level folders.

Disk drive icon

Selected folder

Folder icons

Click plus symbol to show lower-level folders.

Left pane: Network, computers, disk drives, and folders

Right pane: Contents of item selected in left pane

Scroll bars to adjust the panes

Folder icons

File icons

NOTE: The right pane of your Windows Explorer window might look different than the one shown in Figure B-2. Windows Explorer enables you to control the way in which files and folders are displayed in the right pane. The icons might be sized differently, or the contents of the folder might be arranged in a column format, showing details such as file type, date, and size.

Navigating Using Windows Explorer

Practice navigating through your computer's files and folders using the Windows Explorer:

1. Click the Plus symbol ⊞ next to a folder or disk drive icon. The lower-level branches under that folder or drive display.

TIP: Any folder displaying a Plus symbol ⊞ contains one or more folders within that folder.

2. Click the Plus symbol ⊞ next to other folder icons.

Notice that as you display the branches of the hierarchy, the symbol next to the folder icon changes to a Minus symbol ⊟.

3. Click a Minus symbol ⊟ next to a folder icon. The hierarchy under the folder collapses and the lower-level branches under it are hidden.

4. Click a folder icon. The contents of the folder display.

Folders selected in the left pane are displayed in the right pane.

5. Use the scroll bars on the right sides of the two panes if the contents of either pane extend beyond the viewing area.

Copying Files and Folders

You can use Windows Explorer to manage files and folders on you computer. Common management tasks include copying files or folders, moving files or folders to new locations, renaming files or folders, deleting unneeded files or folder, and creating new file folders.

To copy a file or folder from one location to another:

1. In the left pane, click the folder icon containing the file you wish to copy. The files within that folder appear in the right pane.

NOTE: You might have to click several folders in the hierarchy to finally display the folder containing the file you wish to copy.

2. Locate the file in the right pane and right-click it. A shortcut menu appears.

TIP: You can select multiple files to copy. When files are adjacent to one another, select the first file, press and hold Shift, and click the last file. All files between the first and last files will be selected for copying. To select nonadjacent files, select the first file, press and hold Ctrl, select the remaining files, and then click.

3. Select Copy from the shortcut menu.

4. In the left pane, locate the folder to which you will copy the file. Right-click the folder icon. A shortcut menu appears.

TIP: Use the Plus symbols ⊞ and the scroll bar to adjust the viewing area if the folder isn't displayed.

5. Choose Paste from the shortcut menu. The file is copied to the new folder. The file is now located in both the original location and the new location.

Copying Files on to Floppy Disks

To transport a file from your school to your home, you will typically need to copy the file onto a floppy disk. To copy a file from your computer to a floppy disk:

1. Insert a floppy disk in your floppy disk drive (typically this is Drive A).

2. In the left pane, click the folder icon containing the file you wish to copy. The files within that folder appear in the right pane.

NOTE: You might have to click several folders in the hierarchy to finally display the folder containing the file you wish to copy.

3. Locate the file in the right pane and right-click it. A shortcut menu appears.

TIP: You can select multiple files to copy to a floppy disk. When files are adjacent to one another, select the first file, press and hold Shift, and click the last file. All files between the first and last files will be selected for copying. To select nonadjacent files, select the first file, press and hold Ctrl, select the remaining files, and then click.

4. Choose Send To from the shortcut menu.

5. Choose 3½ Floppy (A) from the submenu. The file is copied to the disk.

Moving Files and Folders

You can also move file or folders from one location to another. This process is very similar to copying a file to another location. However, rather than choosing Copy from the shortcut menu when you right-click the file, you choose the Cut command.

To move a file or folder from one location to another:

1. In the left pane, click the folder icon containing the file you wish to move. The files within that folder appear in the right pane.

> **NOTE:** You might have to click several folders in the hierarchy to finally display the folder containing the file you wish to move.

2. Locate the file in the right pane and right-click it. A shortcut menu appears.

> **TIP:** You can select multiple files to copy. When files are adjacent to one another, select the first file, press and hold Shift, and click the last file. All files between the first and last files will be selected for copying. To select nonadjacent files, select the first file, press and hold Ctrl, select the remaining files, and then click.

3. Select Cut from the shortcut menu.

4. In the left pane, locate the folder to which you will move the file. Right-click the folder icon. A shortcut menu appears.

> **TIP:** Use the Plus symbols ⊞ and the scroll bar to adjust the viewing area if the folder isn't displayed.

5. Choose Paste from the shortcut menu. The file is moved to the new folder. The file is located in only the new location. It has been moved from the original location.

Files can also be moved using the drag-and-drop method:

1. In the left pane, click the folder icon containing the file you wish to move. The files within that folder appear in the right pane.

> **NOTE:** You might have to click several folders in the hierarchy to finally display the folder containing the file you wish to move.

2. Locate the file in the right pane and select it.

3. Hold down the left mouse button and drag the file to the left pane. Position the pointer over the desired folder. The folder icon is highlighted.

> **TIP:** If the folder contains lower-level branches and your target location is within a lower level, the lower level will automatically display after a few moments. You can move the pointer near the top or bottom edge of the pane to scroll if the desired folder doesn't appear on-screen.

4. Release the mouse button when the desired folder is highlighted. The file is moved from the original location into the highlighted folder.

> **NOTE:** You can only move a file from one location to another on the same disk when using the drag-and-drop method. If the target location is a different disk, a copy is made. You can also use the drag-and-drop method to copy a file by pressing Ctrl and holding down the left mouse button when selecting the file to copy.

Deleting Files and Folders

When you delete a file or folder, it is placed in the Recycle Bin. To delete a file or folder:

1. Locate the file or folder. A folder can be located in the left or right pane. A file will always be in the right pane.

2. Right-click the file or folder.

3. Choose <u>D</u>elete from the shortcut menu.

TIP: If you mistakenly delete a file or folder (and you haven't emptied the Recycle Bin), you can restore it by clicking the Recycle Bin to open it, right-clicking the item you want to restore, and choosing Restore from the shortcut menu.

Renaming Files and Folders

A common file management task is renaming files and folder. Often companies develop a unique naming structure for their files.

1. Locate the file or folder and right-click it. A shortcut menu appears.

2. Choose Rena<u>m</u>e from the shortcut menu.

3. Key the new name. Delete the old filename.

4. Press Enter to complete the process.

Creating New Folders

Creating folders is a necessary part of file management. They are like folders in a file cabinet. Some people like to use many folders, with a few items in each one. Others use fewer folders with many files in each. You will develop your own system, but try to be consistent in your folder structure. Consistency makes it easier to locate files easily.

To create a new folder:

1. Select (highlight) the disk or folder in the left pane where you want to locate the new folder.

2. Choose <u>F</u>ile from the menu bar.

3. Choose <u>N</u>ew from the File menu.

4. Choose <u>F</u>older from the submenu. The folder is created in the folder or disk you selected. You can now rename the folder.

APPENDIX C

Speech Recognition

The *speech recognition* feature in Microsoft Office enables you to dictate text into any Office program. You also can use your voice to select menu commands, toolbar buttons, dialog box selections, and task pane items. The speech recognition feature is not intended for completely hands-free operation. It is best used in combination with the mouse or keyboard.

To use speech recognition, your computer must be equipped with the following:

- A high-quality close-talk (headset) microphone with gain adjustment. (You use gain adjustment to make your input louder for use by the system.)
- A 400 megahertz or faster computer.
- 128 MB or more of memory.
- Windows 98 or later or Windows NT 4.0 or later.
- Microsoft Internet Explorer 5 or later.

Installing the Speech Recognition Feature

The speech recognition feature is installed in Word (typically by performing a custom installation). To install the speech recognition in Word:

1. Start Word.
2. Choose **Tools** from the menu, and then choose **Speech**. (You might need to click the down arrow at the bottom of the **Tools** menu to display the entire menu.) You'll be asked if you wish to install the feature.
3. Click **Yes**. After the feature is installed, it is available in the **Tools** menu in all Office programs.

NOTE: Installation requires the Office XP CD-ROM.

Speech Training

You increase speech recognition accuracy by training the computer to recognize how you speak. You are offered training when the speech recognition feature is first installed. You also can train the computer at any time after installation.

Speech training helps the computer learn to recognize how you speak. You train the computer by reading text out loud. Microsoft Office listens to your voice and creates a speech recognition user profile. A *user profile* is information created and stored by the speech recognition training program that the computer uses in recognizing your unique voice. After you've created the profile and have completed the initial training, you can improve the computer's accuracy by completing additional voice training sessions. There are eight different voice training sessions. The more training sessions you complete, the more accurate the computer will be in recognizing your voice.

Microsoft Office lets you create multiple speech recognition user profiles. This is particularly useful when more than one individual uses the speech recognition feature on a single computer.

To create your user profile and begin speech recognition training, complete the following steps:

1. Press the Start button [Start].

2. On the **Start** menu, choose **Settings**, and then choose **Control Panel**. The Control Panel appears.

3. Double-click the Speech icon. The Speech Properties dialog box appears. One or more Recognition Profiles might already be listed. You now will create your own profile.

FIGURE C-1
Speech Properties
dialog box

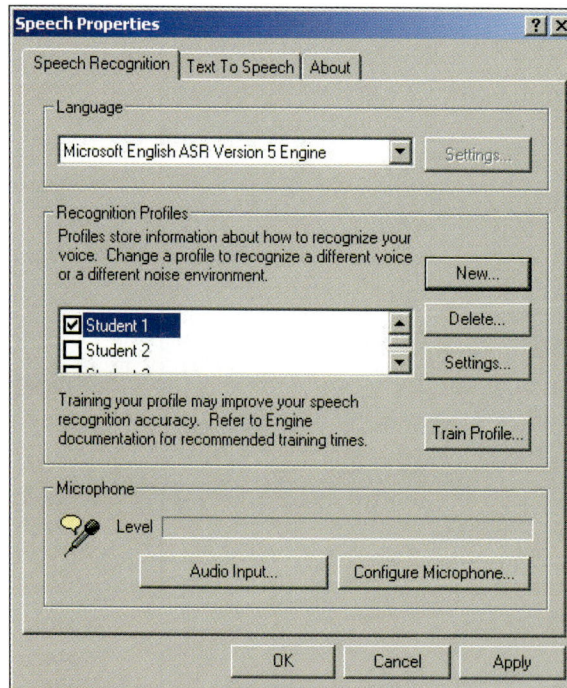

NOTE: You can also access the Speech Properties dialog box by clicking the Tools button [Tools] on the Language toolbar and then choosing Options from the menu.

4. Click **New**. The Profile Wizard dialog box appears.

5. In the Profile text box, key *[your name]* and then click Finish. The Speech Properties dialog box reappears. Your profile is added to the list of available profiles.

6. Make sure your profile is the currently selected profile shown under Recognition Profiles. This means your profile is the profile the computer will use when speech recognition is activated in any Microsoft Office program.

> **NOTE:** To begin voice training, you could have clicked Next instead of Finish in the Profile Wizard dialog box. However, Office requires users with new profiles to complete voice training the first time they activate speech recognition, even if they have already completed training in the Profile Wizard dialog box. You will be prompted to begin voice training the first time you use the speech recognition feature in any Office program.

7. Click OK to close the Speech Properties dialog box, and then close the Control Panel.

8. Click the Start button 🏁Start on the Windows taskbar. Choose Programs on the Start menu, and then choose Microsoft Word. (You can open any Office program in which you want to use speech recognition; in this exercise, you will use Word.) When Word opens, the Language bar is displayed automatically.

> **TIP:** If the speech recognition feature has been installed and the Language bar does not appear in the Office programs, its display has been turned off. To redisplay the Language bar, click the Start button 🏁Start on the Windows taskbar, choose Settings from the Start menu, and then choose Control Panel. On the Control Panel, double-click the Text Services icon 🖰, and then click Language Bar. Select Show the Language bar on the desktop.

9. Click the Microphone button 🎤 Microphone on the Language toolbar to activate speech recognition training. The Welcome to Office Speech Recognition dialog box appears.

> **NOTE:** If the Welcome to Office Speech Recognition dialog box does not appear when you click the Microphone button 🎤 Microphone, you need to make sure Office considers you the current user and is using your profile. Click the Tools button 🔧Tools on the Language toolbar, choose <u>C</u>urrent User, and then select your profile. Now when you click the Microphone button 🎤 Microphone, you will activate the speech recognition training.

10. Click Next to begin the Office Speech Recognition training. There are two parts to the training: microphone training and voice training. The Microphone Wizard dialog box appears first. This wizard helps you adjust your microphone for the best results in speech recognition.

11. Click **Next** and complete the Microphone Wizard. When you click **Finish** at the last Microphone Wizard screen, the Voice Training dialog box for the Microsoft Speech Recognition Training Wizard appears. This wizard trains the computer to recognize your voice.

FIGURE C-2
Voice Training

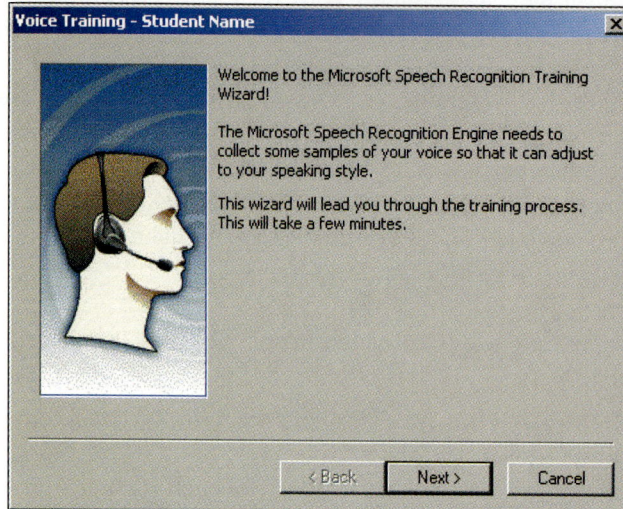

12. Click **Next** to begin the voice training. You'll first be asked some questions about your gender and age, and then you'll read some text out loud.

13. When you complete the voice training, click **Finish**. A short video follows that demonstrates the use of the speech recognition feature. To improve the computer's accuracy in recognizing your speech, it is recommended that you conduct additional training sessions.

NOTE: The video that follows the voice training requires the Flash Player plug-in to run. This is a free program by Macromedia that is used to play movies. If this program is not already installed on your computer, your browser might automatically connect you to the Macromedia Web site. You'll be prompted to begin downloading the plug-in. The video appears only once, after you complete your first speech recognition voice training session.

14. To conduct additional training sessions, click the Tools button [Tools] on the Language bar, and then choose <u>T</u>raining. The Voice Training dialog box appears. Notice that there are eight different sessions. Each contains different material for you to read aloud. You can perform sessions more than once. After you have used speech recognition, you might wish to do more training.

FIGURE C-3
Voice Training,
additional sessions

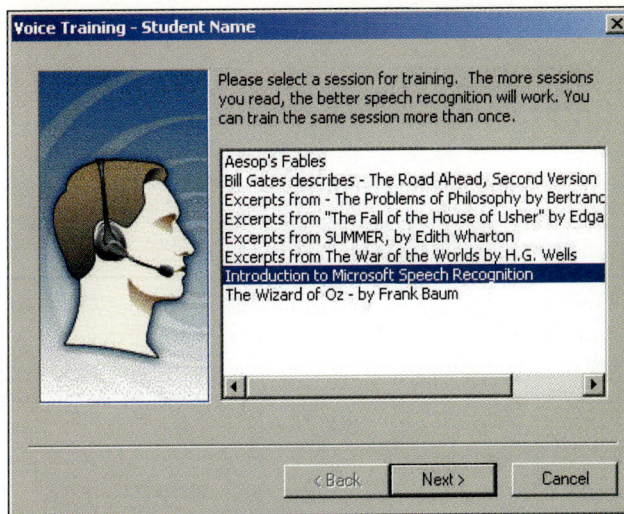

Voice Training - Student Name

Please select a session for training. The more sessions you read, the better speech recognition will work. You can train the same session more than once.

Aesop's Fables
Bill Gates describes - The Road Ahead, Second Version
Excerpts from - The Problems of Philosophy by Bertranc
Excerpts from "The Fall of the House of Usher" by Edga
Excerpts from SUMMER, by Edith Wharton
Excerpts from The War of the Worlds by H.G. Wells
Introduction to Microsoft Speech Recognition
The Wizard of Oz - by Frank Baum

< Back   Next >   Cancel

15. Click **Cancel** to close the Voice Training dialog box, and close Word.

Beginning Speech Recognition: Dictation Mode

After the speech recognition feature is installed and you have completed your initial training, you can use it in any Microsoft Office program. There are two modes of speech recognition:

- *Dictation mode* lets you dictate text into any Office program. For example, you can use the Dictation mode to dictate a Word document or an Outlook e-mail message.
- The *Voice Command mode* lets you select menu commands, toolbar buttons, dialog box options, and task pane items by using your voice.

Speech recognition commands are activated by using the buttons on the Language toolbar. The Language toolbar is displayed automatically in all Office programs if the speech recognition feature has been installed. Table C-1 on the next page describes each of the buttons on the Language toolbar.

To begin using the speech recognition feature, perform the following steps:

1. Start Word. (You can open any Office program in which you want to use speech recognition; in this exercise, you will use Word.) When Word opens, the Language bar is displayed automatically.

2. If the microphone is not already turned off, click the Microphone button [Microphone] on the Language toolbar to turn it off.

3. Click the Tools button [Tools] on the Language toolbar, and then choose Current User. Select your profile if it is not already selected.

TABLE C-1   Language Toolbar

BUTTON	PURPOSE
Correction	Presents correction options for selected text. (Not present in applications where there is no text entry.)
Microphone	Turns the microphone on and off.
Dictation	Turns on the Dictation mode so the words you speak are turned into text.
Voice Command	Turns on the Voice Command mode so you can select menu, toolbar, dialog box, and task pane items using your voice.
Tools	Displays a drop-down menu for various options, including selecting the current user profile and performing additional voice training.

NOTE: Make sure the computer is using your voice profile before you begin using speech recognition.

4. Position your microphone.

5. Click the Microphone button [Microphone]. The microphone is activated, and the Language toolbar expands.

6. Click the Dictation button [Dictation] on the Language toolbar or say *"Dictation."* You are now in the Dictation mode.

7. Say *"I am now using Microsoft Office speech recognition."* As you speak, the computer displays a blue bar for text it is processing. The words appear when processing is completed.

FIGURE C-4
Speech recognition processing spoken text in Dictation mode

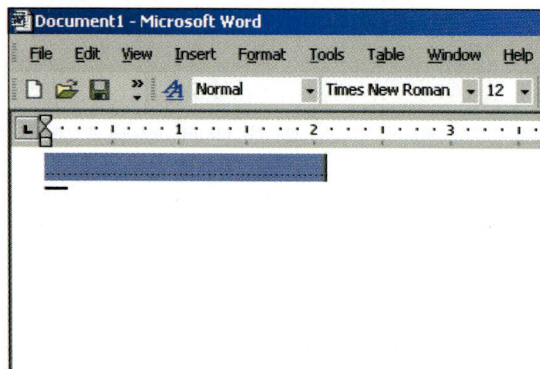

8. Say *"Period."* The computer places a period at the end of the sentence and adds a space for the next sentence.

Correcting Mistakes

Correction

Mistakes can be corrected in several ways:

- You can place the insertion point on the incorrect word and click the Correction button [Correction] on the Language toolbar. You'll be shown a list of correction alternatives.
- You can select the incorrect word or phrase and dictate the correct text.
- You can key over errors by using the mouse or keyboard. In Dictation mode, you can select the text, say "*Spelling mode,*" pause slightly, and then spell the correction.

The computer recognizes many common punctuation and keyboard symbols. For example, "semicolon," "question mark," and "open parenthesis" all generate the appropriate characters in Dictation mode.

1. Say "*As I speak, comma, the words I speak appear on the screen. Period.*" The computer places a comma after the first phrase and a period at the end of the sentence, and the first letter in the sentence is capitalized.
2. If the computer has made any mistakes in the text you dictated in the previous step, try using some of the techniques just described to correct them.

Using Voice Command Mode

In Voice Command mode, you can activate menus, toolbar buttons, dialog box and task pane items, and certain keystrokes. Table C-2 provides some other useful voice commands.

TABLE C-2	Useful Voice Commands
COMMAND	**RESULT**
Say "spelling mode"	In Dictation mode, lets you spell a word.
Say "new line"	In Dictation mode, inserts a line break and places the insertion point at the beginning of the new line.
Say "force num"	In Dictation mode, lets you dictate all numbers as digits.
Say "new paragraph"	In Dictation mode, inserts a new paragraph and places the insertion point at the beginning of the new paragraph.
Say "expand"	In Voice Command mode, displays an entire menu when all commands on a menu are not visible.
Say "escape"	In Voice Command mode, cancels a menu.

1. Say "*Voice Command.*" The computer is now in Voice Command mode.

> **NOTE:** You can switch between Dictation mode and Voice Command mode by saying "*Dictation*" or "*Voice Command.*"

2. Say "*Return.*" The computer places a Return (Enter) after the sentence. The insertion point is now on the next line.

3. Say "*Backspace.*" The computer backspaces to the end of the sentence.

4. Use the mouse to select "speech recognition" in the first sentence.

5. Say "*Italic.*" The selected text is italicized. In Voice Command mode, you can activate toolbar buttons.

6. Move the insertion point to the end of the second sentence.

7. Say "*Return.*" The computer places a Return after the sentence.

8. Say "*Return.*" The computer moves the insertion point down another line.

9. Click the Dictation button [Dictation] or say "*Dictation.*" The computer switches back to Dictation mode.

10. Say "*Speech recognition is a powerful tool. Period.*"

FIGURE C-5
Text dictated into a Word document

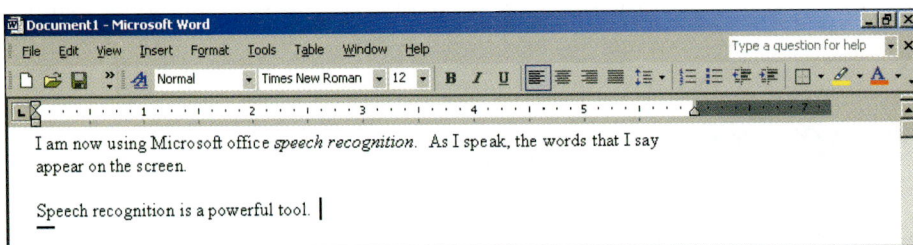

11. Click the Voice Command button [Voice Command] or say "*Voice Command.*"

12. Say "*File.*" The <u>F</u>ile menu displays. You can activate menu commands in Voice Command mode.

13. Say "*Print.*" The <u>P</u>rint command on the <u>F</u>ile menu is selected, and the Print dialog box displays.

14. Say "*OK.*" The document prints. You can make dialog box selections by using your voice in the Voice Command mode.

15. Click the Microphone button [Microphone] or say "*Microphone*" to turn off the microphone. It is good practice to turn off the microphone when it's not in use.

16. Close Word without saving the document.

> **NOTE:** If you find the computer making a significant number of mistakes, make sure your microphone is adjusted correctly. You can also improve the computer's accuracy by completing more training sessions.

APPENDIX D

Proofreaders' Marks

PROOFREADERS' MARK		DRAFT	FINAL COPY
¶	Start a new paragraph	ridiculous! If that is so	ridiculous!
			If that is so
⌒	Delete space	to gether	together
#	Insert space	It may be	It may not be
(move arrow)	Move as shown	it is not true	it is true
∿	Transpose	beleivable	believable
		is it so	it is so
◯	Spell out	2 years ago	two years ago
		16 Elm St.	16 Elm Street
∧	Insert a word	How much is it?	How much is it?
─ϱ OR ─	Delete a word	it may not be true	it may be true
∧ OR ⅄	Insert a letter	temperture	temperature
ϑ OR ∋	Delete a letter and close up	commitment to buy	commitment to buy
─ϱ OR ─	Change a word	but and if you can't won't	but if you can't
Stet	Stet (don't delete)	I was very glad	I was very glad
/	Make letter lowercase	Federal Government	federal government
≡	Capitalize	Janet L. greyston	Janet L. Greyston
∨	Raise above the line	in her new book*	in her new book*
∧	Drop below the line	H2SO4	H_2SO_4

PROOFREADERS' MARK		DRAFT	FINAL COPY
⊙	Insert a period	Mr.Henry Grenada	Mr. Henry Grenada
∧	Insert a comma	a large old house	a large, old house
∨	Insert an apostrophe	my childrens car	my children's car
∨∨	Insert quotation marks	he wants a loan	he wants a "loan"
= OR ≚	Insert a hyphen	a first-rate job	a first-rate job
		ask the coowner	ask the co-owner
M̲	Insert an em-dash	Here it is cash!	Here it is—cash!
N̲	Insert an en-dash	Pages 1-5	Pages 1–5
___	Insert underscore	an issue of Time	an issue of Time
(ital) ___	Set in italic	(ital) The New York Times	*The New York Times*
(bf) ~~~	Set in boldface	(bf) the Enter key	the **Enter** key
(rom) ___	Set in roman	(rom) the *most* likely	the most likely
{ }	Insert parentheses	left today (May 3)	left today (May 3)
⊐	Move to the right	$38,367,000 ___	$38,367,000
⊏	Move to the left	___ Anyone can win!	Anyone can win!
ss [	Single-space	ss [I have heard / he is leaving	I have heard he is leaving
ds [	Double-space	ds [When will you / have a decision?	When will you / have a decision?
(+ 1 line)	Insert 1 line space	Percent of Change / (+ 1 line) 16.25	Percent of Change / 16.25
(– 1 line)	Delete (remove) 1 line space	Northeastern / (– 1 line) regional sales	Northeastern regional sales

APPENDIX E

MOUS Certification

TABLE E-1

Core MOUS Activities Related to Lessons

CODE	ACTIVITY	LESSON
OL2002 1	**Creating and Viewing Messages**	
OL2002 1-1	Display and print messages	1
OL2002 1-2	Compose and send messages to corporate/workgroup and Internet addresses	1, 4, 6, 7
OL2002 1-3	Insert signatures and attachments	1, 4, 7
OL2002 1-4	Customize views	4
OL2002 2	**Scheduling**	
OL2002 2-1	Add appointments, meetings, and events to the Outlook calendar	2, 5, 7
OL2002 2-2	Apply conditional formats to the Outlook calendar	6
OL2002 2-3	Respond to meeting requests	5
OL2002 2-4	Use categories to manage appointments	6
OL2002 2-5	Print calendars	2
OL2002 3	**Managing Messages**	
OL2002 3-1	Move messages between folders	4, 7
OL2002 3-2	Search for messages	4
OL2002 3-3	Save messages in alternate file formats	6
OL2002 3-4	Use categories to manage messages	6
OL2002 3-5	Set message options	4
OL2002 4	**Creating and Managing Contacts**	
OL2002 4-1	Create and edit contacts	1, 3, 7
OL2002 4-2	Organize and sort contacts	3
OL2002 4-3	Link contacts to activities and journal entries	3, 7
OL2002 5	**Creating and Managing Tasks and Notes**	
OL2002 5-1	Create and update tasks	2, 5, 7
OL2002 5-2	Modify task organization and Task view	5, 6, 7
OL2002 5-3	Accept, decline, or delegate tasks	5
OL2002 5-4	Create and modify notes	5, 6
OL2002 5-5	Use categories to manage tasks and notes	5

TABLE E-2

Lessons Related to MOUS Activities

LESSON	CODES*
1 Introduction to Outlook and E-Mail	OL2002 1-1, 1-2, 1-3, 4-1
2 Calendar and Tasks	OL2002 2-1, 2-5, 5-1
3 Working with Contacts	OL2002 4-1, 4-2, 4-3
4 Managing E-Mail	OL2002 1-2, 1-3, 1-4, 3-1, 3-2, 3-5
5 Working with Others and Using Notes	OL2002 2-1, 2-3, 5-1, 5-2, 5-3, 5-4, 5-5
6 Customizing Outlook	OL2002 1-2, 2-2, 2-4, 3-3, 3-4, 5-2, 5-4
7 Integrating Outlook Features	OL2002 1-2, 1-3, 2-1, 3-1, 4-1, 4-3, 5-1, 5-2

*MOUS Activity codes are abbreviated in this table.
For more information about the Microsoft Office User Specialist (MOUS) program, go to www.mous.net.

Glossary

Appointment   An activity occurring on a specific day and time that does not involve inviting other people to attend or reserving a room. (2)

Appointments Calendar   Left section of the Calendar folder that shows any scheduled appointments, meetings, and events. (2)

Archive   To remove selected items to another location for storage and possible future access. (4)

AutoArchive   An Outlook feature for automatically moving old items to an archive location and discarding expired items whose contents are no longer valid. (4)

Contact   A person, business, or organization with whom you correspond. (1)

Contact list   In the Contacts folder, the list of people and organizations with whom you communicate. (1)

Date Navigator   The upper right section of the Calendar folder that shows two complete months of the year. (2)

Delegate   To assign a task request to someone else, usually a subordinate. You never delegate a task to a supervisor and only rarely to a coworker or equal. (5)

Distribution list   A set of contacts to whom e-mail messages are sent. (3)

Domain name   The mail system of an e-mail sender or recipient. It consists of two or more elements separated by periods, or dots. (1)

Event   An activity that lasts a day or longer without any times being specified. (2)

Field   A unit of information within an item. For example, the fields for an Inbox item include the message sender, the subject, and the date sent. (1)

Filter   Instructions that screen a folder based on conditions you define. (4)

Form   An Outlook window used to display and collect information. (1)

Internet e-mail address   A user name and a domain name, with the two separated by the "at" sign (@). (1)

Item   The basic element for storing information in Outlook. Each appointment, meeting, contact, message received, message sent, and so on, is an Outlook item. (1)

Master Category List   The Outlook-supplied set of keywords for grouping, filtering, finding, or sorting items. It includes general categories such as Business, Phone Calls, and Personal. (6)

Meeting   A Calendar activity that involves inviting other people or reserving resources. (5)

Move handle   The left border of an appointment in the Appointments Calendar, used to drag an appointment to a new time. (2)

Office Clipboard   A Microsoft Office feature that lets you copy text from one document or program and paste it into another. (1)

Outlook Bar   The column on the left side of the Outlook window that shows groups of shortcuts, including Outlook shortcuts. (1)

Personal Folders file   A data file in Outlook containing all the information you create, such as your messages, appointments, and tasks. (1)

Print style   A combination of paper and page settings that determines the appearance of printed material. (1)

Recurring   Occurring repeatedly; used to describe appointments, meetings, tasks, or events that occur time after time. (2)

Resource   A conference room, audio-visual equipment, or other organizational space or equipment used for meetings. (5)

Rule   A set of conditions, actions, and exceptions that organizes messages; an action automatically taken on an item in a folder under certain conditions. (4, 6)

ScreenTip   A box with a button name that is displayed by pointing the mouse at the button. (1)

Signature   Text automatically added to a message you send. (4)

Task   A personal or work-related activity that you want to track to completion. (2)

Task list   The list of tracked personal or work-related activities that appears in the Tasks folder or the TaskPad. (2)

TaskPad   The lower right section of the Calendar folder that shows an abbreviated list of current tasks. (2)

Task request   An e-mail message asking the recipient to complete a specified activity. (5)

Timeline   A view type that displays items from left to right on a time scale, showing when items occur in time, typically in a day, month, or year. (7)

vCard   An Internet standard for creating and sharing virtual business cards. (3)

Views   Ways to look at similar information in different formats and arrangements. There are views for Inbox, Calendar, Contacts, Tasks, Journal, and Notes. (1)

Index

Photo Credits

Page 1: All photos, PhotoDisc, Inc.; Page 3: All photos, PhotoDisc, Inc.; Page 5: Photo-Disc, Inc.; Page 89: PhotoDisc, Inc.; Page 209: PhotoDisc, Inc.; A-1: PhotoDisc, Inc.